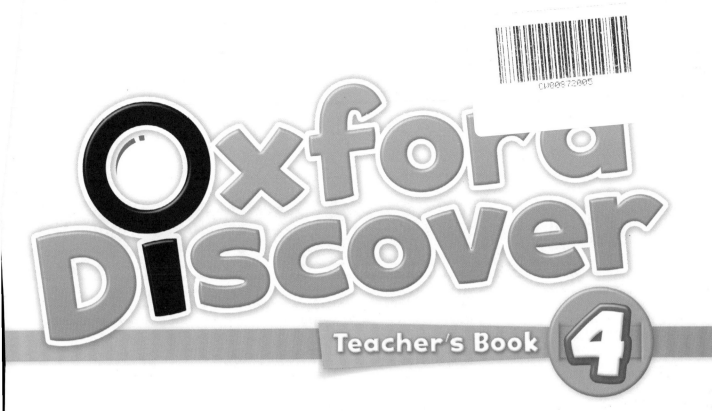

Oxford Discover

Teacher's Book 4

Sarah Bupp

OXFORD
UNIVERSITY PRESS

Scope and Sequence

UNIT	READING	VOCABULARY	GRAMMAR
▶ **BIG QUESTION 1**		**Where are we in the universe?** *Science: Astronomy*	
1 Page 6	**Bella's Home** Science Fiction **Reading Strategy** Visualizing Changes	**Reading Text Words** *moon, asteroid, comet, meteorite, solar system, stars, galaxy, universe, spacecraft, telescope, observatory* **Words in Context** *vast, dwelled, speck, disk* **Word Study** Words with *ei*	**Predictions with *Will*** Future statements *I will visit those places again, Bella thought.*
2 Page 16	**Traveling Together Around the Sun** Science Article (Nonfiction) **Reading Strategy** Compare and Contrast in Science	**Reading Text Words** *astronomer, space probe, core, gravity, orbit, matter, distance, diameter, surface, craters, unique* **Words in Context** *bodies, explore, inner, outer* **Word Study** Words with the suffixes *-ance* and *-ant*	**Future Real Conditional** Future statements and questions *If technology continues to grow, we will travel to these places ourselves.*
▶ **BIG QUESTION 2**		**How do we know what happened long ago?** *Social Studies: History*	
3 Page 26	**Hidden Army: Clay Soldiers of Ancient China** Magazine Article (Nonfiction) **Reading Strategy** Author's Purpose	**Reading Text Words** *army, soldiers, uniform, emperor, armor, treasure, archaeologist, tomb, jade, clay, peasant* **Words in Context** *battle, generals, varnish, coffin* **Word Study** Words with the suffix *-ist*	**Verbs Followed by Infinitives** Simple present and simple past statements and questions *The Chinese government plans to keep it closed for now.*
4 Page 36	**Stumbling upon the Past** Realistic Fiction **Reading Strategy** Predictions	**Reading Text Words** *dinosaur, skull, ravine, examine, discover, excavate, layers, paleontologist, ash, sedimentary rock, pastime* **Words in Context** *favorite, dream, tripped, determine* **Word Study** Words with *ie*	**Verbs Followed by Gerunds** Simple present and simple past statements and questions *Javier enjoyed playing with his friends.*
▶ **BIG QUESTION 3**		**Where does our food come from?** *Social Studies: Geography*	
5 Page 46	**The Breakfast Quest** Humorous Fiction **Reading Strategy** Conclusions	**Reading Text Words** *sugar cane, wheat, cinnamon, butter, vanilla, ingredients, bark, plantation, steamship, spoil, leopard* **Words in Context** *gather, introduce, peel, coax* **Word Study** Phrasal verbs with *drop*	**Present Continuous for Future Plans** Present continuous statements and questions *I'm making a special breakfast today.*
6 Page 56	**From the World to Your Table** Informational Text (Nonfiction) **Reading Strategy** Summarize	**Reading Text Words** *convenient, export, local, process, package, farmer's market, agriculture, corporate farm, decrease, century, chemical* **Words in Context** *grocery stores, food labels, organic food, whole food* **Word Study** Four-syllable wordss	**Polite Offers** Simple present questions and answers *Would you like to know where your food comes from?*
▶ **BIG QUESTION 4**		**Why do we make art?** *Art*	
7 Page 66	**Art Through New Eyes** Magazine Article (Nonfiction) **Reading Strategy** Text Featuress	**Reading Text Words** *sketch, pastels, canvas, paintbrushes, shapes, string, three-dimensional, prodigy, street painter, carpenter, sculptor* **Words in Context** *complex, washable, combines, fascination* **Word Study** Words with the prefix *dis-*	**Indefinite Pronouns** Simple present and simple past statements and questions *I want to paint something in this room.*
8 Page 76	**Sketches in a Gallery** Realistic Fiction **Reading Strategy** Value Judgments	**Reading Text Words** *exhibition, frame, landscape, texture, shading, perspective, contrast, space, stained, brilliant, pale* **Words in Context** *ignore, worries, famous, speechless* **Word Study** Synonyms	**Offers with *Shall* and *Will*** Future statements and questions *"Shall I show you some more sketches?" he asks.*

Jay

Meg

Harry

Anna

LISTENING	SPEAKING	WRITING	WRAP UP

Looking at the Stars A conversation about stars in a galaxy **Listening Strategy** Listening for reasons	**Talking About Differences** *The first picture has a quarter moon.*	**Writing Complete Sentences** *The Earth revolves around the sun.* **Writing Practice** Write about an object in the universe (Workbook)	• **Writing** Write a compare and contrast report (WB) • **Project** Create a model
The Speed of Light A science report about how fast light travels **Listening Strategy** Listening for main idea and numbers	**Asking About Quantity** *How much water is on Jupiter?*	**Choice Questions** *Is Ganymede a planet or a moon?* **Writing Practice** Write about exploring the universe (WB)	• **Review** Units 1 and 2 (WB) Big Question 1 Review

An Ancient Town Children discuss a very old town **Listening Strategy** Listening for similarities and differences	**Giving Reasons** *I'd like to go back to an ancient Maya city.* *I want to see how Maya people made pyramids.*	**Verb Tenses** *The first emperor died when he was 49 years old.* **Writing Practice** Write about something that happened long ago (WB)	• **Writing** Write a descriptive report (WB) • **Project** Create a time capsule
A Nigerian Myth A myth about the sun and the moon **Listening Strategy** Listening for gist and sequence	**Describing with the Senses** *What did dinosaurs sound like?* *They probably sounded very loud.*	**Count and Noncount Nouns** *A lot of volcanic ash was above the bone.* **Writing Practice** Write about something old that people might look for in the ground (WB)	• **Review** Units 3 and 4 (WB) Big Question 2 Review

Where My Food Comes From A girl explains the types of food she eats **Listening Strategy** Listening for examples and numbers	**Giving a Reason for a Preference** *I like oranges, but I prefer bananas because they are easier to peel.*	**Interesting Adjectives** *My chickens lay wonderful eggs.* **Writing Practice** Write about a delicious meal (WB)	• **Writing** Write a research report (WB) • **Project** Create a story
Types of Farms Reporters discuss types of farms **Listening Strategy** Listening for reasons	**Talking About Food in Your Area** *People often grow apples where I live.*	**Prepositional Phrases of Location** *The asparagus is near the carrots.* **Writing Practice** Write about a real or imaginary garden (WB)	• **Review** Units 5 and 6 (WB) Big Question 3 Review

Art Around the World Children discuss art they like to make **Listening Strategy** Listening for reasons	**Talking About a Picture** *What are the children doing?* *They're painting.*	**Compound Predicate** *Picasso painted many masterpieces and created many sculptures.* **Writing Practice** Write about a work of art (WB)	• **Writing** Write an opinion essay (WB) • **Project** Act in a play
An Important Painting A tour guide discusses a famous painting **Listening Strategy** Listening for differences and details	**Expressing a Desire or Wish** *I wish I could paint like Claude Monet.*	**The Articles *A/An* and *The*** *Theo went to see an exhibition.* *Theo went to see the exhibition of Zayan Khan's landscapes.* **Writing Practice** Write about an artist (WB)	• **Review** Units 7 and 8 (WB) Big Question 4 Review 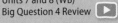

LISTENING	SPEAKING	WRITING	WRAP UP
Cities and Water The reasons why many cities form near bodies of water **Listening Strategy** Listening for reasons	**Giving Reasons** *My city grew because it is next to a river.* *The river was important because people used the water in many ways.*	**Capitalize the Names of Bodies of Water** *River Seine, Lake Texcoco, Pacific Ocean* **Writing Practice** Write about a city near water (WB)	• **Writing** Write a persuasive essay (WB) • **Project** Create a travel brochure.
Benefits of Cities Children share what they like about the cities they live in **Listening Strategy** Listening for facts and opinions	**Asking Questions with *Have To*** *Do people in your city have to recycle bottles and cans?*	**Coordinating Conjunctions: *And, But, Or*** *I play chess with my mother but not with my father.* **Writing Practice** Write about parts of a city (WB)	• **Review** Units 9 and 10 (WB) Big Question 5 Review ▶
Public Service Announcement An announcement on how to stay healthy **Listening Strategy** Listening for advice	**Asking and Answering Personal Questions** *What do you do when you catch a cold?* *I drink a lot of water and sleep as much as I can.*	**Give Advice with Commands** *Eat healthy food every day.* **Writing Practice** Write about good health habits (WB)	• **Writing** Write an interview (WB) • **Project** Conduct an interview
The Body's Bones Facts about the bones in the human body **Listening Strategy** Listening for who's speaking and details	**Explanations with *That* or *Where*** *What is the stomach?* *It's a part of your body that breaks down food.*	**Subject/Verb Agreement with Indefinite Pronouns** *When everyone works together, you can do great things!* **Writing Practice** Write about exercise (WB)	• **Review** Units 11 and 12 (WB) Big Question 6 Review ▶
Creating a Blog An explanation of how to create a blog **Listening Strategy** Listening for gist and details	**Giving Examples** *My dad gets news from the newspaper.*	**Pronouns** *When early humans discovered how to make fire, they told their friends.* **Writing Practice** Write about how news travels (WB)	• **Writing** Write a news story (WB) • **Project** Create a school news program
School News A school news program for students **Listening Strategy** Listening for facts and opinions	**Giving Opinions** *I don't think that all blogs are interesting because some are boring.*	**Regular and Irregular Verbs in the Present Perfect** *George has learned a lot from this science blog.* *I've seen the inside of a television studio.* **Writing Practice** Write about a mass media job (WB)	• **Review** Units 13 and 14 (WB) Big Question 7 Review ▶
Earthquake Preparation An explanation of how to prepare for an earthquake **Listening Strategy** Listening for problems and solutions; main idea and details	**Possibilities** *There might be a lot of rain.*	**Contractions in Present Perfect Sentences** *We've bought extra water in case of a storm.* **Writing Practice** Write about a force of nature (WB)	• **Writing** Write a how-to speech (WB) • **Project** Create an emergency poster
Weather Warnings Reporters give extreme weather warnings **Listening Strategy** Listening for recommendations	**Talking About Needs** *We need to get water bottles.*	**Adverbs of Manner** *The waves were violent. They smashed violently into the hotel.* **Writing Practice** Write about an imaginary, dangerous situation (WB)	• **Review** Units 15 and 16 (WB) Big Question 8 Review ▶
Food Chains Children explain desert food chains **Listening Strategy** Listening for sequence	**Describing a Sequence** *In the spring, the trees are full of small leaves.*	**Complex Sentences with *Until*** *The cheetah ran until it caught the gazelle.* **Writing Practice** Write about someone who visits a biome (WB)	• **Writing** Write a fictional story (WB) • **Project** Act in a play
Life in a Different Biome Children discuss biomes where they would like to live **Listening Strategy** Listening for reasons	**Asking About Needs** *What do I need for my trip?*	**Complex Sentences with *Since* and *Because*** *Since coral reefs are dying, we have to help them.* **Writing Practice** Write about protecting biomes (WB)	• **Review** Units 17 and 18 (WB) Big Question 9 Review ▶

Introduction

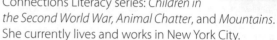

Welcome to *Oxford Discover*

Oxford Discover is a six-level course, created to address the evolving needs of young learners of English in the 21st century. Second language acquisition is now much more than an academic pursuit. It has become an essential skill for global cooperation and problem solving. *Oxford Discover* is centered on the belief that language and literacy skills are best taught within a framework of critical thinking and global awareness, and it aims to guide students toward the broader goals of communication.

Oxford Discover creates a positive and motivating learning environment by:

- providing content that is relevant, informative, and academic.
- offering multiple perspectives on topics across the curriculum.
- allowing students to consider key concept questions that they revisit as they gain more information.
- challenging students to think critically about topics, issues, and questions.
- developing strategies that help students perform well in tests.
- fostering a love of reading and writing.

The *Oxford Discover* Author Team

Lesley Koustaff and Susan Rivers

Lesley and Susan are the authors of *Oxford Discover*, levels 1 and 2.

Lesley is a passionate teacher trainer. She has conducted educational workshops all over the world. Lesley lives in New York and writes and edits material to teach children English.

Susan has over 25 years' experience teaching English in Asia and the United States. Susan is the author of *Tiny Talk* and coauthor of *English Time* as well as many other EFL preschool, primary, and secondary teaching materials.

Kathleen Kampa and Charles Vilina

Kathleen and Charles are the authors of *Oxford Discover*, levels 3 and 4. Both Kathleen and Charles have taught Japanese and International School children for over 16 years. They are both active teacher trainers.

Kathleen and Charles are coauthors of *Magic Time* and *Everybody Up*, primary courses published by Oxford University Press.

Kenna Bourke

Kenna Bourke is the author of *Oxford Discover*, levels 5 and 6. Kenna is the author of *The Grammar Lab* and the *Test it, Fix it* series. Additionally, Kenna has written books for the Oxford Connections Literacy series: *Children in the Second World War*, *Animal Chatter*, and *Mountains*. She currently lives and works in New York City.

Kindergarten Learning Assumptions

It is assumed that students starting at level 1 of *Oxford Discover* will already have some basic literacy and language skills. The three-level kindergarten course *Show and Tell* gets children ready to learn with *Oxford Discover*. If you use this course or another entry-level course, it is expected that children will know the following:

Literacy and Numeracy

Children will know the alphabet and be able to read words and simple sentences. They will be able to write words and short sentences. Children will know digits and words for numbers 1–29.

Vocabulary

Children will know vocabulary relating to basic classroom objects and greetings, but also some word families:

- colors
- shapes
- toys
- animals
- family
- clothes
- nature
- body
- weather
- places and things in a house
- basic verbs and adjectives

Structures

Children will be able to ask and answer basic questions. They will know the present simple, question words, and simple question forms. They will have been introduced to the present continuous for actions happening now.

The Key Principles of *Oxford Discover*

I. Language and Literacy Skills

1. Vocabulary

- *Oxford Discover*'s rich vocabulary is divided between everyday words and curriculum-based words. Students acquire and retain vocabulary through illustrations and definitions, through context, and through pronunciation and spelling work.

- Students need to encounter new words in different contexts a number of times, before they can recall and recognize the words and autonomously produce them. This is why words are presented and practiced with a focus on meaning before they are highlighted in the reading texts where students encounter them in particular contexts. Vocabulary is then rigorously recycled throughout not only the level, but the entire series, so that students can feel confident when meeting those words again in different situations.

2. Grammar

- *Oxford Discover*'s grammar syllabus is fast-paced, carefully sequenced, and high-level.
- The grammar in *Oxford Discover* comes from the texts in each unit. By providing grammar in context, in an implicit manner, students can be exposed to grammar study with a focus on meaning as well as form. Acquiring a language means developing the ability to use language in natural and communicative situations. Structural input is best when integrated into a meaningful syllabus, utilizing familiar vocabulary and situations. The Student Book takes this approach to teaching grammar, with more explicit grammar practice provided in the Workbook to help students apply it in more contexts and to internalize the rules and forms.
- *Oxford Discover Grammar* is a six-level companion series which provides clear structural grammar input and further practice of the grammatical items presented in the corresponding levels of *Oxford Discover*.

3. Literacy

- *Oxford Discover* introduces words and structures through reading texts in each unit. There is a variety of fiction and nonfiction texts and genre types in each level, which helps children to become familiar with different types of language and language use.
- *Oxford Discover* teaches essential literacy skills through the introduction of reading and writing strategies in each unit. These practical strategies encourage students to read critically and efficiently through a broad range of fiction and nonfiction text types and genres.
- *Oxford Discover Writing and Spelling* is a six-level companion series which provides further literacy input and practice, reviewing the vocabulary and grammatical items, and focusing on the writing strategies presented in the corresponding levels of *Oxford Discover*.

II. 21st Century Skills

We live in an age of rapid change. Advances in communication and information technology continue to create new opportunities and challenges for the future. As our world becomes increasingly interconnected, today's young students must develop strong skills in critical thinking, global communication, collaboration, and creativity. In addition, students must develop life and career skills, information, media, and technology skills, as well as an appreciation and concern for the health of our planet and cross-cultural understanding. *Oxford Discover* strives to help students build each of these skills in order to succeed in the 21st century.

The major 21st Century Skills are addressed in *Oxford Discover*. They build on a broad base of academic subjects presented throughout the course.

1. Critical Thinking

Students in the 21st century need to do more than acquire information. They need to be able to make sense of the information by thinking about it critically. Critical thinking skills help students to determine facts, prioritize information, understand relationships, solve problems, and more. *Oxford Discover* encourages students to think deeply and assess information comprehensively. Students are invited to be curious and questioning and to think beyond their normal perspectives. Throughout every unit, questions labelled *Think* encourage students to apply their own experience and opinions.

2. Communication

As a global course for English in the 21st century, *Oxford Discover* offers students plentiful opportunities to become effective listeners, speakers, readers, and writers. Every unit has two pages devoted comprehensively to communication, but these skills are also utilized in general tasks and exercises. In addition, *Oxford Discover* iTools and Online Practice promote online communication and computer literacy, preparing students for the demands of the new information age.

3. Collaboration

Collaboration requires direct communication between students, which strengthens the personal skills of listening and speaking. Students who work together well not only achieve better results, but also gain a sense of team spirit and pride in the process. *Oxford Discover* offers opportunities for collaboration in every lesson, with students working together in pairs, small groups, or as an entire class.

4. Creativity

Creativity is an essential 21st Century Skill. Students who are able to exercise their creativity are better at making changes, solving new problems, expressing themselves through the arts, and more. *Oxford Discover* encourages creativity throughout each unit by allowing students the freedom to offer ideas and express themselves without judgment. In the lower levels, students complete a project which reflects their learning about the Big Question, after every pair of units. In the higher levels, they learn presentation skills and implement learning through creative processes.

III. Inquiry-based Learning

Inquiry-based learning maximizes student involvement, encourages collaboration and teamwork, and promotes creative thinking. Students employ the four skills of listening, speaking, reading, and writing as they identify questions about the world around them, gather information, and find answers.

Oxford Discover supports an inquiry-based approach to learning English. Each pair of units in *Oxford Discover* revolves around a Big Question on a specific curricular theme. The curricular themes come from school subjects such as Social studies (community, history, geography), sciences (life science, physical science, earth science), the arts (music, art) and mathematics. The Big Question is broad, open-ended, and thought-provoking, appealing to students' natural curiosity.

Throughout the process of inquiry-based learning, students play an active role in their own education. Teachers facilitate this learning by guiding students to ask questions, seek information, and find answers. As students work together and share information, they build essential skills in communication and collaboration.

The following guidelines will help teachers create the most effective classroom environment for *Oxford Discover*, ensuring maximum student participation and learning.

1. Facilitate student-centered learning

Student-centered learning gives students an active role in the classroom. The teacher acts as facilitator, guiding the learning and ensuring that everyone has a voice. Students work individually and together to achieve the goals they have set for the lessons. As a result, student participation and dialogue are maximized.

2. Wonder out loud

Curious students are inquirers, ready to look beyond the information on a page. Curiosity can be developed in your students if you are curious, too. As new ideas, stories, or topics encountered, use these sentence starters to help students start wondering:

- *I wonder why these insects are becoming extinct.*
- *I wonder how inventors came up with their first ideas.*
- *I wonder what happens when / if …*

3. Let student inquiry lead the lesson

When students are presented with a topic, invite them to ask their own questions about it. In doing so, they are more motivated to seek answers to those questions. In addition, as students find answers, they take on the added role of teacher to inform others in the class.

4. Explore global values

Children need to understand the importance of values at an early age. Taking an inquiry-based approach means that they are encouraged to think about different situations and the effect that particular behavior has within those situations. *Oxford Discover* promotes global values throughout the series, with texts and activities prompting children to examine values from an outside and a personal perspective. The discussion questions in the teaching notes help to make children aware of their own beliefs and the importance of contributing in a positive way to civil society. There are also nine values worksheets per level, one for each Big Question. The values are drawn from the content of the readings in each pair of units and help students develop a personal and in-depth understanding of the topic. Teachers can use the worksheets flexibly, either while studying the two units, or afterwards.

5. Focus on thinking, not memorizing

Oxford Discover is based on the belief that critical thinking is the key to better learning. While retention of words and structures is important for language development, allowing students to access knowledge on a deeper level is equally important and will further encourage effective learning in the classroom. The critical-thinking activities in *Oxford Discover* help students make sense of the information presented to them, ultimately leading to greater understanding and retention.

6. Build strong student-teacher relationships

While maintaining class discipline, it is important to develop a mutual relationship of trust and open communication with students. In this way, students begin to look at themselves as partners in learning with their teacher. This gives them a sense of shared responsibility, creating a dynamic and highly motivating learning environment.

7. Take time to reflect

Every *Oxford Discover* lesson should begin and end with student reflection. The lesson can begin with the question *What have we learned up to now?* and end with *What have we learned today?* The answers are not limited to content, but can also explore methods, strategies, and processes. As students become more aware of how they learn, they become more confident and efficient in their learning.

8. Make connections

Deep learning occurs when students can connect new knowledge with prior knowledge and personal experiences. Give your students opportunities to make connections. For example:

We learned about the explorer Jacques Cousteau. How is he similar to other explorers we've read about? What qualities do you think explorers have? Could you be an explorer?

Connections can be made between units, too. For example: *How are explorers similar to inventors?*

By making such connections, students will be able to understand new vocabulary and grammar input in a contextualized way and retain language and content knowledge.

9. Cooperate instead of compete

Competitive activities may create temporary motivation, but often leave some students feeling less confident and valued. By contrast, cooperative activities build teamwork and class unity while boosting communication skills. Confident students serve as a support to those who need extra help. All students learn the value of working together. Cooperative activities provide win-win opportunities for the entire class.

Assessment for Learning

Overview of the Assessment Program

The *Oxford Discover* approach to assessment offers teachers and students the tools needed to help shape and improve the students' learning, as well as a means to monitor learning goals, through a shared ongoing and creative process. The *Oxford Discover* assessment program includes five categories of tests for each level of *Oxford Discover*: diagnostic placement tests, progress tests, review tests, achievement tests, four-skill assessments, and portfolio self-assessments. The items in these tests have been reviewed by assessment experts to ensure that each item measures what it is intended to measure. As a result, each test provides an accurate assessment of students' ability in English and their progress in *Oxford Discover*.

Oxford Discover levels 1 – 4 correspond to Cambridge English: Young Learners.

Oxford Discover level 5 corresponds to Cambridge English: Key for Schools.

Oxford Discover level 6 corresponds to Cambridge English: Preliminary for Schools.

The assessment audio is found on the Class Audio CD.

Entry Test and Entry Review Worksheets

- The four-page Entry Test is administered at the beginning of each level and is designed to serve as a diagnostic placement test.
- The test assesses mastery of the key grammar topics from the preceding level that will be reintroduced and expanded on in the new level curriculum. Testing these points on entry can help identify each student's readiness for the new level and thus serve as a baseline for individual student performance as well as class performance.
- There is one Entry Review worksheet for each of the grammar points on the Entry Test.
- The review worksheets can be used to give individualized instruction to students or classes that, based on the Entry Test, have not mastered material from the previous level.
- The worksheets can also be used as additional review and practice throughout the course, even for students or classes that have demonstrated success on the Entry Test.

Unit Tests

- The Unit Tests are grammar and vocabulary progress tests.
- There is one Unit Test after each unit.
- Each test is two pages long.

Review Tests

- The Review Tests are grammar and vocabulary accumulative tests.
- There is a Review Test after Unit 6 and Unit 12.
- Each test focuses on the grammar and vocabulary of the preceding six units.
- Each test is four pages long.

Final Test

- This is a Final Achievement Test for the level.
- It is administered after Unit 18.
- It focuses on the grammar and vocabulary of the entire level.
- This test is four pages long.

Skills Assessments

- The Skills Assessments are contextualized four-skills tests using the vocabulary, grammatical structures, and themes in the Student Book.
- These assessments measure acquisition of listening, reading and writing, and speaking.
- The assessments are based on the style of the Cambridge English: Young Learners (YLE), Cambridge English: Key (KET) for Schools, and Cambridge English Preliminary (PET) for Schools.
- There is a Skills Assessment after Units 6, 12, and 18.
- Each assessment is four pages long.

Portfolio Assessment

- The Portfolio Assessment is a continuous and ongoing formative assessment and self-assessment.
- The purpose is to allow students to be creative, collaborative, communicative, and to be critical thinkers – all 21st Century Skills.
- Portfolio items can include: projects, tests and quizzes, self-assessment worksheets, writing samples, lists of books read, audio or video.

- In addition, the Assessment for Learning CD-ROM contains self-assessment worksheets for students to create their own portfolio cover and to assess their own learning every two units by using can-do statements and responding to Big Question cues.

Answer Keys

- A simple answer key for all tests is provided.

Differentiation

Differentiation helps to ensure that all students find success in the classroom. There are many ways to differentiate instruction. In *Oxford Discover*, differentiation strategies are built into the structure of the course to help you instruct your students in the most effective way possible.

The goal is to:

- Offer a clear pathway for students who are at different levels, with regular checking stages to assess progress against a list of competences at the end of every unit.
- Offer both whole-group work and small-group differentiated activities in the first language tradition to meet the needs of varied teaching styles.

Each lesson spread in the Teacher's Book provides an activity to vary the content difficulty for below-level, at-level and above-level students. These differentiated activities build upon each other. The below-level activity provides support and scaffolding for less confident students before moving on to a task that is at-level. The at-level task then provides support for students to deal with the greater challenge of above-level. This is a practical way of dealing with classroom management of mixed abilities. Teachers may choose to teach the whole class with one activity, and then continue with the additional activities. Alternatively, three separate simultaneous activities can be set up, as in L1 classrooms.

To help teachers meet the needs of students with varying ability levels, differentiation strategies are found consistently throughout the following strands:

- An Entry Test, taken at the start of the year and useful for diagnostic and placement testing, will result in a level diagnosis (below-level, at-level, and above-level).
- Review worksheets (grammar and reading) are provided for below-level students to bring them up to the level needed.
- Additional differentiation strategies are found throughout the course. The wrap up projects invite students to express their ideas through different learning styles (visual, auditory, kinesthetic). Throughout the course, students have opportunities to work alone, in pairs, and in small groups to support differentiated instruction.

Reading and Writing

Reading

Literacy is the ability to read and write and think critically about the written word. *Oxford Discover* promotes greater literacy through a focus on interesting and engaging texts, both fiction and nonfiction, about a variety of subjects.

The texts have been carefully graded so that they are at an appropriate reading level for students. The word length, vocabulary, and structures used gradually increase in difficulty throughout each level.

Text types

Students need to be exposed to different types of texts. In its broadest form this is a focus on introducing them to both fiction and nonfiction. In *Oxford Discover* each Big Question has two texts to help students find their own answers to the question. One text is nonfiction and corresponds to a school subject such as math, life science or music. The other one is fiction and is written in a particular genre, encouraging students to relate to and enjoy the content.

The nonfiction texts are presented through different text types such as a brochure, magazine article, or website. This helps students understand not only that writing comes in many forms in daily life, but also that that tone and register (formal and informal language) change depending on the way the information is presented.

The fiction texts come from a variety of genres. This includes fairy tales, fables, historical fiction, and realistic fiction. These genres reflect the types of stories that students are exposed to reading in their native language and provide variety throughout the course.

Authentic texts

In every level of *Oxford Discover* there is a range of authentic texts. These have been carefully chosen to add more information to the Big Question. They come from a variety of sources and from well-respected writers and authors. Authentic texts expose students to real contexts and natural examples of language. The texts chosen are of an appropriate language level and encourage students to read with a focus on meaning and understanding language in context.

Reading Strategies

Reading strategies help students approach a text, improve their comprehension of the text, and learn how to read for specific and detailed information. Strategies such as prediction, compare and contrast, summarizing, and focusing on characters can inspire students to not only master the meaning of unfamiliar concepts but expand their own vocabulary as well.

Reading strategies tie in closely to critical thinking as they encourage students to reflect on what they are reading. As students grow more comfortable using a variety of reading strategies they learn to make conscious decisions about their own learning process.

Multimodality

Multimodal texts help to support students's literacy. Texts which include words, images, and explicit design are a very effective way of engaging students in purposeful interactions with reading and writing.

Multimodal is the use of 'two or more communication modes' to make meaning; for example, image, gesture, music, spoken language, and written language.

In everyday life, texts are becoming increasingly visual or multimodal in nature. Websites, magazines, advertisements, and informational literature are relying more and more upon visual stimulation and clear use of design, in headlines, through different types of fonts, and in stylized images.

Oxford Discover has included multimodality in its use of DVD and posters to support the Student Book, but even within the texts themselves, the use of words, images and design, and the way they interact with each other helps to keep students stimulated while reading and also helps to exemplify meaning.

Intensive Reading

Intensive reading generally occurs in the classroom and focuses not only upon meaning and strategies used to deduce meaning, but language acquisition in the form of understanding new vocabulary or new grammatical structures. Texts need to be at the correct level and long enough to convey enough information or plot to be interesting, but not so long as to tire the student. *Oxford Discover* takes the approach that intensive reading should be instructional but enjoyable and should encourage students to do more extensive reading.

Extensive Reading

Extensive reading generally occurs outside the classroom and is all about reading for pleasure. Students are encouraged to choose to read about topics that interest them and to employ reading strategies explicitly taught through intensive reading, to help them understand the text more effectively. Reading the different genres and text types in *Oxford Discover* will inspire students to read more in their own time.

Extensive reading is often most effective when students are reading at a level that is appropriate and comfortable for them. If students are reading a book that is too high in level they quickly lose interest. It can be helpful to provide students with access to a collection of graded readers that they can read at their own pace. The recommended readers for use with *Oxford Discover* are the nonfiction selection of *Read and Discover* and the fiction selection of *Read and Imagine*.

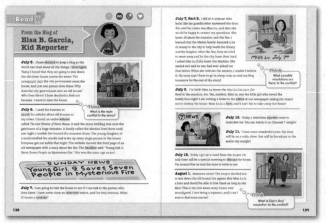

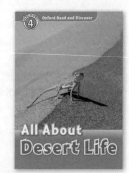

Text Readability

	Level 1	Level 2	Level 3	Level 4	Level 5	Level 6
Flesch Reading Ease Level (F)	85–100	85–95	75–90	70–80	65–80	60–80
Flesch Reading Ease Level (NF)	85–100	80–95	70–85	70–85	60–75	60–75
Flesch-Kincaid Grade Level (F)	0–3	1. 5–3	2– 5	3.5–6	4–7	5–7
Flesch-Kincaid Grade Level (NF)	1–3	2–4	3–5	4–6	5–7. 5	6–8
Lexile Measure (F)	75–325	250–450	400–675	500–900	600–750	600–900
Lexile Measure (NF)	125–325	300–550	450–750	725–900	750–950	900–1000

Both sets of readers have been developed with similar themes to those in the Student Book and there is a selection of titles for each level of *Oxford Discover*.

Grading scales

The texts in *Oxford Discover* have been carefully graded to make sure that students understand the texts at their level, and to help students progress in their reading, within one level and from one level to another. In accordance with this, the standards of the Flesch Reading Ease Level, the Flesch-Kincaid Grade Level, and the Lexile Measure, have been taken into account.

The **Flesch Reading Ease Level** is a scale which measures readability. The higher the rating, the easier the text is to understand. There are different scores for fiction and nonfiction texts:

- 100: Very easy to read. Average sentence length is 12 words or fewer. No words of more than two syllables.
- 65: Plain English. Average sentence is 15 to 20 words long. Average word has two syllables.

The **Flesch-Kincaid Grade Level** converts the Flesch Reading Ease Level to a U.S. grade-school level. For example, a score of 5 means that a fifth-grader can understand the text. There are different scores for fiction (F) and nonfiction (NF) texts. It is important to remember that students in any grade will be able to understand a variety of texts around the score.

The **Lexile Measure** gives information about a student's reading ability as well as the difficulty level of a text. Higher Lexile measures represent a higher reading ability. A Lexile reader measure can range from below 200 for beginning readers to above 1600 for advanced readers. There are different scores for fiction (F) and nonfiction (NF) texts. The nonfiction texts can be more challenging than the fiction texts in the same level. Nonfiction texts contain factual content and students are reading to learn.

Writing

Oxford Discover encourages a joy of reading through a variety of texts and text types. However, students also need to be encouraged to produce their own texts and this requires a step-by-step process, helping students to graduate from sentence to text-level output.

Oxford Discover provides many opportunities for students to write. The Word Study and Writing Study sections in the Student Book present the strategies and language focus that help students become more successful writers, and the Workbook provides a four-step writing process (brainstorming, organizing ideas, writing, editing) which helps students to create their own writing output.

Process and Product

Writing tasks are often broken down into process or product from level 3 onwards. The process is all about how students develop and implement writing strategies such as paragraph development, focusing on formal or informal language, and general text layout. The process often includes stages of input, practice, and reflection. The product is the actual writing output that students create. It is often said that the former, process writing, provides a focus on fluency whereas product writing focuses on accuracy. Students need to have both to learn to write confidently and correctly.

Oxford Discover has a process approach with clear and definable product outcomes that can easily be marked against established criteria.

Brainstorming ideas

Too often, teachers expect students to write without giving them adequate time to prepare or strategies to help them develop their ideas. The *Oxford Discover* team believe that encouraging students to plan ideas creatively will create more interest in the process, as well as the final product.

Modelling the writing process

Students are provided with a model text for every writing task. This text is designed to show how topics can be approached, but also how discourse markers, paragraph organization, punctuation, and general textual layout can help to sew a text together.

Personalization

As much as possible, students should be asked to write about things that are of personal relevance to them. This means that although the model in the Student Book or the Workbook may relate to something that is outside their everyday world, the writing task itself will be flexible enough for students to respond using their own ideas and experience. In this way it becomes authentically communicative and a more interesting experience overall.

For a further focus on literacy, *Oxford Writing and Spelling* provides more textual input and encourages students to use the reading strategies they have acquired as they study *Oxford Discover*.

Speaking and Listening

Oxford Discover utilizes an inquiry-led approach to learning English. This means that students are encouraged to ask questions and explore answers for themselves. To do this, they need to develop good oral skills that help them formulate discussions and express opinions confidently, and strong listening skills that help them to understand language of discussion and participate effectively.

Promoting Successful Classroom Discussions

Discussions in the classroom can involve student pairs, small groups, or the entire class.

What makes these class discussions successful? First of all, the questions should be interesting and engaging for students. They should relate to their personal experiences. The teacher needs to act as a moderator, keeping the discussions on track and ensuring that each student is given an opportunity to speak.

There are two kinds of questions that are commonly used in the classroom: close-ended and open-ended questions. Close-ended questions can be answered with one word or with a few words. Yes / No questions and multiple-choice questions are examples of this type of question.

Examples of close-ended questions:

What is the answer to question number three?

What is the name of the explorer in our story?

How do you spell "pineapple"?

Open-ended questions usually require a longer response to answer the question. They prompt more discussion time, allow students to apply new vocabulary, and often lead to more questions.

Examples of open-ended questions:

How do bees help the world?

What plants would you like to grow in your own garden? Why?

What do you think are important qualities of a good student?

Here are some possible open-ended questions you could ask about the topic of healthy eating:

1. *What was the last thing you ate? Describe it.*
2. *Does something have to taste good to be good for you?*
3. *What are some things that you didn't like to eat, but now you like?*
4. *How are healthy foods the same?*
5. *Why is pizza popular?*
6. *What can students do to improve school lunch?*
7. *How do you decide if a food is healthy or not?*

The above questions not only generate strong discussions, but encourage students to ask their own questions and think critically as well.

Here are some discussion starters that can be used to introduce a variety of topics. Don't hesitate to bring in hands-on materials to get students thinking.

What do you think this is, and how would it be used?

What do you think would happen if _____ ?

How many different ways can you _____?

How are _____ and _____ the same? Different?

How is _____ similar to something that happened in the past?

Why is _____ the way it is?

What should we do to take care of _____?

How do we know this is true?

If you could have a conversation with anyone about _____, who would it be? What would you ask them?

If you could change one thing about _____, what would it be?

Developing a climate of wondering is important in an inquiry-based classroom. While teachers may be accustomed to asking questions and having students take turns to answer, inquiry-based learning invites both students and teachers to ask engaging questions.

Setting up Pairs and Groups

Many activities in this course encourage students to work in pairs or small groups (three or four students). These structures maximize speaking time in a classroom. Students are encouraged to be active rather than passive learners. In groups, they develop collaborative and cooperative skills.

At the beginning of the class year, consider several ways of setting up pairs or small groups. Use one type of grouping for a few classes before changing to a new one. Change groupings throughout the year, so that students interact with many different classmates and have a chance to listen to different vocabulary and structures in different contexts.

Setting up pairs
Side-by-Side Partners

If the classroom is set up with desks in rows, students may work with a partner next to them. If there is an odd number of students, make a group of three.

1 ←→ 2   3 ←→ 4   5 ←→ 6
7 ←→ 8   9 ←→10   11←→12

Front and Back Partners

Instead of working with partners next to each other, students work with the partner in front of (or behind) them.

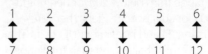

Diagonal Partners

Students work with a partner located diagonally in front of (or behind) them. For ease in discussion, a student may wish to trade seats with the student next to him / her. For example, student 1 and 8 will be partners. Students 1 and 2 might switch seats.

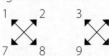

Setting up small groups

Double Partner Groups

Using the partner groups established in pair work above, students form groups of four.

Random Groups

Create random groups of four students by dividing the class size by four, and then having students count off up to that number. For example, if there are 24 students in class, 24 ÷ 4 = 6. Students count off from 1 to 6, and then begin again until all have counted off. Point out where each group will have their discussion in the classroom.

Picture Card Groups

Create a set of picture or word cards. Make five of the same card. Pass four out to students and put the fifth card in the location where those students will work. One card per student will be needed. Use topics from the units, such as instruments, colors, biomes, and explorers. Topic cards are fun to use throughout the unit. This grouping is particularly successful with younger students.

Level Groups

Grouping students of similar ability level to work together is a strategy for differentiation. Leveled groups can be reated based on teacher assessments from the Assessment Grid and from your class observations. There are differentiated tasks in the Teacher's Book to allow all students to work at their appropriate level.

Teacher's Role in Setting up Pairs and Groups

1. Explain the task and form groupings. Write the amount of time students will have to complete this task on the board, or set a timer.

2. As students are discussing the prompt or are involved in the activity, walk around the classroom. First of all, be aware of any groups that may have difficulties. If there are personality conflicts or difficulties, deal with this immediately. Secondly, assess student work. Stop and listen to each group. Are students on task? Can errors be corrected individually? Are there any points that need revision with the entire class?

3. On the Assessment Grid, note the level the students are at for this task. Some students may require additional practice.

4. Take note of points for discussion with the entire class.

5. Keep track of the time. Use a signal, such as a raised hand 'quiet signal', to stop small group discussion.

6. Check in with the entire class. Some questions to use:

What was the most interesting thing your partner shared with you?

What was difficult for you, and did you find a solution?

What new questions do you have?

Working in groups may be new for students. The student poster models some effective ways for students to interact. Student "agreements" should be created together with students, but here are some ideas to get started.

Student Agreements

We will . . .

1. Take turns speaking.
2. Listen to our partner or group members.
3. Stay on task.
4. Raise our hand when we see the 'quiet signal' and stop talking.
5. Treat each member of the class with respect. We are a class community.

Functional Language

Students need to learn how to discuss issues and express opinions, but they also need to learn the different elements of functional language. Functional language includes areas such as apologizing, offering and receiving help, transactions, and clarification and explanation.

Learning functional language helps students to understand language 'chunks' and that language often has a very specific purpose. The main function of language is to help students interact and communicate. Dialogues provide models through which students can see and hear authentic communication. Transposition and substitution of vocabulary then allows students to personalize the dialogues through meaningful oral production.

Integrated Component Overview

Student Book
The Student Book contains 18 units. Each pair of units presents students with a different Big Question, encouraging students to examine the world more critically within an inquiry-based learning environment.

Workbook
The Workbook provides students with extra practice of the language and structures taught in class.

Student Online Practice
The Online Practice is a blended approach to learning where students can use online, interactive activities to further practice the language and ideas taught in the Student Book.

For the Student

Recommended Readers
Oxford Read and Discover is a graded, six-level, nonfiction reading series. *Oxford Read and Imagine* is a graded six-level, fiction reading series. Both draw upon themes and language found in the Student Book.

Dictionaries
Levels 1–4 *Oxford Basic American Dictionary*
Levels 5–6 *Oxford American Dictionary*

Show and Tell
A three-level kindergarten course which introduces children to the 21st Century skills and prepares children for *Oxford Discover*.

Oxford Discover Grammar
A six-level companion series which follows and supports the grammar syllabus and provides further practice opportunities.

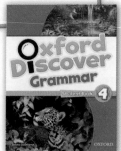
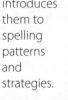

Oxford Discover Writing and Spelling
A six-level companion series which supports students throughout the writing process and introduces them to spelling patterns and strategies.

Teacher's Book

The Teacher's Book is a clear guide for the teacher in all aspects of the course.

Big Question DVD

The Big Question DVD covers each Big Question in the Student Book. Each pair of units has two videos, one with a presenter and one without.

Assessment CD-ROM

Students' progress can be evaluated through continuous assessment, self-assessment and more formal testing.

Posters

The posters initiate and support classroom discussions and act as visual aids; provide support for learning; and document evidence of learning.

Teacher Online Practice

Teachers have complete access to students' online practice, with a gradebook which enables instant marking.

For the Teacher

Picture Cards

(Levels 1 and 2 only)

The picture cards include all the main unit vocabulary from the Student Book. They can be used to present and recycle vocabulary.

Audio CD

The Class Audio CDs support teaching in class and contain recordings of all the listening texts, reading texts, songs, and speaking dialogues.

iTools

The *Oxford Discover iTools* is a DVD-ROM which contains digital class resources. All the iTools resources can be used either on an Interactive Whiteboard or on a projector.

Teacher Website

The Teacher Website provides additional materials for students and teachers to supplement all the other components available.

Parent Website

The Parent's Website provides support and materials for parents of students studying with *Oxford Discover*.

Tour of Units

Big Question

These pages present the theme and objectives of the following two units. The big picture acts as an introductory visual representation of many of the ideas and language that students will go on to discover in the following pages.

Preview

The preview introduces students to the theme and main objectives of the Big Question. It also gives students information about what they will do and learn throughout the following two units.

In units **7** and **8** you will:

WATCH
a video about art and artists.

LEARN
about the reasons artists create art.

READ
about real artists and a boy who loves art.

66 *Big Question 4*

A. Big Question DVD

Students watch a DVD about the Big Question in order to stimulate their thinking about the topic. The DVD can be used to elicit vocabulary and to introduce the theme of the following two units. This first viewing of the DVD is silent, as students are encouraged to respond individually to the clips and images. This will also help the teacher determine what students already know and what they want to know.

B. The Big Picture

Students look at the Big Picture. The Big Picture helps students to think about what they already know and what they want to know about the topic. It can be used to elicit familiar vocabulary and to motivate students about the theme of the following two units.

WRITE an opinion essay.

ACT in a play.

BIG QUESTION 4
Why do we make art?

A Watch the video. ▶

B Look at the picture and talk about it.

1 Where are the girls? What do you see in this place?

2 What are they doing? What are they using to do this?

C Think and answer the questions.

1 What kind of art do you make at school?

2 How is art class different from science class?

D Fill out the **Big Question Chart**.

What do you know about art? What do you want to know?

67

Discover Poster
The Discover Poster should be used to elicit familiar vocabulary and to stimulate interest in the topic

C. Answer the Questions
Students answer questions that ask about their personal knowledge and life experiences. This starts children interacting personally with the theme of the units and encourages them to make connections to help their learning.

D. The Big Question Chart
Students share what they already know and what they want to know about the Big Question and their ideas are recorded on the Big Question Chart.

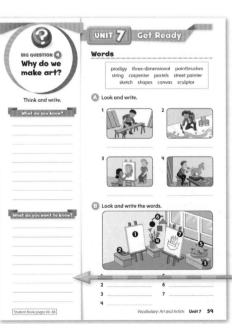

Workbook
Students write about what they know and what they want to know.

Get Ready

This page teaches and helps students practice a vocabulary set. It also encourages students to think critically about the language.

A. Words

Students are introduced to new vocabulary and have the opportunity to connect the words to the pictures and hear them spoken on the Audio CD.

B. Comprehension

Students complete an activity that tests their understanding of the words presented in Exercise A.

C. Critical Thinking

Students complete a critical thinking activity that measures their understanding of some or all of the words.

Workbook

Students complete a variety of activities that build and test their knowledge of the new vocabulary.

UNIT 7 — Get Ready

Words

A Listen and read the words. Listen again and say the words. 🔊 2-02

sketch   pastels   canvas   paintbrushes   shapes   string

three-dimensional   prodigy   street painter   carpenter   sculptor

B Circle True (T) or False (F).

1 You can tie things together with string.   T   F
2 Circles, squares, and triangles are shapes.   T   F
3 A prodigy is usually an adult person.   T   F
4 A photograph is three-dimensional.   T   F
5 You need paint to make a sketch.   T   F
6 Carpenters work with clay.   T   F
7 Street painters work outdoors.   T   F
8 Paintbrushes only come in one size.   T   F

C Three of the four words are correct. Cross out the wrong answer.

1 This person creates something new.
   street painter   shapes   carpenter   sculptor

2 Artists use these things to make art.
   pastels   paintbrushes   sketches   canvases

68   Unit 7 *Vocabulary: Art and Artists*

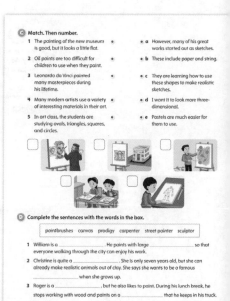

Before You Read

Students are introduced to a reading strategy which they will then apply to help them understand the text on the following pages. They are also introduced to the text type and information about genre.

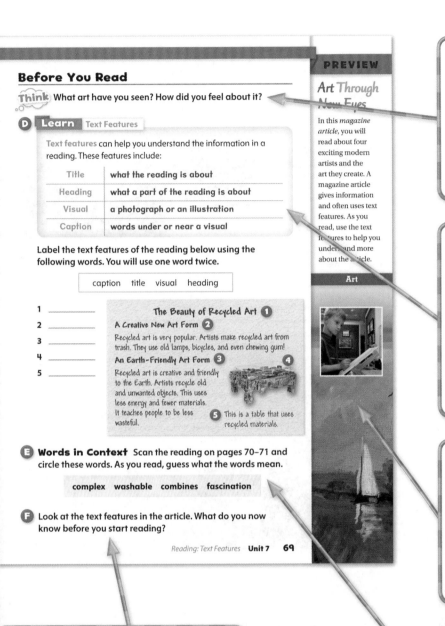

Think. Critical Thinking

These questions act as a lead-in to the reading text. Students use their personal knowledge and life experiences to answer This activates interest in the topic of the text, and immediately connects it to the students own lives.

D. Reading Strategy

Students learn and practice a reading strategy that they will apply to the upcoming reading. This helps students develop reading skills which can be applied to any text and to learn how to focus on the micro and macro meanings contained, whether in class or at home.

Reading Preview

Students read a preview bar about the upcoming reading. This provides information about the text and helps to build interest. Students are introduced to text genre and understand how texts fulfil different learning needs.

F. Pre-reading

Students answer a pre-reading question that builds interest in the upcoming reading. This question also activates students' existing knowledge about the text's subject matter which helps overall understanding of the text.

E. Words in Context

Students are encouraged to understand the link between vocabulary and reading by building a greater understanding of how they can approach difficult or unfamiliar words in a meaningful context.

Read

The reading texts are either fiction or nonfiction. Students are encouraged to focus on meaning, before focusing on the reading strategy. This is followed by general comprehension. The vocabulary presented on the *Get Ready* page is highlighted in yellow to help students understand the words in context.

Before Reading

Students are introduced to a text. They engage in pre-reading activities and examine the reading's features and visuals in order to familiarize themselves with the text before reading it.

During Reading

Students read and listen to the unit's text. Each unit has either a fiction or a nonfiction reading that helps students find answers to the Big Question. The texts are designed to supplement students' learning in different subject areas and to help them make connections between other cultures and their own lives. They are graded to an appropriate vocabulary and grammatical level and meet U.S. readability standards. Students are encouraged to take different approaches to reading the text.

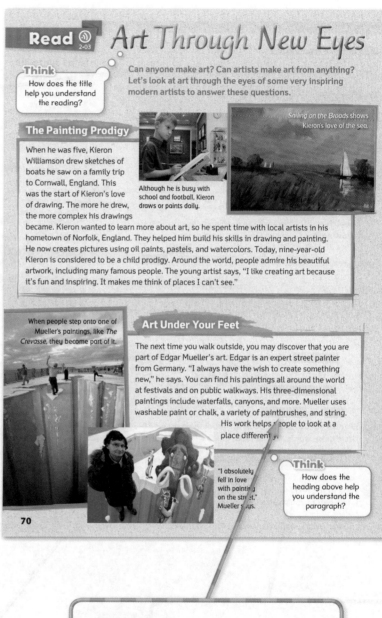

Read 2·03 **Art Through New Eyes**

Think
How does the title help you understand the reading?

Can anyone make art? Can artists make art from anything? Let's look at art through the eyes of some very inspiring modern artists to answer these questions.

The Painting Prodigy

When he was five, Kieron Williamson drew sketches of boats he saw on a family trip to Cornwall, England. This was the start of Kieron's love of drawing. The more he drew, the more complex his drawings became. Kieron wanted to learn more about art, so he spent time with local artists in his hometown of Norfolk, England. They helped him build his skills in drawing and painting. He now creates pictures using oil paints, pastels, and watercolors. Today, nine-year-old Kieron is considered to be a child prodigy. Around the world, people admire his beautiful artwork, including many famous people. The young artist says, "I like creating art because it's fun and inspiring. It makes me think of places I can't see."

Although he is busy with school and football, Kieron draws or paints daily.

Sailing on the Broads shows Kieron's love of the sea.

Art Under Your Feet

The next time you walk outside, you may discover that you are part of Edgar Mueller's art. Edgar is an expert street painter from Germany. "I always have the wish to create something new," he says. You can find his paintings all around the world at festivals and on public walkways. His three-dimensional paintings include waterfalls, canyons, and more. Mueller uses washable paint or chalk, a variety of paintbrushes, and string. His work helps people to look at a place different y.

When people step onto one of Mueller's paintings, like The Crevasse, they become part of it.

"I absolutely fell in love with painting on the street." Mueller says.

Think
How does the heading above help you understand the paragraph?

70

Vocabulary

The vocabulary presented in the *Get Ready* spread is highlighted in yellow throughout the text. This encourages students to focus on the language in context and helps them to understand the meaning of the text.

Stick Sculptures

Patrick Dougherty is a unique sculptor. He combines his love of nature with his skills as a carpenter. His goal is "to build a great sculpture that excites people's imaginations." You can see his large-scale sculptures in many places around the world.

Dougherty's sculptures are made of young trees, or saplings. The saplings are flexible, can bend them into rounded shapes. He keeps them together by weaving the saplings around each other. Building the sculpture is a big job, so the local community helps Dougherty with his project. Many volunteers help to collect the saplings, mark out the space, and build the sculpture. The sculptures are temporary. They will decompose, or break down, over time.

Dougherty creates large-scale sculptures like *Call of the Wild*.

"Sticks are something we all have in common," Dougherty says.

Painting the Universe

When you look at the artwork of Korean artist Sung Hee Cho up close, you see small pieces of brightly colored paper on a large canvas. It may seem disorderly with colors scattered around. However, as you step back, you can imagine the stars, galaxies, and the beauty of the universe. Cho combines *hanji*, traditional Korean paper, with paint. First, she paints the canvas. Then, she cuts out pieces of *hanji* into small shapes, such as flower petals. Next, she dyes and paints the small pieces of paper in a different color. Then she glues thousands of them onto the canvas in layers to capture the glimmer of light. She repeats this process over and over again. She wants to create artwork that is as magical as stars.

By carefully observing the stars, Cho created *The Star in the Cosmos*.

Cho wants to share her fascination with the universe through her artwork.

Think
How do the photos and captions in this section help you to understand Sung Hee Cho's art?

Inspiring artists come from every part of the world. Each one inspires us in a different way. By creating and sharing their art, they help us appreciate and understand the world around us.

71

Understand

This page checks students' understanding of the text through personal response, application of the reading strategy, general comprehension, and critical thinking.

Think. Personal Response
Students answer personal response questions that allow them to discuss their opinions and feelings about the reading.

A. Reading Strategy
Students apply the reading strategy that they learned in an activity about the reading, which helps to connect general reading skills with overall comprehension.

B. Reading Comprehension
Students demonstrate their comprehension of the reading through an additional activity. This will show the teacher and the student the level of understanding gained through reading the text. This exercise may also focus further on the reading strategy.

C. Words in Context
Students complete an activity that helps them to work more closely with the words in context and to develop skills of understanding the meaning of vocabulary from the words, phrases, and structures used around it.

Workbook
Students complete activities that build and test knowledge of the workbook reading and the reading strategy.

Understand

Comprehension

Think Which artist would you like to talk to? What questions would you ask him or her?

A Match a heading to an artist. Then match an artist to a sentence.

1	The Painting Prodigy	a	Edgar Mueller	e	People can walk on this artist's paintings.
2	Art Under Your Feet	b	Sung Hee Cho	f	This artist is interested in the universe.
3	Stick Sculptures	c	Kieron Williamson	g	This artist makes art from natural things.
4	Painting the Universe	d	Patrick Dougherty	h	This artist is very young, but he's a skilled painter.

B Answer the questions.

1 Who helped Kieron Williamson build his skills?
2 How do people become a part of an Edgar Mueller painting?
3 Who helps Patrick Dougherty build his sculptures?
4 What is the Korean name for the paper Sung Hee Cho uses?

C **Words in Context** Complete each sentence with a word from the box.

complex   washable   combines   fascination

1 The artist _____ blue and yellow paint to make green paint.
2 Many artists have a _____ with nature.
3 Jackie spilled paint on her sweater, but the paint is _____ .
4 Sara's sketch is more _____ than Ronald's.

72 **Unit 7** *Comprehension*

Understand

Comprehension

A Which artist's work do you like and why?

_____

B Match a text feature to an example from the reading. Then match the example to its meaning.

Text Feature	Example	Meaning
1 Title	a Art from Trash	f Artists get their ideas from the world around them.
2 First heading	b "I don't see waste."	g This artist paints the beauty of the surrounding culture.
3 Second heading	c Thursday Market Day	h This person says that everything is useful.
4 Visual	d Creating Art from Life	i This artist makes art from things other people don't want.
5 Caption	e Painting African Life	j This painting shows a scene of African women shopping.

C Answer the questions.

1 What does Linda Wise show through her art?

_____

2 What does Robert Aswani show through his art?

_____

D **Words in Context** Read and write.

complex   washable   combines   fascination

1 I have a _____ with African paintings.
2 Linda Wise _____ trash with art.
3 The artist's sketch is very _____
4 Kindergarten classrooms use _____ paint.

62 **Unit 7** *Comprehension*

Student Book page 72

Grammar In Use

Students are introduced to a grammar structure through the context of a song or cartoon story before working with the structure more closely with a grammar presentation and practice activities that allow them to produce the language in a collaborative situation.

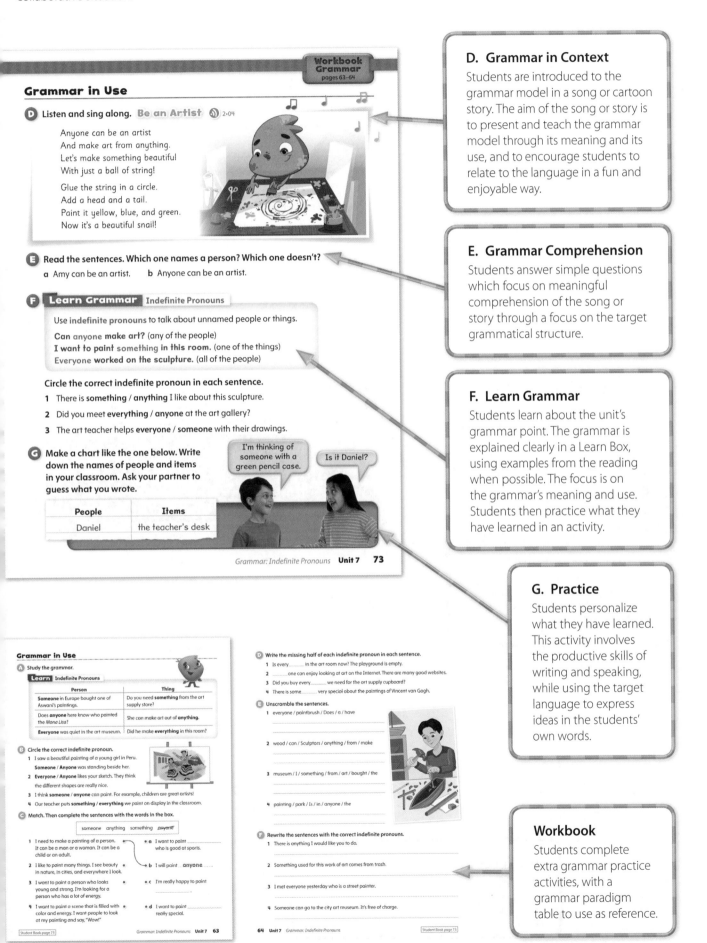

D. Grammar in Context
Students are introduced to the grammar model in a song or cartoon story. The aim of the song or story is to present and teach the grammar model through its meaning and its use, and to encourage students to relate to the language in a fun and enjoyable way.

E. Grammar Comprehension
Students answer simple questions which focus on meaningful comprehension of the song or story through a focus on the target grammatical structure.

F. Learn Grammar
Students learn about the unit's grammar point. The grammar is explained clearly in a Learn Box, using examples from the reading when possible. The focus is on the grammar's meaning and use. Students then practice what they have learned in an activity.

G. Practice
Students personalize what they have learned. This activity involves the productive skills of writing and speaking, while using the target language to express ideas in the students' own words.

Workbook
Students complete extra grammar practice activities, with a grammar paradigm table to use as reference.

Communicate

This page teaches and helps students implement and practice listening strategies, and to practice functional language through spoken production.

Think: Critical Thinking

These questions act as a lead-in to the listening text. Students use their personal knowledge and life experiences to answer. This activates interest in the topic of the text, and immediately connects it to the students' own lives.

A. B. Listening

Students listen to a script that continues to help them find answers to the Big Question. They complete activities which encourage them to listen for detail or specific information, in this way helping them to develop the micro skills of listening.

C. Speaking

Students develop their functional speaking skills in this section. They can read and understand a dialogue which presents useful chunks of language before practicing the dialogue by either choosing substitute words or expressing their own ideas.

Workbook

Students complete a variety of activities that build and test their knowledge of the new vocabulary.

Communicate

Listening

Think Why do people like to look up at the stars at night?

A **Learn** | Listening for Reasons

When you listen for reasons, first listen for questions starting with the word *why*. The answer to each question will usually have a reason.

Listen. Match each question with a reason. 🔊 1-05

1 Why are stars so easy to see on Grandpa's farm? •
    • a It's close to Earth and has clouds that bounce sunlight to Earth.

2 Why is Venus so bright? •
    • b It's shaped like a disk. We are in the disk, and we can look through it.

3 Why can we see the Milky Way galaxy when we're in it? •
    • c There are fewer lights shining outside of a big city.

B **Listen again. Why is our galaxy called the Milky Way? Write your answer.** 🔊 1-06

_____

_____

Speaking 🔊 1-07

C Look at the two pictures. Talk about the differences with your partner.

> In the first picture, I see the Milky Way.

> In the second picture, I see ...

> The first picture has ...

> The second picture doesn't have ... , but ...

14 **Unit 1** *Listening: Reasons • Speaking: Talking About Differences*

Communicate

Word Study

A Match. Then write the words. Write the verbs in the correct tense.

> dissatisfied disorganized dishonest ~~disprove~~ disability distrust

1 dis + prove •
    • a The art teacher was very unhappy with his students because the art room was so messy and _____ .

2 dis + organized •
    • b The tourists were _____ with the museum tour because some of the exhibitions weren't open to the public.

3 dis + trust •
    • c Many famous artists painted beautiful works of art even though they had a _____ , such as poor eyesight.

4 dis + satisfied •
    • d Jack thought Michelangelo painted the *Mona Lisa*, but I **disproved** it by showing him the painting in a book about Leonardo da Vinci.

5 dis + ability •
    • e The _____ artist said that he painted the landscape, but actually his wife painted it.

6 dis + honest •
    • f The art dealer said that all of the sculptures he sold were from ancient Rome, but Paul _____ him.

B Complete the paragraph with the words in the box.

> prove honest disorganized dissatisfied trust ability

I really enjoy painting in art class, but I'm _____ with my paintings. I don't think I have a great _____ . Also, my oil paints are very _____ , so I often can't find the right color. I was _____ with my teacher and told her I wasn't a good artist. She said that she was a good teacher, however, and that I should _____ her teaching ability. I'm going to work harder and _____ that she is right!

Student Book page 73

Vocabulary: Words with the Prefix dis- **Unit 7** **65**

Students focus on word patterns and writing strategies in order to build greater fluency and accuracy. They then personalise the learning by writing about something that links back to the Big Question.

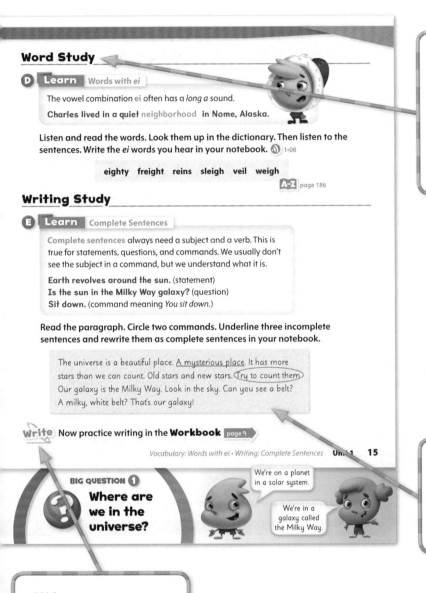

D. Word Study
Each Word Study section focuses on word patterns. This complements and often provides links between vocabulary and grammar learning. Students complete an activity which requires them to utilise their new understanding of the way words work.

E. Writing Study
The Writing Study section helps students learn about different writing strategies and helpful language prompts to help them write fluently and accurately.

Write
Students write about one aspect of the Big Question, using vocabulary and structures taught within the unit.

Workbook
Students complete one page of activities that build and test knowledge of the Writing Study. Students then complete activities that focus on writing output.

Wrap Up - Writing

These pages always come at the end of two units which focus on a Big Question. Students are exposed to vocabulary and grammatical structures learned throughout the previous two units and focus on writing and oral presentations.

A. Text

Students read a particular genre of text in order to focus on the layout, presentation and writing strategies that this type of text requires.

B. Comprehension

An activity helps students to check their understanding of the meaning of the text, before they are expected to produce a similar type of text themselves.

Learn

A learn box provides step by step guidance for students before they write their own text.

Write

Students use writing process techniques to help them plan and write a text in their workbook.

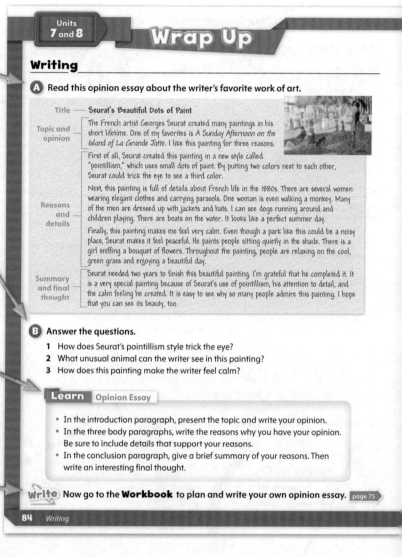

Workbook

Students are guided through writing a particular text type, with a model text, scaffolded activities and a writing task.

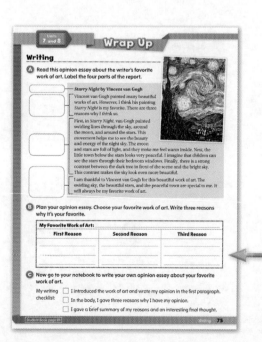

Wrap Up – Project

Students complete a project which recycles the language and ideas of the previous two units and leads to a productive outcome.

Project: Acting in a Play

C Create a short play about artists working in a studio. Then act it out.

- In your group, create a play about artists in a studio.
- Think about different types of art, what artists do, and what kind of artist you want to be in the play. Give yourself a unique name and choose what tools you will need.
- Create a drawing of a piece of art. It can be any type of art.

- Think about what artists would say to each other in a studio. Talk about your ideas with your group. Write down words that you want to remember. Then practice the play with your group.
- Perform the play for your class. Remember to speak clearly, show the artwork you created, and act like you are a real artist.

Can I borrow some of your paint? I ran out of mine!

I have lots of paint! Which colors do you need?

I'm sorry. I only have a little bit left, and I need to finish this portrait.

BIG QUESTION 4
Why do we make art?

A Watch the video.
What did you learn about art?

B Think more about the Big Question. What did you learn?

C Complete the **Big Question Chart.**

Acting in a Play • Big Question 4   **85**

C. Project

A hands-on project with a creative outcome which showcases the previous unit's input of language and ideas. Projects provide opportunities for consolidating learning using all four skills and a focus on accuracy as students feel pride in presenting their productive output. Students are given a set of guidelines to follow to produce an effective project.

Model

A short dialogue is presented so that students understand what they need to do and functional language input on how to present it successfully.

The Big Question, Big Question Poster, Big Question Chart, and DVD

Students return to the Big Question with new answers in order to describe the images with newly gained knowledge and vocabulary, and they complete the final column in the Big Question Chart with what they have learned. This provides a summing up of learning points throughout the previous units and helps students to critically examine their own learning path

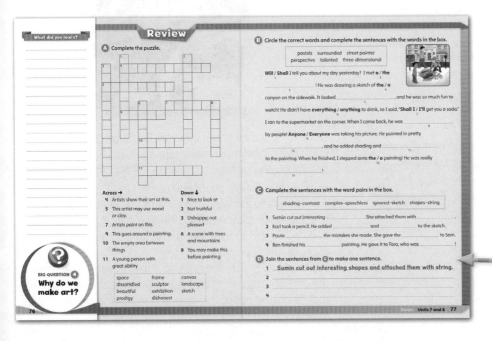

Workbook

Students do a number of review activities to recycle the language from the previous two units.

DVD and Posters

The DVD and posters are key to reinforcing the content of the Student Book. They stimulate interest in the Big Question, and they help students to predict, infer, and check the meaning of the main learning points. The learning points are about content not language. Students will think critically and more fully about the process of language when they see interesting and thought-provoking images.

The images on the DVD and posters encourage students to recall, recognize, and acknowledge new concepts and vocabulary. Students analyze the images themselves to understand the meaning. This leads to a greater impact upon the long-term memory as students continue to make associations between pictures and language.

Big Question DVD

Students watch videos about the Big Question in order to stimulate their thinking about the topic and revise what they have learned. This will help the teacher determine what students already know and what they want to know.

The DVD should be used in two places in each pair of units. Play the Opener video at the beginning of the first unit to activate background knowledge and encourage interest in the topic. Play the Wrap Up video at the end of the second unit to help students summarize their understanding of the topic and to underscore all the learning points which have been studied during the two units.

Suggested Procedure: Beginning of Units

- Explain that students will watch a video about the Big Question, and that it will have pictures but no words. Ask students to write in their notebooks one or more things that they find interesting in the video as they watch it. Explain that words and phrases are acceptable and that full sentences are not necessary.
- Play the video.
- Ask students to compare what they wrote with a partner.
- Elicit some of students' ideas. Write these on the board.
- (Optional) Play the video a second time. Ask students to write down one new thing they see in the video as they watch it. After the video, students talk to their partners and then share their thoughts with the class.

Suggested Procedure: End of Units

- Explain to students that they will now see the video again, this time with a presenter. Play the video. It can be played more than once.
- Ask students to discuss what they learned from the video with a partner.
- Ask students to share what they learned from the video with the whole class.
- Write this information on the Big Question Chart.

Expansion ideas

- Elicit and write useful chunks of language which students can use in discussions about the learning points. Put students into groups and have them make posters with the language and illustrations to help them understand and remember the meaning. Put the posters on the wall and draw students' attention to them before future discussions.
- Have students work in small groups to write a list of their own learning points for the units. Tell them to find or draw pictures to represent the learning points visually. Have each group present their ideas to the class, or create a poster to be put on the wall.
- Make a class DVD based on the Big Question DVD, showing images which represent the learning points. Have different students act as the presenter on camera.

Posters

Discover Posters

There is a Discover Poster for every Big Question in the Student Book. They all have the main learning points for two units with accompanying pictures to illustrate the learning points.

The Discover Poster should be used at the beginning of each pair of units to motivate students' interest in the topic and to elicit existing knowledge around the Big Question. It can also be referred to throughout the units to remind students of the learning points as they come up and to build upon the knowledge they are gaining. Finally, it should be used at the end of each pair of units to summarize all of the learning that has come out of the units and to help students prepare to fill in the Big Question Chart.

Suggested Procedure

It is a good idea to have a list of questions which help students to think critically about the images and learning points. Students can answer individually or be encouraged to share their ideas in pairs or small groups before participating in a general class discussion.

General Discussion Questions

- *What can you see in this picture?*
- *How many ... can you see?*
- *Where do you think it is?*
- *What do you think is happening?*
- *What does it mean?*
- *What does this learning point mean?*
- *Can you see the learning point in the picture?*
- *Do you know about this already?*
- *What else would you like to know?*

Big Question Chart

The Big Question Chart has been designed to follow the KWL methodology. K = What do you know about the topic? W = What do you want to know about the topic? L = What did you learn or what have you learned about the topic?

The Big Question Chart can be written on with board pens and then wiped clean so that it can be reused. If possible, keep it up displayed on the classroom wall.

Suggested Procedure: Beginning of Units

- Have students brainstorm what they already know about the topic surrounding the Big Question. This can be done individually by writing ideas down, or by setting up pair or small group discussions.
- Elicit the ideas and write them on the poster.
- Ask each student to think about something they would like to know about the topic. These could be grouped into categories or headings to help students learn to classify more effectively.
- Write some of the ideas on the chart.
- Don't fill in the final column, as this will be completed once learning has taken place.

Suggested Procedure: End of First Unit

- Look closely at the middle column: *What do you want to know about the topic?* Ask students if they now know the answer to some of those questions. If they do, this information can be moved over to the first column.

- Some ideas can also be elicited to start filling in the third column so that students can see that learning has already taken place around the theme of the Big Question.

Suggested Procedure: End of Units

- Have students look at the middle column and decide if they can answer any more questions they had about the topic. If they have learned about aspects they expressed interest in, this information can be moved over to the column on the right: *What did you learn or what have you learned about the topic?*
- Elicit more information about what they have learned and add it to the third column.

Talk About It! Poster

This poster should be used when students are having a discussion in pairs or groups. If possible, keep it on the wall so that students can refer to it themselves.

In the Student Book it can be used during the Communicate reading pages when students are practicing speaking skills, but also during post-reading discussion tasks and during the Wrap Up project section.

Suggested Procedure

Remind students about the language often and drill the language and practice the intonation. Students begin to acquire authentic process language to then help them express their own ideas and opinions. When introducing it for the first time, elicit possible ways to substitute different opinions while using the sentence frames from the poster. Explain that these prompts can help them to present ideas and to agree and disagree politely with others.

When students are participating in a discussion, point to the sentence frames on the poster and ask them to express their own ideas after using the language indicated.

Dictionary Activities

There is an old proverb which is: *Give a man a fish, and feed him for a day. Teach a man to fish and you feed him for a lifetime.*

Dictionary skills need to be mastered by students learning English, even in the primary years. When students have learned how to successfully use a dictionary, they are able to become more independent and autonomous learners, able to increase their own vocabulary and read and write at a higher level.

Dictionary skills are important, not only because the dictionary itself is important but also because it is an introduction into the world of reference materials. Learning how to use common reference materials will help your students' research and writing skills.

A dictionary entry has several parts. It lists the syllabic divisions in a word, the pronunciation, the part of speech, and of course the definition. Students need to learn how to identify and work with all of these components.

Learner training and encouraging the habit of using a monolingual dictionary is an essential element of current classroom practice. Learner training can focus on various aspects, from understanding abbreviations to interpreting symbols, recognizing and understanding syllable indicators and stress marks, to effectively finding a particular meaning of an item of vocabulary.

Oxford Basic American Dictionary

This dictionary is suggested for students in levels 1–4 of *Oxford Discover*. It is written specifically for students who want to improve their English language skills and has extra help boxes included with related synonyms, collocations, and word families. It is designed to help students' transition from using picture dictionaries by using words that are easy to understand as well as illustrations. It has a focus on content words from different subject areas such as math, geography and history.

Oxford American Dictionary

This dictionary is suggested for students in levels 5–6 of *Oxford Discover*. It has more than 350,000 words and phrases, with lots of explanatory notes and more than a thousand illustrations. Unlike in more traditional dictionaries, where meanings are ordered chronologically according to the history of the language, each entry plainly shows the principal meaning or meanings of the word, organized by importance in today's English. This makes it relevant and easily understood by primary-aged students.

Student Book Dictionary Activities

The Student Books in levels 3–6 of *Oxford Discover* have dictionary pages referencing the words used throughout the units in the book. This is a good introduction to general dictionary use and students should be encouraged to use these pages as a reference. Additionally there are activities and games which can help students to become more familiar and confident when using the dictionary pages.

Do you know?

- Have students work in pairs and choose a word from the dictionary pages at the back of the Student Book.

- Tell them to write the word and the meaning in their notebook.
- Tell students to write two more meanings which they make up, but which look as if they could also match the word.
- Put pairs together and have them read out their word and the three definitions.
- The other pair must guess the correct definition.
- To exploit the game further, keep moving the pairs around so that they work with everyone in the class.

Put it in a Sentence
- Have students open their Student Books to the dictionary pages at the back.
- Tell them to choose one word from the list of words.
- Have students write a sentence using that word, concentrating on understanding the definition as they do so.
- Ask students to read out their sentence to the class.
- Have the class look up that word in the dictionary pages and decide if the sentence matches the definition and if it is used correctly.

Taboo
- Have students open their Student Books to the dictionary pages at the back.
- Tell them to choose one word from the list of words.
- Make sure that students choose a word where they understand the definition.
- Have students write down four words which describe the word they chose, without using the word itself.
- Put students into groups of four or five.
- Have them take turns to read out the words in their notebook.
- The other students try to guess the dictionary word.
- The first student to guess correctly wins a point.
- The winner is the student in the group with the most points.

Picture Words
- Put students into groups for four or five.
- Give each group a large sheet of clean paper, or a few sheets of smaller paper. Make sure each group also has a pencil.
- Ask one person from each group to come to the front of the class.
- Choose one word from the dictionary at the back of the Student Book and show it (with the definition) to the students at the front of the class. Don't let the rest of the students see or hear the word.
- Each student goes back to their group and draws the word. They cannot speak or write while they are doing this.
- The rest of the group tries to guess the word.
- The first student in the class to guess it correctly wins a point for their team.
- Continue the game by having a different student come out and repeating the activity until each student in the group has had a chance to draw a word.

General Dictionary Activities
General dictionaries are useful to have in the classroom and can be incorporated into many aspects of the lesson. They can be used when directed by the teacher or kept for reference for students as and when the need arises. Again, it is useful to help students navigate dictionaries with activities and tasks which help them feel comfortable with these reference materials.

Scavenger Hunt
- Write down ten to twelve questions about using a dictionary. Examples can include:
  What is the first word in the dictionary?
  How many pages of words starting with "x" are in the dictionary?
  Look up the word "supermarket." How many syllables does it have?
  Find the first adjective in your dictionary which has three syllables.
  Find a word which has more than one meaning.
  Find a word which can be a verb and a noun.

Word Search
- Put students into pairs and give each pair a dictionary.
- Call out a word (preferably a familiar or recognizable word).
- Each pair of students must try to find the word as quickly as possible.
- The first pair to call out the correct page number where the word can be found is the winner.

Mystery Word
- Choose a word in the dictionary that will be familiar to students.
- Give a dictionary to each pair or small group of students in the class.
- Read out a series of clues to help students find the word. Read the clues out one at a time, as students are following the previous clue, e.g.:
  I begin with the fourth letter of the alphabet.
  I have three syllables.
  My second letter is "o."
  I come before "dog" in the dictionary.
  My last letter is "t."
- Students use the dictionary to follow the clues and find the word.
- The first pair or group of students to find and say the word correctly wins a point.
- Continue with more words.

Words, words, words!
- Give a dictionary to each pair or small group of students in the class.
- Read out (or write on the board) a series of clues at the same time, e.g. *A word that begins with "s." It has to have double letters, be two syllables long, and be an adjective.*
- Students use the dictionary to find the word. There may be more than one answer as more than one word may fit the description.
- Have pairs say their words to the class to check if they are correct.

Units 1 and 2

Where are we in the universe?

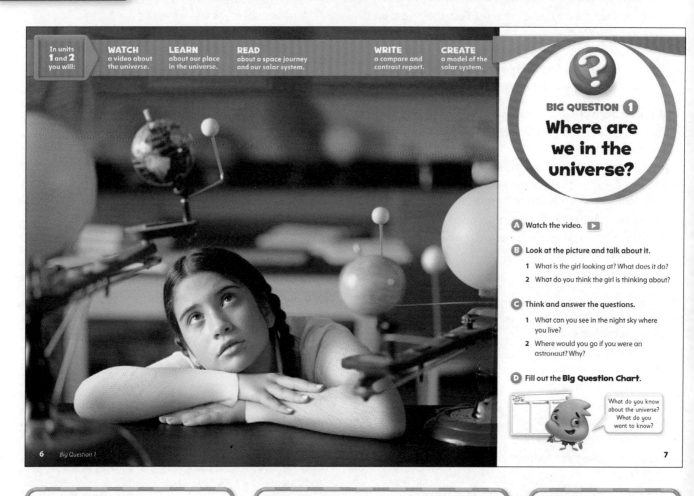

Reading Strategies

Students will practice:
- Visualizing changes
- Comparing and contrasting in science

Vocabulary

Students will understand and use words about:
- The universe

Grammar

Students will understand and use:
- Predictions with *will*
- Future real conditional

Review

Students will review the language and Big Question learning points in Units 1 and 2 through:
- A compare and contrast report
- A project (creating a model of the solar system)

Units 1 and 2
Where are we in the universe?

Students will understand the Big Question learning points:
- We are on a special planet, Earth.
- Earth is in a solar system.
- Our solar system is in a galaxy.
- Our galaxy is in the universe.
- We are far away from other planets, stars, and galaxies.

Listening Strategies

Students will practice:
- Listening for reasons
- Listening for main idea and numbers

Writing

Students will be able to:
- Identify and write complete sentences (statements, questions, commands)
- Write choice questions with *or*

Students will produce texts that:
- Compare and contrast two things

Word Study

Students will understand, pronounce, and use:
- Words with *ei*
- Words with the suffixes *-ance* and *-ant*

Speaking

Students will understand and use expressions to:
- Talk about differences
- Ask about quantity

Units 1 and 2 Big Question page 6

Summary

Objectives: To activate students' existing knowledge of the topic and identify what they would like to learn about the topic.

Materials: Big Question DVD, Discover Poster 1, Big Question Chart

Introducing the topic

- Introduce students to the theme and objectives for the module.
- Introduce the Big Question to the students. Ask *Where are we in the universe?* Take answers from the class.

- Display **Discover Poster 1**.
- Have students discuss the poster in small groups.
- Each group should 1) identify what they see in each picture and 2) identify something interesting or special in each picture.
- Assign roles: a "secretary" writes down ideas; a "monitor" makes sure everyone contributes at least one idea; a "presenter" shares the group's ideas with the class.

A Watch the video.

- Play the video and when it is finished ask students to answer the following questions in pairs:
  What do you see in this part of the video?
  What do you think is happening in this part of the video?
  What do you know about what you just saw?
  Does this part of the video remind you of anything?

B Look at the picture and talk about it.

- Students look at the big picture and talk about it. Ask *What do you see? What looks interesting? What do you think the girl is thinking about?*

Below level:

- Have students write down words that they see in the picture.
- Elicit the words from the students and help them to put their ideas into sentences.

At level:

- Have students write down sentences about what they see in the picture.
- Put students into small groups.
- Have students compare their sentences and check how many are the same or similar.
- Ask students to share their sentences with the class.

Above level:

- Conduct a class discussion about what students can see in the picture.
- Ask students to take three ideas and write a short paragraph.
- Ask individual students to read their paragraphs to the class.

C Think and answer the questions.

- Ask students to think about the first question. Model an answer.
- Put students in small groups to tell each other what they can see in the night sky where they live.
- Have students answer the second question and tell their partner where they would go if they were an astronaut and why.

D Fill out the Big Question Chart.

- Display the **Big Question Chart**.
- Have students write what they know and what they want to know about the Big Question in their Workbooks.
- Write their ideas on the **Big Question Chart** and discuss their ideas as a class.

- Students may have prior knowledge from movies and books. Help them draw connections.
- Ask *Do you know any movies or books that are set in outer space / on another planet? In the movie / book, why do the characters travel to outer space? What problems do they face?*

Discover Poster 1

1 Boys exploring in a field; 2 A solar system model at the Museum of Natural History in New York; 3 Stars of the Milky Way in the night sky; 4 Galaxies and nebulae in the universe; 5 An astronaut on a space walk

Further Practice
Workbook page 2
Online practice · Big Question 1
Oxford **iTools** · Big Question 1

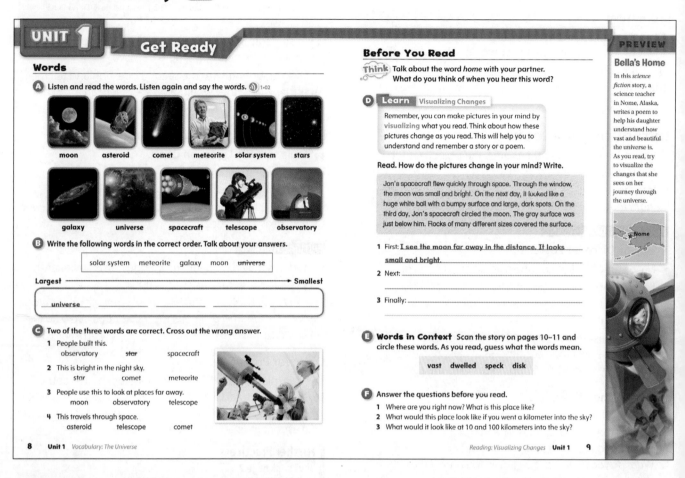

Summary

Objectives: To understand words about the universe; to apply own experience and a reading strategy to help comprehension of a text.

Vocabulary: *moon, asteroid, comet, meteorite, solar system, stars, galaxy, universe, spacecraft, telescope, observatory, vast, dwelled, speck, disk*

Reading strategy: Visualizing changes

Materials: Audio CD

Words

A Listen and read the words. Listen again and say the words. 🎧 1·02

- Play the audio. Ask students to point to the words as they hear them.
- Play the audio a second time and have students repeat the words when they hear them.

CRITICAL THINKING

- Put students into pairs.
- Have each pair write down three stories or movies they know that are about space and are about any of the words in A.
- Elicit the names of the stories or movies from the class.
- Check how many students have either read the most popular book about space or seen the most popular movie about space.

B Write the following words in the correct order. Talk about your answers.

- Refer to the pictures in A to guide students in completing this exercise.
- Students write the words in order from largest to smallest.
- Elicit answers from the class.

ANSWERS

universe, galaxy, solar system, moon, meteorite

C Two of the three words are correct. Cross out the wrong answer.

- Have students complete the exercise individually before checking with a partner.
- Elicit answers from the class.

ANSWERS

1 star   2 meteorite   3 moon   4 telescope

DIFFERENTIATION

Below level:

- Focus on the meaning and pronunciation of the words.
- Have students count and mark the number of syllables in each word.

At level:

- After students finish the exercise put them into pairs or small groups to brainstorm any other words they know about space.
- Draw a word web on the board. Put the word "space" in the middle and elicit all the words that students offer around this word.

Above level:
- Ask students to add more words to each category in C.
- Focus on things people build to help them see the universe, the things they can see in the night sky, and things that travel through space.
- Elicit the answers and make a chart on the board. Check answers with the whole class as words are added.

Before You Read

Think
- Have students think about their answer to the question individually before putting them with a partner to discuss their ideas.
- Elicit some ideas about what *home* is from the class.

D Learn: Visualizing Changes
- Read the *Learn* box together.

Read. How do the pictures change in your mind? Write.
- Encourage students to shut their eyes after they read each sentence of the paragraph.
- Tell them to visualize what happens and to really see it inside their mind before reading the next sentence.

POSSIBLE ANSWERS

Next: The moon is closer. It looks like a huge white ball with a bumpy surface and large, dark spots.
Finally: The moon is close. The gray surface is just below, covered with rocks of different sizes.

CRITICAL THINKING
- Ask each student to think about a favorite story.
- Ask them to choose one where they find it easy to visualize the characters and what happens.
- Put students into pairs.
- Students tell each other how the story made them visualize different things and why it was so easy to visualize changes.

E Words in Context: Scan the story on pages 10–11 and circle these words. As you read, guess what the words mean.
- Ask students to circle the words before they begin reading. They will use the context of the selection to guess the meanings.

COLLABORATIVE LEARNING
- Put students into groups of three or four.
- Ask each group to write a new sentence using the words from the Words in Context exercise.
- Tell them to erase the words in context words and to write blanks in their place in the sentences.
- Each group swaps their sentences with another group and tries to insert the correct word in each sentence.
- Once they have completed the activity, the groups give back their sentences and correct them.
- Elicit some example sentences from the class.

F Answer the questions before you read.

COMMUNICATION
- Ask students to think about the questions individually.
- Put students into pairs or small groups to discuss their answers.
- Elicit different answers from the class.

Reading Preview
- Read the preview bar together. Find Nome, Alaska on a map. Can students name the country, continent, and hemisphere?
- Have students read the title of the story and the short paragraph that follows it.
- Ask students why they think someone would write a poem to explain the universe.
- Then ask students *What do you think the pictures mean? How are they related to the text?*

Further Practice
Workbook pages 2–3
Online practice Unit 1 · Get Ready
Oxford iTools Unit 1 · Get Ready

Bella's Home

Charles Kunayak was a high school science teacher who lived with his family in a quiet neighborhood in Nome, Alaska. In his free time, he studied the secrets of the universe. Charles had a powerful telescope, and he often visited observatories, so he learned more and more about the universe. What an amazing universe!

Yet how could Charles help his daughter Bella understand that our sun was just one of billions* of stars? How could she realize that the small meteorite on display in his classroom traveled to Earth from beyond Mars? How could he explain that we live in a universe so vast, it would take a spacecraft 100,000 years to cross our Milky Way galaxy while traveling at the speed of light!

Charles decided that the best way to show Bella was not through numbers and charts, but through a poem. He sat down and wrote what he knew about the universe. He called it "Bella's Home."

Bella's Home

Bella lived in a white wooden house
On a street in the city of Nome.
Bella sat in her bedroom and thought to herself,
Where in the world is my home?

What I need, she thought, is a spacecraft
To give me a better view.
So in her mind, she climbed inside
And up in the sky she flew.

Her white wooden house was tiny indeed,
And Nome was as small as a pie.
As Bella flew up, she saw that Alaska
Looked like a bear from the sky.

Higher she flew, and Alaska, too,
Became part of something so grand.
She saw islands, countries, and continents
With blue oceans around the land.

Bella now saw her beautiful planet,
A blue ball floating in space,
And a shining moon that circled the earth
With the light of the sun on its face.

She noticed the earth was not alone;
With seven more planets it dwelled.
In a great solar system, they circled the sun
With asteroids and comets as well.

Bella's spacecraft flew higher and higher.
Now the sun was a speck of bright light
In the Milky Way galaxy shaped like a disk.
Bella thought, What a wondrous sight!

Then billions of galaxies appeared everywhere,
Each one filled with billions of stars!
What Bella observed was the vast universe.
Her spacecraft had taken her far.

Suddenly Bella was back in her room
In her white wooden house in Nome.
I will visit those places again, Bella thought,
For wherever I go is my home!

Think How do the pictures in your mind change as you read?

Think What final pictures do you see in your mind?

*Note: one billion = 1,000,000,000

Summary

Objectives: To read, understand, and discuss a fictional text; to apply a reading strategy to improve comprehension.

School subject: Science: Astronomy

Text type: Science fiction

Reading strategy: Visualizing changes

Big Question learning points: *We are on a special planet, Earth. Our solar system is in a galaxy.*

Materials: Audio CD

Before Reading

- Write the title of the poem on the board. Remind students of the information in the Preview on page 9.

- Ask the class questions to check their understanding of the genre. Ask *What is a poem?* (A poem uses special features, such as rhyme, meter, alliteration, rhythm, and artistic language to express an idea. Note that prose is the normal, nonpoetic, form of written and spoken language.)

- Now ask the students the following questions:
  Look at the poem. How does it look different from the introduction? (The introduction is laid out in regular paragraph form. The poem is divided into four-line verses.)
  Have you ever read a poem? How did you know it was a poem?
  Have you ever written a poem? What was difficult about it? What was easy?

During Reading 1·03

- Play the audio. Students listen and read and focus on the rhythm of the poem. Snap along to the beat to reinforce the cadence.

- To improve reading fluency, invite groups to repeat the text of each verse after listening to the audio.

- Encourage them to mimic the rhythm, intonation, and pronunciation of the speakers.

- Help students summarize what is described in each verse:
  Bella sits at home and thinks about her place in the universe. She begins to imagine …
  … getting into a spacecraft so she can fly into space.
  … looking down at Alaska from high in the sky.
  … flying higher and seeing the outlines of continents in oceans.
  … flying so far away that Earth looks like a blue ball.
  … seeing the other planets in the solar system, all circling the sun.
  … flying farther into the Milky Way galaxy so the sun appears tiny.
  … flying farther to where she can see billions of other galaxies.
  Then her imaginary journey ends.

- After you complete each verse, have students find at least one descriptive word or phrase that helps them create a mental image.

- Point out that descriptive language is often used in poetry.

- Remind students to stop and read the *Think* boxes.

Below level:

- Pair confident readers with less confident readers.
- Have confident readers read the verse through and the less confident partner follow them and repeat.

At level:

- Put students into pairs and stop them after each verse.
- Ask them to tell each other what they think it means in their own words.
- Elicit some ideas from the class.

Above level:

- Have students choose their favorite verse in the poem.
- Conduct a show of hands to see which verse is the most popular.
- Elicit the reason why from the class.
- Have students tell each other what they see in their mind as they read this verse.

After Reading

Ask the following questions to check comprehension:

- Is the telescope that Charles uses big or small?
  In the poem, when does Bella cross the Milky Way?
- How long do you think this journey would take in "real life"?
- Bella is using the telescope to study the universe at night. Why doesn't she use the telescope during the day?
- Pair the students and ask them to discuss the *Think* boxes.

CRITICAL THINKING

Discussion questions:

- *Bella's father, Charles, enjoys using a telescope to study the secrets of the universe. If he visited your town, where would you suggest he go?*
- *Why do you think Charles wants to help Bella understand about the universe? Do you think Bella wants to learn about it? Does anyone in your family try to help you understand things that are important to them?*
- *Charles uses a poem instead of "numbers and charts." Why do you think he uses a poem to teach Bella? Would you rather learn something new in an expressive way, such as through a poem or song, or in a less expressive way, such as through charts and graphs?*

COLLABORATIVE LEARNING

- Put students into groups of three or four.
- Have groups create a visual summary of the poem by "drawing" each verse. They can use the illustrations on pages 10–11 for ideas.
- The whole group brainstorms an image for each verse.
- Divide the poem so each group member is drawing one or two verses.
- Combine the images in order, either in a booklet or a poster format.
- Plan for a presentation where each group decides how they want to read the poem (all together, taking turns, or in pairs) while they show their artwork.

CULTURE NOTE

Alaska is the largest state in the United States by area. It is also one of the least populous states and many of the residents live in a relatively small area within the state.

Alaska has many lakes, some active volcanoes, and miles and miles of shoreline. It is home to different species of bears, moose, caribou, and an abundant variety of birds and fish. The weather in Alaska can be very cold, especially in the interior.

Nome was a city in Alaska. It was once the most populated city in Alaska, home to approximately 20,000 people, mostly due to the Gold Rush, which started in 1898. Now Nome is a small town with about 3,000 people.

Further Practice
Workbook page 4
Online practice Unit 1 · Read
Oxford **iTools** Unit 1 · Read

Unit 1 Understand page 12

Understand

Comprehension

Think Do you understand the universe better after reading the poem about Bella's travels? Why or why not?

A In the poem, what did Bella see? Fill in the chart.

First	Next	Finally

B Match each question to an answer.

1 What looks like a bear from the sky?   a the moon
2 What is a blue ball floating in space?   b Alaska
3 What has the light of the sun on its face?   c the sun
4 What is a speck of bright light in the Milky Way?   d the universe
5 What has billions of galaxies?   e Earth

C **Words in Context** Read each line of poetry. Circle the word that has the same meaning as the underlined word.

1 What Bella observed was the vast universe.
   cold   huge   silent
2 With seven more planets it dwelled.
   lived   sang   fell
3 Now the sun was a speck of bright light.
   large ball   warm fire   small spot
4 The Milky Way galaxy was shaped like a disk.
   star   triangle   round plate

Grammar in Use

Workbook Grammar pages 6–7

D Listen and read along. 1·04

Harry, what do you want to do in your life?

I want to travel through the universe.

Harry, do you want to sleep under the stars tonight?

No. I will miss my bed too much.

E Read the sentences. Which one is about what Harry believes?
a I will miss my bed too much.   b I want to travel through the universe.

F **Learn Grammar** Predictions with *Will*

Use will to make a prediction. A prediction is something you believe about the future. A prediction is not a fact.
I will visit those places again, Bella thought.

Three of the following sentences are predictions. Write P beside them. Write X beside the sentence that is not a prediction.
1 Scientists will send a person to Mars someday. _____
2 The sun will rise tomorrow morning. _____
3 She will become an astronaut when she grows up. _____
4 Eric will go to space camp next summer. _____

I think scientists will find new solar systems in our galaxy.

G Make a list like this one. Make predictions and then talk to your partner about them.

Things I Predict
Scientists will find new solar systems.

Summary

Objectives: To demonstrate understanding of a text; to understand the meaning and form of the grammar structure.

Reading: Comprehension

Grammar input: Predictions with *will*

Grammar practice: Workbook exercises

Grammar production: Writing and talking about predictions

Materials: Audio CD

Comprehension

Think

- Have students think about the question and their answer to it individually before putting them into pairs to discuss it.
- Elicit answers from the class.

A In the poem, what did Bella see? Fill in the chart.

- Encourage students to work individually to think about what Bella saw.
- Have them check their ideas in small groups.
- Elicit answers from the class.

POSSIBLE ANSWERS
First she saw Alaska.
Next she saw the planet Earth.
Finally she saw a galaxy and then many galaxies.

B Match each question to an answer.

- Ask students to answer individually and then check their answers with a partner.
- Encourage students to point to the parts in the text that helped them decide their answer when they are discussing it.

ANSWERS
1 b   2 e   3 a   4 c   5 d

C Words in Context. Read each line of poetry. Circle the word that has the same meaning as the underlined word.

- Encourage students to look back at the poem to find the words in context.
- Elicit answers from the class and discuss the surrounding words and phrases that help to make the definition clear.

ANSWERS
1 huge   2 lived   3 small spot   4 round plate

CRITICAL THINKING

- Ask students to reread the text and circle a word or phrase that helps them to understand the words in context.
- Write the words and phrases on the board.
- Discuss how these words help them to understand the other words.

Grammar in Use

D Listen and read along. 🔘 1·04

CREATIVITY

- Have students read the comic strip and listen to the audio at the same time.
- Have three more confident students act it out for the class.

E Read the sentences. Which one is about what Harry believes?

- Write the two sentences on the board.
- Circle the word *believes* in the direction line.
- Explain that *believe* and *think* are similar in meaning. Explain that Harry is predicting that he will miss his bed too much, using *will*.
- Elicit the correct answer from the class.

ANSWER

I will miss my bed too much.

F Learn Grammar: Predictions with *Will*

- Read the *Learn Grammar* box together.
- Have students read the example.

Three of the following sentences are predictions. Write P beside them. Write X beside the sentence that is not a prediction.

- Have students do the activity individually before checking their answers with a partner.
- Remind students of the difference between a fact and a prediction.
- Ask if a prediction can become a fact.
- Elicit the answers from the class.

ANSWERS

1 P   2 X   3 P   4 P

G Make a list like this one. Make predictions and then talk to your partner about them.

- Have students make a list of predictions individually.
- Put students into pairs and have them share their predictions.
- Ask students to stand up and tell the class one of their own predictions, and one of their partner's predictions.

Workbook Grammar

- Direct students to the Workbook for further practice.

DIFFERENTIATION

Below level:

- Put students into small groups. Put the less confident students into the same groups.
- Provide a list of topics to help them complete the charts, e.g. *money, jobs, holidays, weather*.
- Allow students to complete the charts together, writing the same information as other students in the group.

At level:

- Brainstorm different topics for making predictions with the class.
- Write a list on the board and leave it there for students to refer to while completing their charts.

- Encourage students to check their ideas with a partner before completing the chart.
- Put students into pairs and ask them to check each other's sentences for grammatical accuracy as well as meaning.

Above level:

- Have students complete the chart individually.
- Conduct a mingle activity where students stand up and try to find other students with the same predictions.
- When they find a student with the same prediction, they write down the student's name.
- When the mingle activity is completed, ask the class to say the most common predictions.

Further Practice
Workbook pages 5–7
Online practice Unit 1 · Understand
Oxford iTools Unit 1 · Understand

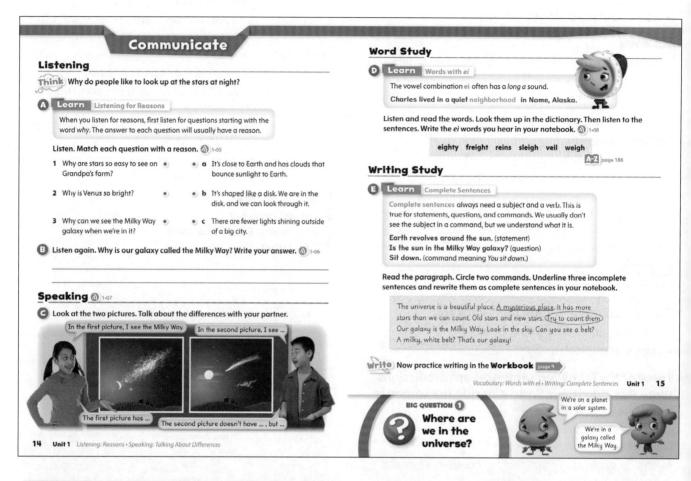

Summary

Objectives: To learn and practice listening, speaking, and writing strategies to facilitate effective communication.

Vocabulary: *eighty, freight, reins, sleigh, veil, weigh*

Listening strategy: Listening for reasons

Speaking: Talking about differences

Word Study: Words with *ei*

Writing Study: Writing complete sentences

Big Question learning point: *Our galaxy is in the universe.*

Materials: Discover Poster 1, Audio CD Big Question Chart

Think

- Open the discussion by talking about the different things you can see at night.
- Put students into pairs.
- Ask them to tell their partner three reasons that people might want to look up at the stars at night.

A Learn: Listening for Reasons

- Have a confident student read the *Learn* box to the class.

Listen. Match each question with a reason. 🔊 1·05

- Play the audio after asking a gist question to focus on general meaning, e.g. *What is light pollution?*
- Play the audio again and ask students to listen and match the sentences.

ANSWERS
1 c   2 a   3 b

B Listen again. Why is our galaxy called the Milky Way? Write your answer. 🔊 1·06

- Have students work individually.
- Once students have completed their writing, put them into pairs to check their answers.

POSSIBLE ANSWER
It's called the Milky Way because there are so many stars that it looks like milk.

Speaking 🔊 1·07

C Look at the two pictures. Talk about the differences with your partner.

COMMUNICATION

- Have students use the speech bubbles as guides for talking about differences. Highlight the specific language used to talk about differences.
- Have students listen to the dialogue as a class.
- Model the dialogue with a confident student in front of the class. Have students practice the dialogue in pairs.
- If necessary, brainstorm some vocabulary in the pictures so that students can choose from this vocabulary when conducting the dialogue.

Answers will vary but should reflect the following:
The second picture doesn't have Venus or the Milky Way.
The second picture has a full moon, not a quarter moon.
The second picture has a comet.

COLLABORATIVE LEARNING

- Have students individually draw two similar pictures.
- Put students into pairs so they can practice a new dialogue to talk about the differences in the two sets of pictures.
- Swap students around so they work with a new partner and repeat the activity.

Word Study

D Learn: Words with *ei*

- Read the *Learn* box together.
- Ask students to identify the *ei* spelling and sound in the word *neighborhood*.

Listen and read the words. Look them up in the dictionary. Then listen to the sentences. Write the *ei* words you hear in your notebook. 🔊 1·08

- Ask students to listen and read individually.
- Have them look up the words in the dictionary section of the Student Book on page 186.
- Have students listen to the sentences. Stop the audio to give them time to write the words in their notebooks.

CRITICAL THINKING

- Have students write new sentences using the words from the Word Study exercise.
- Ask individual students to read their sentences to the class.
- Have the class tell you the definition of the words without looking at the dictionary pages or in their notebooks.

Writing Study

E Learn: Complete Sentences

- Have a confident student read the *Learn* box to the class.
- Ask students to think of other examples of common commands in the classroom.
- Elicit some examples, such as: *Stand up. Open your books. Be quiet. Pens down.*

Read the paragraph. Circle two commands. Underline three incomplete sentences and rewrite them as complete sentences in your notebook.

- Have students do the activity individually and then check with a partner. Elicit answers from the class.

ANSWERS
Two commands: Try to count them. Look in the sky.
Three incomplete sentences: A mysterious place. Old stars and new stars. A milky, white belt?
Complete sentences: The universe is a beautiful and mysterious place. It has more old and new stars than we can count. Can you see a milky, white belt?

DIFFERENTIATION

Below level:

- Review subjects and verbs in sentences by identifying them in written sentences on the board.
- Have students write simple sentences using subjects and verbs.
- Ask them to swap their sentences with a partner to identify the subjects and verbs.

At level:

- Put students into pairs. Have each pair write simple sentences with subjects and verbs.
- Ask each pair to swap their sentences with another pair to identify the subjects and verbs.
- Have each pair stand up and read a sentence where they have identified the subject and verb to the class.

Above level:

- Put students into pairs. Ask each pair to write a short paragraph about something they are interested in, making sure they include one or two commands and one or two incomplete sentences.
- Ask each pair to swap their sentences with another pair to identify the commands and incomplete sentences. Have them correct the incomplete sentences.
- Have each pair swap back their sentences and correct them.

Write

- Direct the students to the Workbook for further practice.

Big Question 1 Review

Where are we in the universe?

- Display **Discover Poster 1**. Point to familiar vocabulary items and elicit them from the class. Ask *What is this?*
- Return to the **Big Question Chart**.
- Ask students what they have learned about where we are in the universe while studying this unit.
- Ask what information is new and add it to the chart.

| **Further Practice**
| Workbook pages 8–9
| **Online practice** Unit 1 · Communicate
| Oxford **iTools** Unit 1 · Communicate

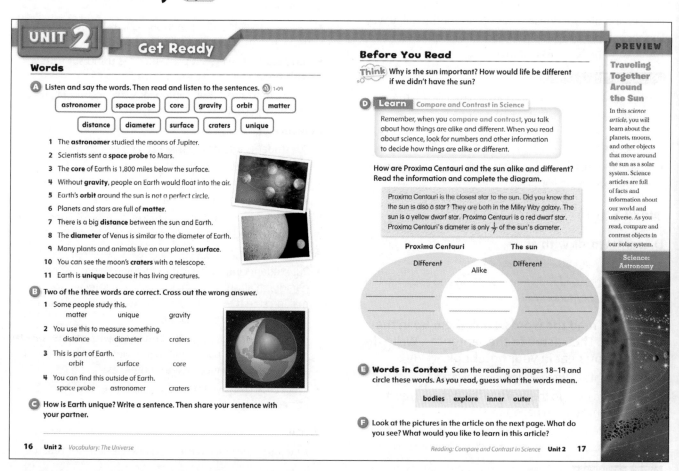

Summary

Objectives: To understand words about astronomy; to apply own experience and a reading strategy to help comprehension of a text.

Vocabulary: *astronomer, space probe, core, gravity, orbit, matter, distance, diameter, surface, craters, unique, bodies, explore, inner, outer*

Reading strategy: Compare and contrast in science

Materials: Audio CD

Words

A Listen and say the words. Then read and listen to the sentences. 🎧 1·09

- Have students point to and say the words they know.
- Play the audio. Ask students to point to the words as they hear them.
- Play the audio a second time and have students repeat the words when they hear them.
- Pay particular attention to the syllable stress in the multi-syllable words *astronomer*, *diameter*, and *gravity*.

CRITICAL THINKING

Ask the following questions to check understanding:

- Which words are about measuring something?
- Are the moon's craters on its surface or in its core?
- Name three other things that would happen if Earth lost gravity.
- Earth is unique in the solar system because it has living creatures. What else makes Earth unique?

B Two of the three words are correct. Cross out the wrong answer.

- Do the first one together to make sure students know what to do.
- Have students complete the activity on their own.
- Ask them to compare with a partner.
- Check answers with the class.

ANSWERS

1 unique 2 craters 3 orbit 4 astronomer

COLLABORATIVE LEARNING

- Divide the class into small groups.
- Have each group copy the vocabulary words from page 16 and the words from page 8 on separate sheets of paper.
- Tell them to work together to sort the words into categories. Students can devise their own categories, or you can suggest some, such as tools or bodies in space. Encourage them to add other words they know to the categories.
- Not every word needs to fit in a category, as long as students work together to think more deeply about the vocabulary set as a whole.
- When students finish, have groups share their category lists with the class.

Below level:

- Before each sentence in A, give a preliminary definition of the vocabulary word, e.g. *An astronomer is a scientist; a space probe is a machine; the core is the center; gravity is a force,* and so on.

At level:

- Write the words on the board.
- Have individual students stand up and spell the words as you point to them.
- Play a round of "Tell me what you know." Point to a word and invite students to say everything they can about the word. This includes content-specifics, personalization, comments on spelling and pronunciation, or simple definitions.
- For each word, give them 30 seconds to brainstorm before eliciting responses. Accept all responses that are thoughtful and accurate.

Above level:

- Have students write sentences about the vocabulary words following the model of B, but using more specific details.
- Tell them not to include the words in the sentences, e.g. *She is a scientist that studies the stars* could be a sentence for *astronomer.*
- Collect the sentences and play a class game where you read aloud the sentence and the class names the word.

C How is Earth unique? Write a sentence. Then share your sentence with your partner.

- Have students write the sentence individually.
- Put students into pairs to compare their sentences.
- Ask for a show of hands if partners wrote sentences with the same meaning.

Before You Read

Think

- Put students into pairs. Ask them to think of two possible consequences for the world if we didn't have the sun.
- Put one pair with a different pair and have them discuss their ideas.
- Elicit ideas from the class and decide upon the most serious consequence for the world.

D Learn: Compare and Contrast in Science

- Have students read the *Learn* box together.

How are Proxima Centauri and the sun alike and different? Read the information and complete the diagram.

- Read the paragraph on Proxima Centauri together. Before reading, focus on the key question that determines their purpose for reading: *How are Proxima Centauri and the sun alike? How are they different?*
- Have pairs complete the Venn diagram and then check answers with the class.

Proxima Centauri: Red dwarf star. Smaller than the sun.
The Sun: Yellow dwarf star. Bigger than Proxima Centauri.
Alike: Both are stars. Both are in the Milky Way galaxy.

- Ask the following questions to check understanding about the text on page 17:
  What do Proxima Centauri and the sun have in common? How are they different?

E Words in Context: Scan the reading on pages 18–19 and circle these words. As you read, guess what the words mean.

- Have students circle the words in the reading on the following pages.

F Look at the pictures in the article on the next page. What do you see? What would you like to learn in this article?

- Help students preview the reading text by focusing on the pictures.
- Point to different images and elicit *planet, Saturn, orbit, asteroid, Earth, Venus.*
- Ask students what they would like to learn about the images they see in the reading text.

Reading Preview

- Read the title of the unit's reading text.
- Have students silently read the content of the preview bar.
- Ask *What type of text is it? What does this type of text do?*
- Tell students to look for sentences that compare and contrast as they read the text the first time.

Further Practice
Workbook pages 10–11
Online practice Unit 2 • Get Ready
Oxford **iTools** Unit 2 • Get Ready

Traveling Together Around the Sun

The sun is a star, and it is very important for our planet Earth. It gives us light and heat. However, Earth is not alone. It shares the sun with seven other planets. Together, these planets revolve around the sun in a solar system. Other bodies travel in this solar system, such as moons, asteroids, and comets. They all move around the sun because the sun's gravity is very strong.

Each planet's path around the sun is called an orbit. The planets that are closer to the sun have smaller orbits, so they take less time to go around it. Mercury takes 88 days to complete one orbit. Earth completes one orbit in 365 days, or one year. Neptune's orbit takes 60,200 days, or almost 165 years!

Each planet in our solar system is unique. For example, Mercury is the smallest planet. It has lots of craters, just like our moon. Jupiter is the biggest planet. Its diameter is eleven times bigger than Earth's. Saturn has giant rings of matter around it. Neptune is the farthest planet from the sun.

Mars is a neighboring planet, and scientists are learning a lot about it. They send many space probes to Mars. A space probe called Curiosity landed on Mars on August 6, 2012. Curiosity is as big as a car, and it moves over the surface of Mars. It recently found rocks that had strange shapes. Running water made these shapes. This is an important discovery. Space probes like Curiosity continue to explore the planets, moons, and other bodies in our solar system. If technology continues to grow, we will travel to these places ourselves.

Iron and rock make up most of the four smaller inner planets of our solar system. Gas and water make up most of the four larger outer planets. This means that you can stand on the surface of Earth, but you can't stand on Saturn. In fact, if you tried to stand on Saturn, you would sink down to the core of the planet.

Drawings of our solar system show the planets close to the sun. However, the distance between the planets and the sun is very far. For example, it would take 176 years to drive a car from Earth to the sun. It would take 5,300 years to drive from Neptune to the sun!

Astronomers think that there are many solar systems in our Milky Way galaxy. However, our solar system is special to us. It is our home.

Think
How are the inner planets the same? How are they different from the outer planets?

Think
How are some of the planets different from Earth?

The Asteroid Belt
An asteroid belt runs between the inner and outer planets. Scientists have discovered over 7,000 asteroids there, and there may be millions more. Asteroids travel around the sun, just like planets.

The Sister Planets
Did you know that Earth and Venus are called "sister planets"? This is because they are almost the same size, and Venus is the closest planet to Earth. However, Venus is much hotter than Earth, and it is always covered in thick clouds.

18   19

Summary

Objectives: To read, understand, and discuss a nonfiction text; to apply a reading strategy to improve comprehension.

School subject: Science: Astronomy

Text type: Science article (nonfiction)

Reading strategy: Compare and contrast in science

Big Question learning point: *Earth is in a solar system.*

Materials: Talk About It! Poster, Audio CD

Before Reading

- Preview and review some clues that let the reader know the author is comparing or contrasting.

- When contrasting, authors may use: *-er* and *-est*; *more* and *less*; *however* and *but*.

- When telling how things are alike, authors may use: *together, all, like, just / as … as, both*.

- Provide a few examples of sentences comparing and contrasting, e.g. *The Sun is hotter than Earth. Earth has living creatures, but Mars doesn't.*

During Reading 🔊 1·10

- Ask a gist question to check overall understanding of the text, and allow students a few minutes to skim the text, e.g. *Think about Earth and another planet. What is one thing that the planet and Earth have in common? What's one thing that's different?*

- Give students a few minutes to skim the text before answering.

- Remind students that they are reading to compare and contrast.

- Play the audio. Students listen as they read along.

- Play the audio a second time if necessary.

DIFFERENTIATION

Below level:

- Put students in mixed-ability pairs.

- Have students take turns reading the text aloud to each other, with the more confident reader helping the less confident one to sound out and pronounce the words and phrases.

At level:

- Put students into small groups of four or five. If possible, have them sit in a circle.

- Have students take turns reading a sentence out loud as the text is read around the circle.

- After each paragraph, ask the groups to pause and discuss what they have just read.

Above level:

- Have students read the text individually and underline any sentences that they don't understand.

- Move around the room and provide help as necessary.

- Ask for any sentences that students couldn't work out and provide an explanation for the whole class.

Discussion questions:

- *If a year on Earth is 365 days, how long would a year be on Mercury? On Neptune?*
- *Why is the length of a year different for different planets?*
- *Why couldn't you stand on Saturn?*
- *Do you think it's important to learn about the solar system and the planets? Why or why not?*
- *What did the space probe "Curiosity" find out about Mars? Why is this an important discovery?*
- *Why do you think Venus is hotter than Earth?*

After Reading

- Have students look again at the reading text.
- Ask them to work with partners to list three questions they still have about the solar system.

COLLABORATIVE LEARNING

- Display the **Talk About It! Poster** to help students form appropriate sentences for a discussion.
- Put students into pairs to discuss how each planet is similar to and different from Earth.

COLLABORATIVE LEARNING

- Put students into pairs and ask them to work together to write a mock interview with an astronomer based on the information in the text.
- Each partner should draft a few questions that are answered in the text.
- Partners share the questions with each other, making any spelling or grammatical corrections as needed.
- Partners work together to write the answers. They combine their questions into one coherent interview.
- They decide who will play the astronomer and who will play the interviewer.
- Encourage students to create a context for the interview, such as a school newspaper or a TV news program.
- After practicing, partners perform their interviews for the class.

CULTURE NOTE

Everyone knows the Earth's moon, but other planets in the solar system have moons, too. Mars has two moons; Jupiter, Saturn, Uranus, and Neptune have several moons each.

The Earth's moon is shaped like a ball, but other planets' moons can be irregularly shaped. All moons orbit around their planet, but some orbit in the same direction the planet spins, while others orbit in the opposite direction. Moons orbit their planets because of the gravitational pull of the planet.

Further Practice
Workbook page 12
Online practice Unit 2 · Read
Oxford **iTools** Unit 2 · **Read**

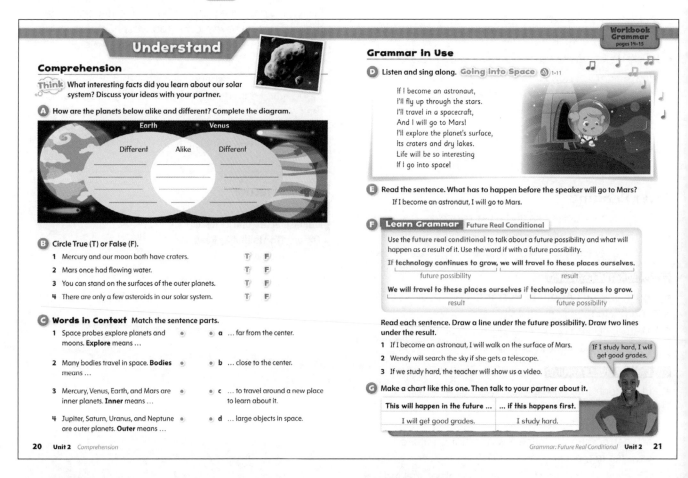

Summary

Objectives: To demonstrate understanding of a nonfiction text; to understand the meaning and form of the grammar structure.

Reading: Comprehension

Grammar input: Future real conditional

Grammar practice: Workbook exercises

Grammar production: Writing personal information

Materials: Audio CD

Comprehension

Think

- Have students share what they found most interesting about the reading on the previous pages.
- Make a note of common answers and then summarize: *Several students thought it was interesting that … Only one student thought it was interesting that … .*

A How are the two planets below alike and different? Complete the diagram.

- Tell students to revisit the reading to find details they can use to complete the diagram.
- Review answers as a class.

ANSWERS

Earth: Not as hot, not as many thick clouds

Venus: Much hotter, covered in thick clouds

Alike: Almost the same size

Below level:

- Review some of the words and phrases that writers use to signal comparison and contrast from the *Before Reading* on Teacher's Book page 44. Show the students how to revisit the reading text to find details they can use to complete the chart.

At level:

- Have students work independently to complete the chart.
- Ask students to check their work with a partner.
- Review the answers together as a class.

Above level:

- First have students complete the diagram on their own.
- Challenge them to write sentences about Venus and Earth using the information in the diagram. Ask students to share their sentences.

B Circle True (T) or False (F).

- Have students complete the exercise individually and then check with a partner.
- Elicit answers from the class.

ANSWERS

1 T   2 T   3 F   4 F

C Words in Context: Match the sentence parts.

ANSWERS

1 c   2 d   3 b   4 a

Grammar in Use

D Listen and sing along. 🎵 1·11

- Listen to the song once and then sing it together as a class.
- Divide the class into two groups. Have each group sing four lines.
- Ask questions about the song to check understanding, e.g. *Where will the speaker go if she becomes an astronaut? How will she get there? What will she see on Mars's surface?*

E Read the sentence. What has to happen before the speaker will go to Mars?

- Draw students' attention to the first part of the sentence: *If I become an astronaut, … .*
- Have students look back at the song and ask: *What else will happen if she becomes an astronaut?*

F Learn Grammar: Future Real Conditional

- Read the *Learn Grammar* box together to the class.
- Write the example sentences on the board. Draw an arrow from *If technology continues to grow,* to *we will travel to these places ourselves* to show the relationship between the future possibility and the result.

Read each sentence. Draw a line under the future possibility. Draw two lines under the result.

- Complete number 1 together. Then have students complete numbers 2 and 3 on their own.
- Check the answers with the class.

> **ANSWERS**
> 1 If I become an astronaut, I will walk on the surface of Mars.
> 2 Wendy will search the sky if she gets a telescope.
> 3 If we study hard, the teacher will show us a video.

DIFFERENTIATION

Below level:

- Point out the agreement between *I* and *become* in the first line of the song and between *technology* and *continues* in the *Learn Grammar* box.
- Point out that *will* is an auxiliary verb that does not have to agree with its subject (*I will, you will, he / she will, it will, we will, they will*).

At level:

- Put students into small groups of three or four.
- Ask them to create two more sentences with the future real conditional.
- Have one person from each group write a sentence on the board.
- Ask the class to tell you if the sentences are correct and to explain why or why not.

Above level:

- Put students into small groups of three or four. Ask each group to think of two possible future situations and to write them down on a piece of paper, e.g. *It gets hotter and hotter. Robots become teachers. We run out of oil.*
- Each group swaps their paper with another group, and writes two sentences for the possible future situations outlined. They give their sentences back.

- Students look at the sentences the other group has written and decide if they are grammatically correct, and if they agree with the meaning of the sentence.

G Make a chart like this one. Then talk to your partner about it.

- Divide the class into pairs.
- Have partners take turns suggesting ideas for the chart. Ask them to record their ideas on a separate piece of paper.
- Make sure that students discuss the ideas. If they need ideas, remind them to think about everyday life. Their charts do not need to be about the solar system.

CRITICAL THINKING

- The grammar presents future real conditional sentences with one future possibility and one result. Challenge students to think of additional future possibilities and / or results for the sentences on the page.
- For example, for the sentence *If technology continues to grow, we will travel to these places ourselves,* an alternate future possibility could be *If I get a spaceship for my birthday* and an alternate result could be *we will see the moon's surface on our smartphones.*
- Encourage students to brainstorm other sentences with several alternate future possibilities and results.

COLLABORATIVE LEARNING

- Have students write the answers for the chart on slips of paper. Ask them to cut the sentences in half so the future possibility and the result are separated.
- In groups, have students mix up their sentence pieces and then work together to see how many possible and logical sentences they can make.

Further Practice
Workbook pages 13–15
Online practice Unit 2 · Understand
Oxford iTools Unit 2 · Understand

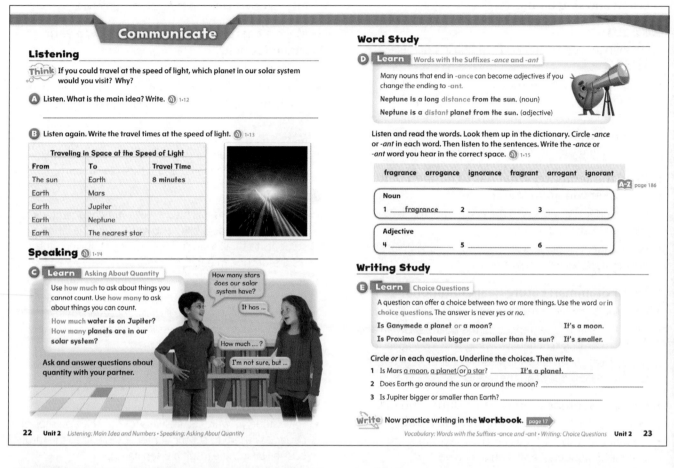

Summary

Objectives: To learn and practice listening, speaking, and writing strategies to facilitate effective communication.

Vocabulary: *fragrance, arrogance, ignorance, fragrant, arrogant, ignorant*

Listening strategy: Listening for main ideas and numbers

Speaking: Asking about quantity

Word Study: Words with the suffixes *-ance* and *-ant*

Writing Study: Choice questions

Big Question learning point: *We are far away from other planets, stars, and galaxies.*

Materials: Audio CD

Listening

Think

- Ask students the *Think* question. Give them one minute to think about their answers. Then select volunteers to share their ideas with the class.
- Encourage answers such as *I would visit Saturn because I want to see the rings up close* instead of *I would visit Saturn because I like it.*

A Listen. What is the main idea? Write. 🔘 1·12

- Break down the question by first asking what the report is about. Then help students create a sentence about it, e.g. *The speed of light is very fast – almost 300,000 kilometers per second.*

B Listen again. Write the travel times at the speed of light. 🔘 1·13

- Listen to the audio again. Pause to allow students time to complete the chart.
- Check the answers with the class.

ANSWERS

Sun to Earth: 8 minutes
Earth to Mars: 4 minutes
Earth to Jupiter: 35 minutes
Earth to Neptune: 4 hours
Earth to the nearest star: 4 years

CRITICAL THINKING

Ask the following questions to check understanding:

- *Traveling at the speed of light, how long do you think it would take to get from the sun to Venus?* (Estimating answers should reflect (A) the understanding that Venus is closer to the sun than Earth, so it would take less than 8 minutes, and (B) that Mars and Venus are roughly the same distance from Earth (see page 18). Earth to Mars is 4 minutes. A reasonable estimate would thus be close to 5 light minutes.)
- *How would it feel to travel at the speed of light?* (Answers will vary, but should reflect the understanding that this is

faster than students have ever moved and faster than any man-made object has ever moved.)

- Focus on the last sentence of the listening passage: *If you wanted to travel across our own Milky Way Galaxy, it would take thousands of (light) years.*
- Ask students to say a future real conditional sentence that uses this fact or another fact in the selection.
- Present some math problems for a curricular connection, e.g. *How long would it take to travel from Mars to Jupiter?* (31 light minutes) *How long would it take to travel from Jupiter to Neptune?* (3 light hours and 25 light minutes).

Speaking 🔊 1·14

C Learn: Asking About Quantity

COMMUNICATION

- Have students read the *Learn* box along with the narrator as they listen to the audio.
- Model the dialogue with a confident student in front of the class.
- Focus on the phrases *How much* and *How many* in the questions. Ask *Why do we use "How much" to ask about water? Why do we use "How many" to ask about planets?*

Ask and answer questions about quantity with your partner.

- Put students into pairs and tell them to practice the dialogue, taking turns speaking the different roles.
- After each pair has practiced the dialogue a few times, have the pair ask and answer questions on different topics.

Word Study

D Learn: Words with the Suffixes *-ance* and *-ant*

- Read the *Learn* box together.

Listen and read the words. Look them up in the dictionary. Circle *-ance* or *-ant* in each word. Then listen to the sentences. Write the *-ance* or *-ant* word you hear in the correct space. 🔊 1·15

- Have students complete the listening activity individually, completing the chart with nouns and adjectives from the list.
- Students can check their answers with a partner.

ANSWERS

Noun: 1 fragrance 2 arrogance 3 ignorance
Adjective: 4 fragrant 5 arrogant 6 ignorant

DIFFERENTIATION

Below level:

- Review the parts of speech. As you go over the presentation, return to this idea to help clarify the teaching point.
- Have students go to the dictionary section in the Student Book (page 186) to help them understand the meaning of the words. Reinforce the part of speech in the definition.
- Guide students through the listening activity and in completing the chart. Stop after each sentence to highlight clues about the meaning of each word and its part of speech.

At level:

- Have students complete the activity on their own and then check their work with a partner.
- For the adjectives, ask them to identify the nouns they describe, e.g. *ignorant* describes *man*.

Above level:

- Play the sentences from the audio one at a time.
- Challenge students to rewrite the sentences, changing target adjectives to nouns and target nouns to adjectives, e.g. *This flower has a nice fragrance* can become *This flower is fragrant.*

Writing Study

E Learn: Choice Questions

- Have a confident student read the *Learn* box to the class.

Circle *or* in each question. Underline the choices. Then write.

ANSWERS

1 Is Mars <u>a moon</u>, <u>a planet</u>, ⓐr <u>a star</u>? It's a planet.
2 Does Earth go around <u>the sun</u> ⓞr around <u>the moon</u>? It goes around the sun.
3 Is Jupiter <u>bigger</u> ⓞr <u>smaller</u> than Earth? It's bigger.

COLLABORATIVE LEARNING

- Have students each prepare a choice question using *or*. They should write their questions on slips of paper.
- Collect the questions and have students sit in a circle.
- Have them take turns choosing a question and reading it aloud to the person next to them. That person answers and chooses the next question.

Write

- Direct students to the Workbook for further practice.

Further Practice
Workbook pages 16–17
Online practice Unit 2 • Communicate
Oxford **iTools** Unit 2 • Communicate

Units 1 and 2 Wrap Up page 24

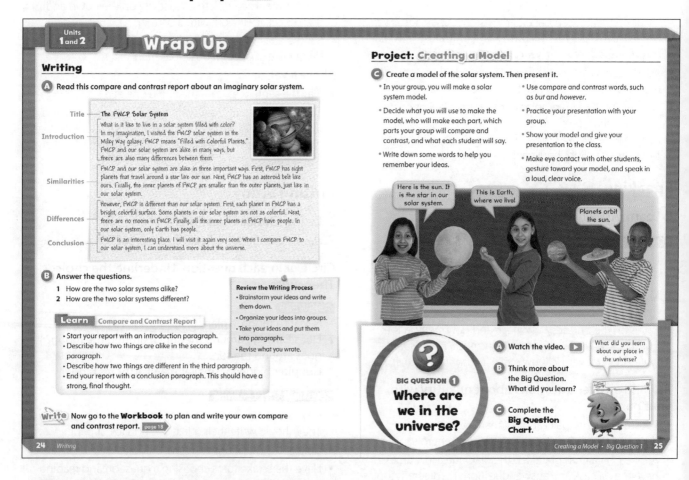

Summary

Objectives: To show what students have learned about the language and learning points of Units 1 and 2.

Reading: Comprehension of a compare and contrast report

Project: Create a model of the universe

Writing: Write a compare and contrast report

Speaking: Talk about the models

Materials: Big Question DVD, Discover Poster 1, Talk About It! Poster, Big Question Chart

Writing

A Read this compare and contrast report about an imaginary solar system.

- As students read, highlight elements from the module objectives. Have students do the following:
  1 Underline key and context vocabulary in the passage.
  2 Review definitions. (See pages 8–9, 16–17.)
  3 Focus on descriptive language. Can they visualize each solar system in their mind? (See page 9.)
  4 Identify facts versus predictions in the passage.
  5 Identify a reason for why things are the way they are. Ask *Why is the second solar system called FWCP?*
  6 Talk about the differences between the two solar systems. Remind students to use the language found on page 14.
  7 Find a word in which *ei* stands for the long a sound.
  8 Identify the subject and verb in a few examples. (See page 15.)

9 Find an example of a sentence that talks about a possible future situation and what will happen as a result.
10 Find an example of quantity. Ask *How many planets are in each solar system?*

B Answer the questions.

- Have students answer the questions individually and then check with a partner.
- Elicit the answers from the class.

POSSIBLE ANSWERS

1 Both have eight planets that travel around a star like the sun; both have an asteroid belt between the inner and outer planets; the inner planets are smaller than the outer planets in both solar systems.
2 The planets in FWCP are all colorful, but the planets in our solar system are not as colorful; many of the planets in our system have moons, but the planets in FWCP do not have moons; there are people on all the inner planets of FWCP, but in our solar system only Earth has people.

CRITICAL THINKING

- Put students into pairs.
- Have partners create a Venn diagram to show the similarities and differences between our solar system and the imaginary FWCP.
- Elicit ideas from the class and draw a Venn diagram on the board, adding different answers to it.

Learn: Compare and Contrast Report

• Read the *Learn* box together.

Write

• Direct students to the Workbook to plan and write their own compare and contrast report.

Project

C Create a model of the solar system. Then present it.

CREATIVITY

• Have two or three confident students take turns reading aloud the instructions to the class.

• Ask if anyone in the class has any questions about the instructions.

• Have partners work together to brainstorm some ideas for their reports.

• Encourage them to consider topics that tie into the Big Question: *Where are we in the universe?* Some ideas are: follow the model in A and compare an imaginary solar system with our own; compare and contrast two related jobs, like an astronomer and an astronaut; compare two places on Earth; compare an imaginary trip in a spacecraft to a real-life trip in an airplane.

DIFFERENTIATION

Below level:

• Elicit the names of the planets and write them on the board.

• Discuss the key differences between the planets. Refer back to the text in the Student Book as necessary.

• Take key sentences from the text in the Student Book and write them on the board, e.g. *Each planet in our solar system is unique.*

• Once the model is completed, allow students to write down their presentation and read it to the class.

At level:

• Ask students to underline the information in the texts in the Student Book that they will need to complete their models.

• Brainstorm the method for creating the models.

• Once the model is completed, allow students to write down key words that they will refer to during their presentation.

Above level:

• Review the information students will need to complete their models.

• Brainstorm the method for creating the models.

• Once the model is completed, give each group time to practice their presentation before doing it in front of the class.

Units 1 and 2 Big Question Review

A Watch the video. ▷

• Play the video and when it is finished ask students what they know about the universe now.

• Have students share ideas with the class.

B Think more about the Big Question. What did you learn?

COMMUNICATION

• Display **Discover Poster 1**. Point to familiar vocabulary items and elicit them from the class. Ask *What is this?*

• Ask students *What do you see?* Ask *What does that mean?*

• Refer to all of the learning points written on the poster and have students explain how they relate to the different pictures.

• Ask *What does this learning point mean?* Elicit answers from individual students.

• Display the **Talk About It! Poster** to help students with sentence frames for discussion of the learning points and for expressing their opinions.

C Complete the Big Question Chart.

COLLABORATIVE LEARNING

• Ask students what they have learned about the universe while studying this unit.

• Put students into pairs or small groups to say two new things they have learned.

• Have students share their ideas with the class and add their ideas to the chart.

• Have students complete the chart in their Workbook.

> **Further practice**
> **Workbook pages 18–20**
> **Online practice • Wrap Up 1**
> **Oxford iTools • Wrap Up 1**

In units 3 and 4 you will:

WATCH a video about uncovering the past.

LEARN how we know about the past.

READ about ancient soldiers and a boy's discovery.

WRITE a descriptive report.

CREATE a time capsule.

BIG QUESTION 2

How do we know what happened long ago?

A Watch the video. ▶

B Look at the picture and talk about it.

1 What is the boy taking a picture of? Why is he taking a picture?

2 Where do you think the boy is? What else do you think is in this place?

C Think and answer the questions.

1 Why do people want to learn about the past?

2 What time in the past do you want to learn more about?

D Fill out the **Big Question Chart**.

What do you know about studying the past? What do you want to know?

26 Big Question 2

27

Reading Strategies

Students will practice:

- Understanding author's purpose
- Predictions

Review

Students will review the language and Big Question learning points of Units 3 and 4 through:

- A descriptive report
- A project (creating a time capsule)

Vocabulary

Students will understand and use words about:

- Discovering the past

Units 3 and 4

How do we know what happened long ago?

Students will understand the Big Question learning points:

- We search for old objects and study them.
- We get knowledge from other people and sources.
- Technology helps us learn about ancient objects and people.
- Stories and myths teach us about life long ago.
- We study images of the past.

Grammar

Students will understand and use:

- Verbs followed by infinitives
- Verbs followed by gerunds

Listening Strategies

Students will practice:

- Listening for similarities and differences
- Listening for gist and sequence

Writing

Students will be able to:

- Keep verb tenses consistent in paragraphs
- Use count and noncount nouns correctly with verbs

Students will produce texts that:

- Describe

Word Study

Students will understand, pronounce, and use:

- Words with the suffix -ist
- Words with ie (the long e sound)

Speaking

Students will understand and use expressions to:

- Give reasons
- Describe with the senses

Units 3 and 4 Big Question page 26

Summary

Objectives: To activate students' existing knowledge of the topic and identify what they would like to learn about the topic.

Materials: Big Question DVD, Discover Poster 2, Big Question Chart

Introducing the topic

- Ask the Big Question: *How do we know what happened long ago?* Write answers from students on the board.

A Watch the video. ▷

- Play the video. When it is finished, ask students to answer the following questions in pairs:
  What do you see in the video?
  Who do you think the people are?
  What is happening?
  Do you like it?
- Have individual students share their answers with the class.

DIFFERENTIATION

Below level:

- After watching, have students list people and things they saw in the video.
- Help them to say sentences describing what they saw.

At level:

- After watching, have students write down five sentences about what they saw in the video.
- Have students rank their ideas based on what seems most interesting.

Above level:

- After watching, have students write down five sentences about what they saw in the video.
- Tell students to stand up and mingle and find someone else with the same sentence (focus on the meaning of the sentence rather than using exactly the same words).
- Have students say their sentences to the class.

B Look at the picture and talk about it.

- Students look at the big picture and talk about the following questions:
  What is the boy taking a picture of?
  Why is he taking a picture?
  Who do you think the boy is?
  What else do you think is in this place?
- Ask the students additional questions about the picture:
  What else can you see in this picture?
  Would you want to go to a place like this? Why or why not?

C Think and answer the questions.

CRITICAL THINKING

- Ask students to think about the first question *Why do people want to learn about the past?* Have students work in small groups to brainstorm answers.
- Encourage them to think of times in their own life when it has been helpful to know about the past. Ideas can be basic or complex.
- Have students answer the second question and tell their partner.

- Encourage them to use specific reasons why they want to learn about a certain time, e.g. *I want to learn more about the mid-twentieth century because my grandparents were children then.*

Expanding the topic

COLLABORATIVE LEARNING

- Display **Discover Poster 2** and give students enough time to look at the pictures.
- Elicit some of the words you think they will know by pointing to different people and objects in the pictures and asking *What's this?*
- Put students into small groups of three or four. Have each group choose a picture that they find interesting.
- Ask each group to say five things that they can see in their picture.
- Have one person from each group stand up and read aloud the words they chose for their picture.
- Ask the class if they can add any more.
- Repeat until every group has spoken.

D Fill out the Big Question Chart.

- Display the **Big Question Chart**.
- Ask the class *What do you know about studying the past? What do you know about history?*
- Record their ideas on the board.
- Ask the class *What do you want to know about studying the past?*
- Ask students to write what they know and what they want to know in their Workbooks.
- Write a collection of ideas on the **Big Question Chart**.

DIFFERENTIATION

Below level:

- Elicit single word answers from students about what they know about studying the past.
- Point to people and things in the big picture and on the poster and ask *What / Who is this?* Write the answers on the board.

At level:

- Elicit complete sentences about the scenes in the poster.
- Write the sentences on the board.

Above level:

- Elicit more details and multiple sentences about the **Discover Poster**.
- Play a game where a student talks about a picture and other students have to guess which picture it is.

Discover Poster 2

1 An archaeologist at work in South Africa; 2 Children learning about an artefact in a museum; 3 A man using a 3D scanner to learn more about an old object; 4 Artwork showing a Viking journey; 5 A woman in an early automobile around 1910

> **Further Practice**
> **Workbook page 21**
> **Online practice • Big Question 2**
> Oxford **iTools** • **Big Question 2**

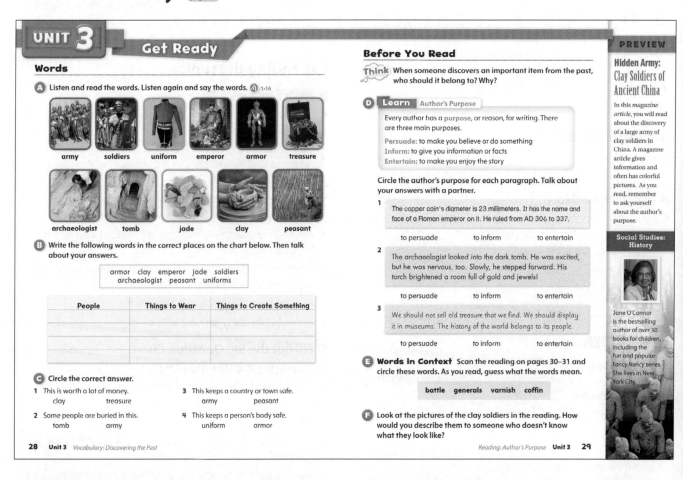

Summary

Objectives: To understand words about archaeology; to apply own experience and a reading strategy to help comprehension of a text.

Vocabulary: *army, soldiers, uniform, emperor, armor, treasure, archaeologist, tomb, jade, clay, peasant, battle, generals, varnish, coffin*

Reading strategy: Author's purpose

Materials: Audio CD

Words

A Listen and read the words. Listen again and say the words. 1·16

- Play the audio. Ask students to point to the words as they hear them.
- Play the audio a second time and have students repeat the words when they hear them.

CRITICAL THINKING

- Have students work individually to put each word into a sentence that they create themselves.
- Put students into pairs. They look at each other's sentences and help to correct them if necessary.
- Ask students to read a sentence to the class and have them explain why they wrote that sentence.

B Write the following words in the correct places on the chart below. Then talk about your answers.

- Have students categorize the words into the chart.
- Have them compare with a partner.
- Check answers with the class.

ANSWERS

People: emperor, soldiers, archaeologist, peasant
Things to Wear: armor, uniforms
Things to Create Something: clay, jade

C Circle the correct answer.

- Have students read each sentence and circle the word it describes.
- Have them compare with a partner.
- Check answers with the class.

ANSWERS

1 treasure   2 tomb   3 army   4 armor

DIFFERENTIATION

Below level:

- Pay particular attention to the silent letters and special spellings in several of the words as these can be confusing:
  In *soldiers*, the *di* stands for a *j* sound.
  In *treasure* and *peasant*, the *ea* stands for the short *e* sound like in *bread* and *heavy*.
  In *archaeologist*, the *ae* stands for a long *e*. It can be written with or without the *a*.

At level:

- After students finish the chart in B, ask them to brainstorm other words they know that might fit in the categories.
- Encourage them to think about the past when they brainstorm ideas. The goal is to name other People, Things to Wear, and Things to Create Something from the past.

Above level:

- Challenge students to follow the style of C and write sentences for some of the other words (*clay, peasant, uniform, jade, archaeologist, soldiers*).
- Have students work with partners and then trade sentences with other groups.
- Then have students share all the sentences and answers with the class.

Before You Read

Think

- It may help to provide an example, such as an archaeologist from the United States who finds an ancient Chinese vase in a tomb in Turkey.
- Discuss the role of museums in sharing archaeological finds with people around the world, as well as universities who keep collections for their own studies.
- Discuss what an archaeological excavation is and why it is difficult, expensive, etc.

D Learn: Author's Purpose

- Have a confident student read the contents of the *Learn* box to the class.
- Invite students to give examples of each kind of writing, e.g.
  1 a commercial, editorial, or letter can be written to persuade
  2 a newspaper, textbook, or dictionary is written to inform
  3 a poem, novel, or comic book is written to entertain.

Circle the author's purpose for each paragraph. Talk about your answers with a partner.

- Have partners read the paragraphs together and choose the purpose for each one.

ANSWERS

1 to inform   2 to entertain   3 to persuade

COLLABORATIVE LEARNING

- Divide students into small groups of three or four. Each group will work together to write a paragraph that informs, entertains, or persuades.
- Give each group a purpose: to inform, to entertain, or to persuade. Assign the purpose quietly or in writing, so that each group is unaware of the other groups' purposes.
- Give students a set amount of time to write a paragraph that informs, entertains, or persuades.
- When students are finished, have one student from each group read the group's paragraph to the class.
- The rest of the groups should guess the purpose of the paragraph.

E Words in Context: Scan the reading on pages 30–31 and circle these words. As you read, guess what the words mean.

- Have students scan the text and circle the words.
- Have students work individually to create four fill-in-the-blank sentences using each word.
- Put students into pairs and tell them to swap their notebooks, completing each other's sentences by writing in the missing words.
- Elicit some of the sentences from the class and discuss the meaning of the words.

F Look at the pictures of the clay soldiers in the reading. How would you describe them to someone who doesn't know what they look like?

COMMUNICATION

- Put the students into pairs and ask them to look at the pictures of the clay soldiers in the reading on page 30.
- Ask them to write a description of the soldiers with their partner. Remind students that they are describing the soldiers to somebody who has never seen them before.
- They need to explain what the soldiers look like and how they are dressed.

Reading Preview

- Have students read the title of the unit's reading text.
- Have students silently read the content of the preview bar. Ask them why they think an army would be called "hidden."
- Then ask students *What do you think the author's purpose will be? Why do you think that? Are there any clues in the title or paragraph?*

Further Practice
Workbook pages 21–22
Online practice Unit 3 • Get Ready
Oxford **iTools** Unit 3 • Get Ready

Hidden Army:

It is 210 BC and the moment before battle. The Chinese emperor's army is ready to charge. The soldiers—thousands of them—are lined up, row after row, as far as the eye can see.

However, the army will never attack. The soldiers are not real. They are the size of real soldiers. But they are made of terra-cotta, a strong kind of clay. They are more than 2,000 years old.

Think
What is the author's purpose in the first paragraph?

Amazingly, no two soldiers are alike. Their faces are different. Some are old; some are young. Some look tired; some look like they can't wait for the battle to start.

Their uniforms are different. The uniforms are exact copies of what real soldiers wore. The archers and foot soldiers were the lowest-ranking soldiers, so they have the plainest uniforms.

The generals, of course, wore the most elegant uniforms. Some of their caps had feathers. Sometimes their shoes turned up at the toes. Their armor had small iron rings that look like fish scales.

Here you see an image of a clay general. It shows how he looked 2,000 years ago. Every single soldier in the emperor's army was painted with bright colors. So were the terra-cotta horses. Now most of the soldiers have only tiny traces of paint left. Scientists are trying to create a special varnish to brush over painted figures to hold the paint in place.

Think
What is the author's purpose for this paragraph?

a computerized image of a clay general

Clay Soldiers of Ancient China

Today, craftsmen near the pits where the soldiers were found make copies of the soldiers. This helps archaeologists learn more about how people made the original army. Modern craftsmen have much better kilns than those in ancient times. Kilns are ovens that bake clay until it hardens. Yet no copies ever come out as hard or shiny as the originals. Why? Nobody knows—it is a mystery.

An even bigger mystery is what lies inside the emperor's tomb. Nobody knows the answer because the tomb has never been opened. The Chinese government plans to keep it closed for now. Work will not start until archaeologists are sure the tomb can be opened without damaging any of the treasures inside.

As for the emperor's body, according to historical records, it rests in a heavy, bronze coffin.

In ancient times, the custom was to dress the dead body of someone important in a suit the Chinese made from hundreds of pieces of thin jade. At that time, jade was more precious than gold.

The emperor died when he was 49 years old. Three years after his death, peasants rose up against the empire. One of their leaders started a new royal family.

Yet now, millions of people come to the emperor's burial place. They visit the covered pits to see the clay soldiers. The emperor lives on in the memory of all who see his amazing hidden army.

Think
What is the author's purpose for the entire reading?

30   31

Summary

Objectives: To read, understand, and discuss a nonfiction text; to apply a reading strategy to improve comprehension.

School subject: Social Studies: History

Text type: Magazine article (nonfiction)

Reading strategy: Author's purpose

Big Question learning points: *We search for old objects and study them. We get knowledge from other people and sources. Technology helps us learn about ancient objects and people.*

Materials: Talk About It! Poster, Audio CD

Before Reading

- Ask *How do we know what happened long ago?* Touch upon the learning point: *We search for old objects and study them.*

- Have students tell you what they see in the pictures. They should be able to identify *soldiers, army, armor, uniform, emperor, archaeologists, tools,* and *clay.*

- Revisit the Preview on page 29, and explain that the reading is about a large army of clay soldiers that was found in China.

During Reading ⊙ 1·17

- Ask a gist question to check overall understanding of the text. Ask *What can we learn about the ancient Chinese army from studying these clay soldiers?*

- Give students a few minutes to skim the text before answering.

- Remind them that they are trying to determine the author's purpose. At each *Think* box, stop and ask about the author's purpose.

- Play the audio. Students listen as they read along.

- Play the audio a second time if necessary.

DIFFERENTIATION

Below level:

- Focus on fluency. Choose one paragraph. Play the audio and pause after each sentence. Have students repeat the sentence after the audio, mimicking the pronunciation, rhythm, and intonation. Make sure they follow the text on the page as they do this.

- Repeat as often as needed until students are very confident reading their paragraph. Invite them to read aloud for the class.

At level:

- Have students read with partners.

- They take turns reading paragraphs and asking each other questions about language they don't understand.

Above level:

- Have students read the text independently.

- As they read, have them jot down comprehension questions they can ask their classmates afterwards. Explain that they are like teachers who need to make sure their students understand the reading.

- Have small groups work together to ask and answer their questions from the reading.

Discussion questions:

- *Why do you think the artists who created these soldiers made them all look different?*
- *Why are modern craftsmen making copies of these soldiers?*
- *What is different about the modern-day figures and the ancient ones?*
- *Do you think the Chinese government is right to keep the tomb closed?*
- *If you could go back in time, what would you ask the artist who created these figures? What would you ask the soldiers they were based upon?*

After Reading

- Have students look again at the text. Ask *What is the author's purpose for this reading? Did the author only have one purpose? Why or why not?*

COLLABORATIVE LEARNING

- Display the **Talk About It! Poster** to help students with sentence frames for discussion and expressing personal opinions.
- Put students into pairs to discuss the author's purpose.
- Have students say one thing about the text that they found interesting and one thing they would like to learn more about.
- Put students into small groups of three or four.
- Have students discuss the value of uncovering ancient artifacts.

CULTURE NOTE

The Terra-cotta Warriors were discovered in 1974. A group of farmers were digging a water-well and stumbled across lots of terra-cotta figures. There had been reports of pieces of these figures being found in the area for many years, but this time, so many were found that the Chinese government decided to investigate.

Many other artifacts have also been found in this area, not just the life-sized figures. Weapons such as crossbows, swords, and shields were buried with the figures and it is believed many of them were actually used on the field of battle. Chariots have also been found. The chariots were used to transport warriors in and around a battle and were designed so that soldiers could shoot crossbows from them as they moved and fight with swords if necessary.

The weapons and transportation provide a very clear picture of wartime life thousands of years ago in China.

A collection of 120 objects have been compiled to travel around the world as the Terra-cotta Army exhibition. Many countries have hosted this exhibition and it has been one of the most popular the world has ever seen.

Further Practice
Workbook page 23
Online practice Unit 3 • Read
Oxford **iTools** Unit 3 • Read

Understand

Comprehension

Think What does the discovery of the terra-cotta soldiers teach you? What else do you want to know about life in China 2,000 years ago?

A What is the author's purpose for each sentence below? Write the number for each sentence in the correct box. Talk about your answers with your partner.

1 The Chinese emperor's army is ready to charge.
2 The emperor died when he was 49 years old.
3 The terra-cotta soldiers are more than 2,000 years old.
4 It is the moment before battle.
5 Some look like they can't wait for the battle to start.
6 Their armor had small iron rings that look like fish scales.

To Inform	To Entertain
	1

B Circle True (T) or False (F).

1 Every terra-cotta soldier looks exactly the same.   T   F
2 The terra-cotta horses were colorful a long time ago.   T   F
3 The original clay soldiers were shinier than the copies.   T   F
4 Archaeologists know what's inside the emperor's tomb.   T   F
5 Many people come to see the terra-cotta soldiers.   T   F

C **Words in Context** Match each word to its definition. Write the letter.

1 battle _____   a a clear liquid that keeps something looking new
2 general _____   b a box that a dead body is put into
3 varnish _____   c a fight between armies in a war
4 coffin _____   d a very important officer in an army

Grammar in Use

D Listen and sing along. **The Archaeologist** 🔊 1-18

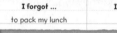

I'm an archaeologist,
And I love to study the past.
I like to hunt and then to dig
And uncover things at last!

A piece of ancient armor,
Or jade or cloth or clay,
I promise to share my treasures
To show the past today.

E Look at **D**. Which verbs start with *to*?

F **Learn Grammar** Verbs Followed by Infinitives

Some verbs are often followed by an infinitive. An infinitive is a verb with the word *to* in front of it.

The Chinese government plans to keep it closed for now.
                  verb   infinitive

Match the two parts of each sentence. Then circle the infinitives.

1 All the students promised   •   • a to find more terra-cotta soldiers.
2 The archeologists tried   •   • b to build the clay army.
3 The emperor decided   •   • c to study hard for the history test.

G Make a chart like this one. Use infinitives with the verbs *forgot* and *promise*. Then talk about your ideas with a partner.

> I forgot to pack my lunch today.

I forgot ...	I promise ...
to pack my lunch	

Summary

Objectives: To demonstrate understanding of a nonfiction text; to understand the meaning and form of the grammar structure.

Reading: Comprehension

Grammar input: Verbs followed by infinitives

Grammar practice: Workbook exercises

Grammar production: Writing and talking about personal information

Materials: Audio CD

Comprehension

Think

- Have students review the text to see what they learned.
- Encourage them to make inferences about the real-life soldiers (i.e. some were old, some were young, some were tired, some were eager to fight); the different ranks in the military (the low-ranking soldiers wore plain uniforms and the higher-ranking officers wore more elaborate uniforms); and what will be found in the tomb when it is opened (likely the emperor's body in a suit of jade).

COLLABORATIVE LEARNING

- Invite students to tell what else they want to know about China 2,000 years ago. Encourage them to think beyond the text.
- In small groups, have students brainstorm one question about each of the following topics: everyday life, growing up, culture, food, art, family, clothing, or another category that the group chooses.

A What is the author's purpose for each sentence below? Write the number for each sentence in the correct box. Talk about your answers with a partner.

- Have students complete the exercise independently and then review their answers in pairs.
- Point out that the sentences that are intended to entertain use language that sounds like a story. The author is only imagining that the "emperor's army is ready to charge."
- By adding a narrative tone, the author makes this informational text more entertaining.

ANSWERS
To Inform: 2, 3, 6   To Entertain: 1, 4, 5

B Circle True (T) or False (F).

- Have students work individually to answer, and then put them into pairs to check their answers before checking answers with the whole class.

ANSWERS
1 F   2 T   3 T   4 F   5 T

DIFFERENTIATION

Below level:

- Help students find the appropriate section to decide if each sentence in B is true or false.
- For number 1, say, e.g. *Look at paragraphs 3 and 4. The word "same" is not there, but what other words do you see that we use to compare or contrast? Read the entire sentence with "alike." Does that mean the soldiers look the same or different. Now read the sentence with "different." Does that mean the soldiers look the same or different?*

At level:

- For B, have students change each false sentence to make it true, e.g. 1 *Every terracotta soldier looks different. / Every terracotta soldier doesn't look the same.*

Above level:

- Have students go back through the text and create new true or false statements for each word.
- Have students share their statements with the class and the other students decide if the statement is true or false, and explain why.

C Words in Context: Match each word to its definition. Write the letter.

- Encourage students to look back at the text to find the words in context.
- Have students work in small groups to discuss the clues that helped them define each word.
- Elicit answers from the class and discuss the surrounding words and phrases that help to make the definition clear.

ANSWERS
1 c   2 d   3 a   4 b

Grammar in Use

D Listen and sing along. 🎵 1·18

CREATIVITY

- Play the audio.
- Listen to the song once and then sing it together as a class.
- Go over the song line-by-line to focus on any words students don't know, and to reinforce comprehension.
- Invite small groups to sing the song together.

CRITICAL THINKING

- Ask *What do you think the singer means by "I promise to share my treasures to show the past today?"*

E Look at D. Which verbs start with *to*?

- Have students look at the song again.
- Have them complete the exercise on their own.
- Check answers with the class.

ANSWERS
to study, to hunt, to dig, to share, to show

F Learn Grammar: Verb Followed by Infinitives

- Read the contents of the *Learn Grammar* box aloud to the class.
- Have students go back to the text and underline all examples of verbs followed by infinitives.
- Write the examples on the board.

Match the two parts of each sentence. Then circle the infinitives.

- Have students complete the activity on their own.
- Check answers together.

ANSWERS
1 c   2 a   3 b

G Make a chart like this one. Use infinitives with the verbs *forgot* and *promise*. Then talk about your ideas with a partner.

- Give students enough time to fill in the chart individually.
- Put students into pairs to discuss the actions.
- Change pairs so that students talk to someone else about their actions.

Workbook Grammar

- Direct students to the Workbook for further practice.

CRITICAL THINKING

- Add two more columns to the chart: *I tried …* and *I decided …*
- Have students brainstorm sentences for each column.
- Encourage them to try to use the sentences in the context of the Big Question and the Unit 3 reading, e.g. *Archaeologists try to find clues about the past. The government promised to protect the ancient tomb. I forgot to visit the museum. The soldiers decided to attack the emperor.*

Further Practice
Workbook pages 24–26
Online practice Unit 3 · Understand
Oxford **iTools** Unit 3 · Understand

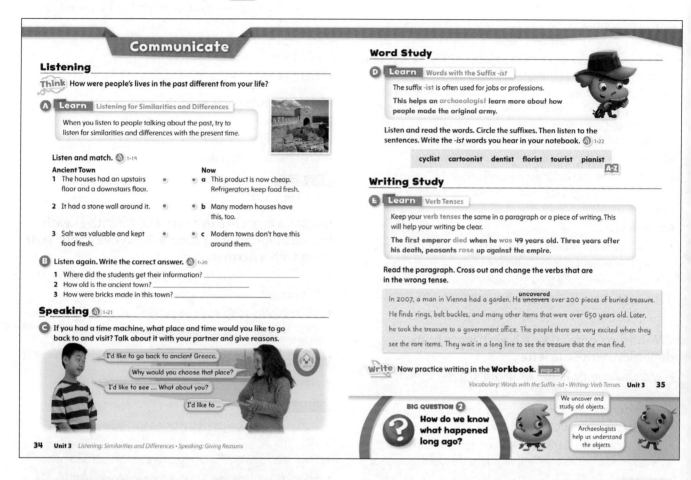

Summary

Objectives: To learn and practice listening, speaking, and writing strategies to facilitate effective communication.

Vocabulary: *cyclist, cartoonist, dentist, florist, tourist, pianist*

Listening strategy: Listening for similarities and differences

Speaking: Giving reasons

Word Study: Words with the suffix *-ist*

Writing Study: Use consistent verb tenses

Big Question learning points: *We get knowledge from other people and sources. We study images of the past.*

Materials: Discover Poster 2, Audio CD, Big Question Chart

Listening

Think

- Open the discussion by talking about the basic things students have to do every day.
- Allow them to answer on their own, then if needed, structure the discussion chronologically. (*In the morning: brush teeth, get dressed, eat breakfast, go to school. In the afternoon …*)
- For each task, discuss how people in the past might have had a different experience. (*Today I turn on the water in my sink. In the past, people had to gather water from a well.*)

A Learn: Listen for Similarities and Differences

- Read the *Learn* box together as a class.
- Recall any ideas from the *Think* discussion above that might be useful, e.g. people today need to eat and people in the past needed to eat. This is a similarity. However, people today usually buy their food at a store, and people in the past probably grew or bartered their food. This is a difference.

Listen and match. 1·19

- Play the audio after asking a gist question to focus on general meaning, e.g. *How are things different and the same now and then?*
- Play the audio again and ask students to listen and match the sentences.
- Check answers with the class.

ANSWERS

1 b 2 c 3 a

B Listen again. Write the correct answer. 1·20

- Have students complete this exercise on their own.
- Check answers with the class.

ANSWERS

1 Through news reports on the Internet.
2 Over 6,000 years old.
3 They were made out of salt.

Below level:

- When you play the audio, pause at the specific parts where students can find the answers for A and B.
- Allow them time to process the language they are hearing, then allow them time to locate the answers on the page.
- Some students may require more concrete guidance.

At level:

- Ask students to guess the answers in A before you play the audio.
- Play the audio for them to check their work.

Above level:

- Ask students to use the information in the listening text to write a paragraph in their own words comparing and contrasting the ancient town with now.
- Revisit the Compare and Contrast Report on page 24 of the Student Book for guidance.
- This will be a challenge for students because they must paraphrase the information in their own words.

Speaking ⊚ 1·21

C If you had a time machine, what place and time would you like to go back to and visit? Talk about it with your partner and give reasons.

COMMUNICATION

- Say each line of the dialogue with students echoing as they hear each line. Model the dialogue with a confident student in front of the class.
- Put students into pairs and tell them to practice the dialogue, taking turns speaking the different roles.
- Have students repeat this exercise, but this time encourage them to use their own information to answer the questions.

COLLABORATIVE LEARNING

- After students have practiced the dialogue in pairs, provide time for them to write notes about what their partner said.
- Have students tell the class about their partner. This requires students to listen to their partner carefully and rephrase his or her answers.
- A sample presentation: *Jenny would like to go back in time to see the woolly mammoths in Asia. She chose that because she loves elephants and wants to see their ancestors in their original habitat.*

Word Study

D Learn: Words with the Suffix *-ist*

- Have a confident student read the *Learn* box to the class.

Listen and read the words. Circle the suffixes. Then listen to the sentences. Write the *-ist* words you hear in your notebook. ⊚ 1·22

- For each word in the word box, help students identify the base, e.g. *cyclist – cycle*, etc.
- Play the audio. Have students write the *-ist* words.

Writing Study

E Learn: Verb Tenses

- Have a more confident student read the *Learn* box to the class.

Read the paragraph. Cross out and change the verbs that are in the wrong tense.

- Have students work individually.
- Ask them to check their answers with a partner before eliciting answers from the class.

ANSWERS

uncovers – uncovered; finds – found; are – were; see – saw; wait – waited; find – found

Write

- Direct the students to the Workbook for further practice.

Big Question 2 Review

How do we know what happened long ago?

- Display **Discover Poster 2**. Point to familiar vocabulary items and elicit them from the class. Ask *What is this?*
- Ask students *What do you see?* Ask *What does that mean?*
- Refer to the learning points covered in Unit 3 that are written on the poster and have students explain how they relate to the different pictures.
- Return to the **Big Question Chart**.
- Ask students what they have learned about studying the past in this unit.
- Ask what information is new and add it to the chart.

Further Practice
Workbook pages 27–28
Online practice Unit 3 · Communicate
Oxford **iTools** Unit 3 · Communicate

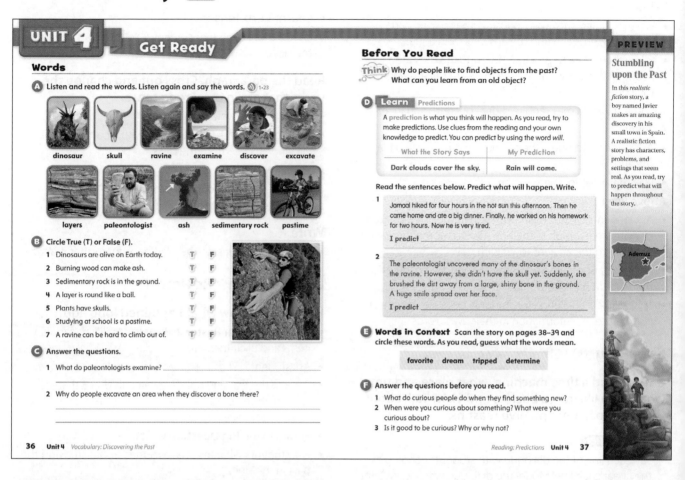

Summary

Objectives: To understand words about archaeology; to apply own experience and a reading strategy to help comprehension of a text.

Vocabulary: *dinosaur, skull, ravine, examine, discover, excavate, layers, paleontologist, ash, sedimentary rock, pastime, favorite, dream, tripped, determine*

Reading strategy: Predictions

Materials: Audio CD

Words

A Listen and read the words. Listen again and say the words. 1·23

- Play the audio. Ask students to point to the words as they hear them.
- Play the audio a second time and have students repeat the words when they hear them.
- If students need help pronouncing the longer words, write the difficult or lengthy words on the board and draw slashes to show the syllable breaks.

CRITICAL THINKING

Ask the following questions to check understanding:

- Which words describe things that archaeologists do?
- Sedimentary rock is characterized by its many layers. Why do you think these layers of rock form over time?
- Is a ravine more like a valley or a mountain? How is it similar?
- What are some of your favorite pastimes

B Circle True (T) or False (F).

- Have students read each statement and circle *T* or *F*.
- Have them compare their answers with a partner.
- Check answers with the class.

ANSWERS

1 F   2 T   3 T   4 F   5 F   6 F   7 T

C Answer the questions.

- Ask a more confident student to read aloud question 1. Encourage students to answer.
- Ask a confident student to read aloud question 2. Again, encourage students to answer.

COLLABORATIVE LEARNING

- Have partners create flashcards for the vocabulary words.
- They write a word on one side and that word's definition on the other.
- Have partners work together and use a dictionary if necessary to create their definitions.
- Ask partners to take turns practicing the words using the flashcards.
- They can also play flashcard games, such as "Concentration" or "Tic-tac-toe."

Below level:

- Say the words in A out of order.
- Have students point to the words as they hear them.
- Say a definition for each word. Use a different order from the order on the page. Have students identify the word you are defining each time.

At level:

- Have students try to use each word in a sentence.
- Have them write their sentences on cards that you can post in the room on a bulletin board.

Above level:

- Challenge students to use two or more words in a sentence.
- Encourage them to go back to page 28 and try to include those words in some of their sentences.
- Offer a prize, such as a sticker, for the student who can use the most vocabulary words in one coherent sentence.

Before You Read

Think

- Ask questions like these to facilitate the discussion:
  Has anybody ever found something from the past, like a fossil or an old bottle? How did you feel when you found it? How does it feel to find an object and hold it and examine it? How is it different from reading about a time and place in history?

D Learn: Predictions

- Read the *Learn* box to the class.

Read the sentences below. Predict what will happen. Write.

- Read the first paragraph together with the class.
- Invite students to write their predictions. Then discuss answers with the class.
- Have students read the second paragraph and write their predictions independently.
- Have them compare predictions with partners.
- Then have students share their predictions with the class.
- For both paragraphs, make sure students can identify the clues they used to make their predictions.

- Ask the following questions to check understanding of the first paragraph:
  Have you ever spent the day doing something active in the hot sun (maybe swimming at the beach, or playing soccer)? How did you feel afterwards?
- Ask the following questions to check understanding about the second paragraph:
  Why do you think there are dinosaur bones in the ravine? Is there any reason the skull would not be in the same ravine with the other dinosaur bones?

Below level:

- Alter the examples in the *Learn* box to change the likely predictions, e.g. instead of "Dark clouds cover the sky" say *There wasn't a cloud in the sky.* Help students see that changing the clue this way changes the predication to *Rain won't come.*

At level:

- Have students complete the predictions using the model texts and check their answers with another student.
- Have a class discussion about the most popular predictions.

Above level:

- Ask students to write their own examples, following the models in D. Have them exchange papers with a partner and try to make predictions.

E Words in Context: Scan the story on pages 38–39 and circle these words. As you read, guess what the words mean.

- Have students skim through the reading and circle the words.
- Ask if anyone already knows any of the definitions.

F Answer the questions before you read.

- Have students discuss the questions in small groups.
- Discuss the answers to the questions in class.
- Write down different answers on the board.

Reading Preview

- Read the title of the unit's reading text.
- Ask students what they think the title means. Elicit the definition of *stumbling* and discuss the idea of finding things accidentally.
- Have students silently read the content of the preview bar.
- Ask *What type of text is it?* Ask *What is the purpose of realistic fiction?*
- Encourage students to try to make predictions as they read the story.
- Point out the map of Ademuz to set the context of the text. If there is a world map in the classroom, point to Spain and see if students can find Ademuz.

Further Practice
Workbook pages 29–30
Online practice Unit 4 • Get Ready
Oxford iTools Unit 4 • Get Ready

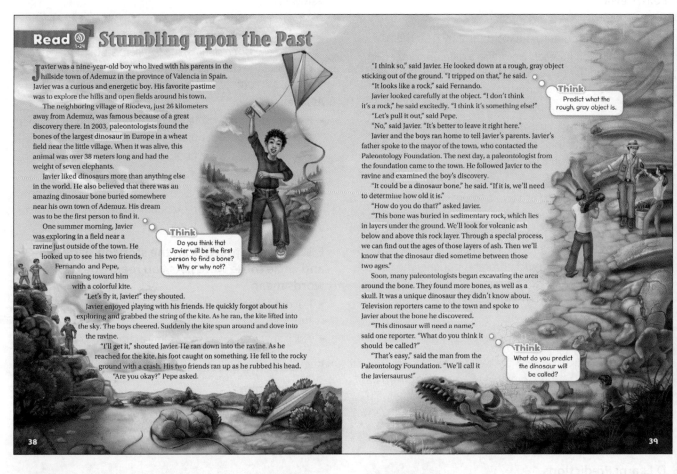

Summary

Objectives: To read, understand, and discuss a fiction text; to apply a reading strategy to improve comprehension.

School subject: Social Studies: History

Text type: Realistic fiction

Reading strategy: Predictions

Big Question learning points: *We get knowledge from other people and sources. We search for old objects and study them.*

Materials: Audio CD

Before Reading

- Review the vocabulary from page 36.
- Look at the pictures on pages 38 and 39 and ask students to predict what might happen in the story.
- Point out that sometimes picture clues can help readers make predictions.

During Reading ⊚ 1·24

- Ask a gist question to check overall understanding of the text, e.g. *What does Javier find?*
- Give students a few minutes to skim the text before answering.
- Remind them that they should revise their predictions as they read more of the text.
- Play the audio. Students listen as they read along. Play the audio a second time if necessary.

Below level:

- Have students read the first paragraph silently to themselves.
- Put students in small, mixed-ability groups.
- Have the groups discuss the first paragraph briefly to clear up any questions about meaning.
- Then students take turns reading the paragraph a second time aloud.
- Continue in this way for the rest of the paragraphs.

At level:

- Students take turns reading each paragraph aloud.
- Have them pause after each paragraph to summarize what's happened so far, and to revise any predictions they've made about what will happen next.

Above level:

- Have students read the text independently. As they read they should jot down any specific clues they find that help them make predictions.
- Have students discuss the specific clues with a partner.
- Have them tell their partner how they answered the *Think* box prediction questions in the story.

- Have small groups work together to create a sequence map of the main events in the story.
- First have them create a chronological list of the main events.
- Group members will divide the events so each person is assigned the same number.
- For each event, the group member designs a card with a sentence describing the event, and an illustration to support the story.
- Groups can display the cards either in book form, or on a bulletin board with arrows between each card.

CRITICAL THINKING

Discussion questions:

- *Why did the mayor of the town contact the Paleontology Foundation?*
- *How were Javier and Pepe different?*
- *Would you be more like Pepe or Javier if you found something like this? Why?*
- *How do you know that Javier is curious? What does he do or say that shows he is curious?*
- *Do you know anyone who is curious like Javier? What is that person curious about?*
- *How do you think Javier felt at the end of the story?*
- *Have you ever felt the same way? What caused you to feel like that?*

After Reading

- Revisit the questions in F on page 37. Have students change their answers after reading the text.
- Ask students to write about their favorite pastime, or discuss their favorite pastime with a partner.
- Have them stand up and walk around the classroom. Ask them to find other people with the same favorite pastime and form groups.
- As a class work out which pastime is the most popular in the class.

CULTURE NOTE

Over the years there have been many famous dinosaur discoveries around the world.

In 1676, a professor at Oxford University found something that he thought was a human giant! Of course, this was identified – 150 years later – as a Megalosaurus.

In 1975, an entire family of dinosaurs was discovered by Jack Horner. He later became the inspiration for the famous dinosaur film, *Jurassic Park*.

In 1997, in China, the first in a famous series of "dino-birds" was unearthed. It shows that some dinosaurs had feathers, and helps us to see how dinosaurs and birds are related.

In 2000, an incredible specimen of Brachylophosaurus was discovered. He was given the name of "Leonardo" and his whole "mummified" body helped scientists to understand better than ever before how dinosaurs looked and moved.

Further Practice
Workbook page 31
Online practice Unit 4 • Read
Oxford iTools Unit 4 • Read

Unit 4 Understand page 40

Understand

Comprehension

Think Talk about the story with your partner. Do you think it could really happen? Why or why not?

A Circle the best prediction for each statement. Talk about your choices with a partner.

1 The paleontologists found all the bones of Javier's dinosaur. What will happen next?
  a They will stop looking and go back to their homes.
  b They will ask Javier to look for more bones.
  c They will look for more dinosaur bones in the ravine.

2 The dinosaur will be called the Javiersaurus. What will happen next?
  a Fernando and Pepe will be angry.
  b Fernando and Pepe will be happy for Javier.
  c Fernando and Pepe will not be friends with Javier.

3 Javier is very interested in dinosaurs. What will happen next?
  a He will become a paleontologist someday.
  b He will become a mayor someday.
  c He will stop looking for dinosaur bones.

B Answer the questions.
1 How was the dinosaur in Riodeva special?
2 Why was Javier in the field when Fernando and Pepe ran up to him?
3 What do paleontologists look for above and below sedimentary rock?

C **Words in Context** Match each sentence to an explanation.
1 His favorite pastime was to explore the open fields. — a This means that he always thought about doing this thing someday.
2 His dream was to be the first person to find it. — b This means that they need to find out or discover this information.
3 "We'll need to determine how old it is." — c This means that he hit his foot against something and fell down.
4 "I tripped on that," he said. — d This means that he enjoyed doing this activity more than any other activity.

40 Unit 4 Comprehension

Grammar in Use

D Listen and read along. 1-25

Anna wants us to help her plant the tomatoes.
Well, I don't like getting my hands dirty.
Look! I just found an old gold ring!
Wow! Now they enjoy digging in the garden!

E Read the sentences below. Which words end in -ing?
a I don't like getting my hands dirty.   b Now they enjoy digging in the garden!

F **Learn Grammar** Verbs Followed by Gerunds
Remember, gerunds are verbs that end in -ing. Gerunds can act like nouns. Verbs like enjoy, finish, and practice are often followed by gerunds.
Javier enjoyed playing with his friends.
  verb   gerund

Read each sentence. Circle the gerunds. Underline the verb in front of each gerund.
1 When it began raining the excavation team went inside.
2 The museum staff finished cleaning the dinosaur bones.
3 Thomas liked examining fossils as a pastime.
4 The paleontologist doesn't like working in the rain.

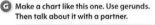 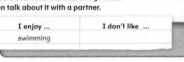
I enjoy swimming in a pool on a hot day.

G Make a chart like this one. Use gerunds. Then talk about it with a partner.

I enjoy ...	I don't like ...
swimming	

Grammar: Verbs Followed by Gerunds Unit 4 41

Summary

Objectives: To demonstrate understanding of a fiction text; to understand the meaning and form of the grammar structure.

Reading: Comprehension

Grammar input: Verbs followed by gerunds

Grammar practice: Workbook exercises

Grammar production: Writing and talking about personal information

Materials: Audio CD

Comprehension

Think

- Have students discuss whether or not this could really happen. If they think it could happen, what do they think would happen next?
- If they think it couldn't happen, ask them if there is any part of the story that could happen (i.e. a boy and his friends playing in a ravine find something interesting).

A Circle the best prediction for each statement. Talk about your choices with a partner.

- Have students complete the exercise independently and then check answers with a partner.
- Check the answers with the class.

ANSWERS
1 c 2 b 3 a

DIFFERENTIATION

Below level:
- Discuss why each prediction in A is the best choice.
- Explain why the incorrect answers are not good predictions, e.g. in question 1, a is not a good choice because if there was one dinosaur there might be another, and the paleontologists would want to keep looking; b is not a good choice because Javier is only a child, and the paleontologists would want a professional with specific tools to keep looking.

At level:
- Have students work in pairs to compare their answers and discuss why they think the prediction they chose is the most appropriate.
- Explain to students that sometimes we can make more than one prediction about things we think will happen in the future.
- Have students work individually to write another prediction for each statement in A. Tell students it should be different from the choices already there, and should be something they think would happen in the story.
- Elicit predictions from the class and see how many students' predictions are the same.
- Have a class vote for the most interesting predictions for each statement.

Above level:
- Tell students to write other questions about the reading that require predictions, e.g. *Who did Javier's parents speak to about the discovery?*

66 Unit 4 · Understand

- Encourage them to think about what else could happen to Javier and his friends, or to the paleontologists after the story ends.
- Have them share their questions with the class and guide the class in making predictions.

B Answer the questions.
- Have students complete the exercise on their own.
- Check the answers with the class.

ANSWERS
1 It was the largest dinosaur in Europe: 38 meters long and as heavy as seven elephants.
2 He was exploring the field.
3 They look for ash because they can date the ash and then estimate the age of the sedimentary rock between it.

COLLABORATIVE LEARNING
- Have small groups choose one of the items in A to role-play, e.g. for question 1, they can role-play the paleontologists talking about what to do next. For question 2, they can role-play Javier telling Pepe and Fernando that the dinosaur will be named after him. And for question 3, they can role-play Javier as an adult paleontologist finding a new dinosaur site.
- Have each group perform their role-play for a different group and have two or three groups perform their role-play for the entire class.

C Words in Context: Match each sentence to an explanation.
- Have the students complete the exercise on their own.
- Check the answers with the class.

ANSWERS
1 d 2 a 3 b 4 c

CRITICAL THINKING
- Return to the reading text on page 30. Ask students to name some of the similarities and differences between the two texts.
- Some similarities include: someone discovered objects in the ground from long ago; scientists use special techniques to learn about the items; people are excited by the discoveries.
- Some differences include: the reading genres; Javier found the bones by accident, we do not know if the clay army was discovered by accident or not; the clay army was made by people, the dinosaur bones were not.

Grammar in Use

D Listen and read along. 🎧 1·25
- Listen to the audio once while students follow along in their books.
- Invite students to repeat the lines using the audio as a model for pronunciation and intonation.
- Help them understand the humor.

E Read the sentences below. Which words end in *-ing*?
- Play the audio and ask students to listen and read.
- Have students find the *-ing* words.
- Check the answers with the class.

ANSWERS
a getting b digging

F Learn Grammar: Verb Followed by Gerunds
- Have a more confident student read the *Learn Grammar* box aloud to the class.
- Substitute the words *finished* and *practiced* for *enjoyed* for additional examples.
- Write more examples of sentences with verb + gerund.

Read each sentence. Circle the gerunds. Underline the verb in front of each gerund.
- Have students complete the exercise on their own.
- Check answers with the class.

ANSWERS
1 When it began raining, the excavation team went inside.
2 The museum staff finished cleaning the dinosaur bones.
3 Thomas liked examining fossils as a pastime.
4 The paleontologist doesn't like working in the rain.

G Make a chart like this one. Use gerunds. Then talk about it with a partner.

DIFFERENTIATION
Below level:
- Brainstorm with the class different activities they might include in their charts.
- Write ideas on the board and encourage students to pick three or four examples to add to their charts.

At level:
- Invite students to share their answers with the class.
- Ask students to keep score of the different activities mentioned.
- Ask the class which activities are the most popular and least popular.

Above level:
- Put students into pairs to discuss their answers.
- Have students report back to the class about their partner.

Workbook Grammar
- Direct students to the Workbook for further practice.

Further Practice
Workbook pages 32–34
Online practice Unit 4 · Understand
Oxford **iTools** Unit 4 · Understand

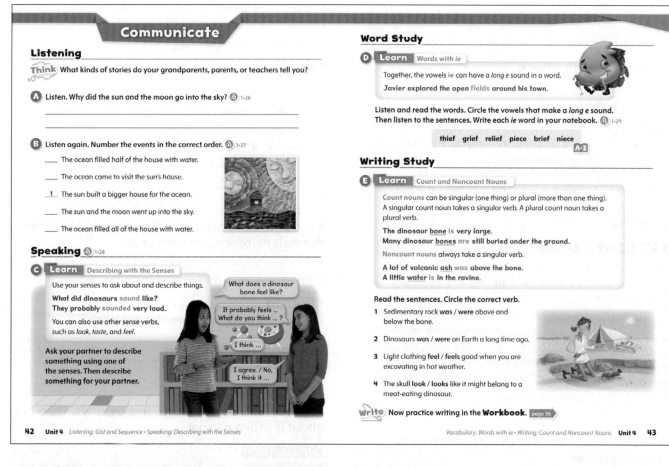

Summary

Objectives: To learn and practice listening, speaking, and writing strategies to facilitate effective communication.

Vocabulary: *thief, grief, relief, piece, brief, niece*

Listening strategy: Listening for gist and sequence

Speaking: Describing with the senses

Word Study: Words with *ie*

Writing Study: Count and noncount nouns

Big Question learning point: *Stories and myths teach us about life long ago.*

Materials: Audio CD

Listening

Think

- Link the discussion to the students' understanding of the author's purpose, e.g. sometimes our parents tell us stories to teach us about something, or to persuade us to behave in a certain way. Friends often want to entertain us with stories.

A Listen. Why did the sun and the moon go into the sky? 🔊 1·26

- Play the audio through one time.
- After students have listened, have them write their answer to the question on the lines.
- Have students share their ideas with the class.
- Check the answer with the class.

ANSWER

The sun and moon went into the sky because the ocean filled their house with water.

B Listen again. Number the events in the correct order. 🔊 1·27

- Have students preview the events in B. Explain that they will need to put these events in order.
- Show them that event 1 has been done for them.
- Play the audio again.
- Check answers with the class.

ANSWERS

Number in this order: 3, 2, 1, 5, 4

DIFFERENTIATION

Below level:

- As you play the audio, pause periodically so students can process what they are hearing.
- Stop the recording after each sentence to give students the opportunity to complete the exercise in the Student Book.

At level:

- Have students take turns retelling the story using the sentences in B as prompts.
- They may add details to their retelling, but remind them that retelling is a shorter version of the original.

Above level:

- Challenge students to add a few sentences to explain what happened before "The sun built a bigger house …"
- Have them share their sentences with the class.
- Write the sentences on the board and in this way create a complete summary of the story.

COLLABORATIVE LEARNING

- Invite small groups to act out the myth for the rest of the class.
- In each group, one student can retell the myth using the sentences in B. Another can be the sun, another the moon, and another the ocean.
- Have groups write out a few lines of dialogue to use during the role-play.

CRITICAL THINKING

- Discuss the importance of myths in culture. Are there any popular myths in the students' cultures? What do those myths attempt to explain?
- Can students think of an alternate myth to explain why the sun and moon are in the sky?

Speaking 🄯 1·28

C Learn: Describing with the Senses

COMMUNICATION

- Review the five senses: *hearing, seeing, touching, tasting,* and *smelling*.
- Read the *Learn* box together. Provide some basic sentence frames to review language, e.g. *It sounds loud. It looks pretty. It smells bad. It tastes delicious. It feels soft.*

Ask your partner to describe something using one of the senses. Then describe something for your partner.

- Play the audio through one time.
- Put students into pairs and tell them to practice the dialogue, taking turns speaking the different roles.
- Provide an additional example if needed.
- Have partners work together to write new dialogues describing something using their senses.

CREATIVITY

- Have students think of a particular item. Give them time to think about how they would describe it to someone else without naming it.
- Put students into pairs. Have one student in each pair describe the item and their partner guesses what it is, e.g. *It is really big. It is round and it feels very hot. It's yellow or sometimes orange. It doesn't smell and you can't hear it.*

Word Study

D Learn: Words with *ie*

- Read the *Learn* box to the class.

Listen and read the words. Circle the vowels that make a *long e* sound. Then listen to the sentences. Write each *ie* word in your notebook. 🄯 1·29

- Play the audio. Have students circle the *ie* in each word as they listen.
- Write the words on the board and circle the *ie* so students can check their work.
- Then have students listen to the sentences and write the *ie* words they hear.
- Check the answers with the class.

ANSWERS
1 rel(ie)f   2 n(ie)ce   3 p(ie)ce   4 br(ie)f   5 gr(ie)f   6 th(ie)f

Writing Study

E Learn: Count and Noncount Nouns

- Read the *Learn* box and examples together.

Read the sentences. Circle the correct verb.

- Have students work individually and then check their answers in pairs.
- Elicit the answers from the class.

ANSWERS
1 was   2 were   3 feels   4 looks

DIFFERENTIATION

Below level:

- Put students into groups of three or four.
- Ask groups to brainstorm a list of ten count nouns or ten noncount nouns.
- Elicit all the words and write them in two columns on the board.
- Ask students to add more words.

At level:

- Return to the vocabulary on pages 28 and 36.
- Have students identify the count nouns (*army, soldier, uniform, emperor, archaeologist, tomb, peasant, dinosaur, ravine, skull, layer, paleontologist, pastime*) and the noncount nouns (*armor, jade, clay, ash, sedimentary rock*). Note that *treasure* can be both count (*How many treasures did you find?*) and noncount (*How much treasure did he find?*). Discuss why this is the case.

Above level:

- Revisit the Speaking lesson on Asking About Quantity on page 22.
- Have students ask and answer some questions about quantity using count and noncount nouns, e.g. *How much ash was above the bone? How many bones did they find?*

Write

- Direct students to the Workbook for further practice.

> **Further Practice**
> Workbook pages 35–36
> Online practice Unit 4 · Communicate
> Oxford **iTools** Unit 4 · Communicate

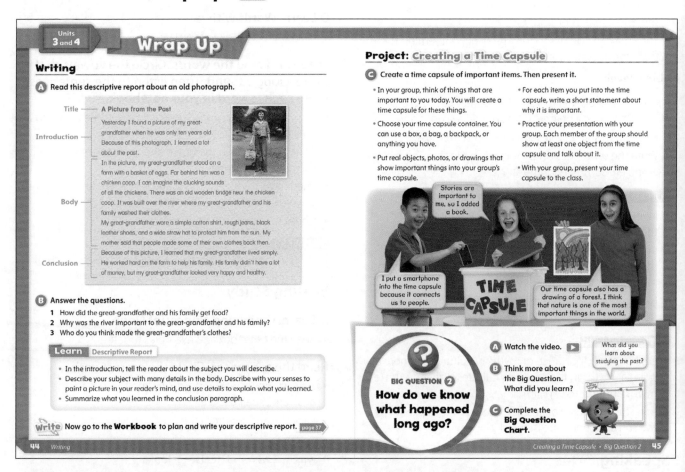

Summary

Objectives: To show what students have learned about the language and learning points of Units 3 and 4.

Reading: Comprehension of a descriptive report

Project: Create a time capsule

Writing: Write a descriptive report

Speaking: Talk about the time capsule

Materials: Video, Discover Poster 2, Talk About It! Poster, Big Question Chart, Big Question DVD

Writing

A Read this descriptive report about an old photograph.

• Put students into groups of three or four.

• Have them sit in a circle and take turns reading a sentence from the report in order.

B Answer the questions.

• Have students complete the answers individually and then check in pairs.

• Elicit the answers and discuss them with the class.

POSSIBLE ANSWERS

1 He got eggs from chicken on a farm.

2 The river was important to the family because that is where they washed their clothes.

3 Maybe the great-grandfather's mother or an older sister or aunt made his clothes. It's possible that the great-grandfather made his own clothes. Ten years old might have been too young to sew, e.g. a shirt, but the times were different back then so it is possible.

Learn: Descriptive Report

• Have one or two confident students read the *Learn* box to the class.

Write

• Direct students to the Workbook to plan and write their description report.

DIFFERENTIATION

Below level:

• Review the different parts of the descriptive report in the model in A.

• Help students understand the difference in content between the introduction (it introduces the photograph and why it's important to the writer), the body (it describes the photograph and its context), and the conclusion (it wraps up the report, tells what the writer learned or felt after looking at the photograph).

At level:

- Have partners discuss possible photographs they might use for their own reports. This isn't a time for them to plan the actual report, rather to choose a good photograph that they will have a lot to write about.

Above level:

- These students can help their classmates edit their reports once they begin writing them.
- Teach some positive phrases to use as they conduct peer reviews, e.g. *I like how you (used descriptive language in this sentence). I would like to see (more details about your father's house). Can you tell me what you meant to say in this sentence? Your (conclusion) doesn't (summarize what you learned). Can I help you with that part?*

Project

C Create a time capsule of important items. Then present it.

CREATIVITY

- Follow the steps on the Student Book page to guide the class through the activity.
- Before groups begin working, discuss with the whole class a few examples of items and drawings that would make good entries for the time capsule.
- Read the sample speech balloons in which students explain why they chose the items they chose. Explain that students will present their time capsules to the class, just as the students in the book do.
- Tell students that everybody has to contribute something to the time capsule.
- Assign one student in each group to be the participation monitor who makes sure everybody contributes.
- For each item or drawing a student contributes, he / she should be able to explain to his / her group why it is important. (Refer again to the model speech balloons on the page.)
- To ensure that students listen to their group peers, structure the presentation so that each student presents at least one item or drawing that another student contributed.
- To prepare, students will have to listen carefully to their group peers to be sure they know what they are including and why it is important.

Units 3 and 4 Big Question Review

A Watch the video. ▷

- Play the video and when it is finished ask students to talk about how we know what happened long ago.
- Have students share ideas with the class.

B Think more about the Big Question. What did you learn?

COMMUNICATION

- Display **Discover Poster 2**. Point to familiar vocabulary items and elicit them from the class. Ask *What is this?*
- Ask students *What do you see?* Ask *What does that mean?*

- Refer to all of the learning points written on the poster and have students explain how they relate to the different pictures.
- Ask *What does this learning point mean?* Elicit answers from individual students.
- Display the **Talk About It! Poster** to help students with sentence frames for discussion of the learning points and for expressing their opinions.

C Complete the Big Question Chart.

COLLABORATIVE LEARNING

Ask students what they have learned about learning about the past.

- Put students into pairs or small groups to say two new things they have learned.
- Have students share their ideas with the class and add their ideas to the chart.
- Have students complete the chart in their Workbook.

Further Practice
Workbook pages 37–39
Online practice • Wrap Up 2
Oxford **iTools** • Wrap Up 2

Reading Strategies

Students will practice:

- Making conclusions
- Summarizing

Vocabulary

Students will understand and use words about:

- Food and farming and the world around us

Grammar

Students will understand and use:

- Present continuous for future plans
- Polite offers with *would like*

Review

Students will review the language and Big Question learning points of Units 5 and 6 through:

- A research report
- A project (creating a story and presentation)

Units 5 and 6
Where does our food come from?

Students will understand the Big Question learning points:

- Food comes from all around the world.
- Some food comes from large farms and plantations.
- Some food comes from small, local farms, or gardens.
- We eat food from plants.
- We eat food from animals.

Listening Strategies

Students will practice:

- Listening for examples and numbers
- Listening for reasons

Writing

Students will be able to use:

- Interesting adjectives
- Prepositional phrases of location

Students will produce texts that:

- Inform

Word Study

Students will understand, pronounce, and use:

- Phrasal verbs with *drop*
- Four-syllable words

Speaking

Students will understand and use expressions to:

- Give a reason for a preference
- Talk about food in their area

Units 5 and 6 Big Question page 46

Summary

Objectives: To activate students' existing knowledge of the topic and identify what they would like to learn about the topic.

Materials: Big Question DVD, Discover Poster 3, Big Question Chart

Introducing the topic

Ask the Big Question. Ask *Where does our food come from?* Write individual words from students on the board.

A Watch the video. ▷

- Play the video and when it is finished ask students to answer the following questions in pairs:
  What do you see in the video?
  Who do you think the people are?
  What is happening?
  Do you like it?
- Have individual students share their answers with the class.

B Look at the picture and talk about it.

- Students look at the big picture and talk about it. Ask students the questions in B.
- Ask additional questions:
  Have you ever been in a place like this?
  Why were you there?
  Who were you with?
  What did you do there?

C Think and answer the questions.

CRITICAL THINKING

- Ask students to think about the first question. If you live in a city where there are no farms, you might need to open up the "area" to mean a region of a country or the country as a whole.
- Ask questions, e.g. *Why do you think farmers grow (oranges) near here? Why aren't there any farms in your town? Is there any way to grow food in a city?*
- Have students discuss the second question in pairs. Tell partners to categorize their favorite foods. Students can create their own categories, or you can suggest they classify by the five food groups, food origin, packaged versus whole, or cooked versus raw.

Expanding the topic

COLLABORATIVE LEARNING

- Display **Discover Poster 3** and give students enough time to look at the pictures.
- Elicit some of the words you think they will know by pointing to different people or objects in the pictures and asking *What's this?*
- Put students into small groups of three or four. Have each group choose a picture that they find interesting.
- Ask each group to say five things that they can see in their picture.
- Have one person from each group stand up and read out the words they chose for their picture.
- Ask the class if they can add any more.

- Repeat until every group has spoken.

D Fill out the Big Question Chart.

- Display the **Big Question Chart**.
- Ask the class *What do you know about where food comes from?*
- Explain that a *source* is where something comes from. Encourage students to think about the word *source* in different ways:
  1 The immediate source of food (*My parents buy our food at the supermarket. We buy food at the farmers' market every weekend.*)
  2 The intermediary source of food (*Corn comes from a farm. Frozen pizza is made in a factory.*)
  3 The base source of food (*Corn grows from a plant. The cheese on pizza comes from a cow.*)
  4 The regional source of food (*Oranges grow in warm climates. Fish are caught in waterfront communities.*)
- Ask students to write what they know and what they want to know in their Workbooks.
- Write a collection of ideas on the **Big Question Chart**.

DIFFERENTIATION

Below level:

- Ask specific questions to help students share what they know, e.g. *Where did you get that apple? Where do you think the supermarket got the apple? Where did the apple farmer get the apple?*
- Add their responses to the "I Know" section of the chart.

At level:

- Have small groups discuss what they know about where food comes from before they share their answers with the class or write them in their notebooks.
- Facilitate completing the second column "What I want to know" by asking questions students may or may not know, *Where do bananas grow? Where does bread come from? Where do hamburgers come from?*

Above level:

- Ask students to consider the questions they wrote in the second column. Can they make educated guesses about any of the answers?
- Encourage partners to work together to predict some of the answers. Tell them to support their predictions with prior knowledge, e.g. a student may want to know where bananas grow. He / She might predict they grow in warm climates. This prediction is based on the prior knowledge that the student lives in a colder climate and there are no banana trees nearby.

Discover Poster 3

1 Produce from different countries for sale in a supermarket in Abu Dhabi; 2 Industrial farmers harvesting wheat; 3 A family harvesting foods from their garden; 4 Food from plants: carrots, peppers, potatoes, gourds, walnuts, and more; 5 Food from animals: eggs, milk, cheese, and eggs.

> **Further Practice**
> Workbook page 40
> Online practice • Big Question 3
> Oxford **iTools** • Big Question 3

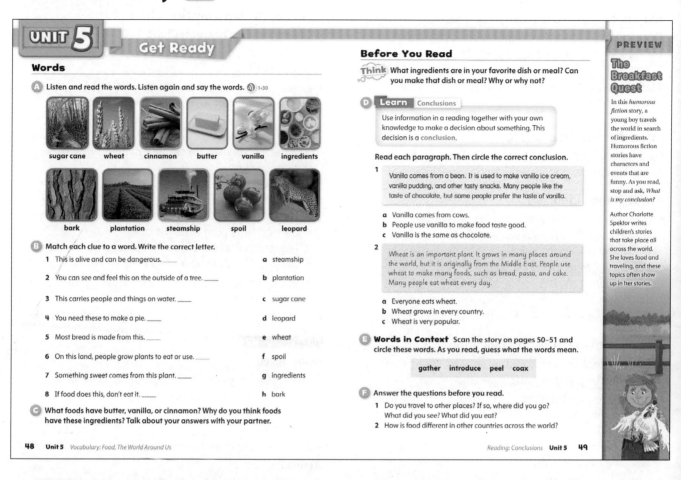

Summary

Objectives: To understand words about food and farming; to apply own experience and a reading strategy to help comprehension of a text.

Vocabulary: *sugar cane, wheat, cinnamon, butter, vanilla, ingredients, bark, plantation, steamship, spoil, leopard, gather, introduce, peel, coax*

Reading strategy: Making conclusions

Materials: Audio CD

Words

A Listen and read the words. Listen again and say the words. 🎧 1·30

- Play the audio. Ask students to point to the words as they hear them.
- Play the audio a second time and have students repeat the words when they hear them.
- Say the words out of order. Ask students to point and repeat.

CRITICAL THINKING

Ask the following questions to check understanding:

- *Which words name food that comes from plants?*
- *Which words might be ingredients for a recipe?*
- *What does the word "steamship" have to do with where food comes from?*
- *Which ingredient is most likely to spoil?*
- *Can you find a base word in "plantation" that gives a clue about its meaning?*

B Match each clue to a word. Write the correct letter.

- Have students complete the exercise independently and then check their work with a partner.

ANSWERS

1 d 2 h 3 a 4 g 5 e 6 b 7 c 8 f

DIFFERENTIATION

Below level:

- For each item, help students choose the best answer by narrowing the options.
- For example, say *Number 1. It is alive and dangerous. Let's look at the choices. Which words name things that are alive? Which of those things are dangerous / can hurt you?*

At level:

- Point out that the sentences substitute pronouns like *it* and *this* for the main vocabulary words.
- Ask students to replace the pronouns with the actual words, e.g. *1 A leopard is alive and can be dangerous. 2 You can see and feel bark on the outside of a tree.*
- Continue with all the items.

Above level:

- Challenge students to use the vocabulary in sentences of their own.
- Have them write their sentences as fill-in-the-blank activities, e.g. *The rice arrived by _____ from Vietnam.* (steamship)
- Students can trade sentences with partners for additional practice.

C What foods have butter, vanilla, or cinnamon? Why do you think foods have these ingredients? Talk about your answers with a partner.

- Answers will vary depending on how experienced students are with cooking and baking.
- Invite students who have more prior knowledge to tell the class about baking with these ingredients.

Before You Read

Think

- Help students break down the ingredients in popular foods like pizza (bread / dough, tomato sauce, cheese) and ice cream (milk / cream, sugar, flavor).
- Invite students who have experience cooking or preparing their favorite meal to share their experience with the class.
- If students have not made or cannot make their favorite dish, help them imagine how it would be prepared.

COLLABORATIVE LEARNING

- Divide the class into small groups. Make sure at least one person in each group knows how to make their favorite dish.
- Have the group create a simple presentation. One student in the group narrates the steps to making their dish, and the others act out the steps.

D Learn: Conclusions

- Read the *Learn* box together.
- On the board write *reading text* and *what you know*. Draw an arrow from each to the word *conclusion* to show that you use what you learn from a reading text and what you already know about a topic to make a conclusion.

Read each paragraph. Then circle the correct conclusion.

- Tell students to complete the exercise first on their own, then check their answers with a partner.
- Remind students that you base your conclusion on evidence in the selection and your own prior knowledge.
- For example: In item 1, choice *a* is incorrect because the first sentence tells that vanilla comes from beans. For choice *c*, while the text does not specifically state that vanilla and chocolate are different, students likely know this from their own prior knowledge. If not, they can figure it out because the text states that some people prefer vanilla; if chocolate and vanilla were the same, nobody would prefer one over the other.
- Have students do number 2 on their own.
- Check the answers with the class.

ANSWERS
1 b   2 c

E Words in Context: Scan the story on pages 50–51 and circle these words. As you read, guess what the words mean.

- Students circle the words in the story.

F Answer the questions before you read.

COMMUNICATION

- Have students discuss the questions in small groups.
- Then have volunteers share their answers to the questions with the class.

Reading Preview

- Have a student read the story's title and guess what it will be about.
- Have students silently read the content of the preview bar.
- Ask *What type of text is it?* Ask *What does this type of text do?*
- Encourage students to make conclusions as they read.

About the Author

- Have students read about the author, Charlotte Spektor.
- Ask students if they think they would like to read stories by this author.

Further Practice
Workbook pages 40–41
Online practice Unit 5 • Get Ready
Oxford **iTools** Unit 5 • Get Ready

Summary

Objectives: To read, understand, and discuss a fiction text; to apply a reading strategy to improve comprehension.

School subject: Social Studies: Geography

Text type: Humorous fiction

Reading strategy: Making conclusions

Big Question learning points: *Food comes from all around the world. Some food comes from large farms and plantations. We eat food from plants. We eat food from animals.*

Materials: Talk About It! Poster, Audio CD

Before Reading

- Revisit the reading strategy by reviewing with students how to make conclusions.
- Explain that making predictions and making conclusions are similar.
- When you make predictions, you use prior knowledge and clues to guess what *will* happen.
- When you make conclusions, you use prior knowledge and clues to make decisions about why things are the way they are. Read the title of the story together and look at the pictures. Have students predict what the story will be about.
- Explain that students will make conclusions as they read.

During Reading 🔊 1·31

- Ask a gist question to check overall understanding of the text, e.g. *Why are the boy and his sister traveling around the world?*

- Give students a few minutes to skim the text before answering.
- Play the audio. Students listen as they read along. Play the audio a second time if necessary.

DIFFERENTIATION

Below level:

- Put students in mixed-ability pairs.
- Have them take turns reading the text aloud to each other, with the more confident reader helping the less confident one to sound out and pronounce the words and phrases.

At level:

- Put students into small groups of four or five. If possible, have them sit in a circle.
- Have students take turns reading a paragraph aloud as the text is read around the circle.

Above level:

- Have students read the text individually and circle any words or sentences they don't understand.
- Put students into pairs to discuss the circled words or sentences.
- Move around the room and provide help as necessary.
- Ask for any words or sentences that students couldn't work out together and provide the meaning for the whole class.

Discussion questions:

- *Why did the boy and his sister travel to different farms? What were they looking for?*
- *Why did Farmer Ray say "You've come to the right place"?*
- *What did Farmer Ray think about his chickens' eggs?*
- *How do the children and other characters get from place to place? Do you think this could really happen? Why or why not?*
- *What happens when Patrick says that he doesn't have any cinnamon? How does the boy solve this problem?*
- *Why is this story considered to be humorous fiction? Did you think it was humorous? Why or why not?*
- *How does the story end? What do you think the boy will do next?*
- *For each "Think" box, ask students what conclusions they made and why.*

After Reading

- Display a map of the world. Trace the journey the boy, his sister, and the other characters make around the world.
- Have students make a timeline naming each place in the story and the ingredient found there.

- Display the **Talk About It! Poster** to help students with sentence frames for discussion and expressing personal opinions.
- Put students into pairs to discuss which place in the story they would want to visit, and then revisit the conclusions they made while reading.

- Have small multi-level groups work together to role-play the journey in the story.
- Structure the activity so each group has a "boy" (from the story) and one or two characters for each place.
- The "boy" in each group should tell the audience where he is going and any other details.
- He should have a brief conversation with the other characters about what he needs and what he has to do, e.g. the "boy" can open with: *First, my sister and I went to Farmer Ray's farm to get some eggs.* The boy and another student, who plays Farmer Ray, should have a conversation about Farmer Ray's eggs.

CULTURE NOTE

Cinnamon is a spice that is popular all around the world and is used in both sweet and savory foods. It has been an important spice for thousands of years and was used in Egypt three thousand years ago.

It is found in the inner bark of special trees. These trees are grown in Sri Lanka, Madagascar, China, India, Vietnam, and the Seychelles. Sri Lanka produces 80–90 percent of the world's supply.

Cinnamon is used in the preparation of cinnamon buns, but also in many other types of food. It can be used in chocolate, coffee, candies, and apple pie.

In the Middle East, it is often used in savory dishes of lamb and chicken.

Further Practice
Workbook page 42
Online practice Unit 5 • Read
Oxford iTools Unit 5 • Read

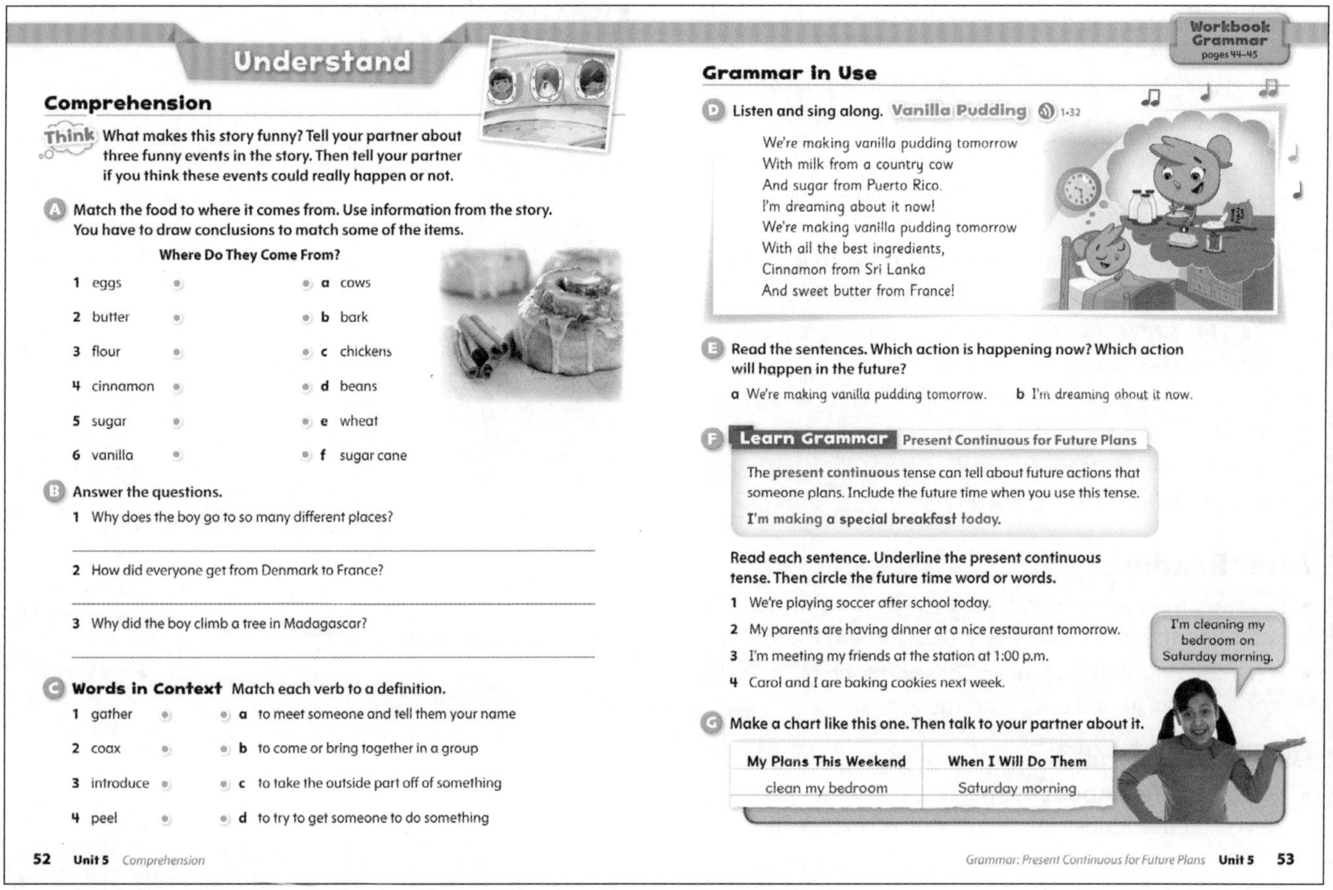

Understand

Comprehension

Think What makes this story funny? Tell your partner about three funny events in the story. Then tell your partner if you think these events could really happen or not.

A Match the food to where it comes from. Use information from the story. You have to draw conclusions to match some of the items.

Where Do They Come From?

1 eggs — a cows
2 butter — b bark
3 flour — c chickens
4 cinnamon — d beans
5 sugar — e wheat
6 vanilla — f sugar cane

B Answer the questions.
1 Why does the boy go to so many different places?
2 How did everyone get from Denmark to France?
3 Why did the boy climb a tree in Madagascar?

C **Words in Context** Match each verb to a definition.
1 gather — a to meet someone and tell them your name
2 coax — b to come or bring together in a group
3 introduce — c to take the outside part off of something
4 peel — d to try to get someone to do something

52 Unit 5 *Comprehension*

Workbook Grammar pages 44–45

Grammar in Use

D Listen and sing along. Vanilla Pudding 1-32

We're making vanilla pudding tomorrow
With milk from a country cow
And sugar from Puerto Rico.
I'm dreaming about it now!
We're making vanilla pudding tomorrow
With all the best ingredients,
Cinnamon from Sri Lanka
And sweet butter from France!

E Read the sentences. Which action is happening now? Which action will happen in the future?
a We're making vanilla pudding tomorrow. b I'm dreaming about it now.

F **Learn Grammar** Present Continuous for Future Plans

The present continuous tense can tell about future actions that someone plans. Include the future time when you use this tense.

I'm making a special breakfast today.

Read each sentence. Underline the present continuous tense. Then circle the future time word or words.
1 We're playing soccer after school today.
2 My parents are having dinner at a nice restaurant tomorrow.
3 I'm meeting my friends at the station at 1:00 p.m.
4 Carol and I are baking cookies next week.

I'm cleaning my bedroom on Saturday morning.

G Make a chart like this one. Then talk to your partner about it.

My Plans This Weekend	When I Will Do Them
clean my bedroom	Saturday morning

Grammar: Present Continuous for Future Plans Unit 5 53

Summary

Objectives: To demonstrate understanding of a fictional text; to understand the meaning and form of the grammar structure.

Reading: Comprehension

Grammar input: Present continuous for future plans

Grammar practice: Workbook exercises

Grammar production: Writing and talking about persona information

Materials: Audio CD

Comprehension

Think

- Have partners work together to decide which parts were funny.
- If students need guidance, ask them to revisit specific paragraphs to find something that stands out, e.g. in the paragraph about riding the cow to the train to France, ask *Is it possible for this many people to ride a cow? Do people ever ride cows? Why do you think the author included this if it's not possible?*

A Match the food to where it comes from. Use information from the story. You have to draw conclusions to match some of the items.

- Have students work independently to do the exercise. Then have them check their answers with a partner before eliciting the answers from the class.

ANSWERS

1 c 2 a 3 e 4 b 5 f 6 d

B Answer the questions.

- Have students reread the story and then answer the questions.
- Check the answers with the class.

ANSWERS

1 He wants to get the best ingredients to make Granny's Famous Cinnamon Buns.
2 They rode a cow to a train. The train took them from Denmark to France.
3 He saw a small piece of bark that could be used for cinnamon.

CRITICAL THINKING

Ask follow-up questions:

- How could you tell if one ingredient was better than another ingredient?
- In the story, which form of travel do you think was the fastest? Which form of travel do you think was the most fun?
- How were all the farmers in the story similar?
- How were all the farmers different?

C Words in Context: Match each verb to a definition.

- Have students work independently to do the exercise. Then have them check their answers with a partner or in a small group before eliciting the answers from the class.

1 b 2 d 3 a 4 c

Below level:

- Have students find the words in context in the story.
- Paraphrase each sentence to provide some additional clues about the meaning of the word.

At level:

- Have students complete the exercise independently and then check their work with a partner.

Above level:

- Have students try to use each word in a new sentence.
- Have them place the sentence in the context of a paragraph to reinforce their understanding of the definition.

Grammar in Use

D Listen and sing along. 🎧 1·32

- Listen to the song once and then sing it together as a class.
- Ask where each ingredient comes from.
- Divide the class into eight groups. Assign each group one line from the song.
- Have groups practice saying their lines without music first.
- Play the music and have groups sing along with the audio.

E Read the sentences. Which action is happening now? What action will happen in the future?

- Point out the time clue in each sentence (*tomorrow* and *now*).
- Point out that the verb form is the same for the "now" sentence and the future sentence.

a This action is happening in the future.
b This action is happening now.

F Learn Grammar: Present Continuous for Future Plans

- Read the *Learn Grammar* box to the class.
- Give more examples of how the present continuous can be used, e.g. *I'm teaching now. I'm taking the bus home today.*
- Ask individual students what they are doing now. Ask them what they are doing after school.

Read each sentence. Underline the present continuous tense. Then circle the future time word or words.

- Have students underline and circle the answers individually.
- Then check answers with the class.

1 We're playing soccer after school today.
2 My parents are having dinner at a nice restaurant tomorrow
3 I'm meeting my friends at the station at 1:00 p.m
4 Carol and I are baking cookies next week

G Make a chart like this one. Then talk to your partner about it.

- Have partners work together to create their charts.

Workbook Grammar

- Direct students to the Workbook for further practice.

Below level:

- Review as needed the conjugation of auxiliary verb *be*.
- Review the spelling rule for adding *-ing* to a verb ending in *e*, e.g. *make*: drop the *e* and add *-ing* (*making*).

At level:

- Have students practice simple dialogues to develop their charts, e.g. *What are you doing this weekend? I'm cleaning my bedroom. When are you cleaning your room? On Saturday morning.*
- Have students tell the class about their chart following the model on the page.

Above level:

- Have students create a schedule for their weekend plans.
- Ask partners to use the schedule as a prompt for a conversation they perform for the class.

- Tell students to stand up and walk around the classroom with their completed charts.
- Students need to find as many people as they can who have the same or similar plans as they do.
- They can mark off how many classmates have similar plans and then tell the class, e.g. *I'm playing soccer on Saturday. So are three other people.*

Further Practice
Workbook pages 43–45
Online practice Unit 5 • Understand
Oxford **iTools** Unit 5 • Understand

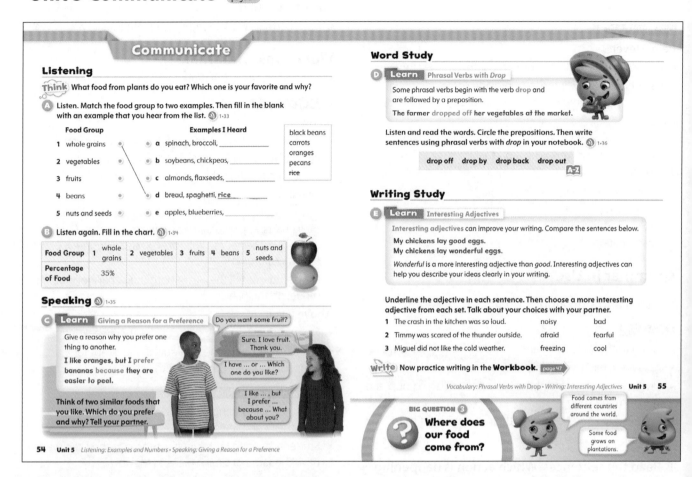

Summary

Objectives: To learn and practice listening, speaking, and writing strategies to facilitate effective communication.

Vocabulary: *drop off, drop by, drop back, drop out*

Listening strategy: Listening for examples and numbers

Speaking: Giving reasons for preferences

Word Study: Phrasal verbs with *drop*

Writing Study: Using interesting adjectives

Big Question learning points: *We eat food from plants. We eat food from animals.*

Materials: Discover Poster 3, Audio CD, Big Question Chart

Listening

Think

- Use a mind map with the class to brainstorm words for foods that come from plants.
- Ask students whether they like each food.
- Make tally marks next to the ones they like to show how many people like each food.
- Challenge them to explain why they like each food.

A Listen. Match the food group to two examples. Then fill in the blank with an example that you hear from the list. 1·33

- Pre-teach number words, if necessary, to prepare students for B, e.g. *35-thirty-five; 30-thirty; 15-fifteen; 10-ten.*
- Write *percent* on the board. Separate the word into *per* and *cent.* Explain that this means "out of a hundred."

- Play the audio once. Tell students to just listen, not write.
- Play it a second time and have students draw lines to match the food group to the 'Examples I Heard' list.
- Tell students to use the words from the word box to finish each list.

ANSWERS
1 d, rice   2 a, carrots   3 e, oranges   4 b, black beans
5 c, pecans

B Listen again. Fill in the chart. 1·34

- Have students fill in the chart on their own.

ANSWERS
1 whole grains 35%   2 vegetables 30%   3 fruit 15%
4 beans 10%   5 nuts and seeds 10%

CRITICAL THINKING

- Challenge students to write out a daily menu for what the girl might eat in an average day.
- Encourage them to consider the percentages as they create the menu, e.g. she gets 15% of her food from fruit and 30% from vegetables, so she eats twice as many vegetables as fruit. Have students guess the percentages of what they eat in a day.

Speaking 🔊 1·35

C Learn: Giving a Reason for a Preference

COMMUNICATION

- Read the *Learn* box together.
- Ask students to identify the preference (*bananas*) and the reason (*they are easier to peel*).
- Model the dialogue with a confident student in front of the class.
- Have students practice the dialogue using the other foods. Make sure they take turns speaking the different roles.

COLLABORATIVE LEARNING

- Ask students to write one food that comes from a plant on a slip of paper.
- Make sure students can identify if their food is a whole grain, a vegetable, a fruit, a bean, or a nut / seed.
- Students walk around the room to find other students who have written food from the same category.
- Once all the groups are together, have them write down all the foods in the category.
- Have them practice the dialogue in C using foods from their list.

Word Study

D Learn: Phrasal Verbs with *Drop*

- A phrasal verb refers to a verb and another word that together form a single-meaning phrase.
- Read the *Learn* box together. Ask students to identify the verb (*drop*) and the "other word," in this case a preposition (*off*).
- Highlight the difference in meaning between *dropped off* and *dropped*, e.g. *The farmer dropped off his vegetables* means he left them there on purpose. *The farmer dropped his vegetables* means they accidentally fell to the ground.

Listen and read the words. Circle the prepositions. Then write sentences using phrasal verbs with *drop* in your notebook. 🔊 1·36

- You may need to provide basic definitions for each phrasal verb before students can write sentences, e.g. *drop off* (leave something somewhere on purpose); *drop by* (to visit unexpectedly or quickly); *drop back* (move back, as in a football game); *drop out* (leave school without finishing).
- Play the audio and ask students to listen and read the words in the box.
- Have them circle the prepositions.
- Check the answers with the class.

ANSWERS

1 off   2 by   3 back   4 out

Writing Study

E Learn: Interesting Adjectives

- Read the *Learn* box together.
- Point out that interesting adjectives are also more descriptive and help a writer get his / her point across.

Underline the adjective in each sentence. Then choose a more interesting adjective from each set. Talk about your choices with your partner.

- Have students underline the adjective in each sentence.
- Ask them to choose a more interesting adjective to use and then ask pairs to talk about their choices.
- Check answers with the class.

ANSWERS

1 loud–noisy   2 scared–afraid   3 cold–freezing

DIFFERENTIATION

Below level:

- Review adjectives as a part of speech. Say *An adjective describes a noun*.
- Brainstorm some common adjectives and the nouns they might describe.
- Ask students to use the adjectives in sentences.

At level:

- Ask students to read each sentence and substitute the more interesting adjective.
- Provide a few other sentences and have the group brainstorm more interesting adjectives for each: *1 Sally is a nice friend. 2 The summer day was hot. 3 Michael's drawing was very good.*

Above level:

- Have students think of other examples of bland adjectives and their interesting replacements.
- Revisit the lesson on Visualizing Changes (page 9) and the poem *Bella's Home* (page 10) in the Student Book.
- Have students identify interesting adjectives in the poem and discuss how they help the reader visualize change.

Write

- Direct students to the Workbook for further practice.

Big Question 3 Review

Where does our food come from?

- Display **Discover Poster 3**. Point to items and elicit them from the class. Ask *What is this?*
- Refer to the learning points covered in Unit 5 and have students explain how they relate to the different pictures.
- Return to the **Big Question Chart**.
- Ask students what they have learned and add it to the chart.

| **Further Practice**
| Workbook pages 46–47
| Online practice Unit 5 • Communicate
| Oxford **iTools** Unit 5 • Commuinicate

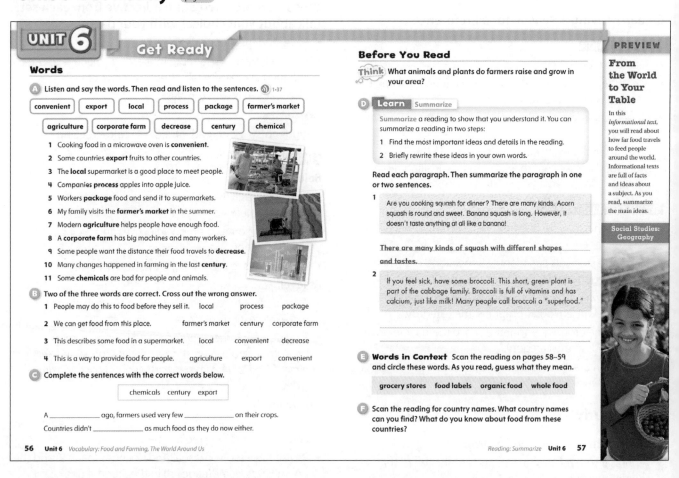

Summary

Objectives: To understand words about food and farming; to apply own experience and a reading strategy to help comprehension of a text.

Vocabulary: *convenient, export, local, process, package, farmers' market, agriculture, corporate farm, decrease, century, chemical, grocery stores, food labels, organic food, whole food*

Reading strategy: Summarizing

Materials: Audio CD

Words

A Listen and say the words. Then read and listen to the sentences. 🎧 1·37

- Play the audio. Ask students to point to the words as they hear them.
- Play the audio a second time and have students repeat the words when they hear them.
- Play the sentences while students read along.
- Ask students to categorize words into parts of speech (nouns, adjectives, verbs).
- Ask volunteers to try to define the words based on the sentences and pictures. Then have students look at the dictionary in the back of the Student Book to see if their definitions were correct.

Ask the following questions to check understanding:

- Which local foods are exported from your country?
- What common root do you see in "century" and "percent," which we learned on page 54?
- Why do people want to reduce the amount of chemicals in their food?
- What are some differences between a corporate farm and the farms that sell food at farmers' markets?

B Two of the three words are correct. Cross out the wrong answer.

- Students can draw conclusions about the part of speech for the correct and incorrect answers, e.g. in number 1, the word *do* lets the reader know that the correct answers will be verbs. *Local* is an adjective, so it couldn't be the correct answer.

ANSWERS

1 local   2 century   3 decrease   4 convenient

COLLABORATIVE LEARNING

- Give small groups the following problem to solve together: *The Ruiz family wants to eat more healthily and help the environment. What can they do?*
- Have groups come up with ideas using as many vocabulary words as possible. They can include words and ideas from Unit 5, as well.
- Facilitate by assigning roles, such as participation monitor, secretary, and timekeeper.

- Have groups save their work to revisit after they complete the *Understand* lesson on page 60.

C Complete the sentences with the correct words below.

- Have students work independently to complete the exercise.
- Check answers with the class.

century, chemicals, export

Before You Read

Think

- Have students name different foods that are grown or raised locally.

D Learn: Summarize

- Have a confident student read the *Learn* box to the class.

Read each paragraph. Then summarize the paragraph in one or two sentences.

- Invite volunteers to read the paragraphs.
- Read the sample answer together before asking students to complete the second one on their own.

Below level:

- To help identify the main idea and details, it can be helpful to draw a simple graphic on the board, e.g. write the main idea at the top of a table and write the details along the legs of the table. (For the second paragraph write the details first, and then guide students to identify the main idea.)

At level:

- Have partners read the second paragraph together. Explain that the main idea is not stated directly, so they will need to figure out the main idea using the details in the paragraph.

Above level:

- Ask students to write a paragraph about a kind of food. Tell them to make sure their paragraph has a main idea and a few details.
- Have students write down a summary of their own paragraph, without showing it to their partner.
- Students exchange paragraphs. Partners summarize each other's paragraphs and then compare summaries.

E Words in Context: Scan the reading on pages 58–59 and circle these words. As you read, guess what they mean.

- Have students skim the reading and circle the words in context.
- As they read, encourage them to guess what the words mean using clues from the surrounding sentences.

F Scan the reading for country names. What country names can you find? What do you know about food from these countries?

- Have students scan the reading to find the country names.
- Ask students to work in pairs to talk about the countries they have found and about the food from these countries.

Reading Preview

- Read the title of the unit's reading text.
- Have students silently read the content of the preview bar.
- Ask *What type of text is it?* Ask *What does this type of text do?*

| **Further Practice**
| Workbook pages 48–49
| Online practice Unit 6 • Get Ready
| Oxford **iTools** Unit 6 • Get Ready

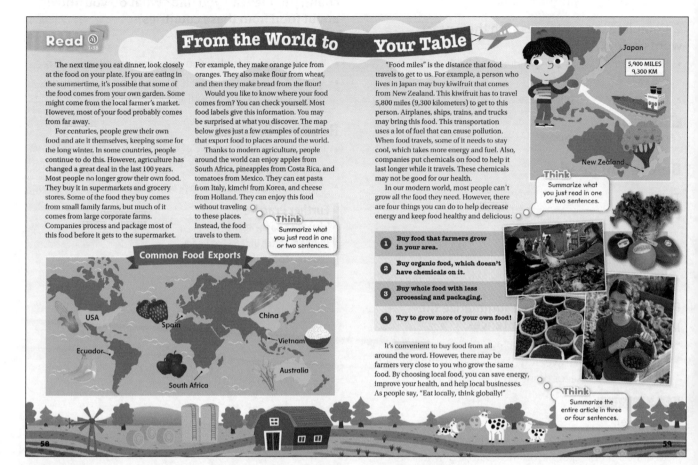

Summary

Objectives: To read, understand, and discuss a nonfiction text; to apply a reading strategy to improve comprehension.

School subject: Social Studies: Geography

Text type: Informational text (nonfiction)

Reading strategy: Summarizing

Big Question learning points: *Food comes from all around the world. Some food comes from large farms and plantations. Some food comes from small, local farms or gardens.*

Materials: Talk About It! Poster, Audio CD

Before Reading

- Ask the students to focus on the maps and pictures.
- Ask questions to generate interest:
  What food does (country) export?
  Why do you think they show the distance from New Zealand to Japan?
  What can you tell me about the photographs?

During Reading 1·38

- Ask a gist question to check overall understanding of the text, e.g. *How has modern agriculture and technology changed the way we get our food?*
- Give students a few minutes to skim the text before answering.
- Remind students that they are going to try to summarize while they read.
- Play the audio. Students listen as they read along.
- Play the audio a second time if necessary.

Below level:

- Put students in small groups.
- Play the audio and have students "echo read" which means that they repeat sentences or a couple of short sentences after they hear them. Make sure you stop the audio often enough to give students time to remember what they have heard and repeat it successfully.
- Support students as they try to summarize at each *Think* box.
- Begin by telling them to first identify important details in each section. After they list the details, guide them in identifying a main idea statement that includes all (or most) of the details.
- Suggest a few possible summaries and ask them to pick the best one.

At level:

- Have partners read together.
- Tell them to focus on identifying the main idea and details in each paragraph in order to properly summarize each one.
- Tell students to work with their partners to identify the main idea and details of each section.
- Once they have the main idea and details, they can create a summary.
- Have groups share their summaries with the class.
- Ask groups to summarize each *Think* box.

Above level:

- Have students read independently.
- Tell them to circle any words, sentences, or sections they do not understand.
- Put students in pairs to work out anything they do not understand together. Tell them to let you know if there's anything they cannot figure out together.
- Challenge them to summarize each *Think* box.
- Ask students to help other groups who are having trouble either identifying the main idea and details, or summarizing.

COLLABORATIVE LEARNING

- Have small groups create "peek-a-boo" posters for each of the four things you can do to reduce energy and keep food healthy and delicious.
- First groups brainstorm reasons why each suggestion will either help the environment or keep food healthy and delicious, e.g. for "Buy food that farmers grow in your area," students will write a reason sentence, such as "It reduces food miles."
- Students will write each suggestion from Student Book page 59 on an index card. They trace the card on a piece of paper and write the reason sentence within the card outline.
- Tape the top of the card to the paper so it covers the outline with the reason sentence. You should be able to lift the card like a flap to reveal the reason sentence hidden under it.
- Have each group swap their cards with another group.
- The groups look at the cards and try to guess the reason sentence before lifting the flaps to check their answers.

CRITICAL THINKING

Discussion questions:

- *In what ways is modern agriculture convenient?*
- *What are some benefits of eating organic food?*
- *What are some of the pros and cons of the modern agricultural system?*
- *Do you have any favorite foods that come from far away? Would you be willing to stop eating those foods to help the planet?*
- *Why do you think the article suggests eating food with less packaging?*

After Reading

- Have students share their summaries from the *Think* boxes. Possible summaries for each *Think* box:
  1 Modern agriculture allows us to eat food from faraway places without leaving our hometown.
  2 A problem with modern agriculture is that food miles create pollution.
  3 Modern agriculture is convenient, but we need to eat locally and think globally to reduce pollution and improve healthy eating habits.

COLLABORATIVE LEARNING

- Display the **Talk About It! Poster** to help students with sentence frames for discussion and expressing personal opinions.
- Put students into pairs to discuss which facts they found most interesting.
- Have students say one thing they can do from now on to eat more healthily and / or to help the environment.

CULTURE NOTE

Some communities use a model called Community Supported Agriculture (CSA). In a CSA, members of a usually urban community partner with a local farm. The CSA members pay the farmers at the beginning of the growing season for a portion of their expected harvest.

During the harvest, the CSA members receive weekly deliveries of fresh local food that they have already paid for. However, if the harvest is poor, the CSA members get less food. Despite the risk, this arrangement benefits the CSA members because they generally receive lots of fresh local produce for a good price. It benefits the farmers because they have a guaranteed market and income source, and they don't carry the burden of risk alone.

Further Practice
Workbook page 50
Online practice Unit 6 • Read
Oxford **iTools** Unit 6 • Read

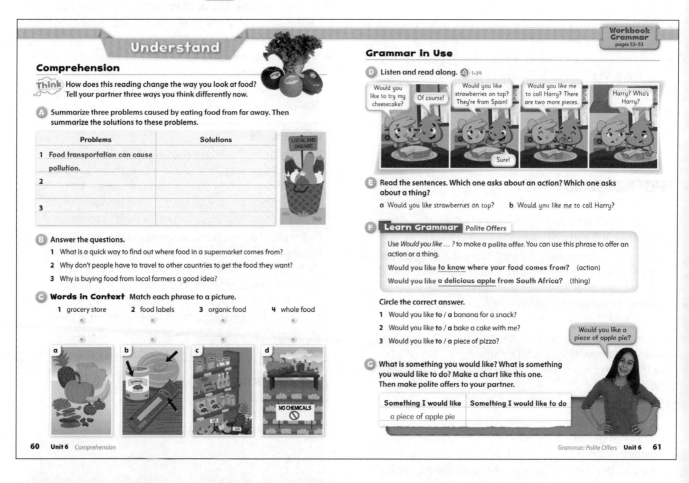

Summary

Objectives: To demonstrate understanding of a nonfiction text; to understand the meaning and form of the grammar structure.

Reading: Comprehension

Grammar input: Making polite offers

Grammar practice: Workbook exercises

Grammar production: Writing and talking about personal information

Materials: Audio CD

Comprehension

Think

- Have partners work together to discuss the question.
- Then have volunteers share their responses with the class.

A Summarize three problems caused by eating food from far away. Then summarize the solutions to these problems.

- Direct attention to the first problem.
- Ask students to look back at the text and find the section that describes about this problem. (See the paragraph that begins "Food miles …")
- As a class, brainstorm possible solutions, such as buying more locally grown food or only buying dry goods from overseas that do not require refrigeration. Have students choose their best idea and write it in the chart.
- Have partners work together to complete the chart.

B Answer the questions.

- Have students reread the text to find the answers to the questions.
- Check answers with the class.

ANSWERS

1 Look at the label.
2 Because modern technology allows us to transport food quickly.
3 It supports local communities and reduces pollution.

CRITICAL THINKING

- Ask a follow-up question:
  Look again at the four things you can do to help reduce energy and keep food healthy on page 59. Why might it be difficult to do these things?

COLLABORATIVE LEARNING

- Have groups revisit the ideas they had for the Ruiz family (see the Collaborative Learning for B on page 56). After reading "From the World to Your Table," do they have any ideas to add?
- Extend the problem. Tell groups that the *entire* Ruiz family wants to follow their advice for healthy eating and environmentally friendly behavior, *except for* Aunt Silda.
- Revisit the reasons students listed above for why it would be difficult to follow the suggestions in the article. Explain that these are the reasons Aunt Silda wants to keep eating packaged food from faraway places.
- Have groups plan a role-play of the Ruiz family at the dinner table trying to persuade Aunt Silda to improve her eating habits and help the environment.

C Words in Context: Match each phrase to a picture.

- Have students match the phrases with the pictures.
- Find the words in the reading. Point out context clues that help define the words.
- Check the answers with the class.

1 c   2 b   3 d   4 a

Grammar in Use

D Listen and read along. 🔊 1·39

- Listen to the cartoon story once while students follow along.
- Have partners take turns repeating the cartoon text after the audio.
- Help them appreciate the joke at the end. Ask *Why does Anna ask "Would you like me to call Harry?" Why does Jay ask "Harry? Who's Harry?"*

E Read the sentences. Which one asks about an action? Which one asks about a thing?

- Sentence *a* asks about a thing and sentence *b* asks about an action.
- Point out the infinitive *to call* in the second sentence. That's the clue that this question asks about an action.

F Learn Grammar: Polite Offers

- Read the *Learn Grammar* box to the class.
- Contrast the polite tone of *Would you like … ?* with the less polite version *Do you want … ?*
- Read each sentence with *Would you like … ?* using a polite and friendly tone of voice.
- Then say the same sentence, but substitute *Do you want … ?* and use a more abrupt and unfriendly tone.
- Explain that we use an infinitive after *Would you like … ?* when we are offering an action, and a noun after it when we are offering a thing. Provide some example sentences, e.g. *Would you like to play a game? Would you like dessert at lunch?*

Circle the correct answer.

- Have students circle the correct answer independently and then check with a partner.
- Elicit the answers from the class.

1 a   2 to   3 a

G What is something you would like? What is something you would like to do? Make a chart like this one. Then make polite offers to your partner.

- Have students fill in the chart on their own to record their own ideas before they begin working with a partner.

- Have partners switch completed charts.
- Partner A asks Partner B *Would you like … ?* questions based on what Partner B wrote on his or her chart and other ideas, e.g. if Partner B wrote *I'd like a piece of apple pie*, Partner A asks, *Would you like a piece of apple pie?* Partner B answers, *Yes*. Then Partner A might ask *Would you like a piece of banana pie?* Partner B has to decide yes or no.
- Allow enough time for both partners to have a turn.

Below level:

- Review the infinitive form of several verbs to reinforce the grammar point.
- Give a few examples and ask students to give you a thumbs up if the construction is correct and a thumbs down if not, e.g. *Would you like watch TV?* (thumbs down) *Would you like to watch TV?* (thumbs up).

At level:

- Review the infinitive form of several verbs to reinforce the grammar point.
- Have students work in pairs to write two sentences, one offering an action and one offering a thing.
- Have each pair stand up and read their sentences to the class. The class decides if the sentence is about an action or a thing.

Above level:

- Have students work in small groups to choose an idea from their chart to use in an original cartoon story.
- Tell them that their group will make a new cartoon. They can use the one at the top of the page as a model. Help them to brainstorm appropriate target language if necessary.
- Have students present and show their cartoons to the class.

Workbook Grammar

- Direct students to the Workbook for further practice.

Further Practice
Workbook pages 51–53
Online practice Unit 6 · Understand
Oxford iTools Unit 6 · Understand

Unit 6 Communicate page 62

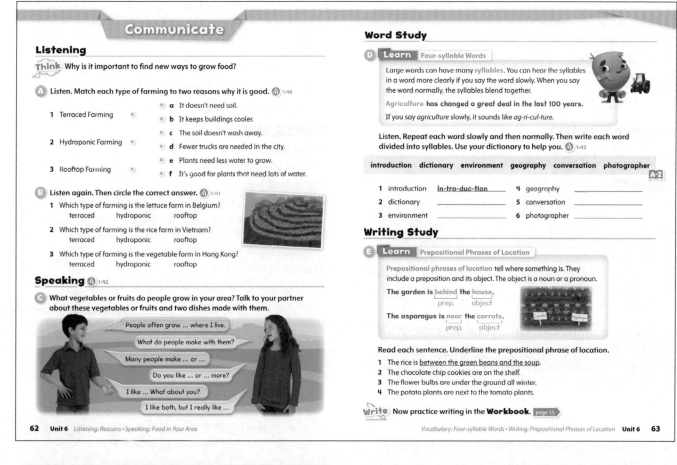

Communicate

Listening

Think Why is it important to find new ways to grow food?

A Listen. Match each type of farming to two reasons why it is good. 1·40

1 Terraced Farming
2 Hydroponic Farming
3 Rooftop Farming

- a It doesn't need soil.
- b It keeps buildings cooler.
- c The soil doesn't wash away.
- d Fewer trucks are needed in the city.
- e Plants need less water to grow.
- f It's good for plants that need lots of water.

B Listen again. Then circle the correct answer. 1·41

1 Which type of farming is the lettuce farm in Belgium?
  terraced   hydroponic   rooftop

2 Which type of farming is the rice farm in Vietnam?
  terraced   hydroponic   rooftop

3 Which type of farming is the vegetable farm in Hong Kong?
  terraced   hydroponic   rooftop

Speaking 1·42

C What vegetables or fruits do people grow in your area? Talk to your partner about these vegetables or fruits and two dishes made with them.

People often grow ... where I live.
What do people make with them?
Many people make ... or ...
Do you like ... or ... more?
I like ... What about you?
I like both, but I really like ...

62 **Unit 6** *Listening: Reasons • Speaking: Food in Your Area*

Word Study

D **Learn** Four-syllable Words

Large words can have many syllables. You can hear the syllables in a word more clearly if you say the word slowly. When you say the word normally, the syllables blend together.

Agriculture has changed a great deal in the last 100 years.

If you say *agriculture* slowly, it sounds like *ag-ri-cul-ture*.

Listen. Repeat each word slowly and then normally. Then write each word divided into syllables. Use your dictionary to help you. 1·43

introduction   dictionary   environment   geography   conversation   photographer

1 introduction   **in-tro-duc-tion**
2 dictionary   _____
3 environment   _____
4 geography   _____
5 conversation   _____
6 photographer   _____

Writing Study

E **Learn** Prepositional Phrases of Location

Prepositional phrases of location tell where something is. They include a preposition and its object. The object is a noun or a pronoun.

The garden is behind the house.
  prep.   object

The asparagus is near the carrots.
  prep.   object

Read each sentence. Underline the prepositional phrase of location.

1 The rice is <u>between the green beans and the soup</u>.
2 The chocolate chip cookies are on the shelf.
3 The flower bulbs are under the ground all winter.
4 The potato plants are next to the tomato plants.

Write Now practice writing in the **Workbook**. page 55

Vocabulary: Four-syllable Words • Writing: Prepositional Phrases of Location **Unit 6** 63

Summary

Objectives: To learn and practice listening, speaking, and writing strategies to facilitate effective communication.

Vocabulary: *introduction, dictionary, environment, geography, conversation, photographer*

Listening strategy: Listening for reasons

Speaking: Describing food in your area

Word Study: Four-syllable words

Writing Study: Prepositional phrases of location

Big Question learning point: *Food comes from all around the world.*

Materials: Audio CD

Listening

Think

- Have small groups discuss the question.
- Then have students offer their ideas to the class and allow other students to respond to the ideas.

A Listen. Match each type of farming to two reasons why it is good. 1·40

- Pronounce each phrase carefully as you point to the words. *Terraced Farming; Hydroponic Farming; Rooftop Farming*. Have students repeat after you.
- Play the audio once. Have students identify which type of farming is discussed in each section.
- Read the directions. Have volunteers read the reasons listed in the second column of the exercise.
- If necessary play the audio a second time.
- Have students complete the exercise while they listen. Review answers as a class.

ANSWERS
1 c, f   2 a, e   3 b, d

B Listen again. Then circle the correct answer. 1·41

- Review the place names. Quickly find the places on the map to give the exercise a little more context.
- Check answers with the class.

ANSWERS
1 hydroponic   2 terraced   3 rooftop

CRITICAL THINKING

Ask the following questions to check understanding:

- Which kind of farming is good in a desert? Why?
- Do you think Vietnam is hilly or flat?
- Why are rooftop gardens popular in cities?
- How might each type of farm help the environment?

88   **Unit 6 • Communicate**

Speaking 🔊 1·42

C What vegetables or fruits do people grow in your area? Talk to your partner about these vegetables or fruits and two dishes made with them.

- Say each line of the dialogue. Have students repeat.
- Model the dialogue with a confident student.
- Put students into pairs and tell them to practice the dialogue, taking turns speaking the different roles.
- Have partners work together. After they practice a few times, have them use the model to discuss other foods and dishes that are common in their area.

Word Study

D Learn: Four-syllable Words

- Read the *Learn* box together with the class.
- Say *agriculture* slowly with the syllable breaks shown on the page. Snap your fingers as you say each syllable.
- Play the audio. Have students listen and repeat the words.
- Play it a second time. Tell them to write the words separated into syllables, following the sample for *introduction*.
- Review answers together as a class.

ANSWERS

1 in-tro-duc-tion   2 dic-tion-ar-y   3 en-vi-ron-ment
4 ge-og-ra-phy   5 con-ver-sa-tion   6 pho-tog-ra-pher

- Have students stand in a large circle.
- Say one of the words. Have students go around the circle, each saying one syllable. They say the word over and over, getting faster and faster each time.
- So for *introduction*, Student 1 says *in*, Student 2 says *tro*, Student 3 says *duc*, and Student 4 says *tion*. Student 5 says *in*, Student 6 says *tro*, Student 7 says *duc*, Student 8 says *tion*, and so on.
- Once you have gone around once, repeat with other words.

Writing Study

E Learn: Prepositional Phrases of Location

- Read the *Learn* box together.
- Clarify by asking *Where is the garden? Where is the asparagus?*

Read each sentence. Underline the prepositional phrase of location.

- Have students answer individually and then check their answers with a partner.
- Elicit the answers from the class.

ANSWERS

1 The rice is <u>between the green beans and the soup</u>.
2 The chocolate chip cookies are <u>on the shelf</u>.
3 The flower bulbs are <u>under the ground</u> all winter.
4 The potato plants are <u>next to the tomato plants</u>.

Below level:

- Review some additional prepositions of location, such as *behind, between, in front of, near, next to, under*.
- First review the words using simple props, like a book, a cup, and a pencil.
- Set the props. Point and say, e.g. *The pencil is behind the cup*. Have students repeat after you.
- Have students work in pairs to describe where things are in the classroom.

At level:

- Put students in pairs.
- Give each student a piece of paper. Tell them to write a sentence as follows at the top of each piece of paper: 1 Use a prepositional phrase of location; 2 Use food as the subject and object of the sentence.
- Point to the examples in the *Learn* box, and remind students that *garden* is the subject and *house* is the object, *asparagus* is the subject and *carrots* is the object.
- Have partners switch papers. Each student draws a picture to illustrate his or her partner's sentence.

Above level:

- Give students pictures to look at or on the board, draw a scene in a park or somewhere with lots of different objects placed around.
- Partners play a guessing game. Partner A describes the location of something in a picture, and Partner B has to guess the object, e.g. Partner A says, *It's between the tree and the car. It's under the umbrella.* Partner B looks at the picture and finds the object that matches the description. He / She guesses, *It's the picnic table*.

Further Practice
Workbook pages 54–55
Online practice Unit 6 • Communicate
Oxford **iTools** Unit 6 • Communicate

Units 5 and 6 Wrap Up page 64

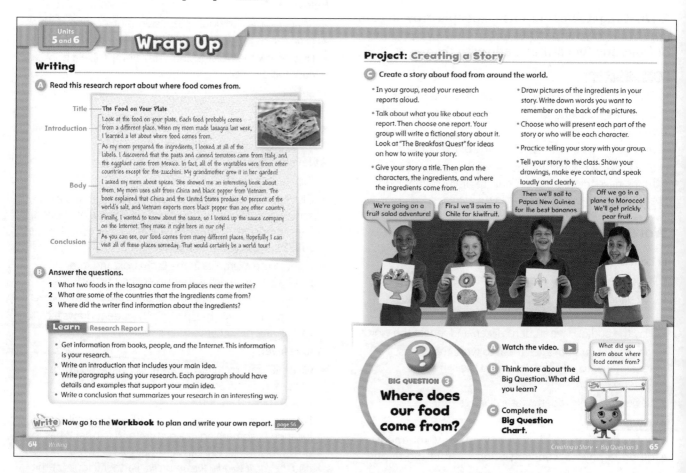

Summary

Objectives: To show what students have learned about the language and learning points of Units 5 and 6.

Reading: Comprehension of a research report

Project: Create a story

Writing: Write a research report

Speaking: Talk about the story

Materials: Big Question DVD, Discover Poster 3, Talk About It! Poster, Big Question Chart

Writing

A Read this research report about where food comes from.

- Before you read, review the parts of the report listed in the sidebar: Title, Introduction, Body, Conclusion.
- Ask *What can you tell me about the (title)?* Invite students to share prior knowledge.
- Go around the room and have students read the research report in turns.

CRITICAL THINKING

- Ask *What are the similarities and differences between this report and "The Breakfast Quest" on page 50?*
- Point out that "The Food on Your Plate" is nonfiction, but the author still does a good job of engaging the reader.
- The report is entertaining, even though its main purpose is to inform.
- Ask *How does the author make this report interesting and engaging?*

B Answer the questions.

- Have students reread the research report in A and answer the questions.
- Check answers with the class.

ANSWERS

1 The zucchini is from her grandmother's garden; the pasta sauce is from a nearby factory.
2 Italy, Mexico, China, Vietnam.
3 She found the information on the labels and on the Internet.

Learn: Research Report

- Read the *Learn* box together.
- Discuss each bulleted step to make sure students understand what to do. Explain that they will use "The Food on Your Plate" text and another research report in the Workbook as a model for their own reports.

COLLABORATIVE LEARNING

- Have small groups brainstorm topics for their research reports. Suggest they consider the dishes they talked about in the *Speaking* lesson on page 62, as well as other favorite meals. Tell them to discuss these points as they brainstorm and discuss:
- **Number of Ingredients.** Point out that having several different ingredients in a dish will make the report more interesting. However, if there are *too many* ingredients, the report might get boring. Tell groups to count the ingredients in each dish they brainstorm to decide if there are too many, too few, or just the right number.

- **Whole Foods or Packaged?** Some students may choose a dish that contains all fresh and whole foods, such as fresh salsa or vegetable soup. Other students might choose something packaged, such as a frozen pizza or boxed cookies.
- **Research Materials.** Where will students find the origin of food when it isn't named on the label? Have them discuss where and how they will research. Likely they will mention searching the Internet, but tell them to describe what steps they will take to search, and what they predict they will find, e.g. *I'll search "Eggplant." I think I will find an Encyclopedia website with information on eggplants. That website will tell me where eggplants are grown.*

Write
- Direct students to the Workbook to plan and write their research report.

Project

C Create a story about food from around the world.

CREATIVITY

- Read and discuss each step with the entire class.
- Put students into groups of four.
- Assign roles in each group to as follows:
  A timekeeper watches the clock and moves the group along when they get off task. The student in this role would use language like *We have ___ minutes. How about we spend ___ minutes picking a story, ___ minutes … ?* etc. *This is fun, but we need to get to work. Everyone has good ideas, but we need to move on to the next thing.*
- A monitor makes sure everyone participates. The student in this role would use language like *Mia, what do you think? Jon, hang on, let Zoe finish. Bill has a lot of good ideas; does anyone else have any ideas?*
- Students write their story, illustrating it if they wish.
- Display the stories on the wall, and let each student in turn present his / her work.

DIFFERENTIATION

Below level:
- Take key sentences from the text on pages 50 and 51 in the Student Book and write them on the board, e.g. *If it's flour you need, the heartiest wheat I know comes from France.*
- Underline the food and place vocabulary, and brainstorm other places and food to substitute.
- Groups decide on word substitutions to create a new story.
- Allow students to write down the sentences they will read to the class if necessary.

At level:
- Ask students to underline and tell you the key sentences from the Student Book that help to structure the story.
- Have each group write down the food and places they want to include in their story.
- Have students write the new sentences in their notebooks.

Above level:
- Have students brainstorm and write down the food and places they want to include in their story.
- Have students tell the story in their own words.
- In their groups, have students put their cards onto poster paper and write the story out, with each sentence under the corresponding picture.
- Put the posters on the wall and give students time to read each other's.

Units 5 and 6 Big Question Review

A Watch the video. ▷
- Play the video and when it is finished ask students what they know about where food comes from.
- Have students share ideas with the class.

B Think more about the Big Question. What did you learn?

COMMUNICATION

- Display **Discover Poster 3**. Point to familiar vocabulary items and elicit them from the class. Ask *What is this?*
- Ask students *What do you see?* Ask *What does that mean?*
- Refer to all of the learning points written on the poster and have students explain how they relate to the different pictures.
- Ask *What does this learning point mean?* Elicit answers from individual students.
- Display the **Talk About It! Poster** to help students with sentence frames for discussion of the learning points and for expressing their opinions.

C Complete the Big Question Chart.

COLLABORATIVE LEARNING

- Ask students what they have learned about where food comes from while studying this unit.
- Put students into pairs or small groups to say two new things they have learned.
- Have students share their ideas with the class and add their ideas to the chart.
- Have students complete the chart in their Workbook.

Further Practice
Workbook pages 56–58
Online practice · Wrap Up 3
Oxford **iTools** · Wrap Up 3

Units 7 and 8 — Why do we make art?

In units 7 and 8 you will:

WATCH a video about art and artists.

LEARN about the reasons artists create art.

READ about real artists and a boy who loves art.

WRITE an opinion essay.

ACT in a play.

BIG QUESTION 4
Why do we make art?

A Watch the video.

B Look at the picture and talk about it.

1 Where are the girls? What do you see in this place?

2 What are they doing? What are they using to do this?

C Think and answer the questions.

1 What kind of art do you make at school?

2 How is art class different from science class?

D Fill out the **Big Question Chart**.

What do you know about art? What do you want to know?

66 Big Question 4

67

Reading Strategies
Students will practice:
- Understanding text features
- Making value judgments

Vocabulary
Students will understand and use words about:
- Art and artists

Grammar
Students will understand and use:
- Indefinite pronouns
- Offers with *shall* and *will*

Review
Students will review the language and Big Question learning points of Units 7 and 8 through:
- An opinion essay
- A project (acting in a play)

Units 7 and 8
Why do we make art?
Students will understand the Big Question learning points:
- We make art to create something new.
- Making art is fun.
- People like to use their imagination.
- Other people can enjoy art we make.
- Art shows what a person is interested in.

Listening Strategies
Students will practice:
- Listening for reasons
- Listening for differences and details

Writing
Students will be able to use:
- Compound predicates
- The articles *a*, *an*, and *the*
Students will produce texts that:
- Give an opinion

Word Study
Students will understand, pronounce, and use:
- Words with the prefix *dis-*
- Synonyms

Speaking
Students will understand and use expressions to:
- Share knowledge
- Express a desire or wish

Units 7 and 8 Big Question page 67

Summary

Objectives: To activate students' existing knowledge of the topic and identify what they would like to learn about the topic.

Materials: Big Question DVD, Discover Poster 4, Big Question Chart

Introducing the topic

- Read out the big question. Ask *Why do we make art?* Write suggestions from students on the board.

A Watch the video.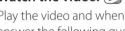

- Play the video and when it is finished ask students to answer the following questions in pairs:
  What do you see in the video?
  Who do you think the people are?
  What is happening?
  Do you like it?
- Have individual students share their answers with the class.

B Look at the picture and talk about it.

- Have students look at the big picture and talk about it. Ask students the questions.
- Ask additional questions:
  Have you ever seen art? Where did you see it? Do you know who made it? Did you like it? Why or why not?
  What are all the girls wearing? Why do you think they are wearing these?
  What is on the wall? Who do you think made these pictures?

C Think and answer the questions.

- Have students think about the questions for a minute or two.
- Then have them discuss the questions in small groups.
- Finally, have groups share their ideas with the class.

DIFFERENTIATION

Below level:

- Review some art supplies and actions that students may or may not know, e.g. *crayons, pencils, markers, paint, watercolor, collage, draw, cut, paint, color, glue / paste*.
- Use real examples or drawings of these objects or pantomime for actions in order to reinforce the meaning of each word.
- Have students use the words in sentences to answer the first question.

At level:

- First, tell students to think of the last few art projects they did in school. What materials and tools did they use? Which project was the most fun to make and why?

Above level:

- Have students extend the discussion to consider the art they have seen in museums, galleries, or other public spaces.
- In addition to asking the above questions, ask them what they think might be the *purpose* of the artwork?

CRITICAL THINKING

- Draw a large Venn diagram on the board to compare and contrast art class and science class.
- Invite the class to brainstorm ideas.
- Write the similarities in the center and the unique differences on the appropriate sides.
- Encourage them to extend the Big Question to help foster ideas, e.g. *Why do we make art? Why do we study science?*

Expanding the topic

COLLABORATIVE LEARNING

- Display **Discover Poster 4** and give students enough time to look at the pictures.
- Elicit some of the words and phrases you think they will know by pointing to different things in the pictures and asking *What's this? What are they doing?*
- Put students into small groups of three or four. Have each group choose a picture that they find interesting.
- Ask each group to say five things that they can see in their picture.
- Have one person from each group stand up and read out the words they chose for their picture.
- Ask the class if they can add any more.
- Repeat until every group has spoken.

D Fill out the Big Question Chart.

- Display the **Big Question Chart**.
- Ask the class *What do you know about art?*
- Draw a mind map on the board, putting *art* in the middle and adding students' ideas around it.
- Then ask the class *What do you want to know about art?*
- Ask students to write what they know and what they want to know in their Workbooks.
- Write a collection of ideas on the **Big Question Chart**.

Discover Poster 4

1 A girl and her grandfather using chalk to create street art; 2 Children having fun while painting a mural; 3 A digital artist creating a new design; 4 A boy enjoying a painting at a museum; 5 A boy taking a photo of tulips

| **Further Practice**
| **Workbook page 59**
| **Online practice • Big Question 4**
| Oxford **iTools** • Big Question 4

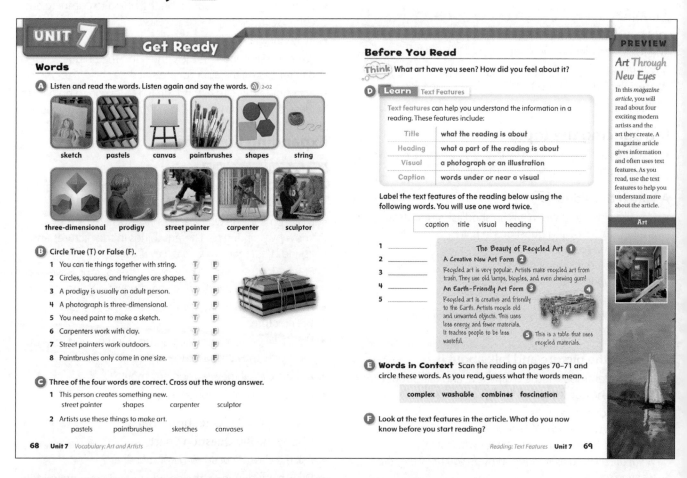

UNIT 7 Get Ready

Words

A Listen and read the words. Listen again and say the words. 2·02

sketch pastels canvas paintbrushes shapes string

three-dimensional prodigy street painter carpenter sculptor

B Circle True (T) or False (F).

1 You can tie things together with string. T F
2 Circles, squares, and triangles are shapes. T F
3 A prodigy is usually an adult person. T F
4 A photograph is three-dimensional. T F
5 You need paint to make a sketch. T F
6 Carpenters work with clay. T F
7 Street painters work outdoors. T F
8 Paintbrushes only come in one size. T F

C Three of the four words are correct. Cross out the wrong answer.

1 This person creates something new.
   street painter   shapes   carpenter   sculptor

2 Artists use these things to make art.
   pastels   paintbrushes   sketches   canvases

68 Unit 7 Vocabulary: Art and Artists

Before You Read

Think What art have you seen? How did you feel about it?

D Learn Text Features

Text features can help you understand the information in a reading. These features include:

Title	what the reading is about
Heading	what a part of the reading is about
Visual	a photograph or an illustration
Caption	words under or near a visual

Label the text features of the reading below using the following words. You will use one word twice.

caption   title   visual   heading

1 _____
2 _____
3 _____
4 _____
5 _____

The Beauty of Recycled Art 1
A Creative New Art Form 2
Recycled art is very popular. Artists make recycled art from trash. They use old lamps, bicycles, and even chewing gum!
An Earth-Friendly Art Form 3
Recycled art is creative and friendly to the Earth. Artists recycle old and unwanted objects. This uses less energy and fewer materials. It teaches people to be less wasteful. 5 This is a table that uses recycled materials. 4

E Words in Context Scan the reading on pages 70–71 and circle these words. As you read, guess what the words mean.

complex   washable   combines   fascination

F Look at the text features in the article. What do you now know before you start reading?

Reading: Text Features Unit 7 69

PREVIEW

Art Through New Eyes

In this *magazine article*, you will read about four exciting modern artists and the art they create. A magazine article gives information and often uses text features. As you read, use the text features to help you understand more about the article.

Art

Summary

Objectives: To understand words about art; to apply own experience and a reading strategy to help comprehension of a text.

Vocabulary: *sketch, pastels, canvas, paintbrushes, shapes, string, three-dimensional, prodigy, street painter, carpenter, sculptor, complex, washable, combines, fascination*

Reading strategy: Text features

Materials: Audio CD

Words

A Listen and read the words. Listen again and say the words. 2·02

- Play the audio. Ask students to point to the words as they hear them.
- Play the audio a second time and have students repeat the words when they hear them.
- Pay particular attention to the pronunciation of the consonant blends in *sketch* and *sculptor*.
- Point out that *paintbrushes* is a compound word: *paint + brushes*.
- Revisit the lesson on Four-syllable Words from Unit 6, page 63. Practice breaking down *three-di-men-sion-al*.

- Have groups work together to create mind maps of the words in A.
- First, they write the vocabulary word in the center. Then they draw lines to words and phrases that tell what they know about the word.
- You might provide dictionaries and art books for ideas, e.g. for the word *sketch*, students might write *plan, pencil and paper, practice, draw, verb or noun, not a lot of detail*.
- You can divide the words among the different groups and then reconvene to share their work.

B Circle True (T) or False (F).

- Read the sentences together.
- Have students complete the exercise on their own and then check their answers with a partner.

ANSWERS

1 T 2 T 3 F 4 F 5 F 6 F 7 T 8 F

Below level:

- First, have students underline the vocabulary word in each sentence in B.
- Then ask them what they know about each word. Refer back to the mind maps the class shared in the Collaboration activity for A.
- Finally, help them break down each sentence. Focus on key words that affect the meaning, e.g. 1 (*tie*), 2 (*circles, squares, triangles*), 3 (*adult*), 4 (*photograph*), 5 (*need paint*), 6 (*clay*), 7 (*outdoors*), 8 (*one size*).

At level:

- Have students rewrite each false statement to make a true statement, e.g.
  3 *A prodigy is usually a child.*
  4 *A photograph is two-dimensional / A photograph is not three-dimensional.*
  5 *You don't need paint to make a sketch.*
  6 *Carpenters work with wood.*
  8 *Paintbrushes come in many sizes.*

Above level:

- Have students write original sentences using the vocabulary words.
- Challenge them to use all the words in one coherent paragraph. The paragraph can be fictional, informative, or persuasive, as long as all the words are used in logical and meaningful sentences.

C Three of the four words are correct. Cross out the wrong answer.

- Have students complete this individually, then check answers with a partner.

ANSWERS
1 shapes   2 sketches

Before You Read

Think

- Create a two-column chart on the board to record some ideas. Column 1: *What kind of art have you seen?* Column 2: *How did this art make you feel?*
- Before you elicit ideas from the class, review some materials, e.g. *paper, pencil, paint, pastel, metal, wood, plastic, cloth*. Now review some feelings, e.g. *happy, sad, angry, confused, curious, interested, impressed*.

D Learn: Text Features

- Read the *Learn* box to the class.
- If possible, look at a newspaper or magazine article together to see the features in context.

Label the text features of the reading below using the following words. You will use one word twice.

- Have partners work through the exercise together.
- Tell students to read the entire text "The Beauty of Recycled Art" first. Then have them write the features on the lines.
- Check the answers with the class.

ANSWERS
1 title   2 heading   3 heading   4 visual   5 caption

Write the following sentences on the board. Ask students under which heading they belong:

- Recycled art wasn't popular 50 years ago because recycling wasn't common.
- Artists express their ideas using many different materials.
- These artists don't add more garbage to the earth; they reuse the garbage to make something interesting.
- Creating recycled art is one more way you can help the planet.
- Point to the vocabulary picture for *prodigy* in A.
- Tell students to imagine this picture in the middle of a newspaper article about child prodigies. Tell them to choose the best caption: *Mark solves a math problem in primary school* or *Mark's parents knew he was a prodigy because he solved difficult math problems in primary school.*
- The first option is a better caption because it is short and to the point, and it describes the picture.
- Have students try to write captions for some of the other vocabulary pictures.
- Each time they should imagine the picture is a visual in an article about a related topic.

E Words in Context: Scan the reading on pages 70–71 and circle these words. As you read, guess what the words mean.

- Direct students to divide the word *washable* into a base (*wash*) and suffix (*-able*). Can they predict what the word means based on those two parts?
- Pronounce the word *fascination* so students know the *c* carries the soft *s* sound.
- It's helpful to do this before they begin reading so they don't mentally mispronounce the word.

F Look at the text features in the article. What do you now know before you start reading?

- Preview the reading with the class.
- Ask *What is the title? Can you predict what the reading will be about based on the title?*
- Say *Look at each heading. What do you think you will read about in each section? Do the visuals and captions in each section help you predict?*

Reading Preview

- Read the title of the unit's reading text and ask students to give their ideas about what the title means.
- Have students silently read the content of the preview bar.
- Ask *What type of text is it?* Ask *What does this type of text do?*
- Tell students to think about how the different text features help them understand the selection.

Further Practice
Workbook pages 59–60
Online practice Unit 7 • Get Ready
Oxford iTools Unit 7 • Get Ready

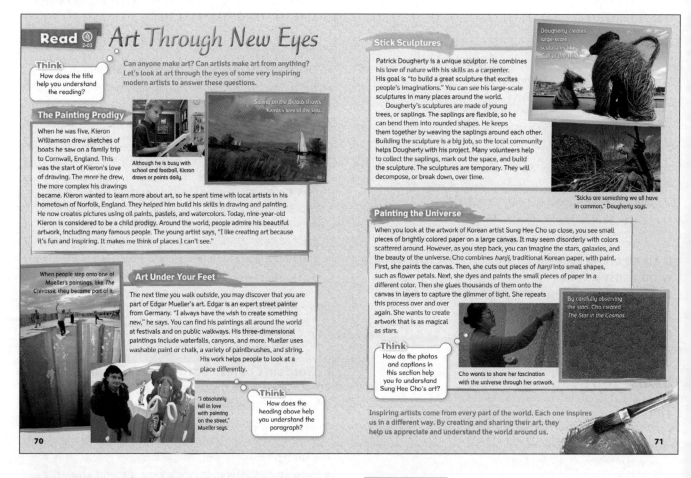

Read 2·03 *Art Through New Eyes*

Think
How does the title help you understand the reading?

Can anyone make art? Can artists make art from anything? Let's look at art through the eyes of some very inspiring modern artists to answer these questions.

The Painting Prodigy

When he was five, Kieron Williamson drew sketches of boats he saw on a family trip to Cornwall, England. This was the start of Kieron's love of drawing. The more he drew, the more complex his drawings became. Kieron wanted to learn more about art, so he spent time with local artists in his hometown of Norfolk, England. They helped him build his skills in drawing and painting. He now creates pictures using oil paints, pastels, and watercolors. Today, nine-year-old Kieron is considered to be a child prodigy. Around the world, people admire his beautiful artwork, including many famous people. The young artist says, "I like creating art because it's fun and inspiring. It makes me think of places I can't see."

Sailing on the Broads shows Kieron's love of the sea.

Although he is busy with school and football, Kieron draws or paints daily.

Art Under Your Feet

The next time you walk outside, you may discover that you are part of Edgar Mueller's art. Edgar is an expert street painter from Germany. "I always have the wish to create something new," he says. You can find his paintings all around the world at festivals and on public walkways. His three-dimensional paintings include waterfalls, canyons, and more. Mueller uses washable paint or chalk, a variety of paintbrushes, and string. His work helps people to look at a place differently.

When people step onto one of Mueller's paintings, like The Crevasse, they become part of it.

"I absolutely fell in love with painting on the street," Mueller says.

Think
How does the heading above help you understand the paragraph?

Stick Sculptures

Patrick Dougherty is a unique sculptor. He combines his love of nature with his skills as a carpenter. His goal is "to build a great sculpture that excites people's imaginations." You can see his large-scale sculptures in many places around the world.
Dougherty's sculptures are made of young trees, or saplings. The saplings are flexible, so he can bend them into rounded shapes. He keeps them together by weaving the saplings around each other. Building the sculpture is a big job, so the local community helps Dougherty with his project. Many volunteers help to collect the saplings, mark out the space, and build the sculpture. The sculptures are temporary. They will decompose, or break down, over time.

Dougherty creates large-scale sculptures like Call of the Wild.

"Sticks are something we all have in common," Dougherty says.

Painting the Universe

When you look at the artwork of Korean artist Sung Hee Cho up close, you see small pieces of brightly colored paper on a large canvas. It may seem disorderly with colors scattered around. However, as you step back, you can imagine the stars, galaxies, and the beauty of the universe. Cho combines *hanji*, traditional Korean paper, with paint. First, she paints the canvas. Then, she cuts out pieces of *hanji* into small shapes, such as flower petals. Next, she dyes and paints the small pieces of paper in a different color. Then she glues thousands of them onto the canvas in layers to capture the glimmer of light. She repeats this process over and over again. She wants to create artwork that is as magical as stars.

By carefully observing the stars, Cho created The Star in the Cosmos.

Think
How do the photos and captions in this section help you to understand Sung Hee Cho's art?

Cho wants to share her fascination with the universe through her artwork.

Inspiring artists come from every part of the world. Each one inspires us in a different way. By creating and sharing their art, they help us appreciate and understand the world around us.

70   71

Summary

Objectives: To read, understand, and discuss a nonfiction text; to apply a reading strategy to improve comprehension.

School subject: Art

Text type: Magazine article (nonfiction)

Reading strategy: Text features

Big Question learning points: *Other people can enjoy art we make. Art shows what a person is interested in.*

Materials: Talk About It! Poster, Audio CD

Before Reading

- Ask the following questions to generate interest in the topic:
  What kind of art do you like to look at or make?
  Do you think all artists make the same type of art? Why or why not?

During Reading ⊙ 2·03

- Ask a gist question to check overall understanding of the text, e.g. for the first section *Why does young Kieron enjoy creating art?*
- Give students a few minutes to skim the text before answering.
- Remind students that they are paying attention to the features of the text and how each helps their overall comprehension.
- Play the audio. Students listen as they read along.
- Play the audio a second time if necessary.

Below level:

- Have students echo read a few sentences at a time, following the audio.
- Students can read together in groups of four or five so you can make sure everyone is participating.

At level:

- Have partners read together.
- Have partners identify the title, headings, visuals, and captions throughout the text. Tell them to pause at each *Think* box to discuss the question.

Above level:

- Have students read the text independently. Tell them to pause after each section and get together with a partner to do the following:
  1 Go over any phrases or sentences that were confusing.
  2 Discuss the question in each *Think* box.
  3 Summarize the main ideas of the section. See Unit 6, page 57 for review

Discussion questions:

- *How did Kieron's artwork change with time? (If needed, note definitions: a waterfall is a drop in a river where water falls from the top level to the bottom level; a canyon is a deep hole in the earth.)*
- *Why do you think Edgar Mueller paints landscape features like waterfalls and canyons?*
- *Why do you think Mueller uses washable paint and chalk?*

- *Which of these materials do you think Patrick Dougherty might use in one of his sculptures? Why or why not? 1 Full-grown tree trunks 2 Vines 3 Metal rods 4 Rubber bands.*
- *Why do you think Sung Hee Cho's process takes a long time?*

COMMUNICATION

- Have small groups work together to compare and contrast the artists from the texts.
- Have them first discuss each text in terms of the questions listed below. A sampling of similarities and differences is listed below, but there are many other ideas students may identify on their own:
  1 *What materials do they use?* (Patrick Dougherty uses material from the natural world. Kieron Williamson uses more traditional things like pastels and paints. Edgar Mueller uses washable paint, chalk, paintbrushes, and string. Sung Hee Cho uses paint, small pieces of paper, and glue.)
  2 *What inspires the artist?* (Sung Hee Cho and Patrick Dougherty are both inspired by the natural world. Sung Hee Cho is inspired by the stars in the universe, and Patrick Dougherty is inspired by things on earth. The text doesn't state Williamson's or Mueller's inspiration, but students can guess.)
  3 *Where can you see their work?* (Edgar Mueller's work and Patrick Dougherty's work are both on display in open public areas. Kieron Williamson's work and Sung Hee Cho's work are probably seen in more traditional indoor places.)
  4 *Is their artwork permanent or temporary?* (Edgar Mueller's work and Patrick Dougherty's work is temporary. Kieron Williamson's work and Sung Hee Cho's work is permanent.)
  5 *Is their artwork two-dimensional or three-dimensional?* (They are all three-dimensional except for Kieron Williamson's.)
  6 *Can you suggest one or two other topics to compare and contrast?*
- After students discuss all the artists in terms of the questions above, have them choose two to compare in a simple Venn diagram.
- Have them share their work with the class.

After Reading

- Have students look again at the four paragraphs about the artists. Ask *How did the features help you understand the text?*

COLLABORATIVE LEARNING

- Display the **Talk About It! Poster** to help students with sentence frames for discussion and expressing personal opinions.
- Put students into pairs to discuss which artist's work they would like to see in person.
- Have students say one thing about each artist in the reading.
- Put students into small groups of three or four.
- Have students discuss other artists they know. Ask *Are they similar to the artists in the text? Are they different?*

CRITICAL THINKING

- Have students rank the artists in the order in which they would like to see their work in person.
- Have students give reasons for how they put the artists in order, e.g. *I want to see Sung Hee Cho's work first because I also love outer space. Next, I want to see Edgar Mueller's art because it is so different. My third choice is Patrick Dougherty's work because it is so big. My last choice is Kieron Williamson's work because the subject matter is not exciting.*

CULTURE NOTE

Sung Hee Cho uses traditional Korean paper in her artwork. This handmade paper is called *hanji*. The paper is made from the bark of the paper mulberry tree and a sticky liquid from the hibiscus manihot flower.

This high-quality paper has been used for almost two thousand years. Throughout history it has been used for official reasons, such as recording history, for everyday purposes in private homes, and for artwork.

Further Practice
Workbook page 61
Online practice Unit 7 · Read
Oxford iTools Unit 7 · Read

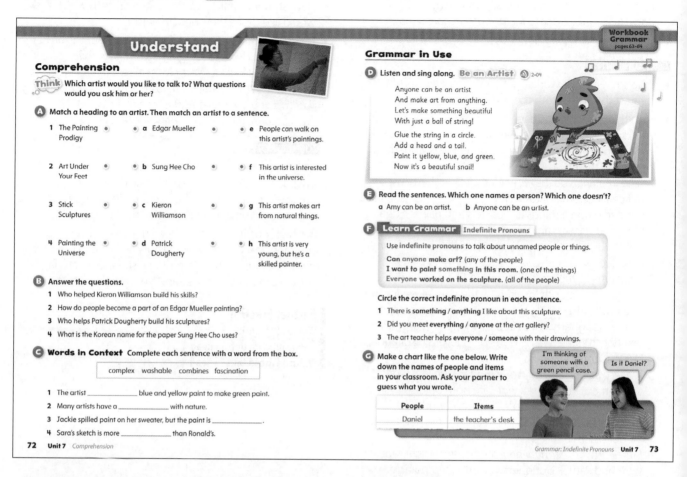

Summary

Objectives: To demonstrate understanding of a nonfiction text; to understand the meaning and form of the grammar structure.

Reading: Comprehension

Grammar input: Indefinite pronouns

Grammar practice: Workbook exercises

Grammar production: Asking about the classroom

Materials: Audio CD

Comprehension

Think

- Have students discuss the questions with partners.
- For an extra challenge, tell them to guess how the artist might answer their questions.
- Invite partners to role-play an interview with one of the artists.

A Match a heading to an artist. Then match an artist to a sentence.

- Have students complete the exercise in groups, then check answers together with the class.

ANSWERS

1 c, h   2 a, e   3 d, g   4 b, f

Below level:

- Read each sentence choice one at a time. Each time, go back to the reading and have students scan each section to see if the sentence is true, e.g. for the first sentence choice, direct them to look at The Painting Prodigy and ask *Can people walk on this artist's paintings?* Continue this way.

At level:

- After they complete A, have students add one detail sentence to each sentence in the third column.
- Here are some sample responses, but students' ideas will vary and you should accept all ideas that are based on the reading: e *People can walk on this artist's paintings. He uses washable paints and chalk to create art directly on the street.* f *This artist is interested in the universe. When you look at her artwork from far away you can imagine stars, galaxies, and the universe.* g *This artist makes art from natural things. The sculptures decompose over time.* h *This artist is very young, but he's a very skilled painter. The local artists in his hometown taught him how to paint and draw better.*

Above level:

- Point out that each heading is a kind of summary or main idea phrase about each section.
- Challenge students to come up with alternate headings for each section. Their headings should reflect the main ideas of the artists' stories.

B Answer the questions.

- Have students go back to the reading to support their answers with evidence from the text.
- Ask students to answer the questions.
- Check the answers with the class.

ANSWERS

1 Artists from his hometown helped him build his skills.
2 People can walk on Mueller's paintings, so they are part of them.
3 Volunteers help Dougherty collect the materials, mark out the space, and build his sculptures.
4 It is called *hanji*.

C Words in Context: Complete each sentence with a word from the box.

- Return to the text to find the Words in Context.
- For each word, help the class form a simple definition and identify the important clues that helped them figure out the meaning, such as:
  complex: not simple; sketches are simple, and Kieron's work got more complex over time.
  washable: not permanent; something you can wash off; break the word into parts *wash* and *able*.
  combines: mixes; she uses paper *with* paint
  fascination: an attraction and interest.
- Tell the class to consider the basic definitions as they complete the exercise independently.
- Check the answers with the class.

ANSWERS

1 combines   2 fascination   3 washable   4 complex

CRITICAL THINKING

- Have students look back at other readings in the Student Book. Ask them to find other examples of text features and discuss how they support meaning.
- Then have partners work together to suggest some text features they would add to some of the different readings.

Grammar in Use

D Listen and sing along. 🔊 2·04

- Play the audio.
- Ask studets to listen to the song once and then sing it together as a class.
- Check comprehension of the song. Ask *Do you have to be famous to be an artist? What does the song tell you to make? What part of the snail is the circle of string?*

E Read the sentences. Which one names a person? Which one doesn't?

- For each example, ask *Who can be an artist?*
- Point out that *Amy* is a specific person, and *Anyone* is general.

F Learn Grammar: Indefinite Pronouns

- Ask a confident student to read the *Learn Grammar* box.

Circle the correct indefinite pronoun in each sentence.

- Help students choose the best answer for each item by providing the following questions and clues:
  1 *Does the speaker like the sculpture? Does he / she know exactly what he / she likes? No, but he / she just feels as if he / she likes it overall. So the answer is "something."*
  2 *Can you meet a thing? No, so the word "meet" lets you know the answer should be "anyone."*
  3 *Does a teacher usually help one person or all people? Does the word "their" refer to one person or more than one person? These clues show that the answer should be "everyone."*

G Make a chart like the one below. Write down the names of people and items in your classroom. Ask your partner to guess what you wrote.

CREATIVITY

- Have students complete the chart by themselves. Tell them to include about five things in each column.
- Put students into pairs. Tell them not to show their charts to their partners.
- Model a conversation to ask and answer questions about the chart:
  A: *I'm thinking of someone with a green pencil case.*
  B: *Is it Daniel?*
  A: *Yes!*
- Point out that because the chart names specific people and things, the questions use the pronouns *someone* and *something*.

Workbook Grammar

- Direct students to the Workbook for further practice.

COLLABORATIVE LEARNING

- Have partners work together to come up with a few questions about people and items in the classroom using *anything* and *anyone*.
- Provide the models below. Point out that in each example, the speaker does not have a specific person / thing in mind, so you use *anything* / *anyone*:
  1 *Is there anyone who can (play guitar)? (Yes, Mike plays guitar or No.)*
  2 *Is there anything you like about that picture? (Yes, I like the colors or No.)*

| **Further Practice**
Workbook pages 62–64
Online practice Unit 7 · Understand
Oxford **iTools** Unit 7 · Understand

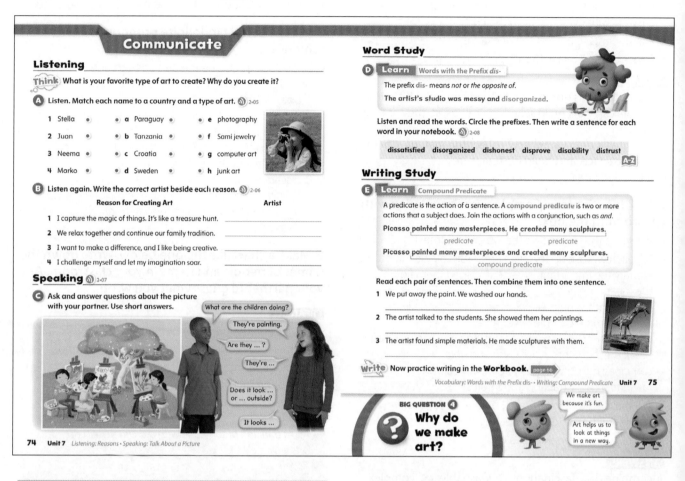

Summary

Objectives: To learn and practice listening, speaking, and writing strategies to facilitate effective communication.

Vocabulary: *dissatisfied, disorganized, dishonest, disprove, disability, distrust*

Listening strategy: Listening for reasons

Speaking: Talking about a picture

Word Study: Words with the prefix *dis-*

Writing Study: Compound predicates

Big Question learning points: *We make art to create something new. Making art is fun. People like to use their imagination. Art shows what a person is interested in.*

Materials: Discover Poster 4, Audio CD, Big Question Chart

Listening

Think

- Have students discuss the questions in small groups.

A Listen. Match each name to a country and a type of art. ⊙ 2·05

- Say each name first so students recognize what they are listening for.
- Have students find each country on a map.
- Play the audio and allow students time to complete the activity.

ANSWERS
1 d, f 2 a, h 3 b, e 4 c, g

B Listen again. Write the correct artist beside each reason. ⊙ 2·06

- Look at the two headings: *Reason for Creating Art* and *Artist*.
- Ask students if they can remember any of the reasons the people in the audio create art.
- Then play the audio.
- Students either check their answers or write them down.
- Check answers with the class.

ANSWERS
1 Neema 2 Stella 3 Juan 4 Marko

DIFFERENTIATION

Below level:

- Pause after the first sentence in each section of the audio track.
- Each time, ask *Who is speaking? Which country are they from?*
- Then play the rest of the section. Just before the speaker identifies the type of art, signal for students to listen carefully. Then pause after the key sentence for them to draw the line from the country to the type of art, e.g. in Stella's section, signal for students to listen carefully as the speaker says *I weave wire and leather together.* Then pause after she says *This is called Sami jewelry.*
- Follow a similar procedure when students complete B.

At level:

- Have students practice discussing the different sections of the listening.
- Have partners practice the following exchange:
  A: *Why does (Stella) create art?*
  B: *(She) creates art to (continue a family tradition).*

Above level:

- Before students work on B, tell them to cover the sentences that are listed on the page in the *Reasons for Creating Art.*
- After you play the audio for the second time, ask them to write down their own summary of why each person creates art.
- Then have them uncover the reasons listed on the page and check their ideas against the ones in the Student Book.

Speaking ⊚ 2·07

C Ask and answer questions about the picture with your partner. Use short answers.

COMMUNICATION

- Say each line of the dialogue with students echoing as they hear each line.
- Model the dialogue with a confident student in front of the class.
- Put students into pairs and tell them to practice the dialogue, taking turns speaking the different roles.
- Have students repeat this exercise, but this time discussing the pictures of the four artists shown on pages 70–71, e.g.
  A: *What is Kieron doing?*
  B: *He's painting.*
  A: *Is he painting inside or outside?*
  B: *He's painting inside.*
  A: *Does it look warm or cool inside?*
  B: *It looks warm.*

Word Study

D Learn: Words with the Prefix *dis-*

- Read the *Learn* box together with students. Ask them if they know anyone who is organized. Give some examples of people or areas of the classroom that are neat and organized.
- Then explain that *disorganized* is the opposite of *organized*.
- Point out the word *messy* is another clue to the meaning of *disorganized*.

Listen and read the words. Circle the prefixes. Then write a sentence for each word in your notebook. ⊚ 2·08

- Have students listen to the audio.
- Make sure students circle the prefix *dis-* in each word.
- Have a volunteer name the base word in each example *(satisfied, organized, honest, prove, ability, trust).*

Writing Study

E Learn: Compound Predicate

- Copy the example sentences from the box onto the board. Review the parts of the first sentence: *Picasso painted many masterpieces. Picasso* is the subject and *painted many masterpieces* is the predicate.
- Ask *Who is the subject of this sentence? And what did Picasso do? What's the predicate?*
- Ask *What else did he do?* (write as students answer, using *and*).
- Circle the word *and.* Explain that *and* joins the two actions in the sentence into a compound predicate.

Read each pair of sentences. Then combine them into one sentence.

- Have students read the sentences and then complete the exercise on their own.
- Check answers with the class.

ANSWERS
1 We put away the paint and washed our hands.
2 The artist talked to the students and showed them her paintings.
3 The artist found simple materials and made sculptures with them.

Write

- Direct students to the Workbook for further practice.

Big Question 4 Review

Why do we make art?

- Display **Discover Poster 4**. Point to familiar vocabulary items and elicit them from the class. Ask *What is this?*
- Ask students *Why is that person making art?* Ask *What inspires him / her?*
- Refer to the learning points covered in Unit 7 which are written on the poster and have students explain how they relate to the different pictures.
- Return to the **Big Question Chart**.
- Ask students what they have learned about making art while studying this unit.
- Ask what information is new and add it to the chart.

| **Further Practice**
Workbook pages 65–66
Online practice Unit 7 · Communicate
Oxford **iTools** Unit 7 · Communicate

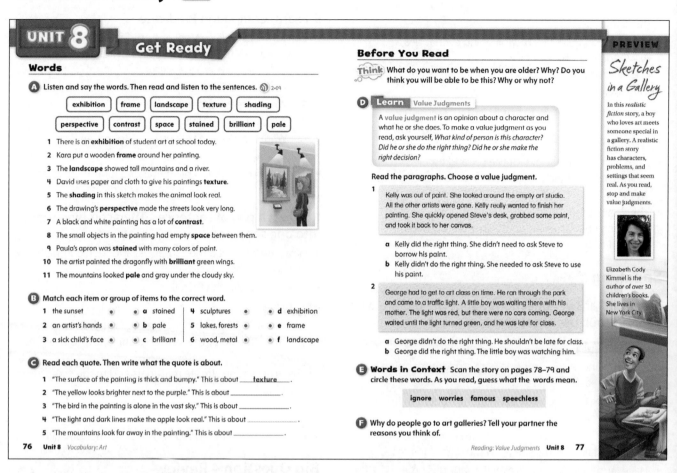

Summary

Objectives: To understand words about art; to apply one's own experience and reading strategy to help comprehension of a text.

Vocabulary: *exhibition, frame, landscape, texture, shading, perspective, contrast, space, stained, brilliant, pale, ignore, worries, famous, speechless*

Reading strategy: Making value judgments

Materials: Audio CD

Words

A Listen and say the words. Then read and listen to the sentences 🔘 2•09

- Play the audio. Ask students to point to and say the words as they hear them.
- Have students silently read the sentences as they listen to them.
- Then read the sentences together. After each sentence, ask students to guess a definition for the word. Fine-tune their definitions as needed.

COLLABORATIVE LEARNING

- Divide the class into small groups. Assign each group a few words from A.
- Have small groups work together to create a "square of meaning" for their words.
- Students write one word in the center of each square. They write one of the following in each corner of the square: a synonym or simple definition, an example, a sentence, and the part of speech, e.g. (center) *Brilliant;* (1st corner: definition / synonym) *bright;* (2nd corner: example) *blue sky;* (3rd corner: sentence) *There were no clouds in the brilliant blue sky;* (4th corner: part of speech) *adjective.*
- Have groups share their squares with the class. If two groups have a square for the same word, compare their answers.

B Match each item or group of items to the correct word.

- Look at the exercise together. Explain that items 1–3 are to be matched with choices a–c, and items 4–6 are to be matched with items d–f.
- Do the first one together. Say *Number 1. The sunset. Look at a, b, and c. Which one matches sunset? Is the sunset stained? Is it pale? Is it brilliant?*
- Then have students complete the rest of the exercise on their own.
- Check the answers with the class.

ANSWERS

1 c, brilliant   2 a, stained   3 b, pale   4 d, exhibition
5 f, landscape   6 e, frame

C Read each quote. Then write what the quote is about.

- Have students discuss the sentences in small groups before they complete the exercise.
- Encourage them to think back to the squares of meaning they created for each word in A.
- If there are any words students do not know, discuss them with the class.
- Check the answers with the class.

1 texture   2 shading   3 space   4 contrast
5 perspective

CRITICAL THINKING

- Have students turn back to the reading selection "Art Through New Eyes" on pages 70–71.
- Following the format of C, say these sentences and have students identify what each sentence is about:
  1 *Edgar Mueller's three-dimensional paintings include waterfalls, canyons, crevices, and more.* (Perspective: note that three-dimensional images always show perspective because they represent height, width, and depth.)
  2 *Sung Hee Cho glues thousands of small pieces of paper onto the canvas. The final product is not flat and smooth.* (Texture: Because her artwork is layered, her paintings capture the glimmer of light with their texture.)
  3 *Kieron Williamson uses pastels and blends them together to create smooth transitions of color.* (Shading: pastel artists use blending techniques to create visual effects.)

Before You Read

Think

- Have students discuss the questions in pairs.
- Encourage them to consider different reasons for choosing a profession, such as helping the world, being good at something, being interested in something, wanting to travel, or following in the footsteps of someone you respect.

D Learn: Value Judgements

- Read the *Learn* box together.
- Focus on the word *opinion*. Point out that a value judgment is an opinion, not a fact, so you and your neighbor may make different value judgments about the exact same situation.

Read the paragraphs. Choose a value judgment.

- Read each paragraph with the group. Have them discuss the options and why each answer might be correct.

ANSWERS
Answers will vary depending on students' opinions.

DIFFERENTIATION

Below level:

- Break down each situation. Ask *What was the person's problem? What did they have to decide?*
- Ask *What decision did they make? What did they do?*
- Ask *Why did they make that decision?*

At level:

- Have students discuss the pros and cons of each decision.
- Kelly taking Steve's paint: pro (she finished her painting and didn't have to wait until the next day); con (she borrowed something without asking).
- George waiting for the green light: pros (it's safer; the little boy will learn that it's good to wait for the green light before crossing the street); cons (he's late for class).
- Do students agree with the decisions that Kelly and George made?

Above level:

- Challenge students to come up with a third scenario.
- Tell them that there shouldn't be an obvious solution to the person's problem; the decision should be a hard one with at least one pro and one con for each possible action.
- Encourage them to use the examples of Kelly and George for ideas, or to come up with their own ideas.
- Share their scenarios with the class, and have students make value judgments.

E Words in Context: Scan the story on pages 78–79 and circle these words. As you read, guess what the words mean.

- Have students scan the story and circle the words.
- Ask if they notice anything familiar about the words, e.g. *speechless* has the base word *speech*, so students may predict that the word has something to do with talking.

F Why do people go to art galleries? Tell your partner the reasons you think of.

COMMUNICATION

- Have students work in pairs to answer the question.

Reading Preview

- Read the title of the unit's reading text.
- Have students silently read the content of the preview bar.
- Ask *What type of text is it?* Ask *What does this type of text do?*
- Remind students to make value judgments as they read.

Further Practice
Workbook pages 67–68
Online practice Unit 8 · Get Ready
Oxford **iTools** Unit 8 · Get Ready

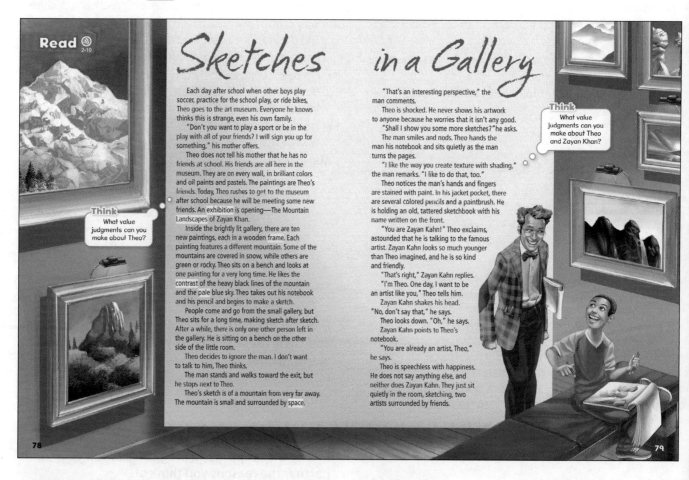

Summary

Objectives: To read, understand, and discuss a fictional text; to apply a reading strategy to improve comprehension.

School subject: Art

Text type: Realistic fiction

Reading strategy: Making value judgments

Big Question learning points: *Other people can enjoy art we make. Art shows what a person is interested in.*

Materials: Talk About It! Poster, Audio CD

Before Reading

- Ask *How do most kids your age like to spend their free time?*
- Tell students that in this story, a boy named Theo spends his time differently from most of the kids his age.

During Reading 💿 2·10

- Ask a gist question to check overall understanding of the text, e.g. *Who does Theo meet in the museum?*
- Give students a few minutes to skim the text before answering.
- Remind students that they will be making value judgments as they read the story.
- Play the audio. Students listen as they read along.
- Stop at each *Think* box for students to discuss the questions.

Below level:

- Have students read in mixed-ability pairs.
- Have the more confident student help the less confident student with pronunciation and comprehension.
- Tell students to pause after every few sentences to discuss the meaning of what they have read so far.

At level:

- Have small groups read the story together, taking turns around a circle.
- Assign a secretary in each group to take notes. Tell the groups to pause at each *Think* box and answer the questions; the secretary writes the group's answers.
- Remind students that when you make a judgment, you use your opinion. For that reason, students may make different judgments, and that's okay.
- Have the class reconvene to share their answers to the *Think* boxes.

Above level:

- Have students read the story on their own, jotting down any phrases or sentences they do not understand.
- Put students with partners to work through anything they jotted down. If they need additional help with comprehension, have them ask you specific questions for clarification.
- As students discuss the questions in the *Think* boxes, tell them to think about the problems that the characters have and the decisions they have to make. Have them discuss the pros and cons of each.

Discussion questions:

- *Do you think Theo will tell his mother about meeting Zayan Khan?*
- *In the third paragraph, Theo rushes to the museum to meet some new friends. … I thought he didn't have any friends.*
- *How can paintings be better friends than people?*
- *How would you treat Theo if he was your brother?*
- *What did everyone think was strange about Theo? Do you agree? Why or why not?*
- *How did Theo change by the end of the story? What did he learn?*
- *What did Zayan Khan say that made Theo so happy? Why do you think this made Theo so happy?*
- *Do you think Theo and Zayan Khan will become friends?*

COLLABORATIVE LEARNING

- Have groups of three work together to role-play the story. Students play the mother, Theo, and Zayan Khan.
- Tell them to write a simple script with dialogue from the story, then practice reading the script and acting out what happens.
- Students can take turns performing for the class.

After Reading

- Return to the *Learn* box on page 77. Have students reread the Value Judgment text.
- Have small groups work together to answer those questions about Theo and Zayan Khan. Within each group of four students, two focus on Theo and two focus on Zayan Khan.
- The group discuss what they've decided.

COLLABORATIVE LEARNING

- Display the **Talk About It! Poster** to help students with sentence frames for discussion and expressing personal opinions.
- Put students into pairs to discuss the characters from the story.
- Have students say one thing about every character in the reading.

CULTURE NOTE

Landscape art is the depiction of natural scenery, such as mountains, rivers, and forests. Often weather is an important element in the painting.

Landscape art comes from two distinct traditions. Chinese ink painting, which goes back thousands of years, often shows spectacular scenery of mountains and waterfalls.

In the Western tradition, the first landscape art was found in frescoes (wall paintings) in Greece, thought to be painted around 2,500 years ago.

In ancient Rome, landscape frescoes were also popular and wealthy people often had them put inside their homes, covering one or more walls.

Further Practice
Workbook page 69
Online practice Unit 8 • Read
Oxford **iTools** Unit 8 • Read

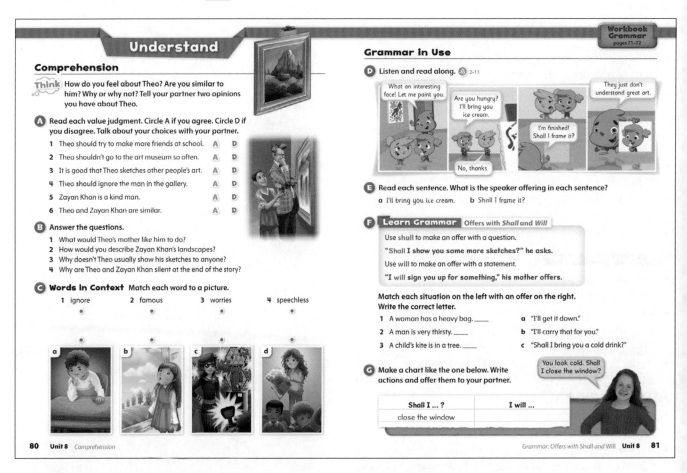

Summary

Objectives: To demonstrate understanding of a fictional text; to understand the meaning and form of the grammar structure.

Reading: Comprehension

Grammar input: Offers with *shall* and *will*

Grammar practice: Workbook exercises

Grammar production: Making offers to others

Materials: Audio CD

Comprehension

Think

• Tell students to write their answers to each question separately and then compare answers with their partners.

• Discuss with the class: *Did partners have similar answers? What do your answers say about your own personality?*

A Read each value judgment. Circle A if you agree. Circle D if you disagree. Talk about your choices with your partner.

• First go over each sentence to make sure students understand the language. Then have students complete the exercise on their own.

• As you discuss each sentence and students' opinions, be sure to reinforce that making judgments requires students to form opinions. There is no right or wrong opinion, so for this exercise there are no right or wrong answers.

B Answer the questions.

• Have students answer the questions and then discuss them with the class.

1 She would like him to make friends by playing a sport or being in a play with other kids his own age.
2 They are mountain landscapes with contrast between thick outlines and pale colors.
3 He worries his artwork isn't very good.
4 Possible answer: They are both happy and don't need to say anything.

DIFFERENTIATION

Below level:

• Review the reading together to complete A.

• Have them scan the text to find supporting details for each statement, e.g.
  1 *How do you know Theo doesn't have friends at school?*
  2 *How do you know Theo goes to museums often?*
  3 *When does Theo sketch other people's art?*
  4 *Does Theo ignore the man in the museum?*
  5 *How does Zayan Khan treat Theo? What does he say?*
  6 *How are they similar and different?*

At level:

• Have students work with partners to discuss the pros and cons of agreeing and disagreeing with each statement. Students' answers will vary, e.g.
  1 *Pro*: School is more fun if you have friends. *Con*: If he is happy the way he is, he shouldn't have to change.

2 *Pro*: He should get exercise and play with kids his own age. *Con*: Going to the museum makes him happy and helps him improve his own artwork.

3 *Pro*: Sketching other artists' work helps you learn. *Con*: Artists should use their own ideas.

4 *Pro*: Children should not talk to strangers. *Con*: People often start conversations about the artwork they are viewing in galleries.

5 *Pro*: He seems kind. *Con*: Children should always be wary of strangers.

6 *Pros*: They are both artists; they both like to create texture with shading; they both enjoy sitting quietly and sketching artwork. *Cons*: One is an adult and one is a child; one is a famous artist and one is a student.

Above level:

- After students complete A and B, have them work in small groups to predict what will happen next, e.g. maybe Theo and Zayan Khan will become friends and Khan will teach Theo how to be a better painter, or maybe Theo will decide to join the art club at school and make some friends his own age.
- Have the groups make judgments about their predictions, e.g. *Why would it be good if that happened? Why would it be bad?*
- Have groups share their predictions with the class, and invite the class to make judgments about each one.

C Words in Context: Match each word to a picture.

- Return to the reading text and have a volunteer read each word in the context of its sentence.
- Invite students to suggest possible definitions for each one, e.g. *ignore, famous, worries, speechless.*
- Check answers with the class.

ANSWERS
1 d 2 c 3 a 4 b

CRITICAL THINKING

- Making value judgments requires us to choose the right thing to do in a given situation. A decision is difficult when the choice is not "black or white," but somewhere in between, or "gray."
- Challenge students to think of times in their own lives when they have had to make difficult decisions. Tell them to consider what factors made the decision complicated, and to discuss how they finally chose what to do.

Grammar in Use

D Listen and read along. ⊙ 2·11

- Play the audio and ask students to quietly read along.
- Have two confident students read it aloud for the class.
- Play the audio again and have volunteers use it as a model for rhythm and intonation as they repeat the dialogue.

E Read each sentence. What is the speaker offering in each sentence?

- Write *I'll bring you ice cream* on the board.
- Explain that the speaker is offering to bring her some ice cream. Note that this isn't a question that requires a response, although it is polite to respond by saying something like, *Thank you* or *OK thanks* or *That's nice of you to offer, but no thanks.*

- Write *Shall I frame it?* on the board.
- Explain the speaker is making an offer, but this time the offer is a question that requires a response, e.g. *Yes, please do* or *No, thank you.*

F Learn Grammar: Offers with *Shall* and *Will*

- Read the *Learn Grammar* box together.
- Go around the room and have students make offers to their partners. Each time, the student decides to use *shall* or *will*, and the partner has to decide an appropriate response.

Match a situation on the left with an offer on the right. Write the correct letter.

- If necessary, discuss the scenarios in more detail, e.g. *You see an older woman. She is holding a heavy shopping bag. What might you offer?*
- Check answers with the class.

ANSWERS
1 b 2 c 3 a

G Make a chart like the one below. Write actions and offer them to your partner.

- Have students complete the chart in small groups.

COLLABORATIVE LEARNING

- Divide the class into small groups.
- Have them use the ideas from their chart to practice conversations. For each conversation, they should set the scene (*You look cold*), make the offer (*Shall I close the window?*), and respond (*Yes, please. Thanks for offering.*)

Further Practice
Workbook pages 70–72
Online practice Unit 8 • Understand
Oxford **iTools** Unit 8 • Understand

Unit 8 Communicate (page 82)

Communicate

Listening

Think In nature, where can you see many colors mixed together?

A Compare Impressionist and traditional paintings. Listen and check (✓). 2·12

	Outdoors	Indoors	More detail	Less detail	Side by side colors	Mixed colors
Impressionist Paintings						
Traditional Paintings						

B Listen again. Answer the questions. 2·13

1 Where is the Marmottan Monet Museum located?
_____

2 How many works of art by Claude Monet does the museum have?
_____

3 When was *Impression: Sunrise* painted?
_____

Speaking 2·14

C Learn Expressing a Desire or Wish

The verb wish can be used to talk about something you want to *do, be,* or *have,* but cannot at this time.

I wish I could paint like Claude Monet.
I wish I were a famous painter.
I wish I had more time to paint.

Do you have a wish? Talk to your partner about it.

I wish I could go to Berlin.

Why do you want ... ?

I want to ...

That sounds fun. I wish I ...

82 **Unit 8** *Listening: Differences and Details • Speaking: Expressing a Desire or Wish*

Word Study

D Learn Synonyms

Remember, synonyms are words that have similar meanings.

They are on every wall in brilliant colors.
They are on every wall in bright colors.

Listen and read the words. Then match the sentences with synonyms. 2·15

beautiful gifted drab pretty talented dreary

1 Manuela thought the painting was *beautiful.*   •   • a Everyone agreed that it was very *dreary.*

2 The sky outside looked *drab* and gray.   •   • b Many of her teachers felt that she was very *gifted.*

3 Damla was a *talented* art student. •   • c Her son thought it was *pretty,* too.

Writing Study

E Learn The Articles *A, An,* and *The*

Use *a* or *an* before a noun if the noun is one of many.
Use *the* before a noun if the noun names one special, or specific, thing.

Theo went to see an exhibition.
(There are many exhibitions. Theo went to see one of them.)

Theo went to see the exhibition of Zayan Khan's landscapes.
(This exhibition is special because it is Zayan Khan's exhibition.)

Read the sentences. Circle the correct article.

1 A / The *Mona Lisa* is Leonardo da Vinci's most famous work of art.
2 I saw a / the sculpture at the Chinese sculpture exhibition yesterday.
3 An / The art of Vincent van Gogh is different from any other art I've seen.
4 I went to an / the art gallery in Paris when I was there.

Write Now practice writing in the **Workbook.** page 74

Vocabulary: Synonyms • Writing: The Articles A, An, and The **Unit 8** **83**

Summary

Objectives: To learn and practice listening, speaking, and writing strategies to facilitate effective communication.

Vocabulary: *beautiful, gifted, drab, pretty, talented, dreary*

Listening strategy: Listening for differences and details

Speaking: Expressing a desire or wish

Word Study: Synonyms

Writing Study: The articles *a, an,* and *the*

Big Question learning points: *We make art to create something new. Art shows what a person is interested in.*

Materials: Audio CD

Listening

Think

- Tell students to close their eyes and picture each of the following: a forest, an ocean, a lake, a river, a desert, a field, an icy tundra. For each scene, can they "see" any colors mixed together?

A Compare Impressionaist and traditional paintings. Listen and check. 🔊 2·12

- Direct students to the chart and read through the different categories so they know what they are listening for.
- Play the audio once through while students just listen.
- Play it a second time and have them complete the chart.

ANSWERS

Impressionist Paintings: Outdoors, Less detail, and Side by side colors.

Traditional Paintings: Indoors, More detail, and Mixed colors.

DIFFERENTIATION

Below level:

- Before playing the audio, read the words on the chart. Clarify meaning: *Impressionist* and *Traditional* refer to styles of painting. *Outdoors* and *Indoors* refer to places. *More detail* and *Less detail* refer to how much is in the painting. *Side by side colors* and *Mixed colors* refer to the technique the artist uses to add color to the page.
- When you play the audio, pause as each section on the chart is addressed so students can process what they've heard.
- Allow them time to add a check mark to the chart before moving on.

At level:

- Ask questions about the audio:
  1 *What are the three reasons Impressionism is important?*
  2 *Why did Monet like to paint outdoors?*
  3 *What do you have to do to see details in his paintings?*

Above level:

- Have students work in pairs to write interviews with Monet. Tell them to imagine an art student is interviewing the famous painter.

B Listen again. Answer the questions. 🔊 2·13

- Have students complete the exercise on their own.
- Check the answers with the class.

1 Paris   2 300   3 1872

Speaking 🔊 2·14

C Learn: Expressing a Desire or Wish

COMMUNICATION

- Read the *Learn* box together.
- Write the sample sentences on the board and underline *could*, *were*, and *had*. Explain that these are the verb forms that usually follow *I wish*.
- Play the audio while students follow along in their books.
- Play it again and have students echo read to mimic the intonation and pronunciation.
- Put students into pairs and tell them to practice the dialogue, taking turns speaking the different roles.

Do you have a wish? Talk to your partner about it.

- Have students follow the model to talk about their own wishes.
- Encourage them to follow up with a *Why* question, like the model's *Why do you want to go there?*

CRITICAL THINKING

- Expand on this opportunity for personalization. Go through the previous units in the Student Book and have students tell a wish that relates to the content of each unit.
- Tell students to use key vocabulary from the units, and to consider the Big Questions. Give them a few minutes to work on their own, then have them fine-tune their ideas with partners. Partners work together to create new conversations following the model on page 82. Have the partners perform the dialogues for the class.

Word Study

D Learn: Synonyms

- Have a confident student read the *Learn* box to the class.
- Ask students if they can think of any other synonyms for *bright* and *brilliant*, e.g. *clear*.
- Ask students why it is important to know and use synonyms. Explain that it makes language more interesting not to always use the same word, especially in writing.

Listen and read the words. Then match the sentences with synonyms. 🔊 2·15

- Play the audio and have students point to the words as they hear them.
- Ask students if they can identify any of the synonyms in the word box.
- Have students complete the exercise on their own.
- Encourage them to use the context of the sentences to help them determine which words are synonyms.

ANSWERS
1 c   2 a   3 b

COLLABORATIVE LEARNING

- Have partners work together to find other words in Units 7 and 8 that have simple synonyms.
- For each word, they write two sentences following the format of D: one uses the original word and one uses the synonym.
- Partners create a new exercise like the matching one in D.
- Each pair of students trades papers with another pair, and they do each other's exercise

Writing Study

E Learn: The Articles *A*, *An* and *The*

- Read the *Learn* box together.
- Give a few more examples using familiar subjects, such as students in the class or landmarks in your town.

Read the sentences. Circle the correct article.

- Have students complete the exercise on their own.
- Check answers with the class.

ANSWERS
1 The   2 a   3 The   4 an

Write

- Direct students to the Workbook for further practice.

| **Further Practice** |
| Workbook pages 73–74 |
| Online practice Unit 8 · Communicate |
| Oxford **iTools** Unit 8 · Communicate |

Units 7 and 8 Wrap Up page 84

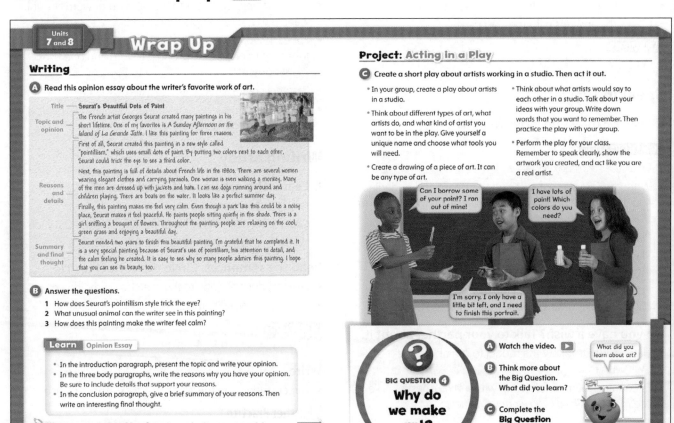

Summary

Objectives: To show what students have learned about the language and learning points of Units 7 and 8.

Reading: Comprehension of an opinion essay

Project: Act in a play

Writing: Write an opinion essay

Speaking: Talk about the plays

Materials: Big Question DVD, Discover Poster 4, Talk About It! Poster, Big Question Chart

Writing

A Read this opinion essay about the writer's favorite work of art.

- Remind students that people have different opinions, and there are no right or wrong opinions.
- Read the sample essay together. Tell students to think about the writer's opinions as they read.

B Answer the questions.

- Have students find the answers in the text.
- Check answers with the class.

ANSWERS

1 By placing two colors next to each other, Seurat could trick the eye to see a third color.
2 a monkey
3 The painting shows people relaxing in a peaceful park, and this makes the writer feel calm.

Below level:

- Have students answer the comprehension questions in pairs.
- Point out the different features of the text.
- Have students underline the opinions in the essay.

At level:

- Put students into pairs. Ask each pair to write another two comprehension questions for the text.
- Have pairs swap questions and answer each other's questions.
- Pairs correct each other's answers.

Above level:

- Have students individually write three more comprehension questions for the text.
- Have students swap questions with another student and answer each other's questions.
- Students correct each other's answers.

Learn: Opinion Essay

- Read the directions in the *Learn* box together.
- Explain that students should follow these guidelines when they plan and write their essays.
- Remind them to refer to the sample as a model.

Write

- Direct students to the Workbook to plan and write their own opinion essay.

- Have students go back to the model to see how the author addressed each requirement.

Ask the following:

- What is the author's topic and opinion?
- What reasons does the author give?
- Does the author summarize the main reasons and add an interesting final thought in the conclusion?

Project

C Create a short play about artists working in a studio. Then act it out.

CREATIVITY

- Read the directions together.
- Encourage students to consider the artists from the reading "Art Through New Eyes" as well as those studied in Unit 8 for ideas.
- Review the sample speech bubbles as examples of the language students may use in their plays.
- Tell students to try to add a problem to the story that requires the characters to make a decision.
- Have groups brainstorm some possible problems that artists in a studio might have, such as running out of materials, sharing a work space, stealing an idea, playing the music too loud, or having trouble coming up with inspiration.
- Tell students to think about how the characters will solve the problem.
- Encourage them to think about the value judgments they can make. Why does the character do what he / she does? Does the character do the "right thing"?

Units 7 and 8 Big Question Review

A Watch the video. ▷

- Play the video and when it is finished ask students what they know about art now.
- Have students share ideas with the class.

B Think more about the Big Question. What did you learn?

COMMUNICATION

- Display **Discover Poster 4**. Point to familiar vocabulary items and elicit them from the class. Ask *What is this?*
- Ask students *What do you see?* Ask *What does that mean?*
- Refer to all of the learning points written on the poster and have students explain how they relate to the different pictures.
- Ask *What does this learning point mean?* Elicit answers from individual students.
- Display the **Talk About It! Poster** to help students with sentence frames for discussion of the learning points and for expressing their opinions.

C Complete the Big Question Chart.

COLLABORATIVE LEARNING

- Ask students what they have learned about art while studying this unit.
- Put students into pairs or small groups to say two new things they have learned.
- Have students share their ideas with the class and add their ideas to the chart.
- Have students complete the chart in their Workbook.

Further Practice
Workbook page 75–77
Online practice • Wrap Up 4
Oxford **iTools** • Wrap Up 4

In units 9 and 10 you will:

WATCH a video about cities in different places.

LEARN about the many features of a city.

READ about Jakarta and a very young mayor.

WRITE a persuasive essay.

CREATE a travel brochure.

BIG QUESTION 5

What is a city?

A Watch the video.

B Look at the picture and talk about it.
1 What do you see in the picture?
2 How is the city similar to and different from where you live?

C Think and answer the questions.
1 What can you do in a city?
2 How are cities different than places that are not cities?

D Fill out the **Big Question Chart**.

What do you know about cities? What do you want to know?

86   Big Question 5

87

Reading Strategies
Students will practice:
- Paraphrasing
- Understanding characters

Vocabulary
Students will understand and use words about:
- The world around us, and life in a city

Grammar
Students will understand and use:
- Negative indefinite pronouns
- Tag questions

Review
Students will review the language and Big Question learning points of Units 9 and 10 through:
- A persuasive essay
- A project (creating a travel brochure)

Units 9 and 10
What is a city?
Students will understand the Big Question learning points:
- Many people live and work in a city.
- A city has businesses and shopping.
- Cities are full of history and culture.
- There are many kinds of transportation in a city.
- A city is often near water.

Listening Strategies
Students will practice:
- Listening for reasons
- Listening for facts and opinions

Writing
Students will be able to use:
- Capital letters for proper nouns
- Coordinating conjunctions *and, but, or*

Students will produce texts that:
- Persuade

Word Study
Students will understand, pronounce, and use:
- Words with *soft c* and *hard c*
- Phrasal verbs using *take*

Speaking
Students will understand and use expressions to:
- Give reasons
- Ask and answer questions with *have to*

Units 9 and 10 Big Question page 86

Summary

Objectives: To activate students' existing knowledge of the topic and identify what they would like to learn about the topic.

Materials: Big Question DVD, Discover Poster 5, Big Question Chart

Introducing the topic

- Read out the Big Question. Ask *What is a city?* Write students' ideas on the board and discuss.

A Watch the video.

- Play the video and when it is finished ask students to answer the following questions in pairs:
  What do you see in the video?
  Who do you think the people are?
  What is happening?
  Do you like it?
- Have individual students share their answers with the class.

DIFFERENTIATION

Below level:

- Pause the video periodically. Point and ask *What's this? Who is this? What's she doing? Where are they?*
- Ask students to answer using complete sentences.

At level:

- After watching, have students write down five things that they saw in the video.
- Elicit the phrases from the class and write them on the board.
- If possible, categorize the things students remember (e.g. objects, colors, people, etc.) and ask them to help you add more to each category.

Above level:

- After watching, have students write down three sentences about what they saw in the video.
- Tell students to choose one sentence.
- Then have students stand up and mingle and find someone else with the same sentence (focus on the meaning of the sentence rather than using exactly the same words).
- Have students say their sentence to the class.

B Look at the picture and talk about it.

- Students look at the big picture and talk about what they see.
- Then students discuss how the "city" in the picture is similar to or different from the city where they live.
- Ask additional questions:
  Is this a real city? Why or why not?
  What would you want to do if you were in this city? What looks interesting?
  Would you want to live in this city? Why or why not?

C Think and answer the questions.

- If your school is not in a city, invite students to share any prior experiences they have visiting cities.

- If your school is in a city, ask students to name some of the things they like and don't like about being in an urban environment.

CRITICAL THINKING

- Ask students to discuss the questions in small groups.
- Encourage groups to think about special activities, like visiting museums or attending live theater, and more everyday activities, like taking a subway / metro or riding an elevator in a skyscraper.
- It may help to show a few pictures of cities, rural areas, and suburbs to spark the discussion.

Expanding the topic

COLLABORATIVE LEARNING

- Display **Discover Poster 5** and give students enough time to look at the pictures.
- Elicit some of the words you think they will know by pointing to different things in the pictures and saying *What's this?*
- Put students into small groups of three or four. Have each group choose a picture that they find interesting.
- Ask each group to say five things that they can see in their picture.
- Have one person from each group stand up and read out the words they chose for their picture.
- Ask the class if they can add any more.
- Repeat until every group has spoken.

D Fill out the Big Question Chart.

- Display the **Big Question Chart**.
- Ask the class *What do you know about cities?*
- Ask students to write what they know and what they want to know in their Workbooks.
- Write a collection of ideas on the **Big Question Chart**.

DIFFERENTIATION

Below level:

- Encourage students to participate using simple phrases or short sentences.
- Point to details in the big picture and on the poster and ask *What is this?* Write the answers on the board.

At level:

- Elicit complete sentences about what students know about cities.
- Write their sentences on the board.

Above level:

- Elicit more detailed responses.
- Challenge students to write their own sentences on the board.

Discover Poster 5

1 A man leaving his house to go to work; 2 A popular, busy shopping district in Shanghai, China; 3 The Parthenon in Athens, Greece; 4 Forms of transportation in Kuala Lumpur, Malaysia; 5 Wasserburg am Inn, Germany: a city surrounded by water

| **Further Practice**
| **Workbook page 78**
| **Online practice • Big Question 5**
| **Oxford iTools • Big Question 5**

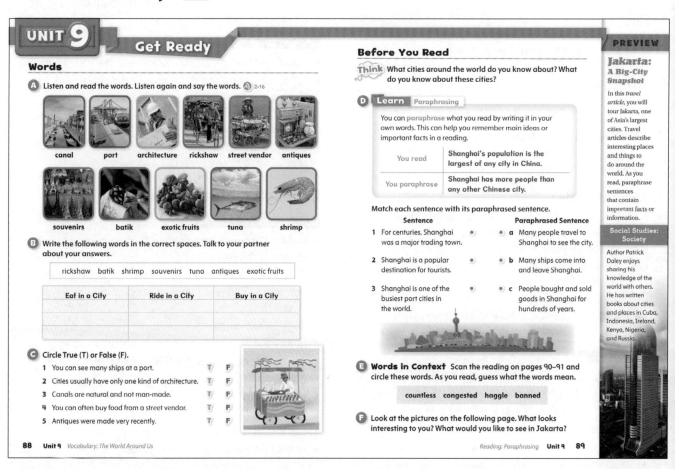

Summary

Objectives: To understand words about cities; to apply own experience and a reading strategy to help comprehension of a text.

Vocabulary: *canal, port, architecture, rickshaw, street vendor, antiques, souvenirs, batik, exotic fruits, tuna, shrimp, countless, congested, haggle, banned*

Reading strategy: Paraphrasing

Materials: Audio CD

Words

A Listen and read the words. Listen again and say the words. 🔊 2·16

- Play the audio. Ask students to point to the words as they hear them.
- Play the audio a second time and have students repeat the words when they hear them.
- Point out the words with origins from non-English-speaking countries: *batik* / Indonesia, *souvenir* / French. *Batik* refers to the craft of using wax while dying cloth to make designs. *Souvenir* in French means *to remember*; we buy souvenirs on trips to remember what we did and saw.
- Say the words out of order and have students race to point to them on the page.

CRITICAL THINKING

Ask the following questions to check understanding:

- Which items would you buy from a street vendor for souvenirs to bring home after a trip?
- Where could you travel in a rickshaw?
- Think about Units 3 and 4 and how we know what happened long ago. What could you look at to learn about the buildings people lived in long ago?
- Put the food words in order from most favorite to least favorite.

DIFFERENTIATION

Below level:

- Have students look up the words in the dictionary pages at the back of the Student Book.
- Tell students to close their books.
- Say a definition for one of the words and have students call out the word together.

At level:

- Tell students to write a sentence for each word.
- Encourage them to make unique sentences that hint at the words' meanings. (*The boat moved through the canal.*)

Above level:

- Tell students to try to write sentences using more than one vocabulary word. (*I bought a batik shirt from a street vendor.*)
- Have them search previous units for words that can be used in sentences with the Unit 9 words, e.g. *I love exotic fruits from faraway cities, but I prefer eating local fruits from the farmers' market. The archaeologist found a treasure when he bought the antique lamp from the street vendor.*

B Write the following words in the correct spaces. Talk to your partner about your answers.

- Have students complete the chart and then compare answers with a partner.

Eat in a city: shrimp, tuna, exotic fruits
Ride in a city: rickshaw
Buy in a city: batik, souvenirs, antiques

COLLABORATIVE LEARNING

- Have small groups work together to add other words to the chart.
- Encourage them to look back at the Poster, and the picture on page 86, and to think about what they saw in the video.

C Circle True (T) or False (F).

- Have students work independently to complete the exercise.
- Then review the answers with the class and discuss what makes each statement true or false.

ANSWERS
1 T   2 F   3 F   4 T   5 F

Before You Read

Think

- Tell students about a city that you know. If possible, talk about a city that is far away and different from the city where students live.
- Talk about the food, some of the famous sites, the modes of transportation, the culture, the architecture, the geography, and anything else that makes the city unique.
- Tell students to follow your model and talk about cities they know about.

D Learn: Paraphrasing

- Read the Learn box together.
- Explain that when you say or write something "in your own words," you keep the same meaning, but you say it differently.
- Have students read the two example sentences and discuss how they are different (the first sentence uses the word population instead of people).

Match each sentence with its paraphrased sentence.

- Read the first sentence together. Break down the sentence for students.
- Tell them to read the choices and choose the best one.
- Point out how the author kept the same verb tense, used some different words, changed the subject from Shanghai to People, and kept the main idea.
- Have students complete the exercise on their own and then compare their work with a partner.
- Check the answers with the class.

ANSWERS
1 c   2 a   3 b

E Words in Context: Scan the reading on pages 90–91 and circle these words. As you read, guess what the words mean.

- Read each word and have students follow your pronunciation.
- Point out the suffix -less in countless. Explain that the suffix -less means without. Tell students to predict what the word might mean based on that clue.
- Point out the -ed ending in congested and banned. Students likely know this ending creates the past tense.
- Explain that this ending can sometimes be used to form an adjective.
- Tell students to decide as they read if these words are used as adjectives or verbs in the reading text.

F Look at the pictures on the following page. What looks interesting to you? What would you like to see in Jakarta?

COMMUNICATION

- Students look at the pictures and discuss them with their classmates.

Reading Preview

- Read the title of the unit's reading text.
- Discuss the meaning of the word snapshot with students.
- Have students silently read the content of the preview bar.
- Ask What type of text is it? Ask What does this type of text do?

Author Biography

- Ask students to read the short bio of Patrick Daley and discuss anything they know about the countries he has written about (Cuba, Indonesia, Ireland, Kenya, Nigeria, and Russia).

Further Practice
Workbook pages 78–79
Online practice Unit 9 • Get Ready
Oxford iTools Unit 9 • Get Ready

Summary

Objectives: To read, understand, and discuss a nonfiction text; to apply a reading strategy to improve comprehension.

School subject: Social Studies: Society

Text type: Travel article (nonfiction)

Reading strategy: Paraphrasing

Big Question learning points: *Many people live and work in a city. A city has businesses and shopping. Cities are full of history and culture. There are many kinds of transportation in a city*

Materials: Talk About It! Poster, Audio CD

Before Reading

- Locate Jakarta on a map. Jakarta is the capital of Indonesia. The country of Indonesia is made up of several islands.

- Ask *What do you notice about Jakarta's location?* (It's on the northwest coast of Java, one of the islands that make up Indonesia.) *What does it usually mean when a city is on the water? Think about food, transportation, and things to see and do.*

During Reading 2·17

- Ask *What are the three main sections of the text? Why do you think the author organizes the text into these three parts?*

- Give students a few minutes to skim the text before answering.

- Remind students that they are going to try to paraphrase as they read.

- Play the audio. Students listen as they read along.

- Play the audio a second time if necessary.

- Note additional information on the "Top 3 Things To Do in Jakarta."

- Help students with definitions of some of the words: *curry* is a spicy dish common in Southeast Asia; *people-watch* means to informally watch interesting people doing what they do; *Monas* is a 433 foot (132 meter) tall obelisk tower in the center of Jakarta.

DIFFERENTIATION

Below level:

- Read with small groups.

- Pause after each paragraph to ask a question, e.g. after the first paragraph, ask *Is Jakarta big or small?*

- Have students identify details in the paragraph to support their answers.

At level:

- Have students read with partners, alternating sections.

- Partner A reads the introduction and Partner B just listens. Then Partner B reads "A Visit to the Old City" and Partner A just listens, and so on.

- At the end of each section, have partners discuss what they read. If there were any sentences that didn't make sense to them, have them try to figure out the meaning together.
- Have each partner choose a different sentence to paraphrase at each *Think* box.

Above level:
- Have students read the text independently and mark any sentences they don't understand.
- Partners work through any sentences they don't understand together. Assist as needed.
- After they paraphrase a sentence for each *Think* box, challenge students to paraphrase an entire paragraph.
- Have them read aloud their paraphrased paragraphs to the class. For each one, tell the class to try to find the original paragraph in the reading text.

COLLABORATIVE LEARNING
- Have small groups work together to list the interesting things to see and do that are mentioned in the article.
- Ask students to go through the article paragraph by paragraph to identify each site and interesting activity.
- The "secretary" records the group's ideas and the "monitor" facilitates by calling on students and making sure everyone contributes.
- Their lists should include: *buying chicken curry from a street vendor, people-watching in the Golden Triangle shopping district, visiting the canals and classical architecture in Kota,* etc.
- Groups assign one student to each item (so students will have two or three each, depending on the size of the group).
- Each student adds a detail to each of his / her items. Encourage them to paraphrase from the article, e.g. the student who has *hire a bajaj to take you around* might add *These are new motorized rickshaws.*
- Finally, the groups present their lists to the class, each taking turns sharing their work.

CRITICAL THINKING

Discussion questions:
- *What does the author think makes Jakarta polluted?*
- *The government banned old-fashioned rickshaws, and they were replaced with bajajs. Why did they ban rickshaws?*
- *Why is the port of Sunda Kelapa located in the northern part of the city? Why would the "original Dutch city" be found near the port?*
- *Would you rather watch people haggling over the price of shrimp or shopping in the fancy Golden Triangle district? Why?*
- *Which area of the city probably has the most skyscrapers?*
- *If you like shopping, where would you go?*

After Reading
- Have students share the different sentences they paraphrased as they read.
- Discuss each sentence in terms of verb tense, key vocabulary, sentence structure, and overall meaning.

COLLABORATIVE LEARNING
- Display the **Talk About It! Poster** to help students with sentence frames for discussion and expressing personal opinions.
- Put students into pairs to discuss which area in the text they would like to visit.
- Have students talk about how each place is similar to and different from their own city or a city they know.

CULTURE NOTE

When a customer and a merchant "haggle" over the cost of something, they negotiate back and forth on the price and terms of the sale.

Haggling is less common in everyday transactions in North America and Europe; it can be more common for large transactions like purchasing a car or a house, or in informal settings like open-air markets.

In Indonesia and other places in Asia, it is more common everywhere, from outdoor markets to department stores, and even hotels.

❚ Further Practice
Workbook page 80
Online practice Unit 9 • Read
Oxford **iTools** Unit 9 • Read

Unit 9 Understand page 92

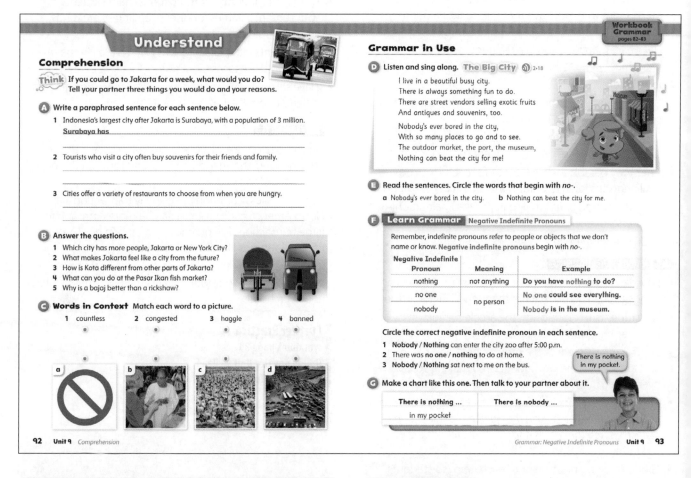

Summary

Objectives: To demonstrate understanding of a nonfiction text; to understand the meaning and form of the grammar structure.

Reading: Comprehension

Grammar input: Negative indefinite pronouns

Grammar practice: Workbook exercises

Grammar production: Speaking

Materials: Audio CD

Comprehension

Think

- As students discuss, tell them to make sure their partner gives specific reasons for their choices.
- For additional discussion practice, partners can rank the activities in order from "must-see" to "only if there's time."

A Write a paraphrased sentence for each sentence below.

- Complete the first example together.
- Remember to focus on verb tense, vocabulary, sentence structure, and meaning.
- Point out that the paraphrase has been started.
- Work through the sentences together. There are several ways to paraphrase each sentence, so encourage alternate ideas.

POSSIBLE ANSWERS

1 Surabaya has 3 million people, making it the second largest city in Indonesia.
2 Buying souvenirs is a popular tourist activity.
3 There are lots of different restaurants in cities.

B Answer the questions.

- For each question, tell students to look back at the reading text and find details to support their answer.

ANSWERS

1 Jakarta
2 There are countless skyscrapers.
3 Kota has old canals and classical architecture, but the rest of the city is modern with skyscrapers.
4 You can inspect strange and exotic fish and watch people haggle.
5 It's faster so it doesn't hold up traffic.

CRITICAL THINKING

Ask follow-up questions:

- Nairobi, Kenya is 269 square miles (696 square kilometers) with a population of a little over 3 million people. How does Nairobi compare with Jakarta?
- Do you prefer a futuristic city, or a more traditional and old-fashioned one?
- Why do you think there are old canals in Kota?
- Think about the Big Question for Module 3: *Where does our food come from?* What new information have you learned about this topic?
- A bajaj is better than a rickshaw because it's faster, but why is a bajaj worse than a rickshaw?

C Words in Context: Match each word to a picture.

- Have students go back and find the words in the reading text.
- Tell them to use the context clues to guess at the meaning of each word.
- Revisit their predictions about the word *countless*. How many students guessed correctly at the meaning?
- Discuss the participles *congested* and *banned*. Ask *Were these words used as verbs or adjectives in the reading text?* (adjectives). *Can you find any other participles used as adjectives?* (polluted, packed, motorized).
- Check the answers with the class.

ANSWERS
1 c   2 d   3 b   4 a

Grammar in Use

D Listen and sing along. 🔊 2·18

- Listen to the song once and then sing it together.
- Ask *What does the singer think about her city?*
- Explain that the phrase *nothing can beat* or *nothing beats* means *nothing is better than*.

E Read the sentences. Circle the words that begin with *no-*.

- Have students read the sentences and circle the correct words. Check answers as a class.
- Tell students to sing the song again. Can they find the words in the song that begin with *no-*?
- Ask students to try to paraphrase the sentences with *nobody* and *nothing*. Help them use the context to figure out the meaning.

F Learn Grammar: Negative Indefinite Pronouns

- Read the *Learn Grammar* box together. Talk about the examples.
- Direct students to the third example sentence. Ask if the subject *Nobody* takes a singular or plural verb.

Circle the correct negative indefinite pronoun in each sentence.

- Read the first sentence together. Read it first using *Nobody* and then using *Nothing*. Ask which one makes sense.
- Repeat for the other items.
- Check the answers with the class.

ANSWERS
1 Nobody   2 nothing   3 Nobody

COLLABORATIVE LEARNING
- Put students into pairs.
- Have each pair work together to create three or four more sentences using the target structure.
- Put pairs together to share their sentences and correct each other's if necessary.
- Elicit some sentences from the class.

G Make a chart like this one. Then talk to your partner about it.

- Students can share charts with partners, and then reconvene to go over them with the whole class.

DIFFERENTIATION

Below level:
- Review the Indefinite Pronouns from Unit 7, page 73: *someone, something, anyone, anything*.
- Brainstorm possible answers with the class and write the ideas on the board.
- Leave the answers there for students to refer to as they fill in the chart for themselves.
- Have students read their chart to a partner before asking some individuals to stand up and read their ideas to the class.

At level:
- Review the Indefinite Pronouns from Unit 7, page 73: *someone, something, anyone, anything*.
- Have students fill in the chart with their own ideas.
- Elicit a selection of answers from the class.

Above level:
- Have students fill in the chart with their own ideas.
- Have them check their sentences with a partner to focus on accuracy.
- Conduct a mingle activity where students stand up and try to find as many other people with the same answers. Ask for a show of hands for the most popular answers.

Workbook Grammar

- Direct students to the Workbook for further practice.

Further Practice
Workbook pages 81–83
Online practice Unit 9 · Understand
Oxford **iTools** Unit 9 · Understand

Unit 9 Communicate (page 94)

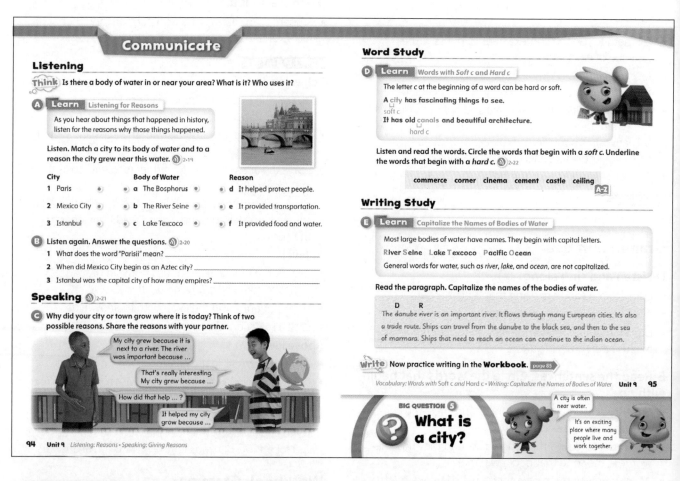

Summary

Objectives: To learn and practice listening, speaking, and writing strategies to facilitate effective communication.

Vocabulary: *commerce, corner, cinema, cement, castle, ceiling*

Listening strategy: Listening for reasons

Speaking: Giving reasons

Word Study: Words with *soft c* and *hard c*

Writing Study: Capitalizing the names of bodies of water

Big Question learning points: *Many people live and work in a city. A city is often near water.*

Materials: Discover Poster 5, Audio CD, Big Question Chart

Listening

Think

- Engage in a class discussion. Encourage students to talk about the different uses of bodies of water, if and why they like to go to the water, and whether or not a body of water is natural or human-made.

A Learn: Listening for Reasons

- Read the *Learn* box together. Ask students to predict what they will hear about in this exercise.
- Focus on the clue *in history*.

Listen. Match a city to its body of water and to a reason the city grew near this water. 2·19

- Before you play the audio, ask students to identify a purpose for listening.
- Play the audio once and have students listen.
- Tell them to raise their finger each time the speaker starts talking about a different city.
- Play the audio again. Have students complete the exercise as they listen.
- Check the answers with the class.

ANSWERS

1 b, f   2 c, d   3 a, e

DIFFERENTIATION

Below level:

- Pause after the first sentence in each section. Ask *Which city name did you hear: Paris, Mexico City, or Istanbul? Which body of water did the speaker say: The Bosphorus, the River Seine, or Lake Texcoco?*
- Have students connect the city and body of water.
- Then continue playing the audio. Pause at the end of the section. Ask students what they remember hearing. After they share, ask *Why did people settle in (Paris) near (the River Seine)?*
- Have them connect the body of water to the reason.
- Continue playing the audio.

At level:

- After students complete the exercise, have them use the information to make sentences on their own: *People settled in (Paris) near (the River Seine) because it (provided food and water).*

Above level:

- Have students complete the exercise after listening to the audio once.
- When you play it a second time, tell students to listen for more details about the history of each city and body of water.
- Tell them to take notes about interesting information they hear. Elicit the interesting information to share with the class.

B Listen again. Answer the questions. 2·20

- Have students answer the questions as they listen.

ANSWERS
1 "Parisii" means "boat people." 2 almost 700 years ago 3 four

Speaking 2·21

C Why did your city or town grow where it is today? Think of two possible reasons. Share the reasons with your partner.

COMMUNICATION

- Say each line of the dialogue with students echoing as they hear each line.
- Model the dialogue with a confident student in front of the class.
- Put students into pairs and tell them to practice the dialogue, taking turns speaking the different roles.
- Have partners first brainstorm reasons why their city might have grown where it is.
- Then have partners practice the dialogue, substituting in their own information.

CRITICAL THINKING

Not every famous or important city grew because of proximity to water. Tell students to think about other reasons why a city might grow in a specific spot. These questions can guide them:

- What else, other than water, can provide protection?
- The Bosphorus provided transportation. If there is no water nearby, what else can be important for transportation?
- The River Seine provided food and water. What else can provide food and water?

Word Study

D Learn: Words with *Soft c* and *Hard c*

- Have a confident student read the *Learn* box to the class.

Listen and read the words. Circle the words that begin with a *soft c*. Underline the words that begin with a *hard c*. 2·22

- Point out that *commerce* has a hard *c* at the beginning and a soft *c* at the end.

COLLABORATIVE LEARNING

- Have groups of two or three students brainstorm other words with soft *c* and hard *c*.
- Tell the group secretaries to list these words in two columns on a piece of paper.
- Have groups look at the words in their two lists and notice any spelling patterns. If necessary, tell them to look at the letter that follows the *c* in each word.

Writing Study

E Learn: Capitalized the Names of Bodies of Water

- Read the *Learn* box together.
- Help distinguish between the specific and nonspecific. Write on the board:
  *There is a **river** in Paris. It is called the **River Seine**.*
  *Mexico City began as an island in a **lake**. The government drained **Lake Texcoco**.*
- For each example, point out the difference between the general / nonspecific term and the proper name.

Read the paragraph. Capitalize the names of the bodies of water.

- Have students complete the activity individually and then check with a partner. Check answers with the class.

ANSWERS
Danube River, Danube, Black Sea, Sea of Marmara, Indian Ocean

Write

- Direct students to the Workbook for further practice.

Big Question 5 Review

What is a city?

- Display **Discover Poster 5**. Point to familiar vocabulary items and elicit them from the class. Ask *What is this?*
- Ask students *What do you see? What does that mean?*
- Refer to the learning points covered in Unit 9 which are written on the poster and have students explain how they relate to the different pictures.
- Return to the **Big Question Chart**.
- Ask students what they have learned about cities while studying this unit.
- Ask what information is new and add it to the chart.

Further Practice
Workbook pages 84–85
Online practice Unit 9 · Communicate
Oxford **iTools** Unit 9 · Communicate

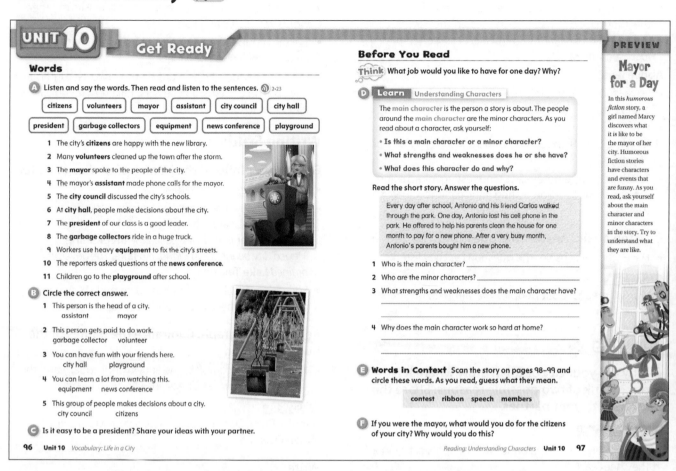

Summary

Objectives: To understand words about cities; to apply own experience and a reading strategy to help comprehension of a text.

Vocabulary: *citizens, volunteers, mayor, assistant, city council, city hall, president, garbage collectors, equipment, news conference, playground, contest, ribbon, speech, members*

Reading strategy: Understanding characters

Materials: Audio CD

Words

A Listen and say the words. Then read and listen to the sentences. 🎧 2·23

- Play the audio. Ask students to point to the words as they hear them.
- Play the audio a second time and have students repeat the words when they hear them.
- Read the sentences together. After each sentence, ask volunteers to guess the definition of the vocabulary word.

COLLABORATIVE LEARNING

- Have small groups work together to sort the words into different categories.
- Encourage them to think of their own ideas for categories first. If necessary, you can suggest they sort into *People, Places,* and *Things.*
- After they sort the words, ask them to think of a few other city words that could fit into each category.

B Circle the correct answer.

- Read each sentence together.
- Tell students to circle the best answer, then check their work with a partner.
- Check the answers with the class.

ANSWERS

1 mayor **2** garbage collector **3** playground
4 news conference **5** city council

DIFFERENTIATION

Below level:

- Focus on some of the sentences in A to practice the words that are not answers in B. Reread the sentences, and ask students guided questions to help them understand the meaning of the words:
  1 *Do you think a citizen is a person who lives in a city, or a person who owns a store?*
  2 *Do you think volunteers are people who visit a city, or people who do work for free?*
  3 *The base word in "assistant" is "assist." Assist means to help. What do you think an assistant does? (Recall the Word Study from Unit 2, page 23, taught words with -ant for adjectives and -ance for nouns. An assistant, however, is a person (noun); assistance follows the rules from page 23 because it is something (noun) that someone provides (help).)*
  4 *Does a president have to be in charge of a country, or can a president be in charge of a company or a school?*
  5 *The word "equipment" can also be used to describe the balls, bats, mitts, and caps used in baseball. Which*

definition do you think is correct: things you use for a specific task or purpose, or things you find in the street?

At level:

- Focus on B. Have students make similar sentences for the other six words in the lexical set.
- Point out that some of the sentences give simple definitions (*This person is head of a city.*) and some are a little looser (*You can learn a lot from watching this*).
- Students can follow either style.

Above level:

- Read the following sentences and have students match each sentence to a Big Question.
  1 *The city council put a giant telescope in city hall so citizens can look at the stars.*
  2 *The president of the museum had a news conference with the mayor to talk about the dinosaur bones found near the river.*
  3 *Many citizens in our city have rooftop gardens to grow their own food.*
  4 *Volunteers painted a mural in the playground to make it look prettier.*
- Have students work alone or with partners to use the words on page 96 in their own sentences about the Big Questions they have learned about so far this year.
- Note that the examples above use complex sentence constructions that students may be able to produce on their own. Tell them that it's okay if they need to use two sentences for each Big Question

C Is it easy to be a president? Share your ideas with your partner.

- Have students discuss the question with their partners. Then have partners share their ideas with the class.

Before You Read

Think

- Students can consider jobs listed on the previous page, in previous units, or from their own experiences.
- Help them explain why they would like each job by providing a few examples, e.g. *I'd like to be the president of a college because I like learning. I'd like to be an archaeologist because I like dinosaurs. I'd like to be a professional artist because I like to paint. I'd like to be a doctor because I'm good at science.*
- Point out the constructions they can use:
  I'd like to be a / an … because I like … (noun).
  I'd like to be a / an … because I like … (infinitive).
  I'd like to be a / an … because I like … (gerund).
  I'd like to be a / an … because I'm good at … (noun)

D Learn: Understanding Characters

- Read the *Learn* box together.

Read the short story. Answer the questions.

- Invite a volunteer to read the story aloud while the class listens.
- Review the answers to the questions together.

CRITICAL THINKING

- Guide students in personalizing the Reading Strategy. Tell students to think of a story they can tell about themselves (true or fictional). They should be the main character in the story, there should be at least one minor character, and the story should show at least one strength and one weakness.
- Have students think quietly, then share a story idea with a partner. Explain that students need to make sure their partner's story meets the criteria above.
- Invite students to tell their stories to the class. After each story, ask *Who is the main character? Who are the minor characters? What strengths and weaknesses does the main character have?*

E Words in Context: Scan the story on pages 98–99 and circle these words. As you read, guess what they mean.

- Have students scan the story and circle the words.

F If you were the mayor, what would you do for the citizens of your city? Why would you do this?

COMMUNICATION

- Put student into pairs to ask and answer these questions.

Reading Preview

- Read the title of the unit's reading text.
- Have students silently read the content of the preview bar.
- Ask *What type of text is it?* Ask *What does this type of text do?*
- Remind students to think about the main and minor characters as they read.

Further Practice
Workbook pages 86–87
Online practice Unit 10 • Get Ready
Oxford iTools Unit 10 • Get Ready

Mayor for a Day

Marcy was nervous. She was the winner of the Mayor for a Day contest at her school. For one day, she would be the mayor of her city. Marcy's mother drove her to the Glenview City Hall.

"You'll probably walk around with the mayor," her mother said. "Watch what he does and take notes. You'll learn a lot!"

Outside City Hall, Marcy met Mayor Wilson. To her surprise, he was holding a beach ball.

"Congratulations, Marcy!" he said. "Keep the city running smoothly. You'll work hard, won't you?"

Marcy nodded nervously. "I'll do my best, sir."

Think
Who is the main character? What do you know about her so far?

"Then I'm going to the beach. Mr. Clark will be your assistant today. Goodbye!"

It was a busy morning. Mr. Clark took Marcy to the new city library, which was about to open for the first time. Marcy cut a celebration ribbon and made a short speech. "Citizens of Glenview, read books every day," she declared. "Reading makes you smarter!"

As the crowd clapped, Mr. Clark tapped on his watch. "You have a meeting in ten minutes with the president of the Terrific Toy Company. We want them to build a factory here in Glenview. Many people could get jobs there."

"Let's go," said Marcy.

Think
Who are three minor characters?

In the mayor's office, Marcy spent one hour talking to Hilda Hanson, the president of Terrific Toys. "I promise you that the people of Glenview will build interesting and creative toys," Marcy said.

"For such a young mayor, you impress me!" said Hilda. "We'll start building our factory here tomorrow."

As Hilda drove away, Mr. Clark ran up to Marcy.

"The garbage collectors are unhappy!" he exclaimed. "There is too much garbage to pick up. They want more workers. What will we do?"

Marcy realized that she wasn't nervous anymore. She thought for a moment and then snapped her fingers. "We'll start a recycling program," she said. "That will reduce garbage. They won't need more workers."

"Great idea!" said Mr. Clark.

After lunch, Mr. Clark ran into Marcy's office. "You have a city council meeting in five minutes!" he shouted.

At the meeting, the head of the city council looked worried. "The playground equipment at the city park needs fresh paint," she said. "The park needs new flowers. But we have no money for extra workers."

"Do we have money for ice cream?" Marcy asked. The city council members looked confused.

"I will have a news conference today," Marcy explained. "Next Saturday will be our first Glenview Volunteer Day. People can volunteer at the park and enjoy free ice cream. The citizens of our city will paint and plant and get the job done!"

"Wonderful idea, Mayor Marcy!" the members cheered.

At 5:30, Mr. Clark thanked Marcy for her hard work. They walked to the front of City Hall, where Marcy's mother was waiting. Marcy got in the car and stretched her legs.

"Did you have fun, Marcy?" asked her mother.

"I did," said Marcy.

"Who knows?" said her mother. "Maybe you'll be a real mayor someday."

Marcy smiled. "Maybe I will," she said.

Think
What do you know about the main and minor characters?

Summary

Objectives: To read, understand, and discuss a fictional text; to apply a reading strategy to improve comprehension.

School subject: Social Studies: Society

Text type: Humorous fiction

Reading strategy: Understanding characters

Big Question learning points: *Many people live and work in a city. A city has businesses and shopping. Cities are full of history and culture.*

Materials: Talk About It! Poster, Audio CD

Before Reading

- Ask *If you could have any job for a day, what would you do?*
- Tell students that in this story, a girl named Marcy becomes mayor for a day.
- Ask *What does a mayor do everyday?*
- Invite students to predict what will happen in the story.

During Reading 🔊 2·24

- Ask a gist question to check overall understanding of the text, e.g. *What sorts of things does Marcy do as the mayor of Glenview?*
- Give students a few minutes to skim the text before answering.
- Remind students that they are looking for information about the main character and minor characters.
- Play the audio. Students listen as they read along.
- Stop at each *Think* box for students to answer the questions.

Below level:

- As you listen to the text, draw a simple timeline on the board showing what Marcy does throughout the story. Include only basic information:
  1 *meets Mayor Wilson outside City Hall*
  2 *meets Mr. Clark*
  3 *goes to new city library*
  4 *meets president of Terrific Toy Company*
  5 *talks to Mr. Clark about unhappy garbage collectors*
  6 *goes to City Council meeting about playground equipment*
  7 *goes home with Mom*
- Play the audio a second time. Pause at each event on the timeline and ask students to add details from the story.
- Guide them to consider the characters when you pause at each event, e.g. at the first event, ask how Marcy felt when she met the mayor.

At level:

- Have small groups read the story together, taking turns around a circle.
- Assign a "secretary" in each group to take notes. Tell the groups to pause at each *Think* box and answer the questions; the secretary writes the group's answer.
- Between readers, have students pause to talk about what they learned about the characters. The secretary writes down their ideas.
- Have the class share their answers to the *Think* boxes, and to share what they wrote about the characters in the story.

Above level:

- Have students practice reading the story with a narrator and characters.
- Put students into small groups. Each group has a "director" who will assign roles and make sure everyone knows when to speak. (Some characters only have one or two lines, so one student can play several minor characters as long as he / she alters his / her voice!)
- Groups practice reading the story with one student reading Marcy (she reads everything that Marcy says in quotations), one student reading the narrator (he / she reads all the words that are NOT in quotations), and one or two students reading all the quotations for the mother, Mayor Wilson, Mr. Clark, Hilda Hanson, and the head of the City Council.
- Encourage the students reading characters to read with expression that reflects meaning.
- Have the groups read aloud to the class.

COLLABORATIVE LEARNING

- Have one slip of paper for each student in your class. Write a minor character's name on each piece of paper, so you have the same number of papers that say *Mayor Wilson,* the same number of papers that say *Mr. Clark,* and so on. (Do not include Marcy in this activity: there is more information on her so the groups won't be balanced if she is included, and students will examine her character in depth on page 98.)
- Hand out the papers randomly. Students circulate to find others with the same character.
- Students meet in their character groups to list as much information as they can about their character. Have them revisit D on page 97 for ideas.
- Have groups tell the class about their characters.

CRITICAL THINKING

Discussion questions:

- *Why was Marcy surprised to see the mayor with a beach ball?*
- *What would you say if you were Marcy cutting the ribbon on the new library?*
- *Was Marcy's meeting with Hilda Hanson a success?*
- *Marcy comes up with a solution to the garbage collectors' problem. What is it?*
- *Why is the head of the City Council worried? What is Marcy's solution? Will this plan work?*
- *Can you think of any other solutions to the garbage collector problem or the City Council problem?*

After Reading

- Have students predict about what will happen "next." Ask *What will happen tomorrow when Mayor Wilson comes back to work? Will the volunteer for ice cream plan be a success? Will Marcy become mayor?*

COLLABORATIVE LEARNING

- Display the **Talk About It! Poster** to help students with sentence frames for discussion and expressing personal opinions.
- Put students into pairs to discuss the characters from the story.
- Have students say one thing about each character in the reading.

CULTURE NOTE

Research local volunteer opportunities in your community. There may not be an ice-cream-for-work exchange like the one Marcy suggests in the story, but it is likely that there are other organizations that welcome student and family volunteers, e.g. some parks have seasonal clean-ups and plantings, libraries have book drives, schools have bake sales, and senior centers have programs for children to read to and visit seniors.

Remind students that *one* of the things that makes a city is its citizens, and by volunteering, even the youngest citizens can help improve their neighborhoods and communities.

Further Practice
Workbook page 88
Online practice Unit 10 · Read
Oxford **iTools** Unit 10 · Read

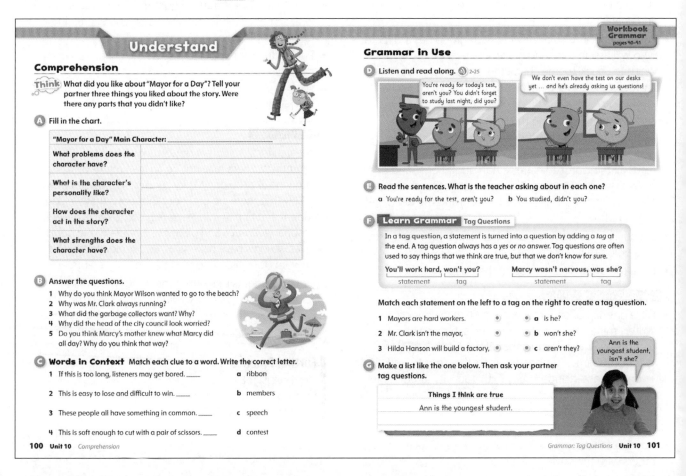

Summary

Objectives: To demonstrate understanding of a fictional text; to understand the meaning and form of the grammar structure.

Reading: Comprehension

Grammar input: Tag questions

Grammar practice: Workbook exercises

Grammar production: Writing opinions; asking tag questions

Materials: Audio CD

Comprehension

Think

- Have students make a list or brainstorm three things they liked about "Mayor for a Day" and then tell these three things to their partners.
- Make sure students explain why they liked these parts.
- Ask pairs to discuss any parts of the story that they didn't like and why.

A Fill in the chart.

- Ask *Who is the main character?* Have everyone answer together.
- Have students fill in the chart on their own.
- Check the answers with the class.

Main Character: Marcy

What problems does the character have? She has to make a speech; she has to convince the president of a toy company to build a factory in Glenview; the garbage collectors are unhappy because there is too much garbage; there's no money to paint the benches and plant flowers

What is the character's personality like? Nervous at first; likes reading; positive / optimistic; creative; thoughtful; smart

How does the character act in the story? Nervous at first; polite; friendly; hard-working; brave; calm

What strengths does the character have? Hard-working; brave; positive / optimistic; willing to try things; creative; calm

DIFFERENTIATION

Below level:

- Have students work with partners to fill in the chart.
- Allow students to write the words without having to use full sentences.
- Elicit and write the words on the board.
- Ask students to add any extra words they would like to their charts.

At level:

- Have students work with partners to fill in the chart.
- Divide the reading text in two. One partner uses details from the first half of the story, and one uses details from the second half.
- They get together and compare answers. Each partner can add the other's ideas to his or her chart.

- Ask *Is there any information that both partners found, even though you focused on different parts of the story?*

Above level:
- After students complete the chart about Marcy, have them revisit the story in Unit 4, on page 38 "Stumbling upon the Past."
- Have them complete a similar chart about Javier.
- Invite students to share their charts with the class.

B Answer the questions.

- Put students into pairs to discuss their answers.
- Have students write the answers in their notebooks individually.
- Elicit the answers from the class.

POSSIBLE ANSWERS
1 He was tired of working so hard and being so busy.
2 Because the mayor is so busy and there's so much to do.
3 They wanted more workers because there is too much garbage.
4 Because there wasn't enough money to paint the benches and plant flowers in the park.
5 Answers will vary.

CRITICAL THINKING
- Ask students to name some problems in their own town or city. Help them describe the details of the problems.
- Then ask them to "think like Mayor Marcy." Can they come up with any creative solutions to their town's problems?

C Words in Context: Match a clue to a word. Write the correct letter.

- Help students use their recollection of the story to mentally find the words. Ask *Do you remember where this word (ribbon) was used?*
- Go back to the story and discuss the definitions.
- Read the sentences in C.
- Point out that these sentences aren't exactly definitions; they give additional information about the words.
- Have students match the sentences to the words.

ANSWERS
1 c   2 d   3 b   4 a

Grammar in Use

D Listen and read along. 🔊 2·25

- Listen to the conversation once.
- Have two confident students read it aloud for the class.
- Ask *Does the teacher think Harry studied for the test?*
- Play the audio and have volunteers use it as a model for rhythm and intonation as they echo read.

E Read the sentences. What is the teacher asking about in each one?

- For sentence *a*, write *You're ready for the test, aren't you?* on the board.
- Ask *What does the teacher want to know? What two answers can Jay give? What are the full sentence answers?*
- Repeat with sentence *b*.

F Learn Grammar: Tag Questions

- Read the *Learn Grammar* box together.
- Write on the board: *You'll work hard*. Say *This is the statement*.
- Add a comma and *won't you?* Say *That's the tag*.
- Reread from the *Learn Grammar* box: *Tag questions are often used … .* Ask *Did Mayor Wilson **think** Marcy would work hard? Did he **know** she would work hard?*
- Break down the second sentence the same way.

Match each statement on the left to a tag on the right to create a tag question.

- Have students complete this exercise individually.
- Check the answers with the class.

ANSWERS
1 c   2 a   3 b

G Make a list like the one below. Then ask your partner tag questions.

- Have students complete the list in groups.

- Divide the class into small groups.
- Tell them to write several sentences about the other students in the group in the column "Things I think are true."
- Suggest some ideas, such as whether or not their group mates play any instruments, have siblings or pets, like certain foods, play sports, like specific musical bands, or want to be something when they grow up.
- After they write their sentences, have them follow the model to change each sentence to a tag question.
- Have group members take turns asking their questions to their group mates.

Further Practice
Workbook pages 89–91
Online practice Unit 10 • Understand
Oxford **iTools** Unit 10 • Understand

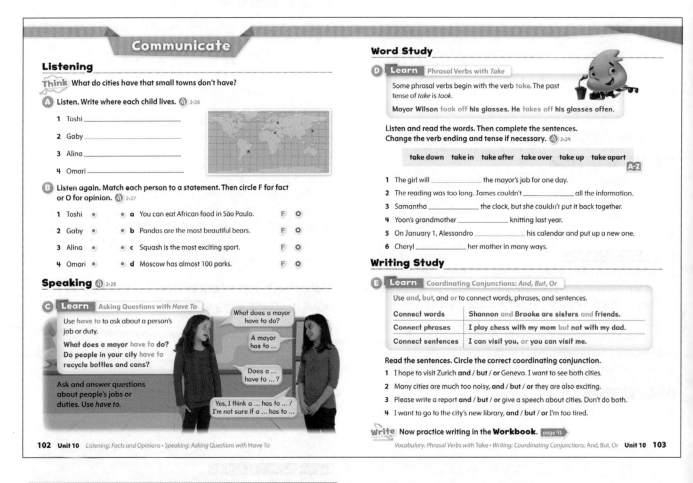

Summary

Objectives: To learn and practice listening, speaking, and writing strategies to facilitate effective communication.

Vocabulary: *take down, take in, take after, take over, take up, take apart*

Listening strategy: Listening for facts and opinions

Speaking: Asking questions with *have to*

Word Study: Phrasal verbs with *take*

Writing Study: Coordinating conjunctions: *and, but, or*

Big Question learning points: *A city has businesses and shopping. Cities are full of history and culture.*

Materials: Audio CD

Listening

Think

- Have students discuss the question in pairs.
- You can provide guidance by focusing on specific needs, such as food, clothing, and shelter.
- Expand the discussion to include non-necessities, like leisure-time activities.

A Listen. Write where each child lives. 2•26

- Play the audio once through while students just listen.
- Play it a second time and have them write where each child lives.

ANSWERS
1 Toshi lives in Tokyo, Japan.
2 Gaby lives in Sao Paulo, Brazil.

3 Alina lives in Moscow, Russia.
4 Omari lives in Cairo, Egypt.

B Listen again. Match each person to a statement. Then circle F for fact or O for opinion. 2•27

- On the board write *Fact* and *Opinion*. Review that a fact is something you can prove, and an opinion is subjective, determined by individual preference.
- Give some examples from your class, such as *Maria is the oldest girl in the class* (fact) or *English is the best subject* (opinion).
- Challenge students to try to match each person with a sentence.
- Play the audio so they can check their work.

ANSWERS
1 Toshi-b-Opinion   2 Gaby-a-Fact   3 Alina-d-Fact
4 Omari-c-Opinion

CRITICAL THINKING

- Read a few other sentences from the audio and have students determine which are facts and which are opinions. For each one, ask students to think about the context and name the person and city:
  1 *The Ueno Zoo also has black bears and polar bears.*
  2 *Nothing is better than sushi for dinner!*
  3 *A park is the best place to read a good book.*
  4 *Here in Cairo, soccer is very popular.*

Speaking 🔊 2·28

C Learn: Asking Questions with *Have to*

- On the board write *have to*, and remind students that this phrase tells about an obligation. Ask *What do you have to do?*
- Go around the room and invite students to name things they have to do, like clean their rooms, go to school, do homework, or practice an instrument.
- Read the *Learn* box together. Then play the audio while students follow along in their books.
- Play it again and have students echo read to mimic the intonation and pronunciation.
- Put students into pairs and tell them to practice the dialogue, taking turns speaking the different roles.

Ask and answer questions about people's jobs or duties. Use *have to*.

- Have students follow the model to ask and answer their own questions about other jobs and duties.

- It may be easier for partners to brainstorm some jobs and duties different people have before they practice the speaking task.
- Have partners write down some ideas they can refer to as they practice the dialogue.

Word Study

D Learn: Phrasal Verbs with *Take*

- On the board write *take*. Pretend to take off your glasses (or really take them off) and say *Let me take off my glasses.* Add the word *off* to the board, *take off*.
- Read the *Learn* box together. Explain that you can take off a coat, your shoes, or other items of clothing.

Listen and read the words. Then complete the sentences. Change the verb ending and tense if necessary. 🔊 2·29

- Play the audio and have students point to the phrases as they hear them.
- Provide a simple definition for each one.
- Have students complete the sentences on their own, then check their answers with a partner.

1 take over   2 take in   3 took apart   4 took up
5 took down   6 takes after

Writing Study

E Learn: Coordinating Conjunctions: *And*, *But*, *Or*

- Read the *Learn* box together. Have the students identify the coordinating conjunction in each example sentence and the two elements in each sentence that are connected by a coordinating conjunction.

Read the sentences. Circle the correct coordinating conjunction.

- Have students complete the exercise on their own.
- Check answers with the class.

1 and   2 but   3 or   4 but

Write

- Have students practice writing in the Workbook.

Below level:

- Help students find clues in each item: In sentence 1, the word *both* is a clue that the answer is *and*.
- In sentence 2, the first clause describes cities as *too noisy*, which is a negative comment. In the second clause the writer says cities *are also exciting*, which is positive. When there is a contrast, the conjunction is *but*.
- In sentence 3, the follow-up sentence says *Don't do both*. If *both* is a clue for *and*, then *not both* means *or*.
- In sentence 4, again there is a contrast, so the conjunction is *but*.

At level:

- Have students think of original sentences that use *and* to connect words, phrases, or sentences.
- Tell them to identify the different words, phrases, or sentences they are connecting, e.g. in the *Learn* box, *and* connects the word *Shannon* with the word *Brooke*; *but* connects the phrase *with my mom* with the phrase *not with my dad*; *or* connects the sentence *I can visit you* with the sentence *you can visit me*

Above level:

- Tell students to come up with original sentences that use *and* to connect words, phrases, or sentences. Add a few requirements to make it more challenging:
  1 The sentences should somehow address this unit's Big Question, *What is a city?*
  2 The sentences should *also* use one of the other Word Study topics from a previous unit.
  3 The sentences should include some target vocabulary from this unit or a previous unit.

| Further Practice
Workbook pages 92–93
Online practice Unit 10 · Communicate
Oxford **iTools** Unit 10 · Communicate

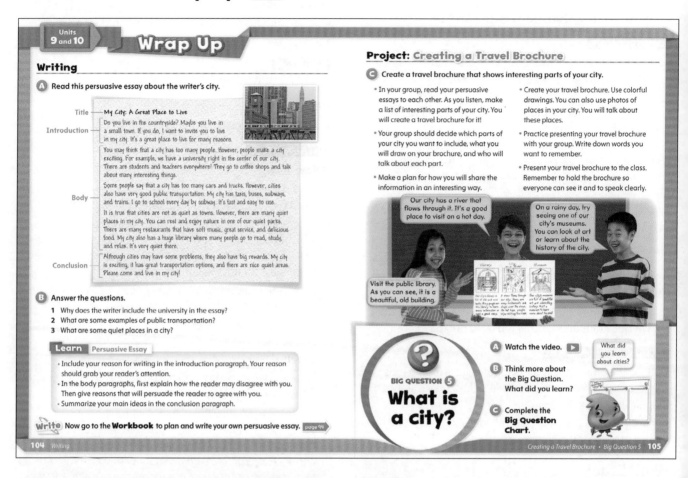

Summary

Objectives: To show what students have learned about the language and learning points of Units 9 and 10.

Reading: Comprehension of a persuasive essay

Project: Creating a travel brochure

Writing: Write a persuasive essay

Speaking: Talk about the travel brochures

Materials: Big Question DVD, Discover Poster 5, Talk About It! Poster, Big Question Chart, Audio CD

Writing

A Read this persuasive essay about the writer's city.

- Remind students about the Author's Purpose they studied in Unit 3, page 29.
- Read aloud the directions and explain that now they will be the writer, and their purpose will be to persuade.
- Point out that even in the title, the author lets you know how he / she feels about the topic.
- Have students go around the room and read the essay.

B Answer the questions.

- Have students find the answers in the text.
- Ask a few other questions to check comprehension.
  Why does the author like having a university in the city?
  How does the author get to school?
  If you lived in this city, where would you go to enjoy some peace and quiet?
- Check the answers with the class.

1 Many students and teachers go to the university, and people make a city exciting.
2 Taxis, buses, subways, and trains
3 Parks, restaurants, libraries

Learn: Persuasive Essay

- Read the directions in the *Learn* box together.
- Explain that students should follow these guidelines when they plan and write their essays.

CRITICAL THINKING

- Have students go back to the model to see how the author addressed each requirement.
- Ask *What is the author's reason for writing? How might the reader disagree with the author's idea? How does the author counter each argument? Does the author summarize the main ideas in the conclusion?*

DIFFERENTIATION

Below level:

- Put students into mixed-ability pairs to brainstorm ways the reader might disagree with the writer's idea.
- Have the more confident student take notes that the less confident student can use as he / she drafts their essay.

At level:

- Have small groups brainstorm some fun reasons for writing the essay, e.g. maybe there is a contest being held by the local newspaper, or maybe a young adult is trying to convince his / her parents to do something.

- Explain that having an interesting purpose will get the writer off to a good start and make it easier to draft an interesting and persuasive essay.

Above level:

- Suggest that some students write essays with a genuine purpose, e.g. they can submit an essay to the principal trying to convince him / her to extend lunchtime, or they can write the essay to try to convince a parent to let them stay up later on Saturday nights.

Write

- Direct students to the Workbook to plan and write their own persuasive eassy.

Project

C Create a travel brochure that shows interesting parts of your city.

CREATIVITY

- If you can gather some real-life travel brochures beforehand, share them with the class.
- Divide the class into small groups.
- Have students take turns reading their persuasive essays to their group.
- After each essay, the group secretary writes down the interesting parts of the city mentioned in the essay.
- After everyone has had a turn, the group votes on which parts they want to include in their brochure.
- Tell students to bring in supplies, like photos or drawings, which they can use to decorate the travel brochure.
- Students should use the sample speech bubbles as models for how they will present their final product.

COLLABORATIVE LEARNING

- Below are some suggestions for facilitating the decision-making process.
- *Decide which parts of the city to focus on.* Have each student in the group choose one place, so if there are four in the group, the brochure will focus on four places.
- *Decide what to draw on the brochure.* All the group members make suggestions for artwork for each place, but the final decision belongs to the student who chose the place.
- *Decide who will talk about each part.* It may be easy to have students talk about the places they chose, but encourage groups to come up with some other ideas.
- *Decide how to share the information in an interesting way.* The group monitor will need to make sure everyone contributes ideas before the group votes. Encourage groups to come up with several ideas: maybe one group will use the information in the brochure to create a rap that could be used for a radio commercial, maybe another will do a skit of someone visiting a travel agent and going over the brochure.

Units 9 and 10 Big Question Review

A Watch the video. ▷

- Play the video and when it is finished ask students what they know about cities now.
- Have students share ideas with the class.

B Think more about the Big Question. What did you learn?

- Display **Discover Poster 5**. Point to familiar vocabulary items and elicit them from the class. Ask *What is this?*
- Ask students *What do you see?* Ask *What does that mean?*
- Refer to all of the learning points written on the poster and have students explain how they relate to the different pictures.
- Ask *What does this learning point mean?* Elicit answers from individual students.
- Display the **Talk About It! Poster** to help students with sentence frames for discussion of the learning points and for expressing their opinions.

C Complete the Big Question Chart.

- Ask students what they have learned about cities while studying this unit.
- Put students into pairs or small groups to say two new things they have learned.
- Have students share their ideas with the class and add their ideas to the chart.
- Have students complete the chart in their Workbook.

Further Practice
Workbook pages 94–96
Online practice • Wrap Up 5
Oxford **iTools** • Wrap Up 5

Reading Strategies

Students will practice:

- Differentiating between theme and main idea
- Sequencing actions

Vocabulary

Students will understand and use words about:

- The body and health

Grammar

Students will understand and use:

- Order of adjectives
- *Used to* versus the simple past

Review

Students will review the language and Big Question learning points of Units 11 and 12 through:

- An interview
- A project (conducting an interview)

Units 11 and 12
How do our bodies work?

Students will understand the Big Question learning points:

- Our body keeps us strong and healthy.
- The respiratory system helps us breathe.
- The circulatory system moves blood and oxygen through our bodies.
- White blood cells fight against infection.
- Bones protect us and help us move easily.

Listening Strategies

Students will practice:

- Listening for advice
- Listening for details

Writing

Students will use and understand:

- Commands for advice
- Subject / verb agreement with indefinite pronouns

Students will produce texts that:

- Inform

Word Study

Students will understand, pronounce, and use:

- Antonyms
- Verbs that end in *-ate*

Speaking

Students will understand and use expressions to:

- Ask and answer personal questions
- Give explanations with *that* and *where*

Units 11 and 12 Big Question

Summary

Objectives: To activate students' existing knowledge of the topic and identify what they would like to learn about the topic.

Materials: Big Question DVD, Discover Poster 6, Big Question Chart

Introducing the topic

- Read out the Big Question. Ask *How do our bodies work?*
- Write students' ideas on the board and discuss.

A Watch the video.

- Play the video and when it is finished ask students to answer the following questions in pairs:
  What do you see in the video?
  Who do you think the people are?
  What is happening?
  Do you like it?
- Have individual students share their answers with the class.

B Look at the picture and talk about it.

- Students look at the big picture and talk about it. Ask students the questions in B.
- Ask additional questions:
  What else can you see in the picture?
  Do you think the boy is alone?
  Have you ever done this?

C Think and answer the questions.

- Have students discuss the questions in small groups, and then with the class.

DIFFERENTIATION

Below level:

- Do a quick vocabulary review for the parts of the body.
- For each word, point to yourself, then have students repeat the word and point to their own bodies.
- You can review words like *eyes, ears, nose, mouth, hair, legs, arms, hands, feet, stomach, neck, shoulders.*

At level:

- Revisit the Speaking lesson in Unit 4, page 42: Describing with the Senses.
- Have students name the parts of the body that are associated with each sense, and say what those parts of the body do, e.g. *The eyes see; the ears hear; the tongue tastes; the nose smells; the skin feels.*

Above level:

- Have students try to describe what parts of the body do using riddles of circumlocution, e.g. *This helps me move my legs and arms when I want to do something* is a description for *muscle.*
- The trick is to have them think of words for specific parts of the body in their native language, then try to describe what those parts of the body do in English.
- Have students jot down in their native language the words they described for which they didn't know the English. If they haven't learned the English

words by the end of the unit, ask them to search in a translation dictionary.

CRITICAL THINKING

- Brainstorm different ways we can keep our bodies healthy.
- Tell students to consider what they learned about healthy food in Module 3. Can they apply any of that knowledge to this topic? (*Eat organic food without chemicals; eat fresh food; eat whole foods instead of packaged and processed food.*)

Expanding the topic

COLLABORATIVE LEARNING

- Display **Discover Poster 6** and give students enough time to look at the pictures.
- Elicit some of the words you think they will know by pointing to different things in the pictures and saying *What's this?*
- Put students into small groups of three or four. Have each group choose a picture that they find interesting.
- Ask each group to say five things that they can see in their picture.
- Have one person from each group stand up and read out the words they chose for their picture.
- Ask the class if they can add any more.

DIFFERENTIATION

Below level:

- Encourage students to participate using simple phrases or short sentences.
- Point to details in the big picture and on the poster and ask *What is this?* Write the answers on the board.

At level:

- Elicit complete sentences about what students know about their bodies.
- Write their sentences on the board.

Above level:

- Elicit more detailed responses.
- Have students write their own sentences on the board.

D Fill out the Big Question Chart.

- Display the **Big Question Chart**.
- Ask the class *What do you know about how your body works?*
- Ask students to write what they know and what they want to know in their Workbooks.
- Write a collection of ideas on the **Big Question Chart**.

Discover Poster 6

1 A man riding a mountain bike up a mountain; 2 A woman using her lungs to blow up a balloon; 3 A model of the human heart; 4 White and red blood cells surrounding a virus; 5 A model showing the human skeletal system and the brain

> ### Further Practice
> **Workbook page 97**
> **Online practice • Big Question 6**
> Oxford **iTools • Big Question 6**

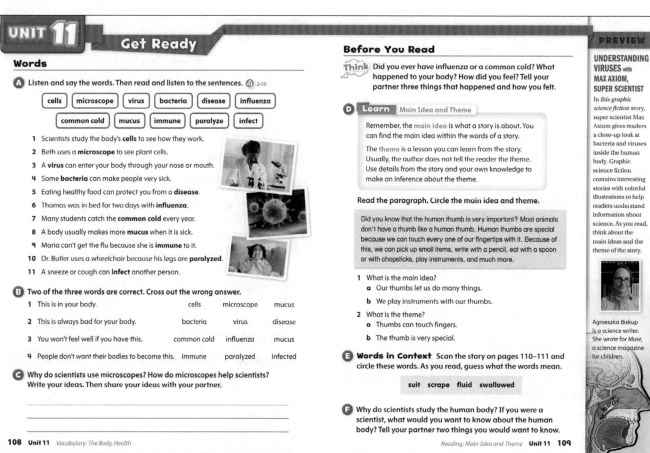

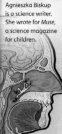

Summary

Objectives: To understand words about viruses and infection; to apply own experience and a reading strategy to help comprehension of a text.

Vocabulary: *cells, microscope, virus, bacteria, disease, influenza, common cold, mucus, immune, paralyze, infect, suit, scrape, fluid, swallowed*

Reading strategy: Main idea and theme

Materials: Audio CD

Words

A Listen and say the words. Then read and listen to the sentences. 🎧 2·30

- Play the audio. Ask students to point to the words as they hear them.
- Play the audio a second time and have students repeat the words when they hear them.
- Say the words out of order and have students race to point to them on the page.
- Point out this special vocabulary connection. Say *Look at the word "microscope." Do you recognize any part of that word?* (*-scope* is also found in *telescope* from Unit 1). *What do you think the connection is?* (The noun-combining form *-scope* means *a tool to look at or observe*. *Tele-* is a combining form that means *faraway*. So a *telescope* is a tool to see far away. *Micro-* is a combining form that means *small*. So a *microscope* is a tool to see something small.

Below level:

- Give students some simple definitions for the words. Because the words are scientific, it can be helpful to draw simple pictures on the board and use students' native language to help clarify many of them.
- Say the definitions and have students call out the words together.

At level:

- Tell students to look at the first sentence in A. Explain that you want them to create a question for which *number 1* is the answer, e.g. *Why do scientists study the body's cells?*
- Brainstorm some questions for the second sentence, such as: *Why does Beth use a microscope?* or *How does Beth see plant cells?*
- Once students understand what to do, have them work with partners to come up with questions for the other sentences.
- Share questions with the class.

Above level:

- Tell students to try to make a connection between two or more words from the list so they can use them in one sentence. Point to sentence 2 as an example, *Beth uses a* **microscope** *to see plant* **cells**.

B Two of the three words are correct. Cross out the wrong answer.

- Read through the items together.
- Have students try the exercise on their own first. Then check answers with the class.
- For item 2, point out that some bacteria is actually healthy and good for your body, e.g. the bacteria found in yogurt is good for your digestive system.

ANSWERS

1 microscope   2 bacteria   3 mucus   4 immune

C Why do scientists use microscopes? How do microscopes help scientists? Write your ideas. Then share your ideas with your partner.

- Encourage students to think about how scientists use microscopes to study the ways bodies work.
- Challenge them to also consider ways scientists might use microscopes to study things from prior units, e.g. some scientists might use microscopes to study ancient artwork or bones; other scientists might use microscopes to learn about different kinds of food.

COLLABORATIVE LEARNING

- Have partners play a guessing game to practice the words. Partner A names three clues about one word, e.g. *These are small. These are in all living things. There is a double letter in this word.* Partner B has to guess the word: *cells*.

Before You Read

Think

- Have partners write down the things that happened to their bodies when they had the flu or a cold.
- Have students share their answers with the class.
- List the answers on the board.

D Learn: Main Idea and Theme

- Read the *Learn* box together.
- Explain that the theme is usually a more general statement, and the main idea is usually specific.

Read the paragraph. Circle the main idea and theme.

- Invite a confident student to read the paragraph aloud for the class.
- Together with the class choose the best answers.
- Write on the board: *Theme: The thumb is very special.* Set this sentence as the center of a mind map.
- Explain that this is a more general idea than the main idea of the paragraph. You could write other paragraphs with other main ideas that would fit into this theme.
- Write the main idea as one offshoot of the theme: *Our thumbs let us do many things.*
- Ask students to name details from the paragraph that support this main idea. List these details by the main idea.
- Then point to the theme again. Say again *The theme is a more general lesson and idea. What other main ideas might work with this theme?*
- Attach another offshoot to the central theme: *Most animals don't have thumbs.* Explain that you could write

another paragraph about which animals besides humans have thumbs. This paragraph would still fit into the theme *The thumb is very special.*

- Ask students to look at their hands. Explain that the thumb and fingers are called *digits*. Tell students to bend their digits. What do they notice? (*The thumb has only one joint; the fingers have two.*) Attach another offshoot to the central theme: *The thumb is the only digit with one joint.* Point out that you could write another paragraph about this topic, and it would still fit into the theme *The thumb is very special.*

CRITICAL THINKING

- Tell students you will give them a theme and a main idea, and they will create a mini-story.
- The theme is, e.g. *It's important to get enough sleep* and the main idea is *Molly had problems because she stayed up late studying.* Ask students to come up with a story that matches this theme and main idea.
- For a second example, the theme is, e.g. *A good friend is loyal through good times and bad times* and the main idea is *Johnny learns that Bill and Juan aren't true friends.* Ask students to come up with a story that matches this theme and main idea.

E Words in Context: Scan the story on pages 110–111 and circle these words. As you read, guess what the words mean.

- Read each word and have students follow your pronunciation.

F Why do scientists study the human body? If you were a scientist, what would you want to know about the human body? Tell your partner two things you would want to know.

COMMUNICATION

- Have students close their eyes and think about the questions for a minute before they begin the discussion.
- Have students share some of their ideas with the class.

Reading Preview

- Read the title of the unit's reading text.
- Have students silently read the content of the preview bar.
- Ask *What type of text is it?* Ask *What does this type of text do?*

Further Practice
Workbook pages 97–98
Online practice Unit 11 • Get Ready
Oxford **iTools** Unit 11 • Get Ready

Summary

Objectives: To read, understand, and discuss a graphic science fiction text; to apply a reading strategy to improve comprehension.

School subject: Life Science

Text type: Graphic science fiction

Reading strategy: Main idea and theme

Big Question learning points: *Our body keeps us strong and healthy. White blood cells fight against infection.*

Materials: Talk About It! Poster, Audio CD

Before Reading

- Write the word *virus* on the board.
- Revisit the idea that viruses are tiny. We need microscopes to see them. Tell students to imagine something much, much smaller than an ant.
- Preview the reading text. Point out that this graphic science text is like a comic book, except it is intended to teach the reader about something.
- Ask students to predict if this format will help them understand the scientific information.

During Reading ⊚ 2·31

- Read the title and introductory text together.
- Point out the numbers in the top-left corner of each section and explain that students should use these to navigate the reading in order.
- Tell students to read the speech bubbles and look at the pictures.

DIFFERENTIATION

Below level:

- Have students read with you in small groups.
- Explain the illustrations to make sure students understand the context of the speech bubbles, e.g.

1 *A scientist named Dr. Lee shows Max Axiom a picture of a virus on a computer.*

2 *Max Axiom shrinks to the size of the virus.*

3 *Max Axiom is tiny like a virus. He shows us different kinds of viruses up close.*

4 *A little boy scraped his leg, and his mother is taking care of it. Max Axiom is still tiny like a virus; now he is on the boy's leg by the scrape.*

5 *Max Axiom explains that the skin is like armor that keeps out viruses. Do you see the virus sitting on the surface of the skin? Remember the word* armor *from Unit 3, page 28? How does that word help you understand what skin does to protect the body?*

6 *Max Axiom shows where the scrape opens into the boy's body. Do you see how the virus is inside the scrape?*

7 *Max Axiom is at the entrance of your nose (nostril). Do you see the hairs?*

8 *Max Axiom shows how mucus can catch viruses that the nose hairs don't stop.*

9 *Max Axiom travels like a virus down the nasal cavity into the throat.*

10 *Max Axiom is like a virus in the stomach.*

11 *Max Axiom swims like a virus through the blood stream with the red blood cells.*

12 *Max Axiom shows white blood cells "fighting" the virus in the blood stream.*

At level:

- Have students read with partners, alternating speech bubbles.
- Have them stop at each *Think* box to discuss the main idea and theme.
- Tell partners to work together to paraphrase a few speech bubbles.

Above level:

- Have students read the text independently.
- Point out that comic books use speech bubbles to tell the story.
- Revisit the lesson on Text Features from Unit 7, page 69. Explain that sometimes comic books include captions to help explain what's going on.
- Challenge students to write captions for the illustrations in "Understanding Viruses." Their ideas will vary, but they should reflect the action and information in the illustration.
- See the descriptions above in the *Below level* section for some ideas.

COLLABORATIVE LEARNING

- List the different steps the immune system takes to prevent a virus from making us sick: skin creates a barrier; nose hairs block the virus; mucus carries the virus to the stomach; stomach acid kills it; white blood cells fight the virus in the blood stream.
- Have groups create simple role-plays to act out a virus trying to get into a body to infect it, and the body's immune system fighting the virus off at each step.

CRITICAL THINKING

Discussion questions:

- *Doctors sometimes check their patients' white blood cell counts (they take some blood and count the white blood cells in the sample). Why do you think they do this?*
- *Why is it important to keep scrapes and cuts clean and covered?*
- *Do viruses infect dead cells?*
- *If you breathe through your mouth, which piece of the immune system are you bypassing?*
- *What else does stomach acid do?*

After Reading

- Ask students if they will act differently now that they understand how the immune system works. Possible answers include: try to keep scrapes clean and covered; blow their nose to blow out viruses stuck in nose hairs; wash their hands so viruses on hands don't accidentally get rubbed into eyes and mouths.

COLLABORATIVE LEARNING

- Display the **Talk About It! Poster** to help students with sentence frames for discussion and expressing personal opinions.
- Put students into pairs to discuss which part of the immune system is most interesting.

CRITICAL THINKING

- Ask students to analyze their own learning styles. Did they find the graphic science book easier to understand or harder to understand than a traditional textbook?
- Encourage them to try to explain what was easy or hard about it. Explain that understanding how we learn helps us be better learners.
- If students found the reading challenging, they might want to look at a traditional textbook to learn more about viruses and the immune system.
- If they found this reading easy to understand, they might want to seek out alternative presentations (such as graphic novels or videos) for other school subjects they find challenging.

CULTURE NOTE

Max Axiom shows the reader the polio virus. Polio is a virus that paralyzes the people it infects. There is no cure for polio, but scientists have created an effective vaccine. This vaccine is one of the standard vaccines that children get in modern times.

Scientists hope that by vaccinating everyone against the disease, they will be able to eliminate it.

Further Practice
Workbook page 99
Online practice Unit 11 • Read
Oxford iTools Unit 11 • Read

Understand

Comprehension

Think Were the pictures in the story useful or interesting? Why or why not? How did the pictures help you understand the information better?

A Circle the main idea and theme for the Max Axiom story.

1 The main idea of the story is:
   a Scientists need electron microscopes to see viruses.
   b Viruses that go into your nose often get trapped there.
   c Viruses are dangerous, but the human body can fight them.
   d Polio is a very dangerous virus.

2 The theme of the story is:
   a The human body works hard to keep you healthy.
   b Viruses and bacteria come in many shapes and sizes.
   c White blood cells are very powerful.
   d Scientists know everything about the human body.

B Circle True (T) or False (F).

1 All bacteria look the same.   T   F
2 The top layer of your skin has dead cells.   T   F
3 Stomach acids can destroy viruses.   T   F
4 White blood cells can hurt us.   T   F
5 You can see viruses with just your eyes.   T   F
6 Mucus helps your body stay healthy.   T   F

C **Words in Context** Match each clue to a word. Write the correct letter.

1 If a person did this, they ate food. _____   a suit
2 You can wear this on your body. _____   b scrape
3 This describes water, juice, oil, or blood. _____   c swallowed
4 If you have one of these, your skin may hurt. _____ d fluid

112 Unit 11 *Comprehension*

Grammar in Use

Workbook Grammar pages 101–102

D Listen and sing along. **Get Back in Bed!** 2·32

It's a nice, warm, and sunny day.
I want to go outside and play.
"You cannot play. Get back in bed!
You're much too sick," my mother said.

She says I have the common cold.
My head aches, and I'm hot and cold.
I sneeze and blow. I blow and sneeze.
More soft, white paper tissues – please!

E Read the sentence. What do the three underlined words describe?

It's a <u>nice</u>, <u>warm</u>, and <u>sunny</u> day.

F **Learn Grammar** Order of Adjectives

You can use more than one adjective to describe a noun. The adjectives must go in a certain order: opinion … size … age … shape … color … kind.

Max Axiom studies these <u>fascinating</u>, <u>tiny</u> visitors.
                           opinion   size

Read each sentence. Write the adjectives in the correct order.

1 The doctor washed his white, new, lab coat. _____
2 Max saw round, red, large viruses. _____
3 It's a tiny, gray, ugly polio virus. _____

G Describe objects in your classroom using two or three adjectives. Make a list like the one below. Then describe the objects to your partner.

There is a long, white, plastic ruler on my desk.

Things in my classroom
long, white, plastic ruler

Grammar: Order of Adjectives **Unit 11   113**

Summary

Objectives: To demonstrate understanding of a text; to understand the meaning and form of the grammar structure.

Reading: Comprehension

Grammar input: Order of adjectives

Grammar practice: Workbook exercises

Grammar production: Describe objects in the classroom

Materials: Audio CD

Comprehension

Think

• Have students point to specific pictures they found helpful or confusing.

A Circle the main idea and theme for the Max Axiom story.

• Revisit the lesson on differentiating between theme and main idea on page 109.
• Read the choices together and discuss why each correct answer is best.
• Check the answers with the class.

ANSWERS
1 c   2 a

B Circle True (T) or False (F).

• For each question, tell students to look back at the reading text and find details to support their answer:
  1 See the illustrations and text in frame 3. The reading is about viruses, but the text says "Just like bacteria" so the reader can infer that bacteria also comes in different shapes and sizes.
  2 See the illustrations and text in frame 5.
  3 See the illustrations and text in frame 10. The text says viruses are *usually* destroyed by stomach acids.
  4 See the illustrations and text in frames 11 and 12. The words *defense*, *fight back*, and *aid* show that white blood cells help us.
  5 See the illustration and text in frame 1.
  6 See the illustration and text in frame 9.

ANSWERS
1 F   2 T   3 T   4 F   5 F   6 T

DIFFERENTIATION

Below level:

• Tell students to go back to the reading text and find specific details that support the main idea that *Viruses are dangerous, but the human body can fight them.* Ask *How do you know viruses are dangerous? How do you know the human body can fight them?*

At level:

• Remind students that the theme is the bigger picture idea or the general lesson of a selection.
• Write the theme on the board: *The human body works hard to keep you healthy.*

- Ask *What other topics might work with this theme?*

Above level:

- Ask students to explain how each of these things supports the theme:
  mucus (carries viruses to the stomach, where they are usually killed by stomach acids)
  stomach (creates an acid that usually kills viruses; this acid also helps breaks down food so your body can use it for nutrition)
  skin (creates a physical barrier so viruses can't enter your body)
  nose hairs (capture viruses before they enter your body)
  white blood cells (fight viruses that enter your blood stream).

CRITICAL THINKING

- Write *immune system* on the board. Underline the word *system*. Ask students what other systems they know about. They may think of systems in their bodies, such as the digestive system or the musculoskeletal system. They may also consider systems related to other Big Questions they have studied, such as the solar system or the transportation system in a city.
- After the class has named other systems they know, guide them in identifying similarities and differences among all systems, e.g. all systems have multiple parts that work together to create a unified whole. In many cases, when one part of the system fails, other parts can compensate for the loss. (If a virus gets past the nose hairs, it may still be killed by stomach acid.) In other cases, when a part of the system fails, the entire system fails. (If you become paralyzed from a disease, your musculoskeletal system won't be able to function at all.)

C Words in Context: Match each clue to a word. Write the correct letter.

- Have students go back and find the words in the text.
- Tell them to use the context clues to guess at the meaning of each word.
- Check the answers with the class.

ANSWERS
1 c 2 a 3 d 4 b

Grammar in Use

D Listen and sing along. 🎵 2·32

- Revisit the symptoms of the common cold that students brainstormed on page 109 for the *Think* question.
- Listen to the song once and then sing it together as a class.
- Ask *What does the singer want to do? Why does her mother tell her she can't go out and play?*

E Read the sentence. What do the three underlined words describe?

- Have students complete the exercise individually and then check with a partner.
- Elicit answers from the class.

ANSWER
The kind of day it is.

F Learn Grammar: Order of Adjectives

- Read the *Learn Grammar* box together.
- Brainstorm a few adjectives that fit in each category.

Read each sentence. Write the adjectives in the correct order.

- Read the first sentence together. Identify what each adjective refers to (*white* is color, *new* is age, *lab* is kind).
- Complete number 1 together. Have students complete 2 and 3 on their own.
- Check answers with the class.

ANSWERS
1 The doctor washed his new, white, lab coat.
2 Max saw large, round, red viruses.
3 It's an ugly, tiny, gray polio virus.

G Describe objects in your classroom using two or three adjectives. Make a list like the one below. Then describe the objects to your partner.

COMMUNICATION

- Students share their lists with their partner and describe the objects.
- Have some students describe their objects to the class.

Workbook Grammar

- Direct students to the Workbook for further practice of the grammar.

Further Practice
Workbook pages 100–102
Online practice Unit 11 • Understand
Oxford **iTools** Unit 11 • Understand

Unit 11 Communicate page 114

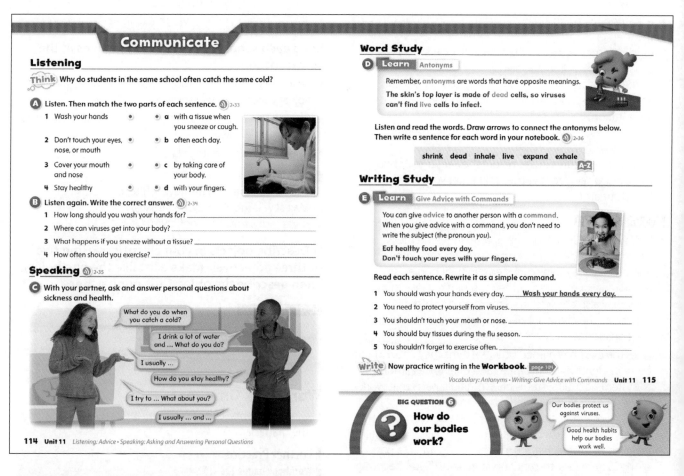

Communicate

Listening

Think Why do students in the same school often catch the same cold?

A Listen. Then match the two parts of each sentence. 2·33
1 Wash your hands • • a with a tissue when you sneeze or cough.
2 Don't touch your eyes, • • b often each day. nose, or mouth
3 Cover your mouth • • c by taking care of and nose your body.
4 Stay healthy • • d with your fingers.

B Listen again. Write the correct answer. 2·34
1 How long should you wash your hands for? _____
2 Where can viruses get into your body? _____
3 What happens if you sneeze without a tissue? _____
4 How often should you exercise? _____

Speaking 2·35
C With your partner, ask and answer personal questions about sickness and health.

What do you do when you catch a cold?

I drink a lot of water and ... What do you do?

I usually ...

How do you stay healthy?

I try to ... What about you?

I usually ... and ...

114 **Unit 11** Listening: Advice • Speaking: Asking and Answering Personal Questions

Word Study
D Learn Antonyms
Remember, antonyms are words that have opposite meanings.
The skin's top layer is made of dead cells, so viruses can't find live cells to infect.

Listen and read the words. Draw arrows to connect the antonyms below. Then write a sentence for each word in your notebook. 2·36

shrink dead inhale live expand exhale
A-Z

Writing Study
E Learn Give Advice with Commands
You can give advice to another person with a command. When you give advice with a command, you don't need to write the subject (the pronoun you).
Eat healthy food every day.
Don't touch your eyes with your fingers.

Read each sentence. Rewrite it as a simple command.
1 You should wash your hands every day. _____Wash your hands every day._____
2 You need to protect yourself from viruses. _____
3 You shouldn't touch your mouth or nose. _____
4 You should buy tissues during the flu season. _____
5 You shouldn't forget to exercise often. _____

Write Now practice writing in the **Workbook.** page 109

Vocabulary: Antonyms • Writing: Give Advice with Commands **Unit 11** 115

BIG QUESTION 6
How do our bodies work?
Our bodies protect us against viruses.
Good health habits help our bodies work well.

Summary

Objectives: To learn and practice listening, speaking, and writing strategies to facilitate effective communication.

Vocabulary: *shrink, dead, inhale, live, expand, exhale*

Listening strategy: Listening for advice

Speaking: Asking and answering personal questions

Word Study: Antonyms

Writing Study: Giving advice with commands

Big Question learning point: *Our body keeps us strong and healthy.*

Materials: Discover Poster 6, Audio CD, Big Question Chart

Listening

Think

- Tell students to think about all the things they touch at school, e.g. door knobs, desks, chairs, pencils, books.
- Then think about how germs enter your body. Every time we touch any opening in the skin (a scrape, our mouth, our eyes, etc.) germs can enter the body.

A Listen. Then match the two parts of each sentence. 2·33

- Play the audio once and have students listen. Ask *What is the purpose of this selection?*
- Tell students to match the sentence parts in A. Then play the audio again so they can check their work.
- Check answers with the class.

ANSWERS
1 b   2 d   3 a   4 c

B Listen again. Write the correct answer. 2·34

- Play the audio so students can complete the exercise.
- Have partners take turns asking each other *Do you wash your hands for 15 seconds / sneeze into a tissue / exercise each day?*
- Check the answers with the class.

ANSWERS
1 at least 15 seconds   2 eyes, nose, mouth
3 virus will go into the air   4 each day

DIFFERENTIATION

Below level:

- Pause after each section to allow the students time to process what they've heard. Ask them to pantomime the healthy habit after each section. (Pantomime washing front, back, and between fingers for 15 seconds; move fingers toward each facial feature but don't touch; sneeze into a tissue; jog in place.)

At level:
- Pause after each section and ask students to tell you the main idea of that section.
- Then ask them to say the best main idea of the entire announcement, e.g. *You can protect yourself from influenza with a few healthy habits.*

Above level:
- Challenge students to name a theme for the selection.
- Encourage answers that touch upon a bigger picture idea or lesson, e.g. *We can help ourselves stay healthy by practicing good habits.*

Speaking 🔊 2·35

C With your partner, ask and answer personal questions about sickness and health.

COMMUNICATION
- Say each line of the dialogue with students echoing as they hear each line.
- Model the dialogue with a confident student in front of the class.
- Put students into pairs and tell them to practice the dialogue, taking turns speaking the different roles.

COLLABORATIVE LEARNING
- Have partners make lists of the different ailments they might have, such as a sore throat, a runny nose, or a high temperature. Then have them brainstorm the things they do to relieve those ailments, such as drink hot tea with honey, take medicine, or get lots of rest.
- Then have partners brainstorm things they do to stay healthy.
- Tell partners to refer to their lists as they practice the dialogue so they have lots of different ideas.

Word Study

D Learn: Antonyms
- Read the *Learn* box together.
- Point out the antonyms *dead* and *live*. Show students how the word *can't* is the negative which contrasts *dead* and *live* in the sentence.

Listen and read the words. Draw arrows to connect the antonyms below. Then write a sentence for each word in your notebook. 🔊 2·36
- Have students draw arrows to connect the antonyms.
- Then ask students to write a sentence for each word, challenge them to write a sentence that includes both antonyms.
- Help them write sentences by suggesting they include a negative word to contrast the antonyms.

ANSWERS
Antonyms: shrink / expand; dead / live; inhale / exhale

Writing Study

E Learn: Give Advice with Commands
- Read the *Learn* box together.
- Write the first sentence on the board. Underneath it write, *(You should) eat healthy foods every day.* Say *This advice tells someone what they should do.*
- Write the second sentence on the board. Underneath it write, *(You shouldn't) touch your eyes with your fingers.* Say *This advice tells someone what they should NOT do.*

Read each sentence. Rewrite it as a simple command.
- Help students identify whether each sentence is positive (*You should … You need to …*) or negative (*You shouldn't …*).
- Have students complete the exercise on their own. Then go over answers with the class.

ANSWERS
1 Wash your hands every day.
2 Protect yourself from viruses.
3 Don't touch your mouth or nose.
4 Buy tissues during the flu season.
5 Don't forget to exercise often.

CRITICAL THINKING
- Tell students you want to create a class advice book with tips for staying healthy.
- Encourage students to look at this unit, the module on food, and their own personal experiences to come up with good ideas for staying healthy.
- Have each student contribute one page to the book: the page includes an illustration or collage and a caption with the piece of advice.

Write
- Direct students to the Workbook for further practice.

Big Question 6 Review

How do our bodies work?
- Display **Discover Poster 6**. Discuss what you see.
- Refer to the learning points covered in Unit 11 which are written on the poster and have students explain how they relate to the different pictures.
- Return to the **Big Question Chart**.
- Ask students what they have learned about their bodies while studying this unit.

> **Further Practice**
> **Workbook pages 103–104**
> **Online practice Unit 11 · Communicate**
> **Oxford iTools Unit 11 · Communicate**

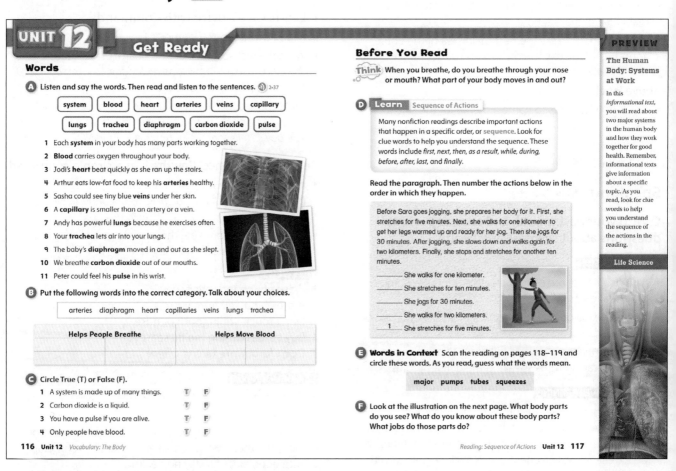

Summary

Objectives: To understand words about the body; to apply own experience and reading strategy to help comprehension of a text.

Vocabulary: *system, blood, heart, arteries, veins, capillary, lungs, trachea, diaphragm, carbon dioxide, pulse, major, pumps, tubes, squeezes*

Reading strategy: Sequence of actions

Materials: Audio CD

Words

A Listen and say the words. Then read and listen to the sentences. ⊚ 2·37

- Play the audio. Ask students to point to the words as they hear them.
- Play the audio a second time and have students repeat the words when they hear them.
- Read the sentences together. After each sentence, ask students to guess the definition of the word. Fine-tune their definitions as needed using discussion points like the following:
  system: The system in the body which controls the central nervous system, the digestive system, and the immune system.
  blood: Ask *What cells in your blood help your immune system?*
  heart: Tap your hand to your chest to imitate the beating of your heart, thump-thump, thump-thump.
  arteries: These carry blood away from the heart.
  veins: These carry blood to the heart.

capillary: This is a tiny tube that connects arteries and veins.
lungs: Take a deep breath and say *I am breathing air into my lungs.*
trachea: Point to the trachea in the X-ray of the respiratory system.
diaphragm: Take an exaggerated breath to demonstrate your diaphragm moving up and down.
carbon dioxide: Use your hand to gesture as you breathe in and out and say *Oxygen in, carbon dioxide out.*
pulse: Have students find their pulse.

B Put the following words into the correct category. Talk about your choices.

- Look at the exercise together to make sure students understand what to do.
- Have partners work together to sort the words.
- Reconvene to share answers and check work.

ANSWERS

Helps People Breathe: lungs, trachea, diaphragm
Helps Move Blood: arteries, heart, capillaries, veins

COLLABORATIVE LEARNING

- Have partners copy the chart from B on a piece of paper and try to add another column to review vocabulary from Unit 11: *These help you stay healthy.*
- Tell them to first try to remember as many words as they can that are related to the immune system. Then have them go back to the previous unit to add any words they forgot.

C Circle True (T) or False (F).

- Have students discuss the sentences before they choose true or false.
- Check the answsers with the class.

1 T   2 F   3 T   4 F

Below level:

- Use visuals to help clarify meaning, e.g. Draw an oval / pear-shaped heart on the board and label it. Draw a tube with word *blood* in it and arrows pointing to the heart and label it *vein*. Draw a tube with the word *blood* in it and arrows pointing away and label it *artery*. If you have colored markers, use red for the artery and blue for the vein.
- From the main artery, branch off a few smaller arteries. The branches become smaller and more web-like, and these tiny web-like branches are the *capillaries*.
- The capillaries connect with the cells of the body (organs) and exchange the oxygen we breathe in and the carbon dioxide we breathe out. You can illustrate this by drawing a cartoon-like arm muscle. The red capillaries and blue capillaries enclose the arm muscle. The blue capillaries become larger and eventually become the larger labeled vein that returns to the heart.

At level:

- Have students write a question for each sentence, e.g. *How is each system in your body similar?*
- Tell them to choose a few sentences for which they write more than one question. They will need to focus on the meaning of the sentence and the word to do this correctly: *What does blood do? What does blood carry throughout your body? What carries oxygen throughout your body?*

Above level:

- Challenge students to write a few more True / False sentences to add to C.
- Tell them to exchange sentences with a partner.
- Have students share the sentences with the class. For each false sentence, have volunteers edit the sentences to make them true, e.g. *Carbon dioxide is not a liquid / is a gas.*

Before You Read

Think

- Have students practice taking deep breaths to see which part of their body moves in and out. Tell them to try breathing in and out through their nose and then their mouth to see how each feels.
- Ask if there's any reason it's better to breathe through one or the other. (Nose hairs filter the air entering your body and help the immune system, so if you breathe through your mouth, you skip this step in the system.)

D Learn: Sequence of Actions

- Read the *Learn* box together.
- Give some examples of the sequence words in the context of a few sentences, e.g. *I sneezed into the tissue. As a result, I didn't spread the virus.* (What happened first? *I sneezed into the tissue.* What happened next? *I didn't spread the virus.*)

Read the paragraph. Then number the actions below in the order in which they happen.

- Read the paragraph. You can have some volunteers pantomime the actions as you read.
- Have students number the actions in order.
- Check answers with the class.

2, 5, 3, 4, 1

- Ask students to share exercise routines they have for playing a sport or exercising.
- First have a volunteer tell the class what they do. Encourage him / her to use sequence words and details. Note the main actions on the board as he / she speaks. Then have the class retell the sequence of events using the notes on the board and sequence words.

E Words in Context: Scan the reading on pages 118–119 and circle these words. As you read, guess what the words mean.

- Have students scan the reading text and circle the words.

F Look at the illustration on the next page. What body parts do you see? What do you know about these body parts? What jobs to those parts do?

- Have students look at the illustration.
- Tell them to check the vocabulary list on page 116 for ideas.
- Have students discuss their ideas in pairs or small groups before checking answers with the class.

Reading Preview

- Read the title of the unit's reading text.
- Have students silently read the content of the preview bar.
- Ask *What type of text is it?* Ask *What does this type of text do?*
- Remind students to pay attention to the sequence of events as they read.

Further Practice
Workbook pages 105–106
Online practice Unit 12 • Get Ready
Oxford **iTools** Unit 12 • Get Ready

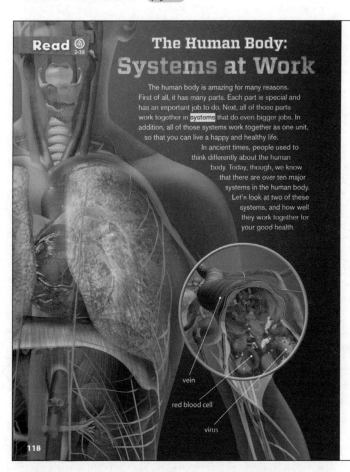

Read 🔊 2·38

The Human Body: Systems at Work

The human body is amazing for many reasons. First of all, it has many parts. Each part is special and has an important job to do. Next, all of those parts work together in **systems** that do even bigger jobs. In addition, all of those systems work together as one unit, so that you can live a happy and healthy life.

In ancient times, people used to think differently about the human body. Today, though, we know that there are over ten major systems in the human body. Let's look at two of these systems, and how well they work together for your good health.

vein

red blood cell

virus

118

The Respiratory System
This system brings oxygen into your body and takes carbon dioxide out of your body. The major parts of the respiratory system are the trachea, the lungs, and the diaphragm.

The Circulatory System
This system carries oxygen and food to all of the cells in your body. It then removes carbon dioxide and other waste products from those cells. The major parts of the circulatory system are the heart, the arteries, the veins, the capillaries, and the blood that moves through those parts.

Two Systems Working Together as One
When you breathe in, your diaphragm first helps your lungs to get bigger. As a result, the air flows into your nose or mouth, through your trachea, and into your lungs. This air has oxygen, which your body needs to live. Next, the oxygen in your lungs passes into the capillaries, which then carry blood to the pulmonary vein. This vein then takes the blood to the left side of your heart.

Your heart pumps this blood into tubes called arteries, which then carry oxygen to all of the cells in your body. Next, these cells use this oxygen to keep your body healthy. They also create carbon dioxide after they use the oxygen. Your body doesn't need carbon dioxide, so your blood takes it away. After veins carry this blood back to the right side of your heart, it is pumped back into your lungs. The carbon dioxide then passes back into the air in your lungs. Finally, when your diaphragm squeezes your lungs, the air rushes out of your body.

Think
What is the sequence of actions up to now?

These two systems work together to bring oxygen-rich blood to every part of your body within one minute. They do this 24 hours a day, while you sleep, eat, study, and play. It is easy to see why the human body is called the most amazing machine in the world.

Think
What is the sequence of actions in this paragraph?

You **BREATHE** about **20,000 times** every day.

Check Your Lung Power!
1. Get a package of large balloons. Make sure they are all the same size. Give one to each friend.
2. Tell everyone to blow ONCE into their balloons, filling them as much as possible. Then measure the balloons. Whose is the biggest?

Put your **two fists together**. This is about the size of your **HEART**.

Check Your Heartbeat!
1. Place two fingers on your wrist below your thumb. Can you feel blood moving through the artery? This is your pulse, which measures your heartbeat.
2. Count the number of beats you feel in one minute. Compare your heartbeat with your friends.

119

Summary

Objectives: To read, understand and discuss a nonfiction text; to apply a reading strategy to improve comprehension.

School subject: Life Science

Text type: Informational text (nonfiction)

Reading strategy: Sequence of actions

Big Question learning points: *The respiratory system helps us breathe. The circulatory system moves blood and oxygen through our bodies. Our bodies keep us strong and healthy.*

Materials: Talk About It! Poster, Audio CD

Before Reading

- Ask students to make predictions about what they will learn in the reading text.
- Tell them to use the words from the vocabulary list on page 116. Revisit their predictions after you finish reading.

During Reading 🔊 2·38

- Play the audio. Students listen as they read along.
- Stop at each *Think* box for students to discuss the questions.
- Have students do the two actions. Say *Check your lung power …; check your heartbeat … .*

DIFFERENTIATION

Below level:
- Have students read in mixed-ability pairs.
- Have the more confident student help the less confident student with pronunciation and comprehension.

- Tell students to pause after every few sentences to discuss what they have read so far.
- Ask questions periodically to check comprehension, such as *What does the respiratory system do?*

At level:
- Have small groups read the text together, taking turns around a circle.
- Assign a secretary in each group to take notes. Tell the groups to pause at each *Think* box and answer the question; the secretary writes the group's answers.
- Tell students to underline the sequence clue words as they read. Pause at each *Think* box and have them look back at the underlined words to help them identify the sequence of actions.
- Have the class share their answers to the *Think* boxes.

Above level:
- Have students read the story alone, jotting down any phrases or sentences they do not understand.
- Put students into partners to work through anything they jotted down. If they need additional help with comprehension, have them ask you specific questions for clarification.
- Challenge students to summarize the main idea of the selection.
- Ask students to try to identify the theme.

- Divide the class into small groups.
- Each group uses a secretary to record the group's ideas, and a monitor to facilitate the discussion.
- Tell groups to paraphrase the different steps in the section *"Two Systems Working Together as One."*
- The secretary writes each step on a separate notecard.
- Collect all the sets of cards and reconvene.
- Invite one group to the front of the room. Give that group another group's cards. Have them work together to quickly arrange the cards in the right order for the class.
- Repeat with the other groups and card sets.

After Reading

- Return to the predictions students made during Before Reading. Check their ideas, and make any content corrections based on the actual reading.

CRITICAL THINKING

Discussion questions:

- *For each* Think *box, ask students what conclusions they made and why.*
- *Why does the author write that the human body is amazing? What is amazing about it?*
- *What would happen if one part of the respiratory or circulatory system didn't work?*
- *How do the illustrations in this informational text help you to understand it more?*
- *What parts of the body are necessary for people to breathe?*
- *Why do you think the author wrote this informational text? What is the author's purpose?*
- *Are these the only two systems in your body? What other systems do you know about?*

COLLABORATIVE LEARNING

- Display the **Talk About It! Poster** to help students with sentence frames for discussion and expressing personal opinions.
- Put students into pairs to discuss the main ideas from the reading text.
- Have students say one thing about every section in the reading.

> CULTURE NOTE
>
> The arteries are more muscular and elastic than the veins. This is because they have to control the flow of blood out of the heart and through the body.
>
> When arteries are clogged or harden, they do not work as well. Healthy eating is one factor that improves arterial health.

Further Practice
Workbook page 107
Online practice Unit 12 · Read
Oxford iTools Unit 12 · Read

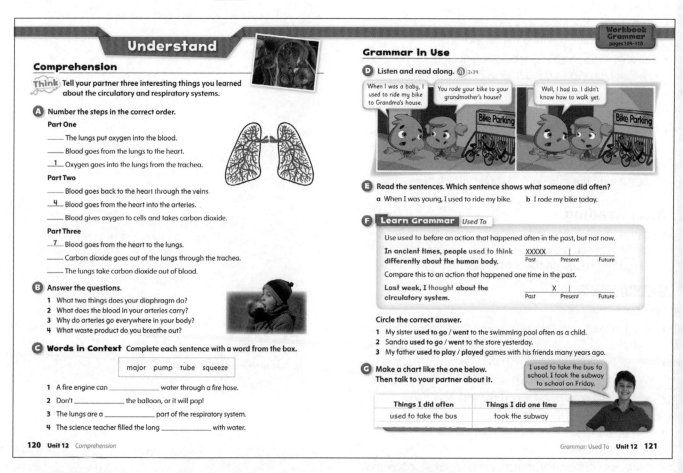

Summary

Objectives: To demonstrate understanding of a nonfiction text; to understand the meaning and form of the grammar structure.

Reading: Comprehension

Grammar input: *Used to*

Grammar practice: Workbook exercises

Grammar production: Use *used to* to talk about actions in the past

Materials: Audio CD

Comprehension

Think

* Tell students to write their answers to each question separately, and then compare answers with their partners.

A Number the steps in the correct order.

* Encourage students to look back at the reading to confirm their answers.
* After you confirm answers, ask *Why are the steps divided into Parts One, Two, and Three?* (Part One tells what happens when oxygen first enters your body; Part Two tells what happens when your heart pumps blood through your body; Part Three tells what happens when the heart pumps the oxygen-depleted blood back to the lungs.)

ANSWERS

Part One: 2, 3, 1   **Part Two:** 6, 4, 5   **Part Three:** 7, 9, 8

DIFFERENTIATION

Below level:

* Review the reading text together to complete A.
* Have students scan the text to find the sentences that support each answer, e.g. in Part One:
  1 In the second sentence under "Two Systems Working Together as One," it says "the air flows … through your trachea, and into your lungs."
  2 In the fourth sentence it says "the oxygen in your lungs passes into the capillaries, which then carry blood to the pulmonary vein."
  3 In the fifth sentence it says, "This vein then takes the blood to the left side of your heart."

At level:

* Have students work with partners to ask and answer *What happens first?* questions, e.g. *What happens first? The lungs put oxygen into the blood or blood goes from the lungs to the heart.*
* For a bigger challenge, have them ask about the sequence of sentences from different parts.

Above level:

* Challenge students to add one more sentence to each of Part One, Part Two, and Part Three in A, e.g.
  Part One, add *The diaphragm helps your lungs get bigger* before *Oxygen goes into the lungs from the trachea.* Part Two, add *Cells use the oxygen to keep your body healthy* between 5 and 6. Part Three, add *Your diaphragm squeezes the carbon dioxide out of your lungs* at the end.

B Answer the questions.

- Have students answer the questions and then discuss them with the class.

1 It expands to help your lungs get bigger and take in oxygen; it contracts to squeeze your lungs and expel carbon dioxide.
2 The blood in your arteries carries oxygen-rich blood.
3 All the cells in your body need oxygen to function.
4 You breathe out carbon dioxide.

CRITICAL THINKING

- There are similarities among many systems in nature. Compare the circulatory system with the rivers, tributaries, and distributaries in a river system, or the root and leaf system in a tree. (If you can, print images from the web to show students.)
- Say *Eating high-fat food is bad for your arteries. The fat builds up in the arteries and makes it harder for them to do their job. What do you think might hurt the arteries of a river system?* (Possible answer: Pollution, dams, or drought.)
- Say *Compare the root and leaf system of a tree with the human circulatory system. Use the words roots, leaves, branches, tree trunk.*

CRITICAL THINKING

- Have students look back at the Max Axiom story from Unit 11, page 110. Tell them to think about how the information from *The Human Body: Systems at Work* could be explained in a graphic novel format. Perhaps Max Axiom could be a single blood cell traveling through the body.

C Words in Context: Complete each sentence with a word from the box.

- Return to the reading text and have a volunteer read each word in the context of its sentence. Use the context to determine meaning.
- Check the answers with the class.

1 pump   2 squeeze   3 major   4 tube

Grammar in Use

D Listen and read along. 🔊 2·39

- Listen to the conversation once.
- Have two confident students read it aloud for the class.
- Play the audio again and have volunteers use it as a model for rhythm and intonation as they echo read.
- Ask students how they know the boy is talking about a time in the past.

E Read the sentences. Which sentence shows what someone did often?

- Point out that *When I was young* covers a long period of time – several years, but *today* only covers one day.
- If the boy used to ride his bike when he was young, it means he did it over and over during that period of time.

F Learn Grammar: *Used to*

- Read the *Learn Grammar* box together.
- Go around the room and have students make sentences about their own lives. Tell them to start with either *When I was (a baby / in first grade / younger) I used to …* or *(Yesterday / Last Monday / This morning) I… .*

Circle the correct answer.

- For each sentence, help students identify the time marker and whether it indicates something that happened regularly over a longer period of time (*used to*) or at one specific time in history (*past tense*).
- Have students complete the exercise on their own.
- Check the answers with the class.

1 used to go   2 went   3 used to play

G Make a chart like the one below. Then talk to your partner about it.

- Have students complete the chart on their own.
- Have partners tell each other about things they used to do often and things they did at one specific time.
- Tell them to follow the model on the page.

COMMUNICATION

- To make sure students listen carefully to their partners, tell them you will ask them to tell the class about their partners, e.g. Maria tells Philip, *I used to eat cereal for breakfast every morning when I was a baby. This morning I ate eggs.* Philip tells the class, *Maria used to eat cereal when she was a baby. This morning she ate eggs.*

Further Practice
Workbook pages 108–110
Online practice Unit 12 · Understand
Oxford **iTools** Unit 12 · Understand

Unit 12 Communicate

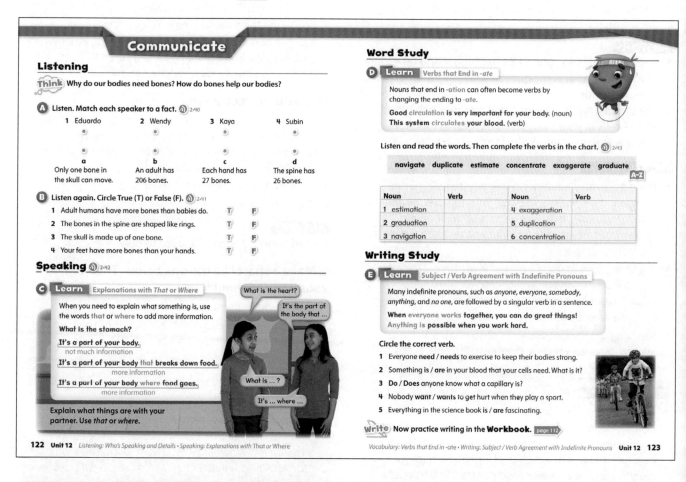

Communicate

Listening

Think Why do our bodies need bones? How do bones help our bodies?

A Listen. Match each speaker to a fact. 2·40

1 Eduardo	2 Wendy	3 Kaya	4 Subin
a	b	c	d
Only one bone in the skull can move.	An adult has 206 bones.	Each hand has 27 bones.	The spine has 26 bones.

B Listen again. Circle True (T) or False (F). 2·41

1 Adult humans have more bones than babies do.   T   F
2 The bones in the spine are shaped like rings.   T   F
3 The skull is made up of one bone.   T   F
4 Your feet have more bones than your hands.   T   F

Speaking 2·42

C **Learn** Explanations with *That* or *Where*

When you need to explain what something is, use the words **that** or **where** to add more information.

What is the stomach?

It's a part of your body.
not much information

It's a part of your body **that** breaks down food.
more information

It's a part of your body **where** food goes.
more information

What is the heart?

It's the part of the body that …

What is … ?

It's … where …

Explain what things are with your partner. Use *that* or *where*.

122 Unit 12 Listening: Who's Speaking and Details • Speaking: Explanations with That or Where

Word Study

D **Learn** Verbs that End in *-ate*

Nouns that end in **-ation** can often become verbs by changing the ending to -ate.

Good circulation is very important for your body. (noun)
This system circulates your blood. (verb)

Listen and read the words. Then complete the verbs in the chart. 2·43

navigate duplicate estimate concentrate exaggerate graduate   A-Z

Noun	Verb	Noun	Verb
1 estimation		4 exaggeration	
2 graduation		5 duplication	
3 navigation		6 concentration	

Writing Study

E **Learn** Subject / Verb Agreement with Indefinite Pronouns

Many indefinite pronouns, such as *anyone, everyone, somebody, anything,* and *no one,* are followed by a singular verb in a sentence.

When everyone works together, you can do great things!
Anything is possible when you work hard.

Circle the correct verb.

1 Everyone **need / needs** to exercise to keep their bodies strong.
2 Something **is / are** in your blood that your cells need. What is it?
3 **Do / Does** anyone know what a capillary is?
4 Nobody **want / wants** to get hurt when they play a sport.
5 Everything in the science book **is / are** fascinating.

Write Now practice writing in the **Workbook**. page 112

Vocabulary: Verbs that End in *-ate* • Writing: Subject / Verb Agreement with Indefinite Pronouns **Unit 12 123**

Summary

Objectives: To learn and practice listening, speaking, and writing strategies to facilitate effective communication.

Vocabulary: *navigate, duplicate, estimate, concentrate, exaggerate, graduate*

Listening strategy: Listening for who's speaking and details

Speaking: Explanations with *that* or *where*

Word Study: Verbs that end in *-ate*

Writing Study: Subject / Verb agreement with indefinite pronouns

Big Question learning point: *Bones protect us and help us move easily.*

Materials: Audio CD

Listening

Think

• Have students discuss the questions in small groups.
• Invite them to share their ideas with the class.

A Listen. Match each speaker to a fact. 2·40

• Play the audio once through while students just listen.
• Play it a second time and have them complete the exercise.
• Check answers with the class.

ANSWERS
1 b   2 d   3 a   4 c

DIFFERENTIATION

Below level:

• Pause after each person's name so students know who is speaking. Tell students to take notes as they listen. Pause after each section and ask students to tell you what they remember hearing.
• Check to see if any of the facts they recall are options for A. If they are, have students match the name to the fact. If not, listen again and help them identify the place in the audio where the fact is mentioned.
• Repeat for each section.

At level:

• Elicit the topic of each student's report.
• Elicit facts from each student's report that are not mentioned in A. Ask *What else did (Eduardo) teach you in his report?* Have students write what they remember on a slip of paper.
• Invite students to take turns reading aloud one of the facts they wrote down. Have the class decide which report it's from.

Above level:

• Have students prepare a similar report on one of the other systems they've learned about. They can share their reports with the class.

CRITICAL THINKING

Tell students to use what they know about systems in the body and the way their bodies work to brainstorm possible answers to the following questions:

- Why do you think babies have more bones than adults?
- Why do you think the vertebrae are shaped like rings, not like a solid rod?
- Why do you think the skull bones mostly don't move?
- Why do you think there are so many bones in the hands and feet?

B Listen again. Circle True (T) or False (F). 2·41

- Write the following numbers on the board: *30, 300, 26, 206, 27, 1, 10.* Ask volunteers to read them aloud, and have the class repeat.
- Have students complete the exercise on their own.
- Check answers with the class.

ANSWERS
1 F 2 T 3 F 4 F

Speaking 2·42

C Learn: Explanations with *That* or *Where*

COMMUNICATION

- Read the *Learn* box together.
- Help students understand the construction. Write *The stomach is a part of your body. The stomach breaks down food.*
- Then cross out *The stomach* in the second sentence and replace it with *that*: *The stomach is a part of your body that breaks down food.*
- Repeat for *where*. Write *The stomach is a part of your body. Food goes to your stomach.*
- Then cross out *to your stomach* in the second sentence and replace it with *where*: *The stomach is a part of your body where food goes.*

Explain what things are with your partner. Use *that* or *where*.

- Have students follow the model to talk about other parts of the body.
- Remind them to talk about the systems they've studied in this module, and to also consider the five senses.

COLLABORATIVE LEARNING

- First have partners list several different body parts in a three-column chart. The word goes in the first column. The second column is labeled *More information / that*; the third column is labeled *More information / where.*
- Students first work together to complete the chart with more information about each body part.
- Then they can refer to the phrases on the chart to help them construct their conversations.

Word Study

D Learn: Verbs that End in -*ate*

- Remind students of the Unit 2 (page 23) Word Study lesson about changing nouns that end in -*ance* into adjectives that end in -*ant*.
- Explain that we often use the same base word to create other words that are different parts of speech.
- Read the *Learn* box together.

Listen and read the words. Then complete the verbs in the chart. 2·43

- Play the audio and have students point to the words as they hear them.
- Have students complete the exercise on their own.
- Check the answers with the class.

ANSWERS
1 estimate 2 graduate 3 navigate 4 exaggerate
5 duplicate 6 concentrate

Writing Study

E Learn: Subject / Verb Agreement with Indefinite Pronouns

- Revisit the lessons on Indefinite Pronouns in Unit 7 (page 73) and Unit 9 (page 93).
- Read the *Learn* box together. Clarify that we use these indefinite pronouns the same way we use *she*, *he*, or *it*.
- Use a traditional drill to conjugate a few regular and irregular verbs to reinforce the singular form. Say *work.* Gesture to a student and say *I*. The student responds with *I work.* Say *be.* Gesture to a student and say *it.* The student responds with *It is.* Continue this way.

Circle the correct verb.

- Have students complete the exercise on their own.
- Check answers with the class.

ANSWERS
1 needs 2 is 3 Does 4 wants 5 is

Write

- Direct students to the Workbook for further practice.

Further Practice
Workbook pages 111–112
Online practice Unit 12 • Communicate
Oxford iTools Unit 12 • Communicate

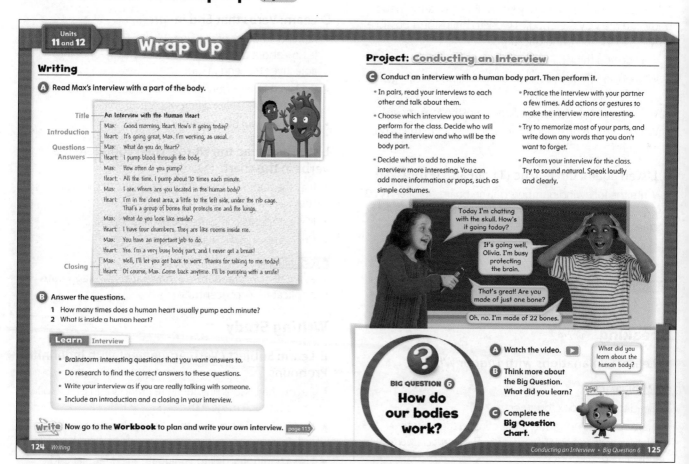

Summary

Objectives: To show what students have learned about the language and learning points of Units 11 and 12.

Reading: Comprehension of an interview

Project: Conduct an interview

Writing: Write an interview

Speaking: Talk about the interviews

Materials: Big Question DVD, Discover Poster 6, Talk About It! Poster, Big Question Chart

Writing

CRITICAL THINKING

• Remind students how to take their pulse (see page 119). Have them take their pulse and measure their resting heart rate for thirty seconds.

• Then have everybody do jumping jacks for 60 seconds. Tell them to count out loud as they jump.

• Have students quickly measure their pulse again for thirty seconds. Ask *What happened? Why do you think that happened? What do you notice about your breathing?*

A Read Max's interview with a part of the body.

• Ask students if they have ever seen an interview, maybe with a politician or a movie star. Ask *What did you notice about the interview?*

• Read the sample interview together.

B Answer the questions.

• Have students find the answers in the text.

• Check the answers with the class.

ANSWERS

1 70 times   **2** four chambers

Learn: Interview

• Explain that students should choose a body part they want to interview.

• Read the directions in the *Learn* box together.

• Remind students to follow these guidelines when they plan and write their interviews. Tell them to refer to the sample as a model.

• If students interview a part of the body that's covered in this module, they can refer to the Student Book for their research. If they choose another body part, they can do research at home or at a library.

DIFFERENTIATION

Below level:

• Focus on the information presented in each question in the sample. Tell students to organize their interviews around the information, e.g.

1 Function (*What do you do?*)

2 Frequency (*How often do you do this?* or *When do you do this?*)

3 Location (*Where are you located in the body?*)

4 Visual (*What do you look like?*)

5 Friendly closing (*You have an important job to do.*)

At level:

- Point out the tone of the model interview. It's friendly and the heart answers as if it is a person. This is called "personification."
- Ask students to try to use language in their interviews that gives the body part some personality.
- Point out examples in the model. Sentences like *I'm working as usual* and *I'm a very busy body part, and I never get a break* help give the heart some personality.

Above level:

- Challenge students to go beyond the basic topics covered in the sample (function, frequency, location, and visual), e.g. they can ask about how the body part works with other body parts or what role the body part plays in a bigger system.

Write

- Direct students to the Workbook to plan and write their own interview.

Project

C Conduct an interview with a human body part. Then perform it.

CREATIVITY

- Read the directions together.
- Have partners work through the steps together.
- Read and practice the sample speech bubbles as examples of how students can perform their interviews.
- After students read their interviews, tell them to practice improvising. This means they use the basic information that they wrote in the interview from C, but they spontaneously add in jokes or other details that make it sound more natural.
- The trick to improvising is to have both partners listen and react to each other. You never know what your partner is going to say, so you have to be flexible and willing to try things.
- One way to facilitate improvisation is to give the body part a personality trait, e.g. it can be cranky, or funny, or busy, or arrogant.
- Tell them to try to match the body part with a personality it might have. (The brain might be arrogant because it's in charge of everything. The foot might be cranky because it's always looking at the ground and never sees the sky.)
- After they try improvising, have them discuss which comments made the interview more interesting and add those to it permanently.

Units 11 and 12 Big Question Review

A Watch the video. ▷

- Play the video and when it is finished ask students what they know about the way the body works now.
- Have students share ideas with the class.

B Think more about the Big Question. What did you learn?

COMMUNICATION

- Display **Discover Poster 6**. Point to familiar vocabulary items and elicit them from the class. Ask *What is this?*
- Ask students *What do you see?* Ask *What does that mean?*
- Refer to all of the learning points written on the poster and have students explain how they relate to the different pictures.
- Ask *What does this learning point mean?* Elicit answers from individual students.
- Display the **Talk About It! Poster** to help students with sentence frames for discussion of the learning points and for expressing their opinions.

C Complete the Big Question Chart.

COLLABORATIVE LEARNING

- Ask students what they have learned about the body while studying this unit.
- Put students into pairs or small groups to say two new things they have learned.
- Have students share their ideas with the class and add their ideas to the chart.
- Have students complete the chart in their Workbook.

Further Practice
Workbook pages 113–115
Online practice · Wrap Up 6
Oxford **iTools** · Wrap Up 6

What is mass media?

In units 13 and 14 you will:

WATCH a video about how people get information.

LEARN about different types of mass media.

READ an interview and a reporter's blog.

WRITE a news story.

CREATE a school news program.

BIG QUESTION 7

What is the mass media?

A Watch the video.

B Look at the picture and talk about it.

1 What does each person have? What can they do with these things?

2 What do you think each person is looking at or reading about?

C Think and answer the questions.

1 Where do you get news and information?

2 What news did you hear today?

D Fill out the **Big Question Chart**.

What do you know about the mass media? What do you want to know?

126 Big Question 7

127

Reading Strategies

Students will practice:

- Understanding the main idea and supporting details
- Understanding conflict and resolution

Review

Students will review the language and Big Question learning points of Units 13 and 14 through:

- A news story
- A project (creating a school news program)

Writing Study

Students will be able to use:

- Pronouns
- Regular and irregular verbs in the present perfect

Students will produce texts that:

- Inform

Vocabulary

Students will understand and use words about:

- Mass media and communication

Units 13 and 14
What is mass media?

Students will understand the Big Question learning points:

- Mass media is information that travels to many people quickly.
- People have had mass media for hundreds of years.
- We can get mass media in many ways.
- The mass media changes a lot.
- We can learn facts, opinions, or both from mass media.

Word Study

Students will understand, pronounce, and use:

- Words with *silent k*
- Synonyms

Grammar

Students will understand and use:

- *must, mustn't, have to, don't have to*
- The present perfect

Listening Strategies

Students will practice:

- Listening for gist and details
- Listening for facts and opinions

Speaking

Students will understand and use expressions to:

- Give examples
- Give opinions

Units 13 and 14 Big Question page 126

Summary

Objectives: To activate students' existing knowledge of the topic and identify what they would like to learn about the topic.

Materials: Big Question DVD, Discover Poster 7, Big Question Chart

Introducing the topic

- Read out the Big Question. Ask *What is mass media?*
- Write students' ideas on the board and discuss.

A Watch the video.

- Play the video and when it is finished ask students to answer the following questions in pairs:
  What do you see in the video?
  Who do you think the people are?
  What is happening?
  Do you like it?
- Have individual students share their answers with the class.

DIFFERENTIATION

Below level:

- Pause the video periodically. Point and ask *What's this? Who is this? What's he doing? Where are they?*
- Ask students to answer using complete sentences.

At level:

- After watching, have students write down five things that they saw in the video.
- Elicit the phrases from the class and write them on the board.

Above level:

- After watching, have students write down three sentences about what they saw in the video.
- Tell students to choose one sentence.
- Tell them to stand up and mingle and find someone else with the same sentence (focus on the meaning of the sentence rather than using exactly the same words).
- Have students say their sentence to the class.

B Look at the picture and talk about it.

- Students look at the big picture and talk about it. Ask *What do you see?*
- Ask additional questions:
  Where are these people?
  What do you think the relationship is between them?

C Think and answer the questions.

- Ask *Do you listen to the radio? Do you read the newspaper or magazines? Do you watch TV news programs? Do you follow anyone on* Twitter *or* Facebook?
- Remind students that "news" does not have to be about politics or the economy; it can be about something local and important to them, e.g. how do students know when a favorite band is playing nearby, or when a local sports team has won?

CRITICAL THINKING

- Ask students to discuss the questions in small groups.
- For the first question, prompt groups to talk about the difference between hearing something on TV or reading it on the Internet versus learning about something through "word of mouth."
- For the second question, have students share any news they heard. If several students learned the same news, where did they get their information?

Expanding the topic

COLLABORATIVE LEARNING

- Display **Discover Poster 7** and give students enough time to look at the pictures.
- Elicit some of the words you think they will know.
- Put students into small groups of three or four. Have each group choose a picture that they find interesting.
- Ask each group to say five things that they can see in their picture.

D Fill out the Big Question Chart.

- Display the **Big Question Chart**.
- Ask the class *What do you know about mass media?*
- Revisit their ideas from C above.
- Ask students to write what they know and what they want to know in their Workbooks.
- Write a collection of ideas on the **Big Question Chart**.

Discover Poster 7

1 A news crew filming a man speaking in Washington, D.C.;
2 An early printing press from the 15th century; 3 A man with a notebook computer, a tablet, and a smartphone;
4 A woman using a hands-free, wearable computer; 5 A meteorologist giving facts and opinions about the weather

| **Further Practice**
| **Workbook page 116**
| **Online practice · Big Question 7**
| Oxford **iTools · Big Question 7**

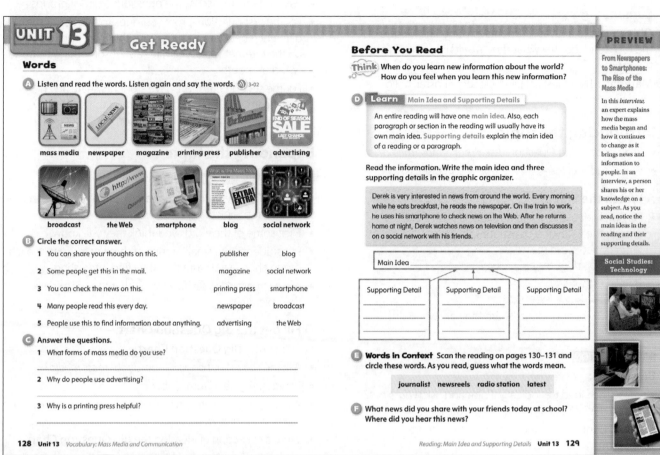

Summary

Objectives: To understand words about the media; to apply own experience and a reading strategy to help comprehension of a text.

Vocabulary: *mass media, newspaper, magazine, printing press, publisher, advertising, broadcast, the Web, smartphone, blog, social network, journalist, newsreels, radio station, latest*

Reading strategy: Main idea and supporting details

Materials: Audio CD

Words

A Listen and read the words. Listen again and say the words. 3•02

- Play the audio. Ask students to point to the words as they hear them.
- Play the audio a second time and have students repeat the words when they hear them.
- The words are all used as nouns, but *broadcast* and *blog* can also be used as verbs.
- Say the words out of order and have students race to point to them on the page.

CRITICAL THINKING

Ask the following questions to check understanding:

- Which things can you buy in a store?
- Which things can you see on a computer or smartphone?
- Think about the Time Capsule project from Unit 4 (page 45). Which items would you add to a time capsule and why?

- A compound word is a word made of two words. Can you find the compound words?
- How do the two words in each compound word help you to understand the meaning?

DIFFERENTIATION

Below level:

- Tell students to look at the images in A. For each one, provide a simple definition, as follows:

  Mass media: newspapers, magazines, websites, and TV shows that give people information. We use the word *masses* to talk about large groups of people. The word *media* is the plural of *medium*; a *medium* is a form of communication.

  Newspaper: set of printed sheets of paper containing news, articles, advertisement, etc. and published every day or every week.

  Magazine: a thin paper book (or online version) with articles about a special topic.

  Printing press: a machine that creates copies of papers quickly.

  Publisher: a company or person that makes books, newspapers, or magazines.

  Advertising: the commercials that try to convince you to buy things.

  Broadcast: send out programs on TV or radio.

  The Web: a system for finding information on the Internet.

  Smartphone: a cell phone that also has some of the functions of a computer.

  Blog: a website where people *post* information and opinions.

Social network: a website where people post pictures and information about themselves, and where people can communicate with their friends and family.

At level:
- Tell students to write a sentence for each word.
- Encourage them to make a unique sentence that hints at the word's meaning (*Jenny posted the pictures from her birthday party on the social network.*)

Above level:
- Tell students to try to write sentences using more than one vocabulary word. (*I read the blog on my smartphone.*)
- Have them search previous units for words that can be used in sentences with the Unit 13 words, e.g. *I read about the comet in a science magazine. The archaeologist posted pictures of the tomb on her blog. There is a story in the newspaper about the chemicals used by corporate farms. I searched the Web for pictures of Monet's landscapes. The garbage collector found an old printing press in the garbage. The company used advertising to make people want to buy the new flu medicine.*

B Circle the correct answer.
- Have students complete the exercise and then compare answers with a partner.
- Check the answers with the class.

ANSWERS
1 blog   2 magazine   3 smartphone   4 newspaper
5 the Web

C Answer the questions.
- Engage in a class discussion before asking students to complete the exercise.
- Check the answers as a class.

POSSIBLE ANSWERS
1 newspaper, magazine, the Web, blog, social network
2 People use advertising to persuade people to buy their products
3 It can create many copies of the same book, newspaper, or magazine in a short time.

Before You Read

Think
- Have students discuss the questions in small groups.

D Learn: Main idea and Supporting Details
- Read the *Learn* box together.

Read the information. Write the main idea and three supporting details in the graphic organizer.
- Have a volunteer read the paragraph aloud.
- Copy the graphic organizer on the board. Ask *What is this paragraph about? What's the main idea?*
- Write each sentence on the board. Point to and read aloud the first detail (*He reads the newspaper while he eats breakfast*). Write *Main Idea?* next to it.
- Say *All the details support the main idea. All the details are about the main idea.*
- Point and ask *Is this sentence "On the train …" about this sentence "He reads the newspaper …?"*

- Repeat with a few other sentences until students understand how the details must support the main idea.
- Finally invite volunteers to complete the graphic organizer on the board while everyone else does so in their books.
- Encourage them to paraphrase the sentences. (See Unit 9, page 89 for this lesson.)
- Check the answers with the class.

ANSWERS
Main Idea: Derek is very interested in news from around the world.
Supporting Details: 1) He reads the newspaper while he eats breakfast. 2) He checks Internet news on his smartphone on the way to work. 3) At night, he watches news on television and discusses it on a social network.

COLLABORATIVE LEARNING
- Have partners practice identifying the main idea and supporting details in other paragraphs they have read in the Student Book this year. Tell them to use a graphic organizer similar to the one on page 129.
- Have the students share ideas with the class.

E Words in Context: Scan the reading on pages 130–131 and circle these words. As you read, guess what the words mean.
- Read each word and have students follow your pronunciation.
- Have students guess at the meaning of each word using prior knowledge and the theme of the unit.

F What news did you share with your friends today at school? Where did you hear this news?

COMMUNICATION
- Give the students time to think about the question.
- Put students into pairs to discuss their ideas.
- Have students share their ideas with the class.

Reading Preview
- Read the title of the unit's reading text.
- Have students silently read the content of the preview bar.
- Ask *What type of text is it?* Ask *What does this type of text do?*

Further Practice
Workbook pages 116–117
Online practice Unit 13 • Get Ready
Oxford **iTools** Unit 13 • Get Ready

Unit 13 Read page 130

Read 🔊 3·03
From Newspapers to Smartphones: The Rise of the Mass Media

Thanks to the mass media, news travels fast. Journalist Megan Michaels interviews Dr. Philip Kendall, a mass media expert.

Megan: Thank you for meeting with me, Dr. Kendall.

Dr. Kendall: You're welcome.

Megan: People like to share news, don't they?

Dr. Kendall: Absolutely. Long ago, when early humans discovered how to make fire, they told their friends. Then those friends told others. Ideas spread from person to person, and in fact, they still do. However, mass media is different. It brings news and knowledge to many people very quickly.

Megan: When did mass media begin?

Dr. Kendall: It began around 1440, when Johannes Gutenberg changed the way news traveled. You see, he invented the printing press. Before the printing press, people had to make copies of books by hand. Suddenly, this invention could make copies of books much more easily. Then, about 150 years later, people printed the first newspapers in Europe. Today, people around the world read newspapers every day.

Megan: How many newspapers are there?

Dr. Kendall: Newspapers, along with magazines, are very popular. There are over 6,000 daily newspapers in the world today. Publishers print almost 400 million copies each day. Magazines are popular because they focus on one subject, such as news, movies, fashion, or sports. Advertising helps to pay for the cost of publishing newspapers and magazines.

Megan: So what happened next in the history of mass media?

Dr. Kendall: Movies were the next form of mass media. People started going to movie theaters about 100 years ago.

Think What is the main idea in this paragraph? What details support it?

These new "moving pictures" amazed people. Often, movie theaters showed newsreels, too. These were short films with news from around the world. People watched the news for the first time this way.

Megan: And then the television came next, right?

Dr. Kendall: Actually, the radio came next. It appeared about the same time as movies, but the first radio station didn't get started until about 1920. Today, there are over 44,000 radio stations around the world.

Think What is the main idea in this paragraph? What details support it?

Megan: Do people still get their news from the radio?

Dr. Kendall: Yes, they do. Many radio stations report the news every hour. Some stations broadcast the news all the time. People can listen to the news while they drive or work.

Megan: When did the television appear?

Dr. Kendall: Television broadcasting started in the 1930s. Now, television is everywhere, bringing news and entertainment to people around the world. Some stations now offer 24-hour news. Events are broadcast live, while they are happening.

Megan: So people have a lot of choices for their news, don't they?

Dr. Kendall: They do, but you mustn't forget the latest choice—the Web! Today, almost one third of the people in the world use the Web, and this number will continue to grow. The Web, or Internet, lets us read news, watch videos, and share information through social networks and blogs. Many people think that the Web is now the most important form of mass media. Also, smartphones give us Web service, so you don't have to carry a computer to check the news.

Megan: We live in very interesting times.

Dr. Kendall: That's true. It will be exciting to see what's next in the world of mass media.

Think What is the main idea of the entire interview? What details support it?

1440s · 1800s · 1900s · 1920s · 1930s · 1950s · 1980s · 2000s

130 · 131

Summary

Objectives: To read, understand, and discuss a nonfiction text; to apply a reading strategy to improve comprehension.

School subject: Social Studies; Technology

Text type: Interview (nonfiction)

Reading strategy: Main idea and supporting details

Big Question learning points: *Mass media is information that travels to many people quickly. People have had mass media for hundreds of years. We can get mass media in many ways. Mass media changes a lot.*

Materials: Talk About It! Poster, Audio CD

Before Reading

- Read the title together. Ask students to predict what the reading will be about.
- Explain that the word *Rise* can be used to describe how something becomes more popular and powerful.
- Revisit the *Writing* lesson on Interviews in Unit 12, page 124.
- Explain that students are going to read an interview. Point to the introduction and ask *Who is the interviewer? Who's asking the questions? Who is being interviewed? Who is answering the questions?*
- Ask *What text features help you understand what you are reading?*

During Reading 🔊 3·03

- Play the audio while students read along.
- Pause periodically to point out the different intonations used for questions and answers.
- Have students mimic the audio to focus on fluency.

DIFFERENTIATION

Below level:

- Have students read in mixed-ability pairs. The more confident student can read Dr. Kendall's lines.
- Pause after each of Dr. Kendall's answers to ask questions about the details, e.g. after the first answer, ask *How did people use to spread the news? How is mass media different?*

At level:

- Have students read with partners, alternating sections.
- Partner A reads Megan Michaels and Partner B reads Dr. Kendall for the first half of the text, then they switch roles.
- At the end of each answer, have partners try to identify the main idea and the supporting details. Tell them that sometimes the main idea is not explicitly written in the paragraph, e.g. the main idea of the first answer can be: *Mass media is different from the way people used to communicate.*

Above level:

- After students read the text and discuss the *Think* boxes with partners, tell them to write a caption for each photo at the bottom of the reading.
- Revisit the lesson on Sequence of Actions in Unit 12, page 117. Have students use sequence words to connect two

or more captions, e.g. *In the 1440s, Johannes Gutenberg invented the printing press. As a result, people could make copies of books more quickly. Then 150 years later, people printed the first newspaper.*

CRITICAL THINKING

Discussion questions:

- *What are two ways in which mass media is different from one person telling another person?*
- *How long do you think it would take to write this book (gesture to the Student Book) by hand?*
- *Do you read any magazines? What hobby or interest does the magazine focus on?*
- *People started watching newsreels in the movies – just like we watch previews before a movie these days. What's the difference between watching newsreels at the movies and watching the news on TV?*
- *Compare and contrast listening to the news on the radio and watching it on TV.*
- *Would you rather read a news blog where you learn people's opinions about the news, or a simple news website where there is no opinion?*
- *What do you think will be the next big thing in mass media? How do you think mass media will change in the future?*

After Reading

- Have students share their responses to the *Think* boxes in the reading text.
- Invite volunteers to name some pros and cons of each form of mass media mentioned in the article.

COLLABORATIVE LEARNING

- Social networks and blogs are often not moderated. This means someone can post a picture or text about somebody without that person's approval. Revisit the lesson on Value Judgments in Unit 8, page 77.
- Tell students the following scenario, and ask groups to discuss whether or not Lina did the right thing.
  Almost everyone at Town Central Middle School used the My Face social network. Lina's friend Julia didn't use My Face because her parents didn't let her. One day, Lina read a post on My Face about Julia. The writer said Julia's clothes were ugly. Lina knew this would hurt Julia's feelings, so she didn't tell her about the post. Did Lina do the right thing? What would you do?

COLLABORATIVE LEARNING

- Display the **Talk About It! Poster** to help students with sentence frames for discussion and expressing personal opinions.
- Put students into pairs to discuss which form of mass media in the reading text they prefer and why.

CULTURE NOTE

The printing press is one of the most important inventions of the past 500 years. It was used as the main method of printing until the late 20th century.

It is a machine that transfers lettering or images that have an inked surface onto paper. It is used for printing many copies of a text onto paper.

Before the printing press, books and pamphlets were written by hand. It could be difficult to find copies of books because it took so long for someone to write them more than once.

Further Practice
Workbook page 118
Online practice Unit 13 · Read
Oxford **iTools** **Unit 13 · Read**

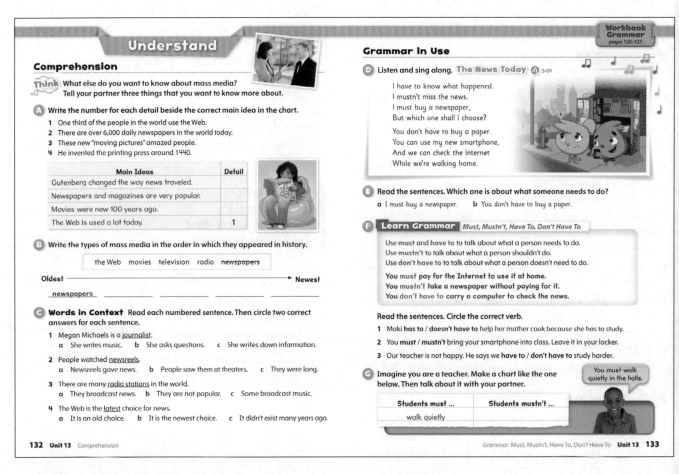

Summary

Objectives: To demonstrate understanding of a nonfiction text; to understand the meaning and form of the grammar structure.

Reading: Comprehension

Grammar input: *must, mustn't, have to, don't have to*

Grammar practice: Workbook exercises

Grammar production: Talk about what students must and mustn't do

Materials: Audio CD

Comprehension

Think

- Have students write down their questions. Encourage them to brainstorm resources where they could find the answers.

A Write the number for each detail beside the correct main idea in the chart.

- Go over the example together.
- Read the remaining sentences together to confirm comprehension.
- Have students complete the exercise independently, then check answers with a partner.

ANSWERS

1 The Web is used a lot today.
2 Newspapers and magazines are very popular.
3 Movies were new 100 years ago.
4 Gutenberg changed the way news traveled.

DIFFERENTIATION

Below level:

- Highlight specific clues that students can use to help them match details with main ideas:
  1 *The words "the Web" appear in the detail sentence and in a main idea sentence. Read the main idea "The Web is used a lot today." Does the detail "One third of the people …" make sense under that main idea?*
  2 *The word "newspaper" appears in the detail sentence and in a main idea sentence. Read the main idea "Newspapers and magazines …" Does the detail "There are over 6,000 …" make sense under that main idea?*
  3 *Find where Dr. Kendall used the phrase "moving pictures" in the reading text. You know that moving pictures and movies are the same thing. Does the detail in number 3 make sense under the main idea "Movies were new 100 years ago"?*
  4 *Look back at the reading text. Who invented the printing press? Does detail in number 4 make sense under "Gutenberg changed the way …"?*

At level:

- Have students go back to the reading text and find additional details that belong with each main idea, e.g.
  1 Gutenberg changed the way news traveled: *Before he invented the printing press, people had to copy books by hand.*
  2 Newspapers and magazines are very popular: *Magazines are popular because they focus on one topic.*
  3 Movies were new 100 years ago: *Movie theaters also showed newsreels.*

4 The Web is used a lot today: *Smartphones let us use the Web without a computer.*

Above level:

- Have students identify the main idea and one or two details for the sections not addressed in A (television and radio). Tell them to try to paraphrase, e.g.
Main Idea: *Television broadcasting is an important modern form of mass media.* Details: *Broadcasting began in the 1930s. Now people all over the world watch TV. There are 24-hour news stations where events are broadcast live.*
Main Idea: *Radio is now one of the most popular forms of mass media.* Details: *The first radio station started around 1920. Now there are over 44,000 radio stations around the world. Some stations report the news 24-hours a day.*

CRITICAL THINKING

- Have partners write one more question and answer for Dr. Kendall's interview. Give them the question: *Which form of mass media is most popular with kids these days, and why?*
- Tell them to write an answer to this question that Dr. Kendall might give.
- Encourage them to review the article and try to match the friendly and informal tone of his answers.

B Write the types of mass media in the order in which they appeared in history.

- Tell students to try to answer from memory first.
- Then have partners return to the interview to confirm their answers together.

ANSWERS

newspapers, movies, radio, television, the Web

C Words in Context: Read each numbered sentence. Then circle two correct answers for each sentence.

- Have students go back and find the words in the reading text.
- Tell them to use the context clues to guess at the meaning of each word.
- Then complete the exercise together.
- Check the answers with the class.

ANSWERS

1 b, c   2 a, b   3 a, c   4 b, c

Grammar in Use

D Listen and sing along. ⊚ 3•04

- Listen to the song once and then sing it together as a class.

Ask questions to check comprehension:

- What does the singer need?
- What choice does she have?
- What solution does her friend suggest?

E Read the sentences. Which one is about what someone needs to do?

- Have students complete the exercise individually and then check with a partner.
- Elicit answers from the class.

ANSWER

a I must buy a newspaper.

F Learn Grammar: Must, Mustn't, Have to, Don't have to

- Read the *Learn Grammar* box together.
- Have students suggest examples of things in their own lives that they must, mustn't, have to, and don't have to do.
- Clarify meaning by paraphrasing and elaborating on their ideas, e.g. if a student says *I have to wash my hands before I eat dinner* say *That's right, you need to wash your hands so you don't spread germs.*

Read the sentences. Circle the correct verb.

- Read the first sentence together. Read it first using *has to* and then using *doesn't have to*. Ask which one makes sense.
- Repeat for the other items.
- Check answers with the class.

ANSWERS

1 doesn't have to   2 mustn't   3 have to

G Imagine you are a teacher. Make a chart like the one below. Then talk about it with your partner.

COLLABORATIVE LEARNING

- Partners can collaborate on each item in the chart. If Partner A suggests an idea for "Students have to," Partner B suggests a related idea for "Students don't have to."
- For example, if Partner A suggests *Students have to do their homework every night*, Student B might suggest *Students don't have to do homework on the weekends.*
- Put two pairs together to compare their ideas.

Further Practice
Workbook pages 119–121
Online practice Unit 13 • Understand
Oxford iTools Unit 13 • Understand

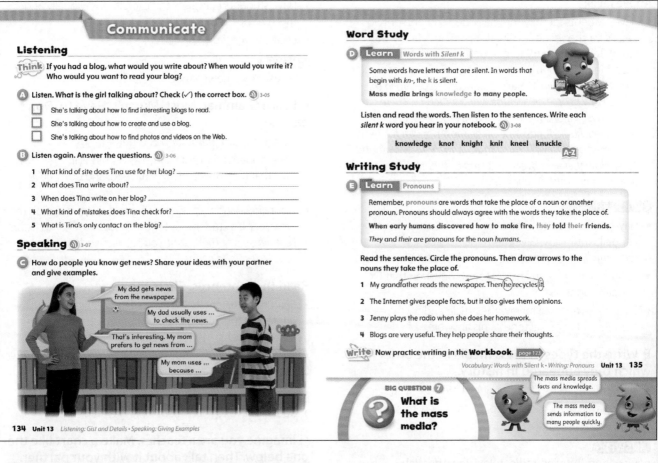

Summary

Objectives: To learn and practice listening, speaking, and writing strategies to facilitate effective communication.

Vocabulary: *knowledge, knot, knight, knit, kneel, knuckle*

Listening strategy: Listening for gist and details

Speaking: Giving examples

Word Study: Words with *silent k*

Writing Study: Writing with pronouns

Big Question learning point: *Mass media is information that travels to many people quickly.*

Materials: Discover Poster 7, Audio CD, Big Question Chart

Listening

Think

- Engage in a class discussion. First invite students to share their experiences with blogs and what they know about them.
- Encourage students to talk about different possible blog topics.

A Listen. What is the girl talking about? Check (✓) the correct box. 3·05

- Play the audio once and have students listen.
- Ask *What is the speaker teaching us?*
- Play the audio again. Have students complete the exercise as they listen.
- Check the answer with the class.

ANSWER

She's talking about how to create and use a blog.

DIFFERENTIATION

Below level:

- Pause after each section. Ask *What is the main idea of this section? What details are about the main idea?*

At level:

- Invent some other details for the same topic.
- Have students work in small groups to think of and write down new details they would add to Tina's details for setting up and maintaining a blog.
- Have students share their new details with the class.

Above level:

- Have students complete the exercise after listening to the audio once.
- Play the audio again so they can check their work.
- Have them try to retell the information in the listening using only the information on page 134 for hints.

B Listen again. Answer the questions. ⊙ 3·06

- Play the audio.
- Have students answer the questions as they listen.
- Check the answers with the class.

1 Her blog is on a children's site.
2 Tina writes about nature in her city.
3 She writes every Saturday afternoon.
4 She checks for grammar and spelling mistakes.
5 Her only contact is her parents' email address

Speaking ⊙ 3·07

C How do people you know get news? Share your ideas with your partner and give examples.

COMMUNICATION

- Play the dialogue once while students follow in their books.
- Then play one line at a time of the dialogue with students echoing as they hear each line.
- Model the dialogue with a confident student in front of the class.
- Put students into pairs and tell them to practice the dialogue, taking turns speaking the different roles.
- Have partners first brainstorm how and from where their friends and family get the news.
- Then have partners practice the dialogue, substituting in their own information.

CRITICAL THINKING

- The reader responses on blogs can be as interesting as the original writer's stories. Students who don't know a lot about nature might be interested in reading.
- Ask students to name some blog topics they would be interested in reading. Have them read Tina's blog again to learn more, and ask if they might even write a comment now and then.
- Lead students to discuss the difference between having your own blog, where you do most of the writing, versus reading and posting on someone else's blog.

Word Study

D Learn: Words with *Silent k*

- Read the *Learn* box together.
- Point out that the *k* in *knowledge* is silent. The *k* in *quickly* works with the *c* to make the hard *k* sound.

Listen and read the words. Then listen to the sentences. Write each *silent k* word you hear in your notebook. ⊙ 3·08

- Play the audio.
- Read each word as the students listen so that they can hear the correct pronunciation.
- Ask the students to listen to the sentences and then write each *silent k* they hear.

ANSWERS
1 kneel   2 knight   3 knuckle   4 knot   5 knit
6 knowledge

Writing Study

E Learn: Pronouns

- Read the *Learn* box together.
- Practice with a few other examples on the board:
  When **Jim** *found the sports blog,* **he** *told* **his** *friends about it.*
  When **Jenny** *watched* **her** *favorite TV show,* **she** *watched with* **her** *parents.*
  I *like reading magazines about entertainment.* **My** *favorite is Celebrity Week.*

Read the sentences. Circle the pronouns. Then draw arrows to the nouns they take the place of.

- If necessary, reread each sentence using the redundant noun, e.g. *Then my grandfather recycles the newspaper.*
- Check the answers with the class.

ANSWERS
1 grandfather: he; newspaper: it
2 Internet: it; people: them
3 Jenny: she, her
4 Blogs: they; people: their

COLLABORATIVE LEARNING

- Have students write sentences about mass media. Then have them exchange papers with a partner.
- Tell the partners to write a follow-up sentence for each one using pronouns. They should use the sentences in E as models.

Write

- Direct students to the Workbook for further practice.

Big Question 7 Review

What is mass media?

- Display **Discover Poster 7**. Elicit words and phrases about the pictures.
- Refer to the learning points covered in Unit 13 which are written on the poster and have students explain how they relate to the different pictures.
- Return to the **Big Question Chart**.
- Ask students what they have learned about mass media that they can add to the chart.

| **Further Practice**
| **Workbook pages 122–123**
| **Online practice Unit 13 • Communicate**
| Oxford **iTools** Unit 13 • **Communicate**

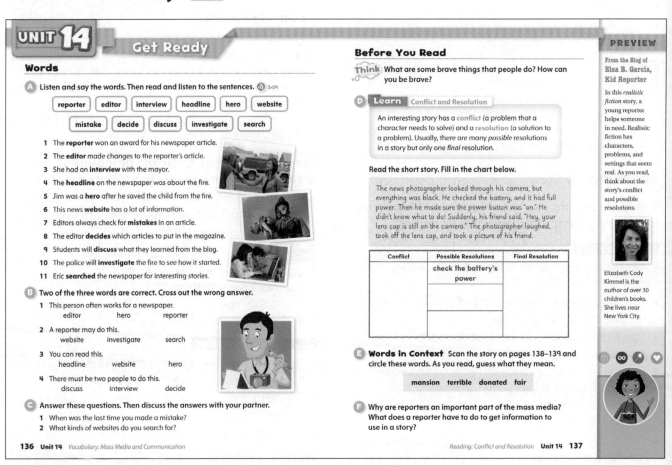

Summary

Objectives: To understand words about mass media; to apply own experience and a reading strategy to help comprehension of a text.

Vocabulary: *reporter, editor, interview, headline, hero, website, mistake, decide, discuss, investigate, search, mansion, terrible, donated, fair*

Reading strategy: Conflict and resolution

Materials: Audio CD

Words

A Listen and say the words. Then read and listen to the sentences. ⊙ 3·09

- Play the audio. Ask students to point to the words as they hear them.
- Play the audio a second time and have students repeat the words when they hear them.
- Read the sentences together. After each sentence, ask volunteers to guess the definition of the vocabulary word.

COLLABORATIVE LEARNING

- Have small groups work together to sort the words into different categories.
- Encourage them to think of their own ideas for categories first. If necessary, you can suggest they sort into *People*, *Actions*, and *Things*.
- After they sort the words on page 136, ask them to think of a few other mass media words that could fit into each category.

B Two of the three words are correct. Cross out the wrong answer.

- Encourage students to consider the categories they sorted the words into to help them.
- Check the answers with the class.

ANSWERS
1 hero   2 website   3 hero   4 decide

DIFFERENTIATION

Below level:

- Create a sentence for each answer in B. Have students choose the word for each one:
  This person does something amazing to help others.
  This is a place on the Internet with information and pictures.
  When you choose something, you do this.

At level:

- Have students write down interesting and familiar things they notice about each word. They can focus on spelling, pronunciation, or meaning.
- Give them the following examples to get started:
  reporter: I notice the word "report." A "reporter" is a person who reports.
  interview: This word has three syllables. The first syllable has the most stress.
  headline: The ea makes the short e sound like in "bread" and "ready."

Above level:

- Read the following sentences and have students match each sentence to a Big Question.
  1 *The astronomer searched for new planets.*
  2 *The archaeologist made a mistake. He broke the clay sculpture!*
  3 *The reporter interviewed a farmer about the chemicals he used in the factory farm.*
  4 *The museum's website had information about the exhibition.*
  5 *The mayor gave the hero an award.*
  6 *Doctors are investigating the new virus.*
- Have students work alone or with partners to use the words on page 136 in their own sentences about the Big Questions they have learned about so far this year.

C Answer these questions. Then discuss the answers with your partner.

- Have students discuss the questions in small groups.
- Have groups share their ideas with the class.

CRITICAL THINKING

Ask other questions to personalize the vocabulary, e.g.

- If you were a reporter, who would you interview?
- Name someone you think is a hero. What makes this person special?
- When you write something important, who is your favorite editor (a friend, teacher, parent) and why?
- What makes a good headline? (e.g. it grabs your attention or it summarizes the main idea or theme of the article.)
- Do you prefer discussing things like which movie to see or what game to play, or would you rather decide by yourself?

Before You Read

Think

- Suggest that to be brave you must be afraid of something first. Bravery is overcoming your fear to do something that seems risky.
- Sometimes we are brave when there's no physical danger, but the risk is emotional, e.g. it takes bravery to stand up for a friend when someone says something mean about him / her, or to give a speech in front of the class when you are nervous about making a mistake.
- Have the students discuss the questions in pairs.

D Learn: Conflict and Resolution

- Read the *Learn* box together.
- Ask students if they can remember any conflicts and resolutions in stories or books they have read.

Read the short story. Fill in the chart below.

- Copy the chart on the board.
- Invite a volunteer to read the first sentence aloud. Ask *What is the conflict, or problem?* Pretend to look through a camera and in confusion say *Hey, it's all black, I can't see anything.* Explain that the reporter's camera seems to be broken.
- Write on the board under *Conflict*: *The reporter cannot see through his camera.*

- Invite another volunteer to read the next sentence. Point to the first possible resolution: *check battery*.
- Have someone read the next sentence and paraphrase the next possible resolution: *check power*. Write it on the board.
- Have another student read the rest of the story. Ask what the third possible resolution is. (*check lens cap*)
- Ask *What is the actual resolution then?*

E Words in Context: Scan the story on pages 138–139 and circle these words. As you read, guess what they mean.

- Have students scan the story and circle the words.

F Why are reporters an important part of mass media? What does a reporter have to do to get information to use in a story?

COMMUNICATION

- Have students discuss the questions in groups.
- Have one person from each group report their ideas back to the class.

Reading Preview

- Read the title of the unit's reading text.
- Have students silently read the content of the preview bar.
- Ask *What type of text is it?* Ask *What does this type of text do?*
- Remind students to think about conflict and resolution as they read.

Further Practice

Workbook pages 124–125
Online practice Unit 14 • Get Ready
Oxford **iTools** Unit 14 • Get Ready

Read 3•10

From the Blog of
Elsa B. Garcia,
Kid Reporter

July 5. I have decided to keep a blog so the world can read about all the things I investigate. Today I heard that they are going to tear down the old stone house across the street. The newspaper says the city government owns the house, and just one person lives there. Why does the city government own an old house? Who lives there? I have decided to find out because I want to save the house.

Think
What is the main conflict in the story?

July 6. I used the Internet to search for articles about old houses on my street. I found an entire website called *The Lost History of Stone House*. It said the stone building was once the gatehouse of a huge mansion. A family called the Martins lived there until one night a terrible fire burned the mansion down. The young daughter of a maid smelled the smoke and woke up every single person in the house. Everyone got out safely that night. The website showed the front page of an old newspaper with a story about the fire. The headline said: "Young Girl, 9, Saves Seven People in Mysterious Fire." She was the same age as me!

SUNDAY NEWS
Young Girl, 9, Saves Seven People in Mysterious Fire

July 7. I am going to visit the house to see if I can talk to the person who lives there. I have never done an interview before, and I'm very nervous. What if I make a mistake?

July 7, Part 2. I did it! A woman who looks like my grandmother answered the door. She said her name was Miss Lu, and that she would be happy to answer my questions. She knew all about the mansion and the fire. I learned that the Martin family donated a lot of money to the city to help build the library and the hospital. After the fire, they decided to move away and let the city have their land. I asked Miss Lu if she knew the Martins. She smiled and said no one had ever asked her that before. When she told me the answer, I couldn't believe it. My mom says I have to go to sleep now, so read my blog tomorrow for the rest of the story!

Miss Lu July 7th

Think
What possible resolutions are there to the conflict?

July 8. I'm back! Miss Lu knew the Martins because she lived in the mansion, too. Yes, readers, Miss Lu was the little girl who saved the family that night! I am writing a letter to the editor of our newspaper asking the mayor not to destroy the house. Miss Lu is a hero, and it isn't fair to take away her home!

7 NEWS

July 10. Today, a television reporter came to interview me. You can watch it on Channel 7 tonight!

July 11. I have more wonderful news. My story will be on a radio show that will be broadcast to the entire city tonight!

July 15. Today I got an e-mail from the mayor. He said there will be a special meeting to discuss the house. I'm amazed that he took the time to write to me!

August 1. Awesome news! The mayor decided not to tear down the old house! He agrees that Miss Lu is a hero and should be able to live there as long as she likes. This is the first news story I have ever investigated. I love being a reporter, and I can't wait to find more stories!

Think
What is Elsa's final resolution to the conflict?

138   139

Summary

Objectives: To read, understand, and discuss a fictional text; to apply a reading strategy to improve comprehension.

School subject: Social Studies: Technology

Text type: Realistic fiction

Reading strategy: Conflict and resolution

Big Question learning points: *Mass media is information that travels to many people quickly. We can get mass media in many ways.*

Materials: Talk About It! Poster, Audio CD

Before Reading

- Preview the story. Point out the dates that help the reader navigate the timeline of the story. Explain that blogs are usually organized by date.
- Look at the illustrations and ask students to predict what will happen in the story.

During Reading 3•10

- Remind students that they should think about the conflict and possible resolutions in the story.
- Play the audio. Students listen as they read along.
- Pause after the July 7, Part 2 entry and ask the class to predict: *Who is Miss Lu?*
- Stop at each *Think* box for students to answer the questions.

Below level:

- As you listen to the story, draw a simple timeline on the board showing the main events in the story. Include only basic information:
  July 5: Elsa decides to find out about the old stone house.
  July 6: Elsa learns about the house from a website: a nine-year-old daughter of a maid saved the wealthy family who lived in a mansion near the house.
  July 7: Elsa decides to visit the house to interview the person who lives there.
  July 7, Part 2: Elsa interviews Miss Lu, an elderly woman who lives in the house.
  July 8: Elsa tells us that Miss Lu was the little girl who saved the family. Elsa decides to ask the mayor not to tear down the house.
  July 10: Elsa is interviewed by a television reporter.
  July 11: Elsa's story is broadcast on a radio show.
  July 15: The mayor tells Elsa he will discuss the house.
  August 1: The mayor decides not to tear down the house.

At level:

- Have small groups read the story together, taking turns around a circle.
- Tell students to stop after each blog entry and work together to summarize what happened. See above for possible ideas.
- Encourage them to take turns reading aloud, mimicking the enthusiasm and expression of the model on the audio.

Above level:

- Have students role-play the action described in a blog entry.
- Put students into small groups. Each group chooses one entry they want to act out.
- Assign a director in each group. The director makes sure everyone has a role. If there are more students than acting roles, the nonactors can write the script or create props.
- Encourage students to elaborate on the details in the blog, e.g. if they act out the July 6 entry, they may add Elsa's mother to help her search the Internet.

COLLABORATIVE LEARNING

- Remind students that in a typical blog format, readers write questions and comments to the blogger. The blog is like an online conversation.
- Have small groups work together to write one question or comment for each entry, e.g. a possible comment after the July 7 entry might be *Are you going with your mom or dad? My parents never let me go anywhere by myself.*
- After each group has written their question or comment, have them exchange papers with another group. Groups pretend to be Elsa and respond to each other's questions and comments.
- Have students share their work with the class.

CRITICAL THINKING

- Focus on some of the reading strategies students have practiced so far this year, e.g.
  Author's purpose: *Why did the author write "From the Blog of Elsa B. Garcia, Kid Reporter"?* (to entertain) *Why did Elsa write her blog?* (to inform)
  Making conclusions: *The blog never says that her letter to the editor was published (see July 8). Do you think the newspaper published her letter?)*
  Making value judgments: *Do you think the mayor should let Miss Lu stay in the house? What if the mayor wanted to tear down the house to build a park for everyone in the city, but the plan would only work if he tore down the house?*
  Understanding characters: *What are some of Elsa's character traits?*
  Theme and main idea: *What's a theme for this story?*

After Reading

- Have students predict what will happen next (after the story ends) in Elsa's life and on her blog.
- Ask *What will Elsa's blog entry be on August 3? What will her entry be on September 1?*

COLLABORATIVE LEARNING

- Display the **Talk About It! Poster** to help students with sentence frames for discussion and expressing personal opinions.
- Put students into pairs to discuss the conflict and resolution from the story.

CULTURE NOTE

In many countries around the world the local or national government can decide that a building is so important that it cannot be destroyed or changed without permission.

In the UK there are over 300,000 listed buildings. Listed buildings are those that are considered important in order to preserve a shared history.

In the United States buildings can be put on the National Register of Historic Places. Properties can be nominated and have to meet different criteria to be put on the register.

| Further Practice
Workbook page 126
Online practice Unit 14 • Read
Oxford **iTools** Unit 14 • Read

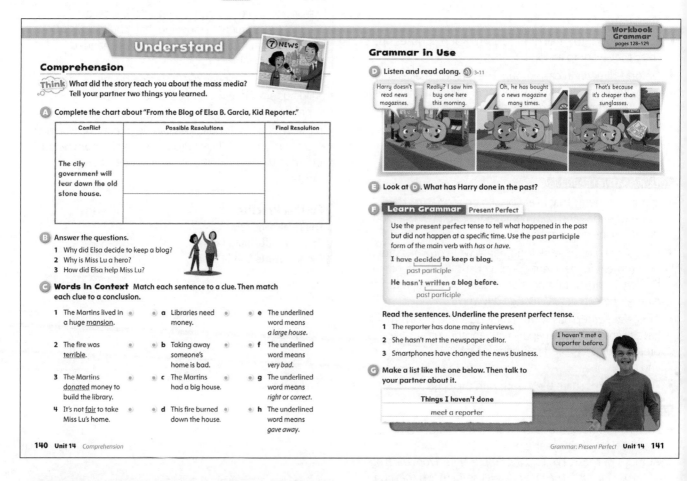

Summary

Objectives: To demonstrate understanding of a fictional text; to understand the meaning and form of the grammar structure.

Reading: Comprehension

Grammar input: Present perfect

Grammar practice: Workbook exercises

Grammar production: Make a list of actions you haven't done and use present perfect to talk about the actions

Materials: Audio CD

Comprehension

Think

• Have students discuss the questions together. Point out that mass media can influence politicians and the public.

A Complete the chart about "From the Blog of Elsa B. Garcia, Kid Reporter."

• Have students revisit the story.
• Copy the chart on the board and fill it in together with the class.

ANSWERS

Possible Resolutions: Miss Lu is friends with the Martins. The Martins will donate money to keep the house standing. The city will agree not to tear down the house.

Final resolution: The city agrees not to tear down the house.

B Answer the questions.

• Have students reread the story and then answer the questions.
• Check the answers with the class.

ANSWERS

1 She wants to tell the world about the things she investigates.
2 She warned the Martins about the fire so they could escape.
3 Elsa convinced the mayor not to tear down the house where Miss Lu lives.

CRITICAL THINKING

• Ask students to consider a different ending to the story: the mayor decides to tear down the house, even though Elsa tells everyone that Miss Lu was a hero.
• Ask *What other steps could Elsa take to help Miss Lu?*

C Words in Context: Match each sentence to a clue. Then match each clue to a conclusion.

• Help students use their recollection of the story to mentally find the words. Ask *Do you remember where this word (mansion) was used?*
• Go back to the story, find the Words in Context, and discuss possible definitions.
• Have students match word to clue to conclusion.
• Check answers with the class.

ANSWERS

1 c, e   2 d, f   3 a, h   4 b, g

Grammar in Use

D Listen and read along. 🎧 3·11

- Listen to the conversation once.
- Have two confident students read it aloud for the class.
- Ask *What does Harry use the news magazine for?*
- Play the audio and have volunteers use it as a model for rhythm and intonation as they echo read.

E Look at D. What has Harry done in the past?

- If necessary, tell students to focus on the first frame of the conversation. Ask *At any time, has Harry read a news magazine?* The students reply in the negative. Say, *That's correct. He's never read a news magazine. The word "never" means "not at any time."*

F Learn Grammar: Present Perfect

- Have a confident student read the *Learn Grammar* box to the class.
- Write the sample sentences on the board. Underline and label the past participle in each sentence. Circle the contractions.

Read the sentences. Underline the present perfect tense.

- Have students complete the activity independently, and then check answers with a partner.
- Elicit answers from the class.

ANSWERS

1 has done   2 hasn't met   3 have changed

Below level:

- Review conjugations of *have / has*: *I have, you have, she / he / it has, we have, they have.*
- Look at the past participles of common verbs, e.g.
  be (present), *was / were* (past tense), *been* (past participle)
  begin, began, begun
  break, broke, broken
  come, came, come
  do, did, done
  drink, drank, drunk
  eat, ate, eaten
  go, went, gone
  make, made, made
  see, saw, seen

At level:

- Provide a few examples on the board and ask students to fill in the blanks with either the past tense or present perfect of the verbs in parentheses, e.g.
  I _____ to the beach yesterday. (go)
  I've never _____ sushi. (eat)
  I have _____ that movie. (see)

Above level:

- Have students write sentence pairs contrasting the past tense and present perfect.
- Tell them to follow your models on the board from the presentation above.

G Make a list like the one below. Then talk to your partner about it.

- Have students complete the list in groups.
- Tell them to focus first on meaning. Ask *What have you never done?*
- Take time to correct verb forms after students have expressed their ideas.

- Tell students to choose one thing they haven't done.
- Put the class into small groups in a circle, and have students take turns saying what they haven't done.
- Tell them to pay close attention to what members of their group say.
- Ask students in the class to talk about a member of their group, e.g. ask Student A about Student B, *What has Molly never done?* Student A answers, *Molly hasn't swum in the ocean.* Confirm with Student B.

Further Practice

Workbook pages 127–129
Online practice Unit 14 • Understand
Oxford iTools Unit 14 • Understand

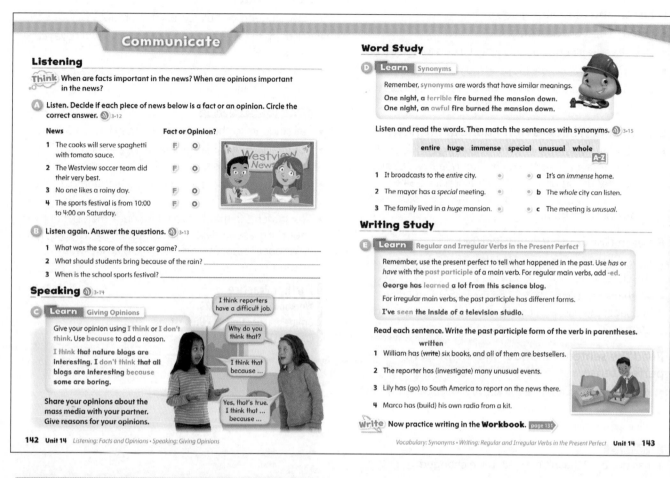

Summary

Objectives: To learn and practice listening, speaking, and writing strategies to facilitate effective communication.

Vocabulary: *entire, huge, immense, special, unusual, whole*

Listening strategy: Listening for facts and opinions

Speaking: Giving opinions

Word Study: Synonyms

Writing Study: Using regular and irregular verbs in the present perfect

Big Question learning points: *Mass media is information that travels to many people quickly. We can learn facts, opinions, or both from mass media.*

Materials: Audio CD

Listening

Think

- On the board write *Fact* and *Opinion*. Review that a fact is something you can prove, and an opinion is subjective, determined by individual preference.
- Have students discuss the questions in pairs. Tell them to try to identify times when they expect to hear opinions (like in editorials or fashion reports) and when they expect to hear facts (like in the weather).

A Listen. Decide if each piece of news below is a fact or an opinion Circle the correct answer. 3·12

- Play the audio once through while students just listen.
- Play it a second time and have them circle F for fact or O for opinion.

- Check the answers with the class.

ANSWERS
1 Fact 2 Opinion 3 Opinion 4 Fact

B Listen again. Answer the questions. 3·13

- Have students complete the exercise individually and then check with a partner.
- Elicit answers from the class.

ANSWERS
1 4–3 2 umbrellas and happy smiles
3 Saturday, October 14, from 10:00 a.m. to 4:00 p.m

DIFFERENTIATION

Below level:

- Pause after each section to check comprehension. Ask questions like the following to focus on facts and opinions:
Fran says spaghetti with tomato sauce is for lunch. Can you prove this? It's a fact because you can prove it.
Jae-Sung says the 4th grade soccer team did their best. Can you prove this? Is it possible someone else might say they didn't do their best? So it's subjective. That makes this sentence an opinion.
Kareena says no one likes a rainy day. Can you prove that? Some people like rainy days. So Kareena's sentence is an opinion.
What does Omar say that's a fact? What does he say that's an opinion?

At level:

- Have students rewrite the sentences in A so the facts become opinions and the opinions become facts, e.g.
  Spaghetti and tomato sauce is boring.
  The Westview soccer team players were sad that they lost.
  Some people like rainy days.
  The sports festival should start at 9:00 a.m.

Above level:

- Have students write one more sentence for each news story, either a fact or an opinion.
- Remind them that you can prove a fact, and it's something everyone will agree upon. An opinion is a statement that some people might disagree with.
- Invite them to share their sentences. Have the class identify each one as a fact or an opinion.

CRITICAL THINKING

- Personalize the lesson by having students write mini-news reports about things going on at their school. Tell them to follow the models on the audio.
- Tell them to include at least one fact and one opinion in their stories.
- Students share their news stories with the class, and the class identifies the facts and opinions.

Speaking 🎧 3·14

C Learn: Giving Opinions

COMMUNICATION

- Read the *Learn* box together.
- Explain that prefacing each opinion with *I think* or *I don't think* signals that you are giving an opinion.
- Point out the role of the word *that* in each sentence. Sometimes in informal dialogue the speaker omits the word *that*, e.g. *I think nature blogs are interesting.* In these cases, the word *that* is implied.
- Play the audio and have students echo, mimicking the pronunciation and intonation of the speakers.

Share your opinions about mass media with your partner. Give reasons for your opinions.

- Have students follow the model to share their opinions about mass media.

COLLABORATIVE LEARNING

- Have students return to the vocabulary lists on pages 128 and 136.
- Tell them to consider all the words on the lists as they formulate opinions about mass media.
- Partners can play a game where Partner A says one of the vocabulary words and Partner B says the first thing that pops into his / her head.
- After they've gone through all the words, they will have already formulated the content and they can focus on the form.

Word Study

D Learn: Synonyms

- Read the *Learn* box together.
- Ask students if they can name any other synonyms for *awful* and *terrible*, such as *bad* or *horrible*.

Listen and read the words. Then match the sentences with synonyms. 🎧 3·15

- Play the audio and have students point to the words as they hear them.
- Have students match sentences.
- Elicit answers from the students.

ANSWERS
1 b   2 c   3 a

Writing Study

E Learn: Regular and Irregular Verbs in the Present Perfect

- Read the *Learn* box together.

Read each sentence. Write the past participle form of the verb in parentheses.

- Have students complete the exercise on their own.
- Check answers with the class.

ANSWERS
1 written   2 investigated   3 gone   4 built

Write

- Direct students to the Workbook for further practice.

Further Practice
Workbook pages 130–131
Online practice Unit 14 • Communicate
Oxford **iTools** Unit 14 • Communicate

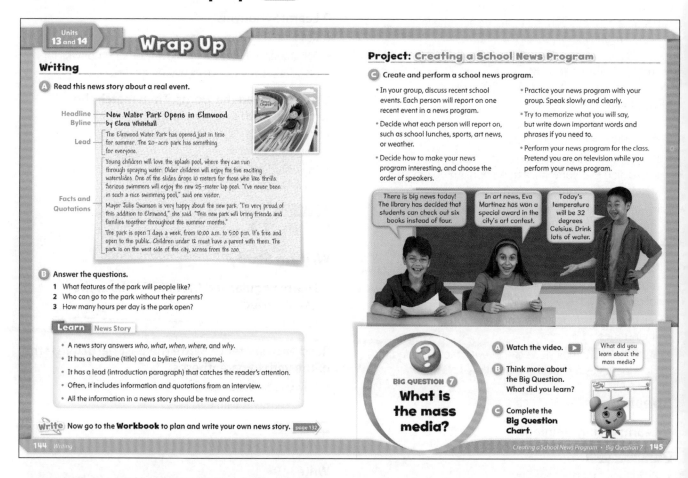

Summary

Objectives: To show what students have learned about the language and learning points of Units 13 and 14.

Reading: Comprehension of an informative newspaper article

Project: Create a school news program

Writing: Write a news story

Speaking: Talking about the school news programs

Materials: Big Question DVD, Discover Poster 7, Talk About It! Poster, Big Question Chart

Writing

A Read this news story about a real event.

- Remind students about the Author's Purpose they studied in Unit 3, page 29.
- Identify the different parts of the article that are labeled: Headline, Byline, Lead (which is like the main idea), and Facts and Quotations.
- Ask *Do you think this news story will have facts or opinions?*

B Answer the questions.

- Have students find the answers in the text.
- Elicit the answers from the class.

ANSWERS

1 The splash pool (young children), the waterslides (older children), the lap pool (serious swimmers)
2 Anyone older than 12
3 Seven hours a day

Learn: News Story

- Read the directions in the *Learn* box together.
- Explain that students should follow these guidelines when they plan and write their news stories.
- Copy the quotations from the sample article on the board. Show students the different formats they can use in their own articles:
  She said, "Quotation."
  "Quotation," she said.
  "Quotation." (When the speaker is understood.)

CRITICAL THINKING

- Have students go back to the model to see how the author addressed each requirement.
- Say *Tell me the who, what, when, where, and why.*
- Ask *What is the headline? What is the byline? What is the lead? How does this grab your attention? Who does Elena quote? Who else do you think Elena might have interviewed? Can the facts in the story be proved? There are opinions in the quotations. Are there any other opinions?*

DIFFERENTIATION

Below level:

- Tell students to write about something they know well, such as a family birthday party or a popular school event. It will be easier to plan and write if students have lots of information about the topic.
- Have them discuss their topics in mixed-ability pairs. Each partner asks the other about each bulleted item in the *Learn* box. The more confident students can help

their partners address each requirement before they start writing.

At level:

- Tell students to use an idea web to help plan their writing.
- First small groups can brainstorm possible article topics.
- Once everyone has chosen a topic, they can use an idea web with *Who, What, When, Where,* and *Why* to plan.
- Have students suggest possible leads to one another. Tell them to ask their partners if the lead grabs their attention and makes them want to read the article.

Above level:

- Challenge students to choose topics for which they can actually interview people for information, e.g. they might interview a parent about an event at home, a teacher about something at school, or a store owner about a new product.
- Tell them to include information from the actual interviews in their articles.
- Remind them to differentiate between facts and opinions. It's OK to include opinions in quotes, but it's important to remember when a source is telling you what he / she thinks versus what he / she can prove.

Write

- Direct students to the Workbook to plan and write their own news story.

Project

C Create and perform a school news program.

CREATIVITY

- Read the directions together as a class. Make sure everyone knows what to do.
- Divide the class into small groups to plan and present their news programs.
- The group monitor should facilitate a discussion of recent events at school that might be fun to include in the program.
- Have groups think about what will make each story more interesting, such as an onscreen interview or a picture.
- Give groups a period of time during which students practice their stories independently. Then tell groups to gather and practice together.

Units 13 and 14 Big Question Review

A Watch the video. ▷

- Play the video and when it is finished ask students what they know about the mass media now.
- Have students share ideas with the class.

B Think more about the Big Question. What did you learn?

COMMUNICATION

- Display **Discover Poster 7**. Point to familiar vocabulary items and elicit them from the class.
- Refer to all of the learning points written on the poster and have students explain how they relate to the different pictures.
- Ask *What does this learning point mean*? Elicit answers from individual students.
- Display the **Talk About It! Poster** to help students with sentence frames for discussion of the learning points and for expressing their opinions.

C Complete the Big Question Chart.

COLLABORATIVE LEARNING

- Ask students what they have learned about the mass media while studying this unit.
- Put students into pairs or small groups to say two new things they have learned.
- Have students share their ideas with the class and add their ideas to the chart.
- Have students complete the chart in their Workbook.

Further Practice
Workbook page 132–134
Online practice • Wrap Up 7
Oxford **iTools** • Wrap Up 7

Units 15 and 16 — What can we learn from nature's power?

In units 15 and 16 you will:

WATCH a video about nature's power.

LEARN about forces of nature.

READ about natural forces and a family that faces one.

WRITE a how-to speech.

CREATE an emergency poster.

BIG QUESTION 8

What can we learn from nature's power?

A Watch the video.

B Look at the picture and talk about it.

1 What do you see? How does it make you feel?

2 If you were in this place, what would you do?

C Think and answer the questions.

1 What types of bad weather or natural forces do you have in your area?

2 What can you do to prepare for bad weather or natural forces?

D Fill out the **Big Question Chart**.

What do you know about nature's power? What do you want to know?

146 Big Question 8

147

Reading Strategies
Students will practice:
- Understanding cause and effect in a series of events
- Making inferences

Vocabulary
Students will understand and use words about:
- Natural forces, safety, and supplies

Grammar
Students will understand and use:
- Present perfect with *ever and never*
- Present perfect with *already, just,* and *yet*

Review
Students will review the language and Big Question learning points of Units 15 and 16 through:
- A how-to speech
- A project (creating an emergency poster)

Units 15 and 16
What can we learn from nature's power?
Students will understand the Big Question learning points:
- Nature's power can be dangerous.
- Nature can destroy buildings.
- Disasters can cause problems in cities or towns.
- We should be prepared for nature's power.
- Warning systems are important for people's safety.

Listening Strategies
Students will practice:
- Listening for problems and solutions; main ideas and details
- Listening for recommendations

Writing
Students will use and understand:
- Contractions in present perfect sentences
- Adverbs of manner
Students will produce texts that:
- Inform / teach

Word Study
Students will understand, pronounce, and use:
- Compound nouns with noun-verb combinations
- Phrasal verbs with *turn*

Speaking
Students will understand and use expressions to:
- Talk about possibilities
- Speak about needs

Units 15 and 16 Big Question page 146

Summary

Objectives: To activate students' existing knowledge of the topic and to identify what they would like to learn about the topic.

Materials: Big Question DVD, Discover Poster 8, Big Question Chart

Introducing the topic

- Read out the Big Question. Ask *What can we learn from nature's power?*
- Write students' ideas on the board and discuss.

A Watch the video. ▷

- Play the video and when it is finished ask students to answer the following questions in pairs:
  What do you see in the video?
  Who do you think the people are?
  What is happening?
  Do you like it?
- Have individual students share their answers with the class.

B Look at the picture and talk about it.

- Students look at the big picture and talk about it.
- Ask additional questions:
  Have you ever seen a storm like this? If so, where was it? When was it? What did you do?
  Should people be outside during a storm like this? Why or why not?

C Think and answer the questions.

- Have students discuss the questions in small groups, and then with the class.

Below level:

- Do a quick vocabulary review for basic weather words (*rain, wind, sun, snow*).
- Have students use the words in sentences.

At level:

- Invite students to share their experiences during any recent weather events, such as hurricanes, floods, or droughts.
- Encourage them to suggest preparation tips they know from television, the news, or school.

Above level:

- Ask students to give mini-news stories about recent weather events in your area.
- Tell them to use what they learned in the Unit 14 Project on page 145.

- Have students discuss how weather and natural events relate to the previous Big Questions in the Student Book. You could write the following on the board, e.g.
  (Units 1 and 2) *Weather satellites orbit Earth and send photos of weather patterns to scientists.*
  (Units 3 and 4) *Earthquakes created changes in the surface of the earth. .*
  (Units 5 and 6) *Farmers need rain to grow food When there is no rain, crops don't grow.*
  (Units 7 and 8) *People take pictures of lightning flashes and tornadoes to show what they are interested in.*
  (Units 9 and 10) *Underground subway systems in cities can be damaged in bad rainstorms.*
  (Units 11 and 12) *If you need medicine to stay healthy, you should have extra in case of an emergency.*
  (Units 13 and 14) *People use mass media to stay informed during serious weather events.*

Expanding the topic

- Display **Discover Poster 8** and give students enough time to look at the pictures.
- Put students into small groups of three or four.
- Have each group choose a picture that they find interesting. Ask each group to say five things that they can see in their picture.

D Fill out the Big Question Chart.

- Ask the class *What do you know about nature's power?*
- Ask students to write what they know and what they want to know in their Workbooks.
- Write a collection of ideas on the **Big Question Chart**.

Discover Poster 8

1 Boats damaged and tossed by Hurricane Katrina;
2 A building severely damaged by an earthquake in San Francisco; 3 A flooded city street; 4 A man using storm shutters to protect his home from a hurricane; 5 A person using a weather warning system on a smartphone

| **Further Practice**
| **Workbook page 135**
| **Online practice · Big Question 8**
| Oxford **iTools · Big Question 8**

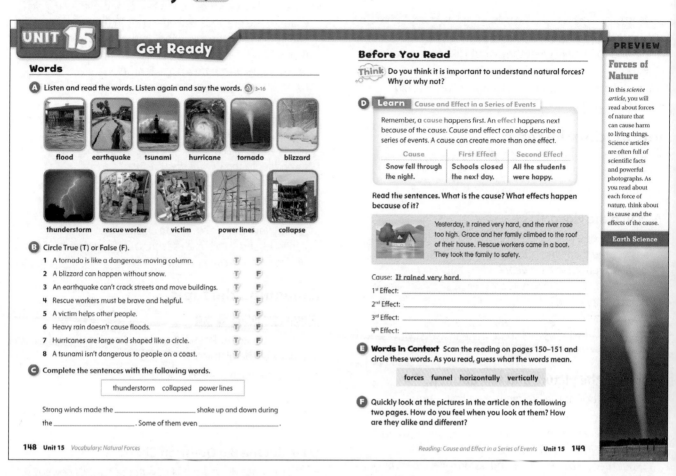

Summary

Objectives: To understand words about nature's power; to apply own experience and a reading strategy to help comprehension of a text.

Vocabulary: *flood, earthquake, tsunami, hurricane, tornado, blizzard, thunderstorm, rescue worker, victim, power lines, collapse, forces, funnel, horizontally, vertically*

Materials: Audio CD

Words

A Listen and read the words. Listen again and say the words. ⊚ 3•16

- Play the audio. Ask students to point to the words as they hear them.
- Play the audio a second time and have students repeat the words when they hear them.
- Say the words out of order and have students race to point to them on the page.

B Circle True (T) or False (F).

- Read through the items together.
- Have students try the exercise on their own first. Then check answers with the class.
- Invite volunteers to edit the false sentences to make them true, e.g. *A blizzard* **can't** *happen without snow.*

ANSWERS

1 T 2 F 3 F 4 T 5 F 6 F 7 T 8 F

Below level:

- Help students break down the meaning of the sentences in B, e.g.
  1 Say *The phrase "is like" tells you they are similar.*
  2 Underline the word *without.* Say *"without" means there isn't any. Can a blizzard happen if there isn't any snow?*
  3 Underline the word *can't.* Read the sentence and ask *Does that make sense?*
  4 and 5 Say *Look at the pictures. Who needs help and who is helping?*
  6 Underline the word *doesn't.* Read the sentence and ask *Does that make sense?*
  7 Point to the picture and trace the circular shape with your finger.
  8 Say *Remember the coast is where the sea meets land. A tsunami is a big wave.*

At level:

- Have student use what they've learned about the words in A and B to play a game of "association."
- To play the game, Partner A says a word. Partner B responds with all the words or phrases he / she associates with that word, e.g. Partner A says *rescue worker.* Partner B says words like *hero, uniform, firefighter, helpful, brave, disaster, danger.*
- Have students count the words they have said and keep score.
- The student with the most words wins the game.

Above level:

- Have students play a more challenging version of "association." Partner A says the words and phrases he / she associates with one of the target vocabulary words, and Partner B has to guess the word, e.g. Partner A says words like *person, hurt, can't move, disaster,* and *needs help.* Partner B says *victim.*

C Complete the sentences with the following words.

- Have students try to complete the exercise independently.
- Check answers as a class.

1 power lines   2 thunderstorm   3 collapsed

Before You Read

Think

- Have partners talk about the questions together first, and then share their ideas in a class discussion.

D Learn: Cause and Effect in a Series of Events

- Read the *Learn* box together.
- Copy the chart on the board. Draw an arrow from "Cause" to "First Effect." Write the number 1 on the arrow and say *first.*
- Draw an arrow from the "First Effect" to the "Second Effect." Write the number 2 on the arrow and say *second.*
- Point out the words *cause* and *because.* Explain that the cause tells you why something happens. Point and say *My school closed because snow fell through the night. All the students were happy because my school closed.*

Read the sentences. What is the cause? What effects happen because of it?

- Invite a confident student to read the paragraph aloud for the class.
- Together with the class list the effects in order.
- Check the answers with the class.

Cause: It rained very hard.
1st Effect: The river rose too high.
2nd Effect: Grace and her family climbed to the roof of their house (to escape the water).
3rd Effect: Rescue workers came in a boat.
4th Effect: They took the family to safety.

- Read aloud the following three events and have students suggest the correct order for a causal sequence:
  1 *Rescue workers come to the city* (3). *There is a sudden tornado* (1). *People are hurt* (2).
  2 *Lots of kids made snowmen* (3). *The blizzard dumped a meter of snow on the town* (1). *School was canceled* (2).
  3 *Buildings by the coast collapsed* (2). *The tsunami hit land in the morning* (1). *Victims were trapped in the buildings* (3).
- Invite students to try to come up with other examples.
- Have them write each event on a separate piece of paper, exchange papers with a partner, and put their partner's sentences in cause-and-effect order.

- Have students write acrostic poems for the target words.
- To create each poem, students write the word vertically on a piece of paper, then use each letter to start a word, phrase, or sentence about the target word.
- This is good to do with partners so students can help each other think of words and phrases, e.g. for the word *flood:*
  Find a boat!
  Lots of water.
  Outside it's wet.
  Open your umbrella.
  Drenched.

E Words in Context: Scan the reading on pages 150–151 and circle these words. As you read, guess what the words mean.

- Read each word and have students follow your pronunciation.
- Have them circle the words in the article.

F Quickly look at the pictures in the article on the following two pages. How do you feel when you look at them? How are they alike and different?

- Have students look at the pictures.
- If they have trouble identifying how they feel, encourage them to imagine they are in the middle of one of the weather scenes on the page. What would they do? What would they say?

Reading Preview

- Read the title of the unit's reading text.
- Have students silently read the content of the preview bar.
- Ask *What type of text is it?* Ask *What does this type of text do?*

Further Practice
Workbook pages 135–136
Online practice Unit 15 • Get Ready
Oxford iTools Unit 15 • Get Ready

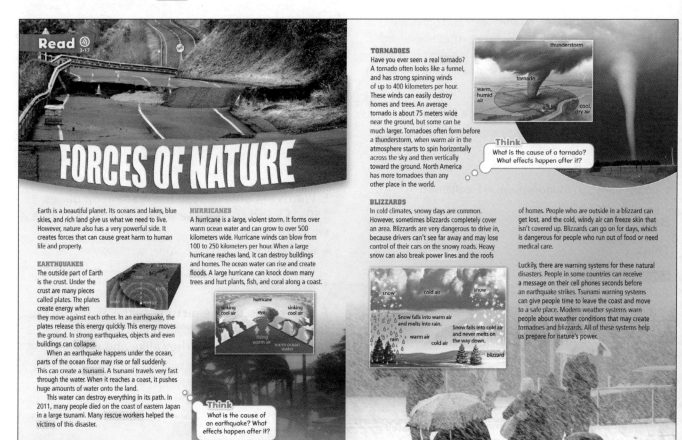

150
151

Summary

Objectives: To read, understand, and discuss a nonfiction text; to apply a reading strategy to improve comprehension.

School subject: Earth Science

Text type: Science article (nonfiction)

Reading strategy: Cause and effect in a series of events

Big Question learning points: *Nature's power can be dangerous. Nature can destroy buildings. Disasters can cause problems in cities and towns. We should be prepared for nature's power. Warning systems are important for people's safety.*

Materials: Talk About It! Poster, Audio CD

Before Reading

- On the board write the title *Forces of Nature*.
- Ask *What is a force?* (the power to make something happen) Say *Nature creates forces that can do wonderful and amazing things. What are some examples?* (Possible answers: The sun's power helps plants grow. Your heartbeat causes blood to circulate throughout your body. Wind can turn windmills to provide electricity.)
- Say *Nature creates forces that can also do great harm to human life and property. In this article, you will learn about some examples.*

During Reading ⊚ 3·17

- Read the title and introductory text together.
- Point out the text features that will help students navigate and understand the article. For example, the subtitle for each section tells the topic of the section, the realistic photos show the impact of nature, and the labeled illustrations give the reader a visual explanation of how things work.
- Remind students that as they read, they should think about cause and effect in each sequence of events.

DIFFERFENTIATION

Below level:

- Have students read in mixed-ability pairs so the more confident student can help explain vocabulary and phrases that are more challenging.
- Write some questions about each section on the board.
- Have students refer to the questions as they read and then elicit answers from the class when they have completed the reading.
- Tell each pair to be sure they can answer the following questions at the end of each section before they move on: Earthquakes: *When plates move against each other, what do they create? What can this energy create?*
Hurricanes: *Does a hurricane form over warm water or cool water? Is there a lot of wind in a hurricane?*
Tornadoes: *Is there a lot of wind in a tornado? What shape is a tornado?*
Blizzards: *What's the weather like in a blizzard? Why are blizzards dangerous to drivers?*

At level:

- Have students read with partners, alternating sections.
- Have them stop at each *Think* box to discuss the cause and effect sequences.
- Have partners try to paraphrase a few sentences in each section.

Above level:

- Have students read the article independently.
- Tell them to focus on the labeled illustrations on the page.
- Have them work with partners and take turns describing what each illustration shows.
- After partners practice, invite volunteers to "present" an illustration to the class and explain what it is showing.

- Have small groups revisit the Project in Unit 14 on page 145, "Creating a School News Program." Tell them to use those guidelines to create a weather report about an imaginary weather event that affects their town.
- Have the group discuss the who, what, where, when, and why of the weather event.
- Group roles: Tell the "group monitor" to make sure everyone contributes ideas and participates. Assign a "fact checker" to make sure the group includes facts and details from the reading selection "Forces of Nature." Assign a "drama monitor" to make sure the group portrays the exciting and urgent nature of the event.
- Groups may have one person present the news story as the reporter, and others can be interviewed as witnesses.

Discussion questions:

- *What causes a tsunami?*
- *Look at the photograph of the road damaged by an earthquake. Name some of the immediate effects from this earthquake.*
- *In a hurricane, what two elements can cause damage?*
- *Why do hurricanes usually form near the equator?*
- *In a tornado, you should go to a safe basement or a windowless area in the lowest and most central area of the building. Why?*
- *Why might people who are outside in a blizzard get lost?*
- *How can you alert people to a dangerous weather event? What if people do not have TVs or cell phones?*

After Reading

- Ask students to put the weather events in order from the scariest to the least scary. There is no right or wrong answer. This is based on students' individual personalities.
- Encourage them to explain what makes one scarier than another.

- Display the **Talk About It! Poster** to help students with sentence frames for discussion and expressing personal opinions.
- Put students into pairs to discuss which weather event is most interesting.

Many people consider rain the most risky source of water damage in a hurricane. Actually, the "storm surge" from a hurricane can cause the worst damage to areas along the coast during a hurricane.

The storm surge is like a giant, long, deep wave of water caused by the wind pushing ocean water toward the shore.

The surge is higher when the hurricane happens at high tide, when the water is naturally higher at the coast. (Natural tides rise and fall based on the lunar cycle and the time of day.)

Further Practice
Workbook page 137
Online practice Unit 15 • Read
Oxford iTools Unit 15 • Read

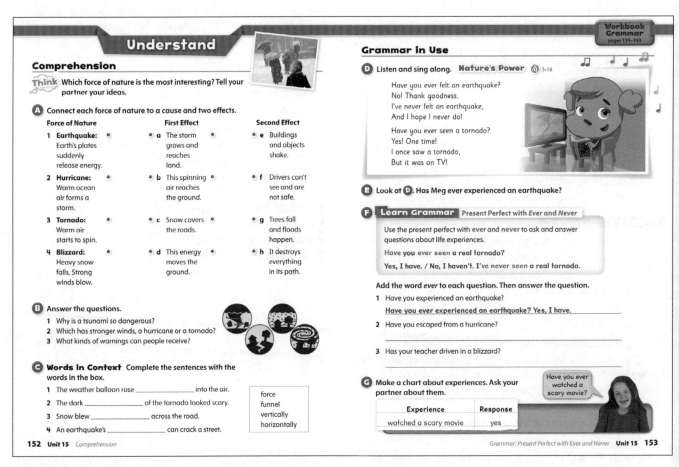

Summary

Objectives: To demonstrate understanding of a nonfiction text; to understand the meaning and form of the grammar structure.

Reading: Comprehension

Grammar input: Present perfect with *ever* and *never*

Grammar practice: Workbook exercises

Grammar production: Use the present perfect with *ever* and *never* to ask about experiences in the past

Materials: Audio CD

Comprehension

Think

• Have students refer to specific details from the reading to support their choices.

A Connect each force of nature to a cause and two effects.

• Read the choices together to make sure students understand the language.
• Have them complete the exercise, then check answers as a class.

ANSWERS

1 d, e   2 a, g   3 b, h   4 c, f

Below level:

• Have students work with partners to ask and answer questions following the model below. They can substitute different language from A in parentheses.
  A: *In (an earthquake), what happens after (the Earth's plates suddenly release energy)?*
  B: *(The energy moves the ground).*
  A: *What happens next?*
  B: *(Buildings and objects shake.)*

At level:

• Have students name one additional detail about each cause or effect in A, e.g.
  Heavy snow falls. Strong wind blows. (Students say *The snow doesn't melt because the air is cold* based on information for the blizzard section.)
  The storm grows and reaches land. (Students say *The storm can grow to over 500 kilometers wide* based on the information in the hurricane paragraph.)

Above level:

• Have students create a fifth example for A to tell about tsunamis. Tell them to include a cause, a first effect, a second effect, **and** a third effect, e.g.
  Cause (an earthquake occurs under the ocean)
  1st Effect (a giant wave of water travels quickly through the ocean)
  2nd Effect (the wave pushes huge amounts of water onto the coast)
  3rd Effect (the water destroys everything in its path).

B Answer the questions.

- For each question, tell students to look back at the reading text and find details to support their answer.
- Ask them to identify which weather event is depicted by each illustration next to B.
- Check answers with the class.

ANSWERS

1 It pushes huge amounts of water onto the land and destroys everything in its path.
2 A tornado
3 Messages on cell phones; weather warning systems

CRITICAL THINKING

- Have small groups name some third, fourth, and fifth effects for each item in A. Encourage them to consider effects on a smaller, personal scale, e.g.
  Earthquake: 3rd Effect (*The elevator in a building breaks.*) 4th Effect (*Someone is trapped in the elevator.*) 5th Effect (*Rescue workers have to rescue the person from the elevator.*)
  Hurricane: 3rd Effect (*The basement floods in a house along the coast.*) 4th Effect (*Old photographs in boxes in the basement are ruined by the water.*) 5th Effect (*Grandchildren can never see photos of their grandparents when they were young.*)

C Words in Context: Complete the sentences with the words in the box.

- Have students go back and find the words in the text.
- Tell them to use the context clues to guess at the meaning of each word.
- Have students complete the exercise independently, then check answers with a partner.

ANSWERS

1 vertically   2 funnel   3 horizontally   4 force

Grammar in Use

D Listen and sing along. ⊚ 3•18

CREATIVITY

- Revisit the Learn Grammar section on the Present Perfect on page 141.
- Listen to the song and then sing it together as a class.
- Help students identify the two roles: one person sings the questions and the other sings the answers.
- Divide the class in two groups: one sings the questions and the other sings the answers.

E Look at D. Has Meg ever experienced an earthquake?

- Have students look back over the song and answer the question.
- Check the answer with the class.

ANSWER

No

F Learn Grammar: Present Perfect with Ever and Never

- Read the *Learn Grammar* box with the class.
- Copy the example sentence on the board: *Have you ever seen a real tornado?* Underline the word *seen* and remind students that this is the past participle of *see*.
- Remind students that the question and answer form will change depending on the subject, e.g.
  Have you ever … ? Yes, I have. No, I haven't.
  Has she / he / it ever … ? Yes, she / he / it has. No, she / he / it hasn't.
  Have they ever … ? Yes, they have. No, they haven't.
  Have we ever … ? Yes, we have. No, we haven't.
- Review other past participles. Do a circle drill where students choose a verb and practice forming the beginning of the question using the past participle, e.g.
  Have you ever seen … ? / Has he ever been … ? / Have they ever eaten … ? / Have we ever read … ?

Add the word *ever* to each question. Then answer the question.

- Read the first question together. Identify the verb (*experienced*). Then read the revised question with *ever*.
- Have students complete the exercise and answer for themselves.
- Tell them to check the exercise with a partner.

ANSWERS

1 Have you ever experienced an earthquake? Yes, I have.
2 Have you ever escaped from a hurricane? Yes, I have. / No, I haven't. I've never escaped from a hurricane.
3 Has your teacher ever driven in a blizzard? Yes, he / she has. / No, he / she hasn't. He's / She's never driven in a blizzard.

G Make a chart about experiences. Ask your partner about them.

- Students fill in the chart individually.

COLLABORATIVE LEARNING

- Encourage students to look through the book for ideas related to each Big Question, e.g. *Have you ever seen a comet? Has your sister ever visited Shanghai? Have you ever read a blog?*
- Put students in pairs to share their ideas.
- Swap pairs so that students can ask the questions to other people.

Workbook Grammar

- Direct students to the Workbook for further practice.

Further Practice
Workbook pages 138–140
Online practice Unit 15 • Understand
Oxford **iTools** Unit 15 • Understand

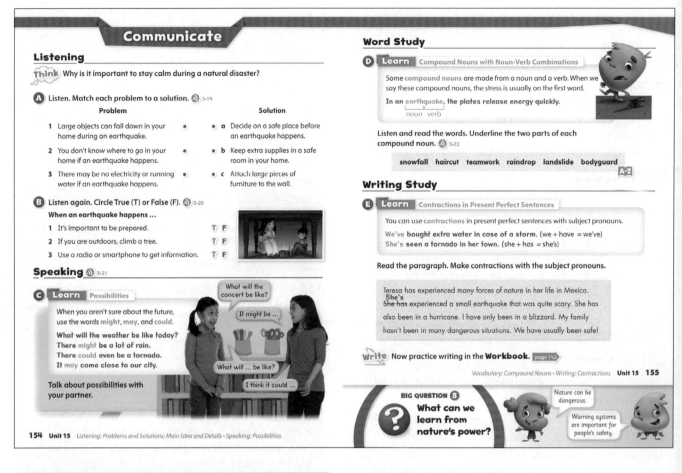

Summary

Objectives: To learn and practice listening, speaking, and writing strategies to facilitate effective communication.

Vocabulary: *snowfall, haircut, teamwork, raindrop, landslide, bodyguard*

Listening strategy: Listening for problems and solutions; main idea and details

Speaking: Talking about possibilities

Word Study: Compound nouns with noun-verb combinations

Writing Study: Contractions in present perfect sentences

Big Question learning points: *Nature's power can be dangerous. Nature can destroy buildings. We should be prepared for nature's power.*

Materials: Discover Poster 8, Audio CD, Big Question Chart

Listening

Think

- Invite a few volunteers to help you role-pay a tornado hitting your school. In the first role-play, students panic and aren't able to follow directions. In the second role-play, they are calm and follow directions.
- Afterwards, help students describe how staying calm allowed them to follow instructions, think clearly, and stay safe.

A Listen. Match each problem to a solution. ⊙ 3·19

- Play the audio once and have students listen. Ask *What is the purpose of this text?*

- Tell students to match the problems and solutions in A.
- Play the audio again so they can check their work.

ANSWERS
1 c   2 a   3 b

B Listen again. Circle True (T) or False (F). ⊙ 3·20

- See if students can complete the exercise without listening to the audio first.
- Then play the audio so they can check their work.
- Ask students which question deals with a main idea of the listening passage.

ANSWERS
1 T   2 F   3 T

DIFFERENTIATION

Below level:

- Pause after each section that addresses one of the problems in A to allow students time to process what they've heard.
- Help them find the problem in the left column of the exercise by focusing on key words and phrases: *fall down, go,* and *electricity or running water.*
- Then look at the solutions together. Replay the section of the audio so students can hear the key words and phrases: *decide on a safe place, safe room,* and *attach … to the wall.*

At level:

- Say *Dr. Demir says there are two ways to be prepared for an earthquake. What are they?*

- Have students use these two ideas to create main idea and detail organizers where the main idea is the "table top" and each detail is written as one of four "legs" on the table.
- Organizers should include this information:
  1 *Main idea*: Make sure your home is ready for an earthquake. *Details*: 1. Attach large objects to the wall. 2. Decide on a safe place to go. 3. Keep food and water in a safe room. 4. Keep a flashlight and batteries.
  2 *Main idea*: Know what to do when an earthquake happens. *Details*: 1. If indoors, go to your safe room. 2. If outside, get away from trees and buildings, and stay low. 3. Use a smartphone or radio to get information. 4. Stay calm.

Above level:

- Tell students to imagine that an earthquake hit your town.
- Rephrase the problems in A as "causes": 1. Large objects fell. 2. You didn't know where to go during an earthquake. 3. There was no electricity or running water after the earthquake.
- Have partners name some possible sequences of effects for each cause.

Speaking ⊚ 3·21

C Learn: Possibilities

COMMUNICATION

- Read the *Learn* box together.
- Play the audio and have students echo the speakers to practice pronunciation and intonation.
- Model the dialogue with a confident student in front of the class.
- Put students into pairs and tell them to practice the dialogue, taking turns speaking the different roles.

Talk about possibilities with your partner.

COLLABORATIVE LEARNING

- Write the following on the board: *What will the earthquake aftermath be like?* Explain that *aftermath* refers to the effects of a given event. Provide a sample answer: *There might be collapsed buildings*.
- Have partners brainstorm other possible answers using the models in C.
- Tell partners to practice the conversation by talking about the aftermath for the other weather events discussed in "Forces of Nature."

CRITICAL THINKING

- Ask students to apply what they learned from Dr. Demir's presentation to come up with ideas for "Preparing Your School for an Earthquake."
- Many of the ideas will be the same, such as deciding on a safe place to go and attaching large furniture to the walls, but others may need to be adapted or invented, e.g. students may decide the school should create a call-tree where parents call one another with updates and important information.

Word Study

D Learn: Compound Nouns with Noun-Verb Combinations

- Read the *Learn* box to the class.
- Ask *In the word "earthquake," which word is the noun? Which is the verb? Is the compound word a noun or verb?*

Listen and read the words. Underline the two parts of each compound noun. ⊚ 3·22

- Play the audio. Have students repeat each word.
- For each word, have students identify the noun and the verb.
- Point out that in each case, the compound word is a noun that tells the effect of the noun and verb working together.

ANSWERS

snow / fall, hair / cut, team / work, rain / drop, land / slide, body / guard

Writing Study

E Learn: Contractions in Present Perfect Sentences

- Have a confident student read the *Learn* box to the class.
- Write the related contractions on the board: *I have / I've, you have / you've, he has / he's, it has / it's, they have / they've*.

Read the paragraph. Make contractions with the subject pronouns.

- Have students complete the exercise. Then check the answers with the class.

ANSWERS

She's, She's, I've, We've

Write

- Direct students to the Workbook for further practice.

Big Question 8 Review

What can we learn from nature's power?

- Display **Discover Poster 8**. Have students explain how the learning points relate to the different pictures.
- Return to the **Big Question Chart**.
- Ask students what they have learned about nature's power while studying this unit.

Further Practice
Workbook pages 141–142
Online practice Unit 15 • Communicate
Oxford **iTools** Unit 15 • Communicate

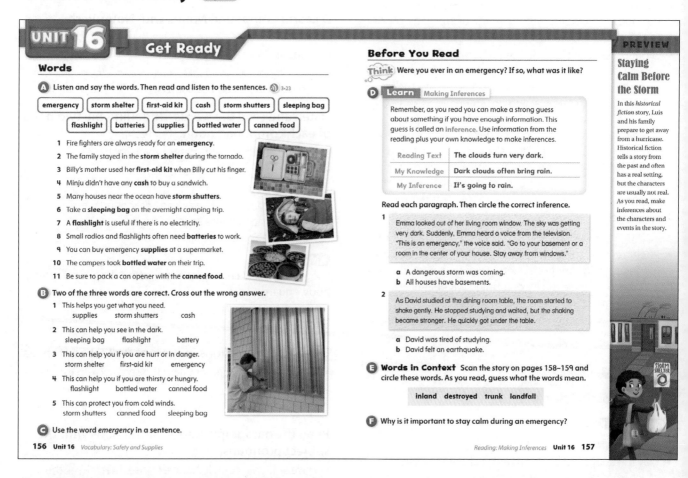

Summary

Objectives: To understand words about emergencies; to apply own experience and reading strategy to help comprehension of a text.

Vocabulary: *emergency, storm shelter, first-aid kit, cash, storm shutters, sleeping bag, flashlight, batteries, supplies, bottled water, canned food, inland, destroyed, trunk, landfall*

Reading strategy: Making inferences

Materials: Audio CD

Words

A Listen and say the words. Then read and listen to the sentences. ⊚ 3·23

- Play the audio. Ask students to point to the words as they hear them.
- Play the audio a second time and have students repeat the words when they hear them.
- Play the sentences and have students echo read them, focusing on pronunciation and intonation.

DIFFERENTIATION

Below level:

- Encourage students to think more deeply about the words by asking *What can you tell me about (storm shelters)?*
- This allows students to share any prior knowledge they have. Students may also simply use the sentences in A for ideas, e.g. ask *What can you tell me about emergencies?*

- Possible answers include sentences like these: *They are dangerous. An earthquake is an emergency. Firefighters help in emergencies. You don't know it's coming.*
- Students' understanding of each word will be more complete the more they listen to others' answers.

At level:

- Have students write a question for each sentence, e.g. *Who is always ready for an emergency?*
- Tell them to choose a few sentences for which they write more than one question.
- They will need to focus on the meaning of the sentence and the word to do this correctly, e.g. *Who stayed in the storm shelter during the tornado? Where did the family stay during the tornado? When did the family stay in the storm shelter?*

Above level:

- Have students write original sentences for the words in A. Instead of actually writing the word, they should substitute a blank line. Have them exchange papers with partners. The partners fill in the blanks.
- For an added challenge, tell students to try to include vocabulary from other units, or to use more than one word from A in each sentence.

- Divide the class into small groups. Assign each group a few words from A.
- Have the groups work together to create "squares of meaning" for their words.
- Students write one word in the center of each square. They write one of the following in each corner of the square: a synonym or simple definition, an example, a sentence, and the part of speech, e.g.
  emergency: (1st corner: definition / synonym) *something bad and surprising that you have to deal with;* (2nd corner: example) *a fire;* (3rd corner: sentence) *The police can help when there's an emergency;* (4th corner: part of speech) *noun.*
- Have groups share their squares with the class. If two groups have a square for the same word, compare their answers.

B Two of the three words are correct. Cross out the wrong answer.

- Look at the exercise together to make sure students understand what to do.
- Have students complete the exercise on their own, then check answers with a partner.

ANSWERS
1 storm shutters 2 sleeping bag 3 emergency
4 flashlight 5 canned food

C Use the word *emergency* in a sentence.

- Have students work in pairs to come up with a sentence.

Before You Read

Think

- Students may want to retell the events of their emergency, but encourage them to focus on the emotions they had and the mood around them, as well.

D Learn: Making Inferences

- Have a confident student read the *Learn* box to the class.
- Point out that we make strong guesses based on clues and what we already know. In the example, we know that dark clouds and thunder usually accompany rainstorms.

Read each paragraph. Then circle the correct inference.

- Have a volunteer read the first paragraph aloud.
- Read the two possible answers.
- Ask students to choose the correct answer. If necessary, point out that the announcement directs everyone to their basement or a room in the center of the house.
- Have a volunteer read the second paragraph. Ask students what clues they can use to choose the correct inference. (*The room shakes gently, then the shaking becomes stronger. Going under the table is a good idea during an earthquake.*)
- Point out that the paragraph doesn't mention David rubbing his eyes or yawning, it doesn't mention him thinking of playing outside, and there are no other hints that he is tired of studying.

ANSWERS
1 a 2 b

Provide two more examples:

- *Jenny shivered and tried to close her coat more tightly around her. She couldn't see the road in front of her, all she could see was white. It was hard to walk because her feet sank deeper and deeper in the snow.* (Jenny is lost in a blizzard.)
- *Dean read the alert on his cell phone. He quickly grabbed a bottle of water, a flashlight, and a bag of chips. He heard the wind howling outside and noticed a giant piece of wood blow past his window. He raced to the bathroom in the center of the house and shut the door.* (There is a tornado.)

E Words in Context: Scan the story on pages 158–159 and circle these words. As you read, guess what the words mean.

- Have students scan the story and circle the words.
- Ask them to find the two compound words in the list (*inland, landfall*). Of the two, which is an example of a noun-verb combination (*landfall*).

F Why is it important to stay calm during an emergency?

- Reinforce the importance of following directions in an emergency.
- Ask students to think about having fire drills at school.
- Put students into pairs and have them discuss what happens and why its important to remain calm.
- Encourage them to use cause and effect sequences in their descriptions.
- Have students share ideas with the class.

Reading Preview

- Read the title of the unit's reading text.
- Have students silently read the contents of the preview bar.
- Ask *What type of text is it?* Ask *What does this type of text do?*
- Remind students to try to make inferences as they read.

Further Practice
Workbook pages 143–144
Online practice Unit 16 • Get Ready
Oxford iTools Unit 16 • Get Ready

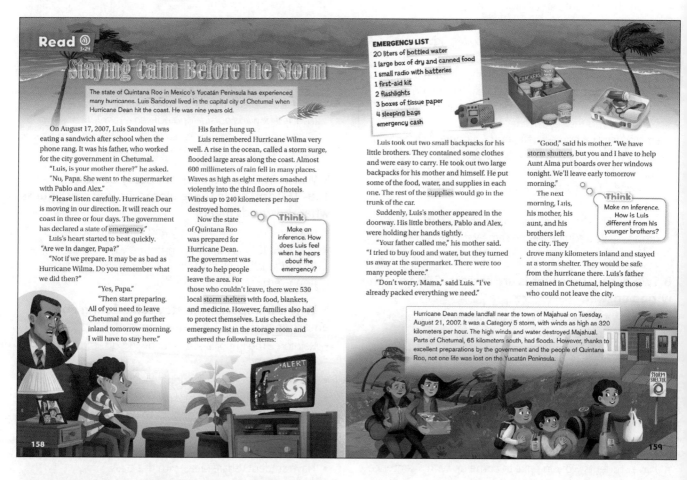

Read 3·24
Staying Calm Before the Storm

The state of Quintana Roo in Mexico's Yucatán Peninsula has experienced many hurricanes. Luis Sandoval lived in the capital city of Chetumal when Hurricane Dean hit the coast. He was nine years old.

On August 17, 2007, Luis Sandoval was eating a sandwich after school when the phone rang. It was his father, who worked for the city government in Chetumal.

"Luis, is your mother there?" he asked.

"No, Papa. She went to the supermarket with Pablo and Alex."

"Please listen carefully. Hurricane Dean is moving in our direction. It will reach our coast in three or four days. The government has declared a state of emergency."

Luis's heart started to beat quickly. "Are we in danger, Papa?"

"Not if we prepare. It may be as bad as Hurricane Wilma. Do you remember what we did then?"

"Yes, Papa."

"Then start preparing. All of you need to leave Chetumal and go further inland tomorrow morning. I will have to stay here."

His father hung up.

Luis remembered Hurricane Wilma very well. A rise in the ocean, called a storm surge, flooded large areas along the coast. Almost 600 millimeters of rain fell in many places. Waves as high as eight meters smashed violently into the third floors of hotels. Winds up to 240 kilometers per hour destroyed homes.

Now the state of Quintana Roo was prepared for Hurricane Dean. The government was ready to help people leave the area. For those who couldn't leave, there were 530 local storm shelters with food, blankets, and medicine. However, families also had to protect themselves. Luis checked the emergency list in the storage room and gathered the following items:

Think — Make an inference. How does Luis feel when he hears about the emergency?

EMERGENCY LIST
- 20 liters of bottled water
- 1 large box of dry and canned food
- 1 small radio with batteries
- 1 first-aid kit
- 2 flashlights
- 3 boxes of tissue paper
- 4 sleeping bags
- emergency cash

Luis took out two small backpacks for his little brothers. They contained some clothes and were easy to carry. He took out two large backpacks for his mother and himself. He put some of the food, water, and supplies in each one. The rest of the supplies would go in the trunk of the car.

Suddenly, Luis's mother appeared in the doorway. His little brothers, Pablo and Alex, were holding her hands tightly.

"Your father called me," his mother said. "I tried to buy food and water, but they turned us away at the supermarket. There were too many people there."

"Don't worry, Mama," said Luis. "I've already packed everything we need."

"Good," said his mother. "We have storm shutters, but you and I have to help Aunt Alma put boards over her windows tonight. We'll leave early tomorrow morning."

The next morning, Luis, his mother, his aunt, and his brothers left the city. They drove many kilometers inland and stayed at a storm shelter. They would be safe from the hurricane there. Luis's father remained in Chetumal, helping those who could not leave the city.

Think — Make an inference. How is Luis different from his younger brothers?

Hurricane Dean made landfall near the town of Majahual on Tuesday, August 21, 2007. It was a Category 5 storm, with winds as high as 320 kilometers per hour. The high winds and water destroyed Majahual. Parts of Chetumal, 65 kilometers south, had floods. However, thanks to excellent preparations by the government and the people of Quintana Roo, not one life was lost on the Yucatán Peninsula.

Summary

Objectives: To read, understand and discuss a fictional text; to apply a reading strategy to improve comprehension.

School subject: Earth Science

Text type: Historical fiction

Reading strategy: Making inferences

Big Question learning points: *Nature's power can be dangerous. Nature can destroy buildings. Disasters can cause problems in cities or towns. We should be prepared for nature's power. Warning systems are important for people's safety*

Materials: Talk About It! Poster, Audio CD

Before Reading

- Ask students to make predictions about the story. Tell them to use the words from the vocabulary list on page 156 and the illustrations. Revisit their predictions after you finish reading.

During Reading ⊚ 3·24

- Play the audio. Students listen as they read along.
- Stop at each *Think* box for students to discuss the questions.
- Point out the clues for the first inference that Luis is nervous. (*Luis's heart started to beat quickly* … when his father told him Hurricane Dean was moving in their direction; Luis remembered the details of Hurricane Wilma, which include lots of flooding and damage.)

- Point out clues for the second inference that he is more responsible and mature than his little brothers. (He packs everything they need; he packs smaller backpacks for his brothers.)

DIFFERENTIATION

Below level:

- Have students read in mixed-ability pairs.
- Have the more confident student help the less confident student with pronunciation and comprehension.
- Tell students to pause after every few sentences to discuss what they have read so far.
- Ask questions periodically to check comprehension, such as *Why does Luis's father call Luis?*

At level:

- Have small groups read the story together, taking turns around a circle.
- Assign a secretary in each group to take notes. Tell the groups to pause at each *Think* box and answer the questions; the secretary writes the group's answers.
- Tell students to identify the clues for each inference as they read.
- Have the students share their answers to the *Think* boxes.

Above level:

- Have students read the story alone, jotting down any phrases or sentences they do not understand.
- Put students with partners to work through anything they jotted down. If they need additional help with comprehension, have them ask you specific questions for clarification.

- Challenge students to list the main events of the story in order on separate pieces of paper. Have them exchange papers and sequence each other's papers.

COLLABORATIVE LEARNING
- Divide the class into small groups.
- Have each group plan a role-play of the story. Assign a director in each group. The director assigns parts (narrator, Luis, his father, his mother, the two little brothers).
- First have groups work together to divide the reading into scenes, or do this as a whole class, e.g.
  Scene 1: *Luis talks to his father on the phone.*
  Scene 2: *The narrator talks about Luis's memory of Hurricane Wilma.*
  Scene 3: *Luis packs their bags.*
  Scene 4: *Luis's mother comes home with his brothers.*
  Scene 5: *The family leaves in the morning.*
- Next have groups write simple scripts for each scene. Assign a secretary in each group. Ideally the secretary will be one of the students who has a smaller part in the role-play.
- Groups practice their role-plays, then perform for the class. They may memorize their lines, improvise, or read directly from the scripts they wrote.

CRITICAL THINKING
Discussion questions:
- *Luis's father stays in Chetumal during the hurricane. Is this the right thing to do, or should he come home and help his family?*
- *How did Luis know what to pack?*
- *Why did the supermarket turn away Luis's mother? Make an inference: Why were so many people at the supermarket? What does this tell you about being prepared for an emergency?*
- *Make an inference: Why do Luis and his mother have to help Aunt Alma?*
- *Were the winds stronger in Hurricane Wilma or Hurricane Dean?*

After Reading
- Return to the predictions students made during Before Reading. Check their ideas.
- Challenge students to predict what will happen next, when Luis and his family return home. Encourage them to use language for talking about possibilities on page 154, e.g. *There could be a lot of damage. There might be some collapsed buildings.*

COLLABORATIVE LEARNING
- Display the **Talk About It! Poster** to help students with sentence frames for discussion and expressing personal opinions.
- Put students into pairs to discuss the events in the story.
- Have students say one thing about each main event in the reading.

CULTURE NOTE

The story mentions that Hurricane Dean was a Category 5 hurricane. Scientists and governments use categories as a scale for measuring and comparing hurricanes.

The categories refer to the wind speed, and the expected resulting damage. The wind speeds are as follows:
Category 1: 119–153 km/hour
Category 2: 154–177 km/hour
Category 3: 178–208 km/hour
Category 4: 209–251 km/hour
Category 5: 252 km/hour or higher

Remember that in a hurricane, the second biggest risk after wind is the storm surge, but because the storm surge is a result of wind, scientists use wind speed to determine intensity.

Further Practice
Workbook page 145
Online practice Unit 16 · Read
Oxford iTools Unit 16 · Read

Unit 16 Understand page 160

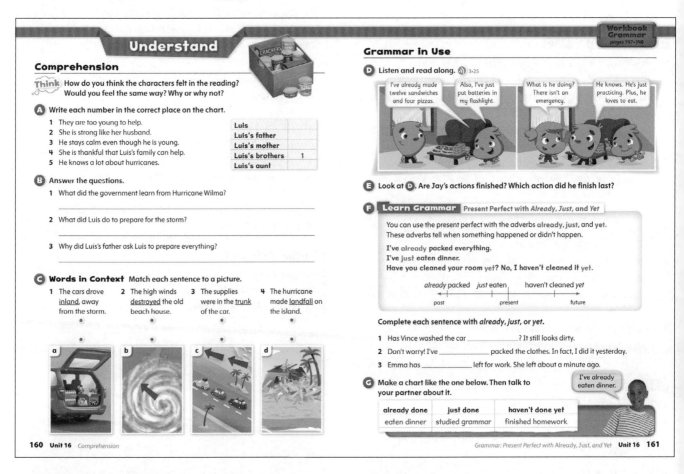

Summary

Objectives: To demonstrate understanding of a fictional text; to understand the meaning and form of the grammar structure.

Reading: Comprehension

Grammar input: Present perfect with *already, just,* and *yet*

Grammar practice: Workbook exercises

Grammar production: Use the present perfect to talk about what happened or didn't happen

Materials: Audio CD

Comprehension

Think

- Tell students to discuss the questions with a partner.
- Tell them to use specific details from the story to support their inferences about how the characters felt.

A Write each number in the correct place on the chart.

- Have students try to complete the exercise on their own.
- Check answers as a class.

ANSWERS

1 Luis's brothers   2 Luis's mother   3 Luis
4 Luis's aunt   5 Luis's father

DIFFERENTIATION

Below level:

- Review the reading together to complete A.
- Have students scan the reading to find the details that support each answer, e.g.
  1 Luis's brothers are too young to help. (Luis takes out two small backpacks for them; he packs larger backpacks with supplies for himself and his mother. Luis is allowed to stay at home by himself, which implies he is older and more responsible. His brothers must stay with their mother.)
  2 Luis's mother is strong like her husband. (She doesn't panic; she helps put boards over Aunt Alma's windows; she takes care of all three children by herself.)
  3 Luis stays calm, even though he is young. (Even though he is nervous, he doesn't panic. He remembers to pack the items on the emergency list, and he is able to help his mother.)
  4 Aunt Alma is thankful that Luis's family can help. (His mother says "you and I have to help," which implies that if they do not help, nobody will.)
  5 Luis's father knows a lot about hurricanes. (He works for the government and has information about Hurricane Dean.)

At level:

- Have students use what they know about understanding characters (see Understanding Characters on page 97) to analyze the characters in the story, e.g.
  Luis is the main character. He is calm and responsible. He helps his family prepare for the hurricane.

186   Unit 16 • Understand

Luis's brothers are minor characters. They are too young to help. They follow their mother and brother.

Above level:

- Have students write one inference for each character, e.g.
Luis: *He wants to be helpful to his mother.* (He packs the bags and tells her not to worry.)
Luis's father: *During Hurricane Wilma he taught Luis how to prepare for an emergency.* (He asks *Do you remember what we did then?*)
Luis's mother: *She felt worried when they turned her away at the supermarket.* (She went to the supermarket after Luis's father called, so she thought they needed supplies.)
Luis's brothers: *They are worried.* (They are holding their mother's hands tightly when they get home.)
Luis's aunt: *She is alone.* (Luis's mother says they have to help Aunt Alma, but she doesn't mention anyone else. This implies she lives alone.)

B Answer the questions.

- Have students answer the questions and then discuss them with the class.

ANSWERS
1 Possible answer: They learned how to prepare.
2 Luis got all the supplies ready for his family.
3 He knew Luis remembered how to prepare for a hurricane.

CRITICAL THINKING

Ask additional questions:

- How do you think the characters will feel the next time there is an emergency?
- What do you think happened to people who did NOT have a plan?

C Words in Context: Match each sentence to a picture.

- Return to the story and have a volunteer read each word in the context of its sentence. Use the context to determine meaning.
- Ask a question about each sentence, e.g. *1 Why do you drive inland during a storm? 2 What is one effect of a house being destroyed? 3 What are some supplies to pack in the trunk? 4 Which noun and verb make this word?*
- Check the answers with the class.

ANSWERS
1 c 2 d 3 a 4 b

Grammar in Use

D Listen and read along. 3·25

- Listen to the conversation once.
- Have two confident students read it aloud for the class.
- Play the audio and have volunteers use it as a model for pronunciation and intonation as they echo read.

E Look at D. Are Jay's actions finished? Which action did he finish last?

- Ask the class what language helps us to understand the action that was finished last (*just*).

ANSWERS
Yes, they are finished. He put batteries in the flashlight last.

F Learn Grammar: Present Perfect with *Already*, *Just*, and *Yet*

- Read the *Learn Grammar* box together.
- Refer to the timeline and ask students to sequence events in their lives, such as book series they have read, movies they have seen, cities they have visited, or grades they have finished, e.g.
I've already read (the first book in the series). I've just finished (the second book in the series). I haven't read (the third book in the series) yet.

Complete each sentence with *already*, *just*, or *yet*.

- For each sentence, help students identify the clue: In sentence 1, the car *looks dirty*, which implies he hasn't washed it *yet*. In sentence 2, the word *yesterday* is a clue that he *already packed the clothes*. In sentence 3, the phrase *a minute ago* is a clue that she *just left for work*.
- Elicit the answers from the class.

ANSWERS
1 yet 2 already 3 just

G Make a chart like the one below. Then talk to your partner about it.

- Have students complete the chart individually.

COMMUNICATION

- Put students into pairs. Have them read their charts to each other and compare them.
- Conduct a mingle activity where students walk around the room and try to find other students with the same answers.
- Ask for a show of hands for the most popular answers and write them on the board.

| Further Practice
Workbook pages 146–148
Online practice Unit 16 · Understand
Oxford iTools Unit 16 · Understand

Unit 16 Communicate page 162

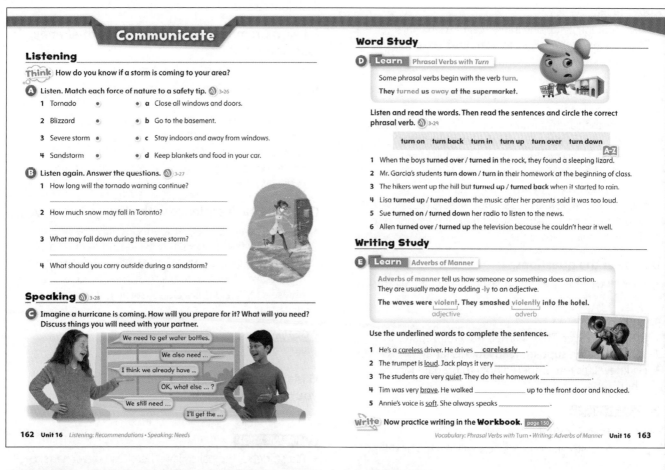

Summary

Objectives: To learn and practice listening, speaking, and writing strategies to facilitate effective communication.

Vocabulary: *turn on, turn back, turn in, turn up, turn over, turn down*

Listening strategy: Listening for recommendations

Speaking: Talking about needs

Word Study: Phrasal verbs with *turn*

Writing Study: Adverbs of manner

Big Question learning points: *Nature's power can be dangerous. Disasters can cause problems in cities or towns. We should be prepared for nature's power. Warning systems are important for people's safety.*

Materials: Audio CD

Listening

Think

• Have students discuss the question in small groups. Invite them to share their ideas with the class.

A Listen. Match each force of nature to a safety tip. ⊚ 3•26

• Play the audio once through while students just listen.
• Play it a second time and have them complete the exercise. Check the answers with the class.

ANSWERS
1 b   2 d   3 c   4 a

Below level:

• Pause after each announcement. Tell students to take notes as they listen. Pause after each section and ask students to tell you what they remember hearing.
• Check to see if any of the details they recall help them to complete A. If they do, have students match the weather to the recommendation. If not, listen again and help them identify the place in the audio where the recommendation is mentioned.
• Repeat for each section.

At level:

• Elicit the *what, when,* and *where* of each announcement, e.g. in the first announcement: *What?* (a tornado warning) *When?* (for the next 60 minutes) *Where?* (Greenhills, Ohio)
• Then elicit the recommendation, e.g. *In a tornado, seek shelter in a basement or room near the center of your house.*

Above level:

• Have students ask partners *Why* questions about each announcement. This requires them to make inferences, e.g.
Why should you close all the windows and doors?
Why should you go to the basement?
Why should you stay indoors and away from the windows?
Why should you keep blankets and food in your car?

B Listen again. Answer the questions. 3·27

- First have students read the questions so they know what information they are listening for.
- Then play the audio and have them complete the exercise on their own.
- Check answers with the class.

ANSWERS
1 60 minutes   2 75 centimeters   3 trees
4 goggles and a dust mask

CRITICAL THINKING

Ask additional questions:

- Why does the tornado warning last 60 minutes?
- Scientists cannot know exactly how much snow will fall. Is it better to overestimate (predict more snow than actually falls) or underestimate (predict less snow than actually falls)?
- What else may fall down during a severe storm?
- Besides a sandstorm, when else might goggles be helpful?
- Of the four warnings you just heard, which event do you think might be the most dangerous? Why?

Speaking 3·28

C Imagine a hurricane is coming. How will you prepare for it? What will you need? Discuss things you will need with your partner.

COMMUNICATION

- Play the audio once. Invite students to echo the dialogue to focus on pronunciation and intonation.
- Then practice the dialogue with a confident student.
- Have partners practice the dialogue together.

COLLABORATIVE LEARNING

- Have partners list items they would need for the four emergencies in A. Tell them to think about the supplies named in the announcements they listened to, as well as their own ideas.
- Tell partners to practice the dialogue, substituting in the other emergencies and supplies.

Word Study

D Learn: Phrasal Verb with *Turn*

- Remind students of the Unit 5 (page 55) Word Study lesson "Phrasal Verbs with *Drop*" and the Unit 10 (page 103) Word Study lesson "Phrasal Verbs with *Take*." Tell them that they will learn some similar expressions with *turn*.
- Read the *Learn* box together.
- Ask *Where did you read this sentence?* (In "Staying Calm Before the Storm," when Luis's mother tried to go to the supermarket.) Ask *What did it mean in the story?* (They wouldn't let her in the supermarket.)

Listen and read the words. Then read the sentences and circle the correct phrasal verb. 3·29

- Play the audio and have students point to the phrases as they hear them, then repeat them.
- Provide some simple definitions: *turn on* (start the power), *turn back* (to return the same way you came), *turn in* (give to someone), *turn up* (make louder), *turn over* (look at the underside), *turn down* (make quieter).
- Have students complete the exercise on their own.
- Check answers with the class.

ANSWERS
1 turned over   2 turn in   3 turned back
4 turned down   5 turned on   6 turned up

Writing Study

E Learn: Adverbs of Manner

- Read the *Learn* box together.
- Copy the sample sentence on the board. Draw an arrow from *violent* to *waves*, and from *violently* to *smashed*.
- Explain that the adjective describes the noun, and adverb describes the verb.

Use the underlined words to complete the sentences

- Have students complete the exercise on their own.
- Check answers with the class.

ANSWERS
1 carelessly   2 loudly   3 quietly   4 bravely   5 softly

Write

- Direct students to the Workbook for further practice.

Further Practice
Workbook pages 149–150
Online practice Unit 16 · Communicate
Oxford **iTools** Unit 16 · Communicate

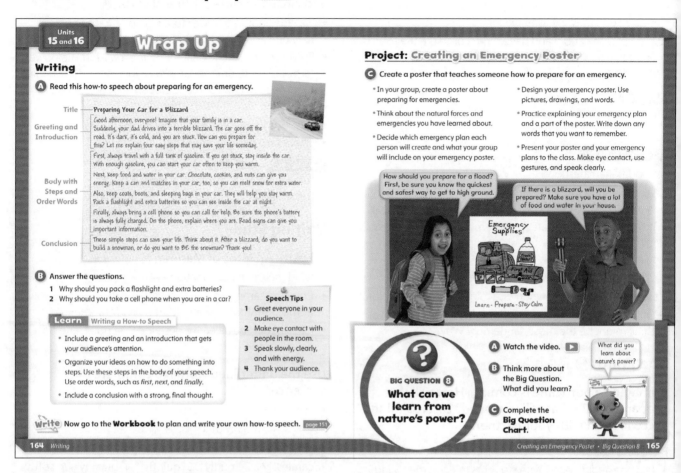

Summary

Objectives: To show what students have learned about the language and learning points of Units 15 and 16.

Reading: Comprehension of how-to speech

Project: Creating an emergency poster

Writing: Write a how-to speech

Speaking: Talking about the emergency posters

Materials: Big Question DVD, Discover Poster 8, Talk About It! Poster, Big Question Chart, Audio CD

Writing

A Read this how-to speech about preparing for an emergency.

- Explain that a how-to speech explains how to do something. In this case, the speech explains how to prepare your car for a blizzard.
- Ask students to predict what tips might be included in the speech.
- Read the speech together.

CRITICAL THINKING

Ask questions to check comprehension:

- How does the writer grab your attention?
- What recommendations does she make?
- The writer suggests that with a full tank of gas, you can start the car to stay warm. Why else is it helpful to have a full tank of gas?
- Of all the recommendations, which one is the easiest to follow? Which is the hardest to follow?

- Of all the recommendations, which is the most important?

B Answer the questions.

- Have students find the answers in the text.
- Elicit the answers from the students.

ANSWERS

1 Pack a flashlight and batteries so you can see in the dark.
2 Take a cell phone so you can call for help.

Learn: Writing a How-to Speech

- Guide students in analyzing the model *Preparing Your Car for a Blizzard* to see how it meets the requirements listed in the *Learn* box, e.g. the writer gets the audience's attention by creating the imaginary context of a family driving in a car and suddenly being caught in a blizzard.
- Have students prepare their speeches.

DIFFERENTIATION

Below level:

- On the board, write a simple outline that students can use to plan their writing:
  1 Greeting
  2 Introduction (grab audience's attention)
  3 Steps in the How-To
    a) Step 1
    b) Step 2
    c) Step 3
    d) Step 4
  4 Conclusion

- Students can work in mixed-ability pairs to plan their speech using the outline.

At level:
- Tell partners to use the Speech Tips on the page to help them practice reading aloud their speeches.
- Have each student rate their partner on a scale of 1–3 for each of the four tips (1 for "You should work on this" and 3 for "You did a great job!").
- After they practice with partners, students can present to the class.

Above level:
- Challenge students to memorize their speeches rather than read them aloud. (They may also use notecards to remind them of specific details.)

Write
- Direct students to the Workbook to plan and write their own how-to speech.

Project

C Create a poster that teaches someone how to prepare for an emergency.

CREATIVITY

- Read the directions together.
- Have groups work together to follow the steps and create the poster.
- Read and practice the sample speech bubbles as examples of how students can present their posters.
- Explain that even though the poster will address different emergencies, there should be some unifying visual plan so the poster is attractive and easy to understand.
- Assign one "layout monitor" in each group to elicit ideas and finalize a plan for how the poster will be unified. Here are some ideas:
  1 Each corner may have an illustration of the natural disaster in the center of a web-like diagram, with four off-shooting sentences that give recommendations for preparations.
  2 Design the text to mimic the "shape" of the disaster: Draw a funnel cloud for a tornado, and write the safety tips in the funnel; draw a cross-section of earth with cracks like an earthquake, and write the safety tips along the crack lines; draw huge snow mounds for the blizzard and have the safety tips contained in snowmen; draw a huge tsunami wave with the safety tips surfing along the crest.
  3 In the center of the poster, create a four-piece pie. Glue a photo of a different disaster in each section. Draw a line from each picture to its corner, where the tips are written. On the line, write *How to stay safe in an earthquake (a hurricane / a tornado / a blizzard / a tsunami)*.

Units 15 and 16 Big Question Review

A Watch the video. ▷
- Play the video and when it is finished ask students what they know about nature's power now.
- Have students share ideas with the class.

B Think more about the Big Question. What did you learn?

COMMUNICATION

- Display **Discover Poster 8**. Elicit key vocabulary and ideas from the class.
- Refer to all of the learning points written on the poster and have students explain how they relate to the different pictures.
- Ask *What does this learning point mean*? Elicit answers from individual students.
- Display the **Talk About It! Poster** to help students with sentence frames for discussion of the learning points and for expressing their opinions.

C Complete the Big Question Chart.

COLLABORATIVE LEARNING

- Ask students what they have learned about nature's power while studying this unit.
- Put students into pairs or small groups to say two new things they have learned.
- Have students share their ideas with the class and add their ideas to the chart.
- Have students complete the chart in their Workbook.

Further Practice
Workbook pages 151–153
Online practice • Wrap Up 8
Oxford iTools • Wrap Up 8

Why are biomes important?

In units 17 and 18 you will:

WATCH a video about biomes.

LEARN about the importance of Earth's biomes.

READ about Earth's biomes and a girl who explores one.

WRITE a fictional story.

ACT in a play.

BIG QUESTION 9

Why are biomes important?

A Watch the video.

B Look at the picture and talk about it.
1 What kinds of life do you see?
2 Where do you think this place is?

C Think and answer the questions.
1 How are parts of Earth different from each other?
2 What types of animals and plants live near you?

D Fill out the **Big Question Chart**.

What do you know about biomes? What do you want to know?

166 Big Question 9

167

Reading Strategies
Students will practice:
- Classifying and categorizing
- Asking open-ended questions

Review
Students will review the language and Big Question learning points of Units 17 and 18 through:
- A fictional story
- A project (acting in a play)

Writing
Students will be able to use:
- Complex sentences with *until*
- Complex sentences with *since* and *because*
Students will produce texts that:
- Entertain

Vocabulary
Students will understand and use words about:
- The world around us and animals

Units 17 and 18
Why are biomes important?
Students will understand the Big Question learning points:
- Biomes make our world interesting.
- Many different animals and plants live in each biome.
- Animals and plants get what they need from biomes.
- Biomes add to Earth's beauty.
- Scientists can discover new medicines in biomes.

Word Study
Students will understand, pronounce, and use:
- Words with -*tch*
- Words with the suffixes -*ent* and -*ence*

Grammar
Students will understand and use:
- Present perfect with *for* or *since*
- Present perfect and simple past

Listening Strategies
Students will practice:
- Listening for sequence
- Listening for reasons

Speaking
Students will understand and use expressions to:
- Describe a sequence
- Ask about needs

Units 17 and 18 Big Question   page 166

Summary
Objectives: To activate students' existing knowledge of the topic and identify what they would like to learn about the topic.

Materials: Big Question DVD, Discover Poster 9, Big Question Chart

Introducing the topic

- Read out the Big Question. Tell students that the picture they are looking at is a picture of a biome, and that they will learn about biomes in these two units.
- Ask *Why are biomes important? Why are the places and things you see in the picture important?*
- Write students' ideas on the board and discuss.

A Watch the video. ▷

- Play the video and when it is finished ask students to answer the following questions in pairs:
  What do you see in the video?
  What is happening?
  Do you like it?
- Have individual students share their answers with the class.

DIFFERENTIATION

Below level:
- Pause the video periodically. Point and ask *What's this? What's it doing? Where are they?*
- Ask students to answer using complete sentences.

At level:
- After watching, have students write down five things that they saw in the video.
- Elicit the phrases from the class and write them on the board.

Above level:
- After watching, have students write down three sentences about what they saw in the video.
- Tell students to choose one sentence.
- Tell them to stand up and mingle and find someone else with the same sentence (focus on the meaning of the sentence rather than using exactly the same words).
- Have students say their sentence to the class.

B Look at the picture and talk about it.

- Students look at the big picture and talk about it. Ask *What do you see?*

Ask additional questions:
- Would you like to visit this place? Why or why not?
- What would you do in this place?
- Do you think people live here? Why or why not?
- Where on Earth do you think this place is?
- Why do you think that?

C Think and answer the questions.

- Ask *How are parts of Earth different from each other?*
- Invite students to consider weather and climate, geographical features, native plants and animals, and the ways humans and animals have adapted to the environment.
- Ask *What types of animals and plants live near you?* Help students distinguish between plants and animals that are wild and native versus ones that are domesticated or cultivated.

CRITICAL THINKING

- If you live in an urban area where most native plants and animals have been displaced by development, find out which plants and animals would be native to your region, then invite students to close their eyes while you describe an imaginary scene from long, long ago.

COLLABORATIVE LEARNING

- Display **Discover Poster 9** and discuss.
- Put students into small groups of three or four. Have each group choose a picture that they find interesting.
- Have each group say five things they can see in the picture.

D Fill out the Big Question Chart.

- Display the **Big Question Chart**.
- Ask the class *What do you know about biomes?*
- Ask students to write what they know and what they want to know in their Workbooks.
- Write a collection of ideas on the **Big Question Chart**.

Discover Poster 9

1 A Japanese macaque in Yamanouchi, Japan; 2 An elephant, a giraffe, a zebra, and plants together in the African savannah; 3 A koala bear eating eucalyptus in Australia; 4 Angel Falls, the highest waterfall in the world, in Venezuela; 5 A scientist gathering research in a forest in Alaska.

Further Practice
Workbook page 154
Online practice · Big Question 9
Oxford iTools · Big Question 9

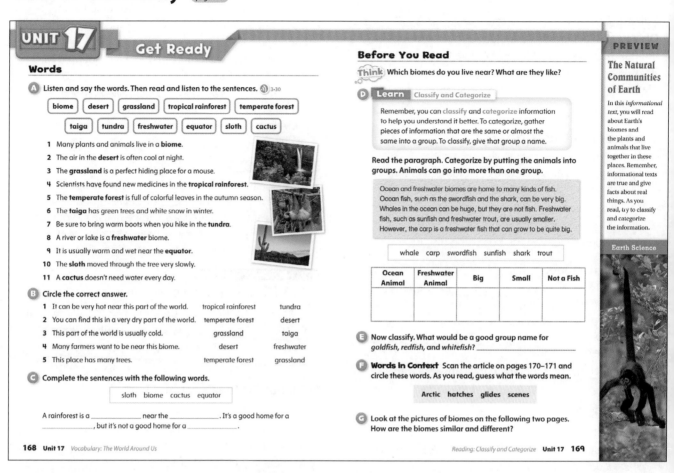

Summary

Objectives: To understand words about biomes; to apply own experience and a reading strategy to help comprehension of a text.

Vocabulary: *biome, desert, grassland, tropical rainforest, temperate forest, taiga, tundra, freshwater, equator, sloth, cactus, Arctic, hatches, glides, scenes*

Reading strategy: Classifying and categorizing

Materials: Audio CD

Words

A Listen and say the words. Then read and listen to the sentences. 🔊 3·30

- Play the audio. Ask students to point to the words as they hear them.
- Play the audio a second time and have students repeat the words when they hear them.
- Say the words out of order and have students race to point to them on the page.
- Play the sentences while students read along.

DIFFERNTIATION

Below level:

- Have students look up the target vocabulary in their Student Book and read the definitions.
- Have students check the definitions against the sentences in A to help them understand the meaning of the words.

At level:

- Have students write the target vocabulary in their notebooks.
- Have students write three more words that they associate with the target vocabulary as well. This will help them to remember and personalize the meaning of the words.
- Elicit ideas for associated words from the class and make a word web on the board.

Above level:

- Tell students to try to write sentences using more than one vocabulary word, e.g. *We saw a cactus in the hot and dry desert biome.*
- Have them search previous units for words that can be used in sentences with the Unit 17 words, e.g. *I wonder if other planets in the universe have different biomes. The surface of the tundra is covered in a layer of ice. Sugar cane grows in warm areas near the equator. The artist painted the brilliant sunset in his grassland landscape. Volunteers cleaned up the freshwater pond in the city park. Scientists used a microscope to study the cactus skin. The headline said "Sloth Found in City Park. Police Don't Know How it Got There!"*

B Circle the correct answer.

- Have students complete the exercise and then compare answers with a partner.
- Check the answers with the class.

ANSWERS

1 tropical rainforest 2 desert 3 taiga 4 freshwater
5 temperate forest

Ask the following questions to guide and check comprehension:

- Find the three compound words in the list. How do the two words in each compound word help you understand the meaning?
- What is the difference between a tropical rainforest and a temperate forest?
- Why do you need warm boots in the tundra?
- Which word names a plant and which names an animal?

C Complete the sentences with the following words.

- Have students work independently, then check answers with a partner.
- Elicit answers from the class.

ANSWERS

biome, equator, sloth, cactus

Before You Read

Think

- Have students discuss the questions in small groups.
- Elicit ideas from the class.

D Learn: Classify and Categorize

- Read the *Learn* box together.
- Point out the two actions: *categorizing* is putting similar things together, and *classifying* is giving those things a name.

Read the paragraph. Categorize by putting the animals into groups. Animals can go into more than one group.

- Have a volunteer read the paragraph aloud.
- Copy the graphic organizer on the board. As you reread the paragraph, have a volunteer write each fish in the proper category or categories.

ANSWERS

Ocean Animal: swordfish, shark, whale
Freshwater Animal: sunfish, trout, carp
Big: swordfish, shark, whale, carp
Small: sunfish, trout
Not a Fish: whale

E Now classify. What would be a good group name for *goldfish*, *redfish*, and *whitefish*?

POSSIBLE ANSWER

Fish named for how they look

- Have partners categorize the vocabulary words on page 168. Encourage them to come up with several different categories.
- Tell them that each word can go into more than one group, some groups may only have one word, and some words may not belong to a group. The idea is for students to think about similarities among words.
- To practice classifying, have Partner A write down a group of words from page 168 or from previous units' vocabulary lists. Partner B must think of a good name for the group of words, e.g. Partner A writes *shrimp, exotic fruits, tuna, wheat, cinnamon, butter*. Partner B writes *Food*.

F Words in Context: Scan the article on pages 170–171 and circle these words. As you read, guess what the words mean.

- Read each word and have students follow your pronunciation.
- Have students guess at the meaning of each word using prior knowledge and the theme of the unit.

G Look at the pictures of biomes on the following two pages. How are biomes similar and different?

- Have students jot down their ideas in Venn diagrams.
- Put students in pairs and have them share their ideas.
- Have students add to the Venn diagram as they read the article.

Reading Preview

- Read the title of the unit's reading text.
- Have students silently read the content of the preview bar.
- Ask *What type of text is it?* Ask *What does this type of text do?*

| Further Practice
Workbook pages 154–155
Online practice Unit 17 • Get Ready
Oxford iTools Unit 17 • Get Ready

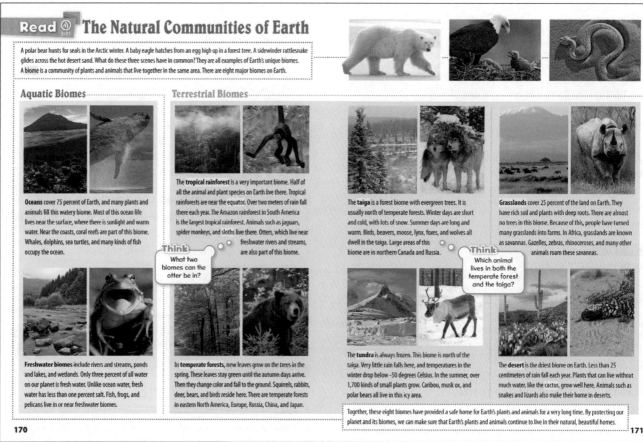

The Natural Communities of Earth

A polar bear hunts for seals in the Arctic winter. A baby eagle hatches from an egg high up in a forest tree. A sidewinder rattlesnake glides across the hot desert sand. What do these three scenes have in common? They are all examples of Earth's unique biomes. A biome is a community of plants and animals that live together in the same area. There are eight major biomes on Earth.

Aquatic Biomes

Oceans cover 75 percent of Earth, and many plants and animals fill this watery biome. Most of this ocean life lives near the surface, where there is sunlight and warm water. Near the coasts, coral reefs are part of this biome. Whales, dolphins, sea turtles, and many kinds of fish occupy the ocean.

Freshwater biomes include rivers and streams, ponds and lakes, and wetlands. Only three percent of all water on our planet is fresh water. Unlike ocean water, fresh water has less than one percent salt. Fish, frogs, and pelicans live in or near freshwater biomes.

Terrestrial Biomes

The **tropical rainforest** is a very important biome. Half of all the animal and plant species on Earth live there. Tropical rainforests are near the equator. Over two meters of rain fall there each year. The Amazon rainforest in South America is the largest tropical rainforest. Animals such as jaguars, spider monkeys, and sloths live there. Otters, which live near freshwater rivers and streams, are also part of this biome.

Think What two biomes can the otter be in?

In **temperate forests**, new leaves grow on the trees in the spring. These leaves stay green until the autumn days arrive. Then they change color and fall to the ground. Squirrels, rabbits, deer, bears, and birds reside here. There are temperate forests in eastern North America, Europe, Russia, China, and Japan.

The **taiga** is a forest biome with evergreen trees. It is usually north of temperate forests. Winter days are short and cold, with lots of snow. Summer days are long and warm. Birds, beavers, moose, lynx, foxes, and wolves all dwell in the taiga. Large areas of this biome are in northern Canada and Russia.

Think Which animal lives in both the temperate forest and the taiga?

The **tundra** is always frozen. This biome is north of the taiga. Very little rain falls here, and temperatures in the winter drop below -50 degrees Celsius. In the summer, over 1,700 kinds of small plants grow. Caribou, musk ox, and polar bears all live in this icy area.

Grasslands cover 25 percent of the land on Earth. They have rich soil and plants with deep roots. There are almost no trees in this biome. Because of this, people have turned many grasslands into farms. In Africa, grasslands are known as savannas. Gazelles, zebras, rhinoceroses, and many other animals roam these savannas.

The **desert** is the driest biome on Earth. Less than 25 centimeters of rain fall each year. Plants that can live without much water, like the cactus, grow well here. Animals such as snakes and lizards also make their home in deserts.

Together, these eight biomes have provided a safe home for Earth's plants and animals for a very long time. By protecting our planet and its biomes, we can make sure that Earth's plants and animals continue to live in their natural, beautiful homes.

170   171

Summary

Objectives: To read, understand, and discuss a nonfiction text; to apply a reading strategy to improve comprehension.

School subject: Earth Science

Text type: Informational text (nonfiction)

Reading strategy: Classifying and categorizing

Big Question learning points: *Biomes make our world interesting. Many different animals and plants live in each biome. Animals and plants get what they need from biomes. Biomes add to Earth's beauty.*

Materials: Talk About It! Poster, Audio CD

Before Reading

- Read the title together. Ask *What other communities have you studied this year? The title of this reading is "Natural Communities." Are cities natural communities?*

During Reading   ⊚ 3·31

- Play the audio while students read along.
- Pause at the *Think* boxes for students to answer the questions.

DIFFERENTIATION

Below level:

- Have students read in mixed-ability pairs.
- Have them ask and answer questions as they read and mark unfamiliar words or phrases.

- Ask students to tell the class the unfamiliar words or phrases and see if other students can help define them. If not, write them on the board and teach the meanings.

At level:

- Have students read with partners, alternating sections.
- As they finish each section, have them jot down one interesting fact about the biome.
- After everyone finishes reading the article, have students read aloud their facts without naming the biome, e.g. *This biome covers 75% of Earth*. Ask the class to name the biome.

Above level:

- Have students create simple webs to categorize the information in each section. Suggest categories, e.g. *What plants and animals live there? What does it look like? Where is it?*
- After they complete their webs, have them come up with a few questions about each biome, e.g. *What animals live in ocean biomes?*
- Invite students to ask their questions to the class.

CRITICAL THINKING

Discussion questions:

- *Is there anywhere that salt water and fresh water can mix?*
- *Are there any biomes that might overlap or coexist?*
- *Do snakes and lizards need a lot of water to survive?*
- *What do you think would happen to the plants and animals in a biome if something in that biome was altered?, e.g. if it started raining in the desert, if the salt content in a*

*lake increased, if it became warm in the tundra or cold in
the rainforest?*

- *Which biome do you think is easiest for a human to live in
  and why?*
- *Which biome do you think is most difficult for a human to
  live in and why? Think about the plants and animals that live
  there. Why can they survive there?*

After Reading

- Have students share their responses to the *Think* boxes in
  the article.

COLLABORATIVE LEARNING

- Display the **Talk About It! Poster** to help students
  with sentence frames for discussion and expressing
  personal opinions.
- Put students into groups to discuss why each biome is
  important, and what they find interesting about it.
- Ask them to create an imaginary country or society.
- Have them decide what type of biomes they live in and
  how they live there.
- Ask each group to tell the class about their society
  and biome.

CULTURE NOTE

Different societies have developed in each biome around
the world. One example is the Bedouin, a traditional
desert-dwelling group in the Middle East. Their society
is organized around family and tribe. Traditionally, the
Bedouins were nomadic, meaning they moved from place
to place rather than setting up permanent villages. They
adopted this lifestyle in response to the lack of water and
good, permanent farming land in the desert. Recently
many Bedouins have started living in cities and taking on
more modern jobs and lifestyles.

Another example of a culture that developed in response
to its biome is the Inuit of the Arctic tundra regions
of North America, Greenland, and Russia. They are
traditionally hunters and fishers. There isn't any good
farming land in the tundra, but the Inuit were able to
gather some native plants for food, as well. They used dog
sleds and boats for transportation in this difficult terrain,
and built temporary shelters made of snow (igloos) in
the winter.

Further Practice
Workbook page 156
Online practice Unit 17 · Read
Oxford **iTools** Unit 17 · Read

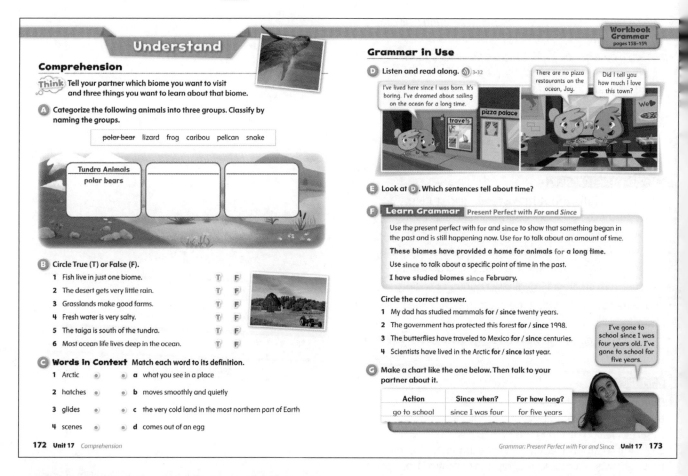

Summary

Objectives: To demonstrate understanding of a nonfiction text; to understand the meaning and form of the grammar structure.

Reading: Comprehension

Grammar input: Present perfect with *for* and *since*

Grammar practice: Workbook exercises

Grammar production: Discussing past actions with the present perfect and *for* and *since*

Materials: Audio CD

Comprehension

Think

• Have students discuss with partners. Ask them to consider where and how they might find answers to their questions. (e.g. if you wanted to learn how the Inuit build igloos, you might interview an elderly Inuit.)

• Have groups work together to write a list of things to pack when visiting the biomes they named in the *Think* discussion.

• Encourage them to consider possible emergencies they might encounter, and to include items that would help in those emergencies. Make sure they keep in mind the weather, food, water, and shelter sources, as well as instruments needed to study the things they want to learn more about.

A Categorize the following animals into three groups. Classify by naming the groups.

• Have students go back to the reading to complete the exercise independently.

• Then check answers with the class.

Tundra Animals: polar bear, caribou
Desert Animals: lizard, snake
Freshwater Animals: pelican, frog

B Circle True (T) or False (F)

• Tell students to try to answer from memory first.

• Then have partners return to the article to confirm their answers together.

• Check the answers with the class.

1 F 2 T 3 T 4 F 5 T 6 F

Below level:

• Help students find the sentences in the article that prove each answer:
Oceans: Whales, dolphins, sea turtles, and many kinds of fish occupy the ocean.
Freshwater biomes: Fish, frogs, and pelicans live in or near freshwater biomes.
Tundra: Very little rain falls here, and temperatures in the winter drop below -50 degrees Celsius.
Desert: Less than 25 centimeters of rainfall each year.
Grasslands: Because of this, people have turned many

grasslands into farms.
Freshwater biomes: Unlike ocean water, freshwater has less
than one percent salt.
Tundra: This biome is north of the taiga.
Oceans: Most of this ocean life lives near the surface, where
there is sunlight and warm water.

At level:

- Have students rewrite each false sentence from B to make it true, e.g. *Fish live in ocean and freshwater biomes. Freshwater has less salt than ocean water.*

Above level:

- Have students write their own True / False sentences about the article.
- Encourage them to try specific techniques, such as using antonyms (north / south, more / less, a little / a lot, only one / many, hot / cold) and mixed-referencing (using a fact from one biome in a statement about a different biome).
- Students can share their sentences with partners, or you can ask the whole class to choose true or false.

CRITICAL THINKING

- The article mentions that *By protecting our planet and its biomes, we can make sure that Earth's plants and animals continue to live in their natural, beautiful homes.*

Discuss the following:

- Why else should we protect the planet and its biomes? Many industrialized and wealthy nations have altered or damaged their natural biomes (chopped down their forests, polluted their rivers).
- Some scientists consider Earth like a system (think about the circulatory system or the immune system), where biomes work together to keep the entire planet healthy.

C Words in Context: Match each word to its definition.

- Have students go back and find the words in the reading.
- Tell them to use the context clues to guess at the meaning of each word.
- Then complete the exercise together.
- Check the answers with the class.

ANSWERS
1 c   2 d   3 b   4 a

Grammar in Use

D Listen and read along. 3·32

- Listen to the audio once. Play it again and have students echo to focus on pronunciation and fluency.

Ask questions to check comprehension:

- Has he ever lived anywhere else?
- Why does he change his mind about sailing on the ocean?
- What can you infer about him?

E Look at D. Which sentences tell about time?

- Point out that the first sentence gives a specific starting point (*the day he was born*) and the other sentence (*I've dreamed … for a long time*) tells how long.

ANSWER
I've lived here since I was born. I've dreamed about sailing on the ocean for a long time.

F Learn Grammar: Present Perfect with *For* and *Since*

- Read the *Learn Grammar* box together.
- Explain that in the example with *for a long time*, the speaker does not name the specific starting point. If you know the starting point and want to use *for*, you use the amount of time, not the starting point: *I've studied biomes for three months.*
- Reinforce that we use *for* when we name the amount of time, and we use *since* when we name the starting point.

Circle the correct answer.

- Read the first sentence together. Read it first using *for* and then using *since*. Ask which one makes sense.
- Repeat for the other items.
- Check the answers with the class.

ANSWERS
1 for   2 since   3 for   4 since

G Make a chart like the one below. Then talk to your partner about it.

- Have students fill in their charts individually.

COLLABORATIVE LEARNING

- Put students into pairs to talk about the chart.
- Have partners brainstorm ideas to include on the chart, such as how long they've studied English or played an instrument, how long they've known a certain person, or how long they've lived in their house.
- Have students share some of their ideas with the class.

| **Further Practice**
| **Workbook pages 157–159**
| **Online practice Unit 17 · Understand**
| Oxford **iTools** Unit 17 · **Understand**

Unit 17 · Understand   199

Unit 17 Communicate page 174

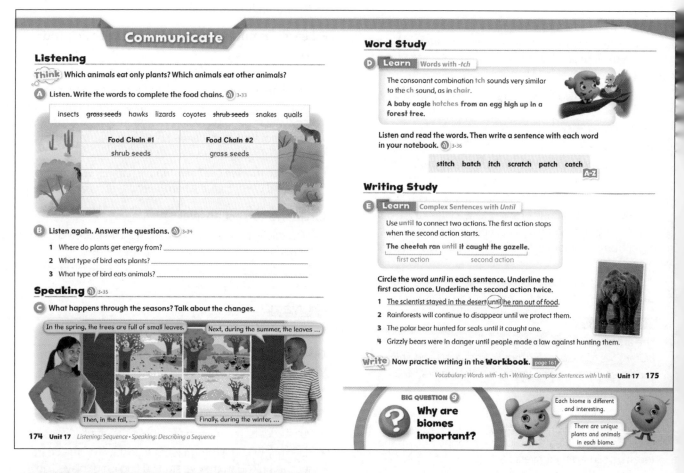

Communicate

Listening

Think Which animals eat only plants? Which animals eat other animals?

A Listen. Write the words to complete the food chains. 3-33

insects ~~grass seeds~~ hawks lizards coyotes ~~shrub seeds~~ snakes quails

Food Chain #1	Food Chain #2
shrub seeds	grass seeds

B Listen again. Answer the questions. 3-34

1 Where do plants get energy from? _____
2 What type of bird eats plants? _____
3 What type of bird eats animals? _____

Speaking 3-35

C What happens through the seasons? Talk about the changes.

In the spring, the trees are full of small leaves.

Next, during the summer, the leaves …

Then, in the fall, …

Finally, during the winter, …

174 Unit 17 Listening: Sequence • Speaking: Describing a Sequence

Word Study

D Learn Words with -tch

The consonant combination tch sounds very similar to the ch sound, as in chair.

A baby eagle hatches from an egg high up in a forest tree.

Listen and read the words. Then write a sentence with each word in your notebook. 3-36

stitch batch itch scratch patch catch

A-Z

Writing Study

E Learn Complex Sentences with Until

Use until to connect two actions. The first action stops when the second action starts.

The cheetah ran until it caught the gazelle.
first action   second action

Circle the word until in each sentence. Underline the first action once. Underline the second action twice.

1 The scientist stayed in the desert until he ran out of food.
2 Rainforests will continue to disappear until we protect them.
3 The polar bear hunted for seals until it caught one.
4 Grizzly bears were in danger until people made a law against hunting them.

Write Now practice writing in the **Workbook.** page 161

Vocabulary: Words with -tch • Writing: Complex Sentences with Until **Unit 17 175**

BIG QUESTION 9

? Why are biomes important?

Each biome is different and interesting.

There are unique plants and animals in each biome.

Summary

Objectives: To learn and practice listening, speaking, and writing strategies to facilitate effective communication.

Vocabulary: *stitch, batch, itch, scratch, patch, catch*

Listening strategy: Listening for sequence

Speaking: Describing a sequence

Word Study: Words with *-tch*

Writing Study: Complex sentences with *until*

Big Question learning points: *Many different animals and plants live in each biome. Animals and plants get what they need from biomes.*

Materials: Discover Poster 9, Audio CD, Big Question Chart

Listening

Think

- Encourage students to think of animals they know that aren't mentioned in this unit, including pets and human beings.

A Listen. Write the words to complete the food chains. 3-33

- Play the audio once and have students listen.
- Play the audio again so they can complete the exercise.
- Check the answers with the class.

ANSWERS

Food chain #1: shrub seeds, quails, coyotes
Food chain #2: grass seeds, insects, lizards, snakes, hawks

DIFFERENTIATION

Below level:

- Help students navigate the two sections by writing the students' names on the board, e.g. *Food chain #1: Jake and Mandy. Food chain #2: Carlos and Fatima.*
- Play the audio and pause after the following lines so students have time to process what they hear and write down the animals in the chart:
  Desert quails are birds that eat shrub seeds.
  The coyote is the final animal on this food chain.
  Insects eat these seeds.
  Lizards, of course.
  Did you know that snakes eat lizards?
  The hawk is the final animal on this food chain.

At level:

- After students complete the chart in A, have them use the information to summarize the food chain in their own words.
- Encourage them to use sequence words in their summaries, e.g. *First the shrub plant gets energy from the*

sun. It produces seeds. Then the desert quail eats the seeds. Finally, the coyote eats the desert quail.

Above level:

- Have students try to complete the exercise after listening to the audio only once.
- Play the audio again so they can check their work.
- Have them write sequence questions about the selections, e.g. *What's the first thing in the food chain? What comes after the desert quail in the food chain? What is the last step in the food chain?*

B Listen again. Answer the questions. 🔊 3·34

- Have students answer the questions as they listen.

ANSWERS

1 the sun   2 desert quail   3 hawk

CRITICAL THINKING

- Explain that a food chain is yet another example of a system where things are interrelated. Ask *What would happen if a piece of the chain stopped working?*, e.g. what if suddenly there were no more coyotes?
- Ask a few similar questions to help students understand how the food chain can be interrupted and how that can have bigger implications for biomes.

Speaking 🔊 3·35

C What happens through the seasons? Talk about the changes.

COMMUNICATION

- Play the dialogue once while students follow in their books.
- Then play one line of the dialogue at a time with students echoing as they hear each line.
- Model the dialogue with a confident student in front of the class.
- Put students into pairs and tell them to practice the dialogue, taking turns speaking the different roles.
- Ask *Which biome do you think is shown here?*

COLLABORATIVE LEARNING

- Have students look at the pictures and identify other changes that happen with the seasons, e.g. students may focus on the birds (and their eggs) and the weather. Have them follow the model to talk about those changes as well.
- Then encourage them to personalize the exercise by discussing seasonal changes in their own lives, e.g. *First, in the spring, I play soccer after school. Then, in the summer, I go to the beach to visit my grandparents. Next, in the fall, I start school. Finally, during the winter, I go ice-skating on our pond.*

Word Study

D Learn: Words with *-tch*

- Have a confident student read the *Learn* box to the class.

Listen and read the words. Then write a sentence with each word in your notebook. 🔊 3·36

- Point out that the *-tch* blend occurs at the end of each word. Explain that no word begins with *-tch*, and the only time it appears in the middle of a word is when it appears at the end of a syllable or base word, as in *scratching* or *patched*.

Writing Study

E Learn: Complex Sentences with *Until*

- Read the *Learn* box together.
- Copy the example sentence on the board. Add the sentence *And then it stopped running.* Circle the word *until*. Say *As soon as the cheetah caught the gazelle, it stopped running.*

Circle the word *until* in each sentence. Underline the first action once. Underline the second action twice.

- Have students complete the exercise on their own, then check their work with a partner.

ANSWERS

1 The scientist stayed in the desert until he ran out of food.
2 Rainforests will continue to disappear until we protect them.
3 The polar bear hunted for seals until it caught one.
4 Grizzly bears were in danger until people made a law against hunting them.

Write

- Direct students to the Workbook for further practice.

Big Question 9 Review

Why are biomes important?

- Display **Discover Poster 9**. Elicit words and phrases about the pictures.
- Refer to the learning points covered in Unit 17 which are written on the poster and have students explain how they relate to the different pictures.
- Return to the **Big Question Chart**. Ask students what they have learned about biomes that they can add to the chart.

Further Practice
Workbook pages 160–161
Online practice Unit 17 · Communicate
Oxford **iTools** Unit 17 · Communicate

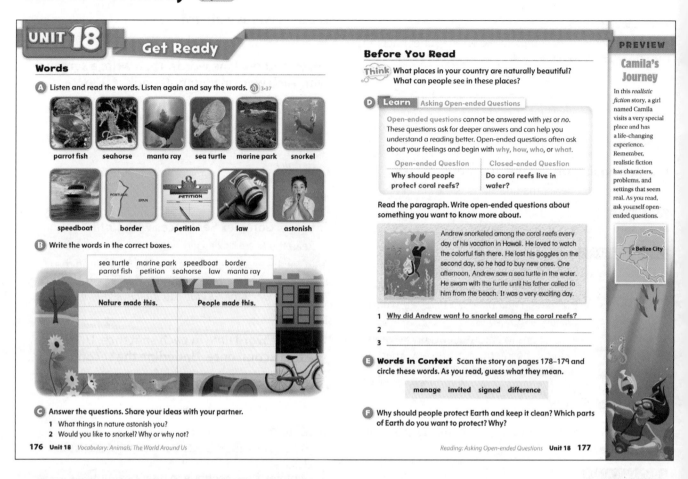

176 Unit 18 Vocabulary: Animals, The World Around Us

Reading: Asking Open-ended Questions **Unit 18 177**

Summary

Objectives: To understand words about the biomes; to apply own experience and reading strategy to help comprehension of a text.

Vocabulary: *parrot fish, seahorse, manta ray, sea turtle, marine park, snorkel, speedboat, border, petition, law, astonish, manage, invited, signed, difference*

Reading strategy: Asking open-ended questions

Materials: Audio CD

Words

A Listen and read the words. Listen again and say the words. ⊚ 3·37

- Play the audio. Ask students to point to the words as they hear them.
- Play the audio a second time and have students repeat the words when they hear them.
- Say *Find some compound words. How do the two words in each one help you to understand the meaning of the word?*
- Some examples: *(Parrot fish: This fish is colorful like a parrot. Seahorse: This animal looks like a horse that lives in the sea. Sea turtle: This is a turtle that lives in the sea. Marine park: Marine means water, so this is a park that has something to do with the water. Speedboat: This is a boat that goes very fast.)*

B Write the words in the correct boxes.

- Look at the exercise together to make sure students understand what to do.
- Have partners work together to sort the words.
- Check answers with the class.

ANSWERS

Nature made this: parrot fish, seahorse, manta ray, sea turtle
People made this: marine park, speedboat, border, petition, law

CRITICAL THINKING

Discussion questions:

- *Parrot fish eat algae that grows on coral reefs. Eels and sharks eat parrot fish. What would happen to the food chain if something harmed the algae?*
- *Sea turtles live in ocean biomes around the world. They need to breathe air though, so sometimes they swim to the surface to breathe. What do you think happens when a sea turtle gets tangled in a fishing net?*
- *The border shown in this picture (on Student Book page 176) is a human-made border between two countries (Portugal and Spain). Sometimes humans use existing geographical features to create borders, e.g. two neighboring countries may use a river as a border. What problems might arise from two countries sharing a border river? What benefits might arise from two countries sharing a border river?*

C Answer the questions Share your ideas with your partner.

- Have students discuss the questions in small groups.

Before You Read

Think

- Have students name some natural features of your area that are beautiful.
- Encourage them to focus on naturally occurring sites, such as the ocean or mountains.

D Learn: Asking Open-ended Questions

- Read the *Learn* box together.
- Give some other examples of open-ended questions (*Why is it fun to ride in a speedboat? Who do you know who would enjoy snorkeling, and why?*) and closed-ended questions (*Is a speedboat fast? Do you have to get wet when you snorkel?*)

Read the paragraph. Write open-ended questions about something you want to know more about.

COMMUNICATION

- Have a confident student read the paragraph aloud while everyone reads along.
- Read the sample question together. Ask *Why is this an open-ended question?* (The answer isn't *yes* or *no*. You have to understand Andrew's personality and know about coral reefs to answer. Several people might answer differently, and they could all be right.)
- Have students write two more questions. Ask them to read their questions aloud, and discuss possible answers with the class.

DIFFERENTIATION

Below level:

- Ask *What can you tell me about Andrew?* (He snorkeled every day of his vacation. He loved to watch the colorful fish. He bought new goggles. He swam with the sea turtle all afternoon.) Ask *What can you tell me about snorkeling?* (You wear goggles to see underwater. You can see lots of fish and other underwater plants and animals. You can snorkel among the coral reefs.)
- Say *Look at the example. There are many different ways to answer this question, and there are lots of possible answers. Who can think of one answer?* Say *Can you think of another question with many possible answers? Try starting with* Why. (Then have them start with *How, Who,* and *What*).
- Discuss their ideas and why they are open-ended or not. Allow students to choose the best questions from the entire groups' ideas.

At level:

- First have partners ask and answer closed-ended questions about the paragraph.
- They can contrast those questions with open-ended questions that require them to think more deeply and perhaps give their opinions.
- Explain that the answer to an open-ended question may not be in the actual paragraph; you may need to make an inference or share your opinion, e.g. *What would you like to see if you snorkeled with Andrew? How did Andrew feel when he lost his goggles? Why is snorkeling popular in Hawaii?*

Above level:

- When they finish D, challenge students to write some open-ended questions about other reading texts in the Student Book.
- Have them share these with partners to check that they are open-ended and not closed-ended. Then have them ask the class.

COLLABORATIVE LEARNING

- Have students write four possible questions for D in their notebook (*Why? What? How? Who?*).
- Put them into small groups to share their questions. After a student reads a question, the group members take turns answering.
- After a student reads all four questions, he / she chooses the two questions that elicited the most varied and interesting answers. Then he / she records those two questions in the Student Book.

E Words in Context: Scan the story on pages 178–179 and circle these words. As you read, guess what they mean.

- Have students scan the story and circle the words.

F Why should people protect Earth and keep it clean? What parts of Earth do you want to protect? Why?

- Encourage students to think about what they learned about biomes as they answer.

Reading Preview

- Read the title of the unit's reading text.
- Have students silently read the content of the preview bar.
- Ask *What type of text is it?* Ask *What does this type of text do?*

Further Practice
Workbook pages 162–163
Online practice Unit 18 · Get Ready
Oxford iTools Unit 18 · Get Ready

Summary

Objectives: To read, understand and discuss a fictional text; to apply a reading strategy to improve comprehension.

School subject: Earth Science

Text type: Realistic fiction

Reading strategy: Asking open-ended questions

Big Question learning points: *Biomes make our world interesting. Many different animals and plants live in each biome. Biomes add to Earth's beauty. Scientists can discover new medicines in biomes.*

Materials: Talk About It! Poster, Audio CD

Before Reading

- Ask students to make predictions about the story. Tell them to use the words from the vocabulary list on page 176 and the illustrations in the story.
- Revisit their predictions after you finish reading.

During Reading ⊚ 3·38

- Play the audio. Students listen as they read along.
- Stop at each *Think* box and tell students to start thinking about some open-ended questions.
- Have students read the story again and jot down their open-ended questions.

Below level:

- Have students read in mixed-ability pairs.
- Have the more confident student help the other with pronunciation and comprehension.
- Tell students to pause after every few sentences to discuss what they have read so far.
- Ask questions periodically to check comprehension, such as *What does Camila's father do for a living?*

At level:

- Have students read in small groups.
- Tell groups to pause after each paragraph to discuss what's happened so far, and what they've learned about the characters.
- Tell them to try to work through any problems with comprehension together first, before they ask you for help.

Above level:

- Have students read the story on their own, jotting down any phrases or sentences they do not understand.
- Put students with partners to work through anything they jotted down. If they need additional help with comprehension, have them ask you specific questions for clarification.
- Challenge students to create a list of questions (closed- and open-ended) that address some of the reading strategies they have studied this year, e.g.
  Visualize changes: *How did the scene change when the motorboat arrived?*

Author's purpose: *What are the purposes of this story? What do you think the author's main purpose is?*
Understanding characters: *Why does Camila want to go with her father to the park?*

CRITICAL THINKING

Discussion questions:

- *Camila's father says that the coral reefs are dying, in part, from overfishing. Why does overfishing hurt coral reefs?*
- *Has Camila gone snorkeling before this trip?*
- *Why doesn't Camila's father stop the speedboat? What does this tell you about rules in the park's border?*
- *How do the coral reefs help humankind?*
- *What did you learn about Camila? What kind of person is she?*
- *Do you think Camila will continue to make a difference in the world? Why or why not?*

COLLABORATIVE LEARNING

- Have small groups read the story together, taking turns around a circle.
- Assign a secretary in each group to take notes. Tell the groups to pause at each *Think* box and discuss possible open-ended questions.
- Tell students to try to answer one another's questions. Which ones elicit the most varied responses? Which were the most difficult to answer?
- Have the students share their questions and answers to the *Think* boxes with the class.

After Reading

- Return to the predictions students made during the Before Reading. Check and revise their predictions based on what happened in the story.

COLLABORATIVE LEARNING

- Display the **Talk About It! Poster** to help students with sentence frames for discussion and expressing personal opinions.
- Put students into pairs to discuss the events in the selection.
- Have students say one thing about every section in the reading.

CULTURE NOTE

Corals are invertebrate (no spine) marine animals. There are many different kinds of corals. Some corals secrete a hard substance (calcium carbonate) which forms hard frames in the reef.

A coral reef is actually a complex community of marine plants and animals. Some scientists call coral reefs the rainforests of the sea because they support a large variety of plants and animals, have different layers, and contain hundreds of species living in symbiotic (cooperative) relationships.

Coral reefs face many natural threats, such as damage from hurricanes or from natural predators. Coral reefs are generally able to recover from damage caused by these natural threats. However, as they are damaged more and more by human activities, they are weaker and less able to recover.

Coral reefs face many threats from human activity. Some threats are very complicated and will take international cooperation to solve, e.g. the fragile ecosystems cannot withstand even small changes in ocean temperature. As temperatures rise on Earth and in its oceans, reefs are damaged.

Other threats are relatively simple to protect against, e.g. ships that drop anchor on reefs damage them, so rules that prohibit dropping anchor in parks and other reef areas can help protect the reefs.

Further Practice
Workbook page 164
Online practice Unit 18 · Read
Oxford iTools Unit 18 · Read

Understand

Comprehension

Think Would you do the same thing as Camila? Why or why not? Tell your partner your answer and reasons.

A Match each open-ended question to two possible answers.

1 How did Camila feel about the coral reef when she first saw it?
2 How did Camila feel about the boat and the people on it?
3 Why did Camila start a petition to help the planet's coral reefs?

- a She felt it was beautiful and exciting.
- b She wanted to protect them.
- c She wanted to ask for people's help.
- d She was very angry and upset.
- e She was astonished by its variety of life.
- f She didn't like what the people did.

B How did Camila help the world's coral reefs?

_____
_____

C **Words in Context** Circle the best ending to each sentence.

1 Camila's father helped to <u>manage</u> the seven marine parks,
   a so he told others what to do to keep the parks clean and safe.
   b so he went fishing in the parks every weekend.
2 When Camila's father <u>invited</u> her to go with him to the marine park,
   a he told her that she had to go with him.
   b he asked her if she wanted to go with him.
3 When 20,000 people <u>signed</u> Camila's petition,
   a they made a sign to put up in their school.
   b they put their names on the petition to show that they agreed.
4 When Camila's father said that Camila made a <u>difference</u>, it meant that
   a she changed something and made it better.
   b she could see how each coral reef was different.

180 Unit 18 *Comprehension*

Grammar in Use

Workbook Grammar pages 166–167

D Listen and sing along. **Speedboat, Speedboat** 3·39

Speedboat, speedboat,
You raced around the reef today.
You scared the parrot fish at play!
We've written a petition – stay away!

Speedboat, speedboat,
You raced across the reef today.
You chased around a manta ray!
We've signed a new law – stay away!

E Read the sentences. Which one tells when the action happened?
a You raced across the reef today.   b We've written a petition.

F **Learn Grammar** Present Perfect and Simple Past

Use the **present perfect** for past experiences, past actions that continue to the present, or actions that happened at an unspecific time.
Camila **has created** a petition. (We don't know when she did it.)
Use the **simple past** for completed actions that happened at a specific time.
When she got home, Camila **created** a petition. (We know when she did it.)

Circle the correct answer.

1 I **read / have read** this article about biomes.
2 They **snorkeled / have snorkeled** this morning.
3 He **went / has gone** to the Arctic last year.
4 The explorer **saw / has seen** a manta ray before.

I have run in a race. I ran in a race last summer.

G Make a chart like below. Talk about it with your partner.

Action I have done	When I did it
run in a race	last summer

Grammar: Present Perfect and Simple Past **Unit 18** **181**

Summary

Objectives: To demonstrate understanding of a fictional text; to understand the meaning and form of the grammar structure.

Reading: Comprehension

Grammar input: Present perfect and simple past

Grammar practice: Workbook exercises

Grammar production: Using the present perfect and simple past to talk about past actions

Materials: Audio CD

Comprehension

Think

- Tell students to write their answers to each question separately, and then compare answers with their partner.

A Match each open-ended question to two possible answers.

- Encourage students to look back at the reading to confirm their answers.
- Ask if they can think of any other possible answers.
- Check the answers with the class.

ANSWERS

1 a, e   2 d, f   3 b, c

DIFFERENTIATION

Below level:

- Review the story together to complete A.
- Have students scan the story to find the sentences that support each answer:
  1 *The beauty and variety of the underwater world astonished Camila. It was the most exciting experience of her life.*
  2 *She was angry and upset. "They'll scare the fish!" shouted Camila.*
  3 *"I'm going to do something for our planet's coral reefs," she said. "We need to help them." Back in Belize City, Camila spoke to her class about coral reefs. When she got home, Camila created a petition on the Internet.*

At level:

- Have students list some closed-ended questions for each open-ended question in A, e.g. *What did Camila see in the coral reef? Who was in the speedboat? How many countries passed laws to protect coral reefs?*
- Point out that sometimes the answers to closed-ended questions like these can help you find answers to more challenging open-ended questions.

Above level:

- Have students work in pairs or small groups.
- Ask them to think about an environmental issue they are interested in and what they think should be done about it.
- Have students write a petition based on Camila's.
- Encourage them to revisit the persuasive essays they wrote in Unit 10 (page 104).
- Ask each pair or group to read their petition to the class.

- Ask the class which petitions they would like to sign and why.

B How did Camila help the world's coral reefs?

- Have students complete the activity individually and then check with a partner.
- Elicit answers from the class.

She raised awareness among her classmates. She started a petition to save the world's reefs. Twenty thousand people in 38 countries signed it.

C Words in Context: Circle the best ending to each sentence.

- Have students complete the exercise and then check answers with a partner.
- Elicit answers from the class.

ANSWERS

1 a   2 b   3 b   4 a

CRITICAL THINKING

- Point out that in the story Camila made a difference. Ask students what they can do to make a difference.
- Encourage them to think not only about saving the coral reefs, but also about protecting other biomes that are either near your town or far away.
- Explain that sometimes we can make a difference simply by talking to people and letting them know why biomes are important.
- Have students share their ideas with the class.

Grammar in Use

D Listen and sing along. 🎵 3·39

- Play the audio once while students listen and read along in their books.
- Play the audio again and have students sing along.
- Ask *What happened today? What have the singers done?*

E Read the sentences. Which one tells when the action happened?

- Point out that the word *today* answers the question, so *a* is the answer.
- Check the answer with the class.

F Learn Grammar: Present Perfect and Simple Past

- Read the *Learn Grammar* box together.
- Invite volunteers to say other sentences with either verb form.
- Remind them to use the simple past when they include a specific time marker, and to use the present perfect when the time is in the past, but not specified.

Circle the correct answer.

- For each sentence, help students decide if there is a time marker or not. Then have them choose the correct verb form.
- Check the answers with the class.

ANSWERS

1 have read   2 snorkeled   3 went   4 has seen

G Make a chart like below. Talk about it with your partner.

- Have students complete the chart on their own.

COLLABORATIVE LEARNING

- Have partners tell each other about things they have done and when they did them. Tell them to follow the model on the page.
- To make sure students listen carefully to their partners, tell them you will ask them to tell the class about their partners, e.g. Maria tells Philip, *I've snorkeled. I snorkeled in Belize last summer.* Philip tells the class, *Maria has snorkeled. She snorkeled in Belize last summer.*

Further Practice

Workbook pages 165–167
Online practice Unit 18 · Understand
Oxford iTools Unit 18 · Understand

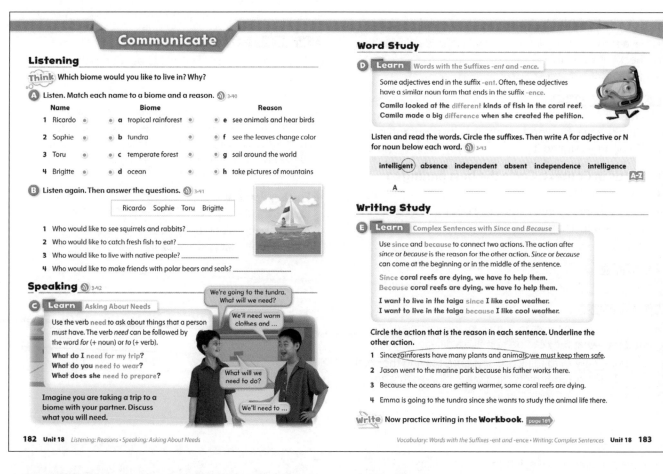

Summary

Objectives: To learn and practice listening, speaking, and writing strategies to facilitate effective communication.

Vocabulary: *intelligent, absence, independent, absent, independence, intelligence*

Listening strategy: Listening for reasons

Speaking: Asking about needs

Word Study: Words with the suffixes *-ent* and *-ence*

Writing Study: Complex sentences with *since* and *because*

Big Question learning points: *Biomes make our world interesting. Many different animals and plants live in each biome. Biomes add to Earth's beauty.*

Materials: Audio CD

Listening

Think

• Have students discuss the questions in small groups.

• Invite them to share their ideas with the class.

A Listen. Match each name to a biome and a reason. 🔘 3·40

• Play the audio once through while students just listen.

• Play it a second time and have them complete the exercise.

ANSWERS

1 d, g   2 a, e   3 b, h   4 c, f

Below level:

• Pause after each person's name so students know who is speaking. If necessary, write the names on the board for them to follow.

• Tell students to take notes as they listen. Pause after each section and ask students to tell you what they remember hearing.

• Check to see if any of the facts they recall are options for A. If they are, have students match the name to the biome to the reason. If not, listen again and help them identify the place in the audio where the answer is mentioned.

• Repeat for each section.

At level:

• After listening, elicit other details that students mention that are not listed as reasons in A. Ask, e.g.
What else does Ricardo say about why he wants to live on the ocean?
What else does Sophie say about why she wants to live in the rainforest?
What else does Toru say about why he wants to live on the tundra?
What else does Brigitte say about why she wants to live in a temperate forest?

Above level:

• Have students prepare a similar answer about one of the other biomes they've learned about.

• Encourage them to use the same tone and style as the others in the exercise.

- Have them read their answers to the class. Have the class name the reasons they gave for why they want to live in that specific biome.

CRITICAL THINKING

- The exercise focuses on why people want to live in each biome.
- Ask students to consider what challenges each person would face, e.g. Ricardo would have to find fresh drinking water; Sophie would need to find a way to communicate with people outside the remote rainforest; Toru would have to figure out a way to stay warm; Brigitte would have to clear some trees to plant a garden.

B Listen again. Then answer the questions. 3·41

COMMUNICATION

- Have students complete the exercise on their own.
- Have students discuss their answers in pairs.
- Check answers with the class.

ANSWERS

1 Brigitte   2 Ricardo   3 Sophie   4 Toru

Speaking 3·42

C Learn: Asking About Needs

- Read the *Learn* box together.
- Play the dialogue once while students listen and follow in their books.
- Then play one line of the dialogue at a time with students echoing as they hear each line.
- Model the dialogue with a confident student in front of the class.
- Put students into pairs and tell them to practice the dialogue, taking turns speaking the different roles.

Imagine you are taking a trip to a biome with your partner. Discuss what you will need.

- Have students follow the model to talk about visiting other biomes.

COLLABORATIVE LEARNING

- First have partners list the things they will need and the things they will need to do before a trip to each biome.
- Once they have made a list for each biome, they can refer to it and substitute language in the model dialogue on the page.

Word Study

D Learn: Words with the Suffixes *-ent* and *-erce*

- Read the *Learn* box together.
- Remind students of the Unit 2 (page 23) Word Study lesson about changing nouns that end in *-ance* into adjectives that end in *-ant*.
- Explain that students will learn about some words with a similar spelling relationship.

Listen and read the words. Circle the suffixes. Then write A for adjective or N for noun below each word. 3·43

- Play the audio and have students point to the words as they hear them.
- Have students complete the exercise on their own.
- Check the answers with the class.

ANSWERS

1 A   2 N   3 A   4 A   5 N   6 N

Writing Study

E Learn: Complex Sentences with *Since* and *Because*

- Read the *Learn* box together.
- Point out that if *since* or *because* is the reason for the other action, this is like a cause and effect relationship.
- Copy the sample sentences on the board. Ask a volunteer to find the reasons (or causes): *the coral reefs are dying; I like cool weather*.

Circle the action that is the reason in each sentence. Underline the other action.

- Have students complete the exercise on their own.
- Check answers with the class.

ANSWERS

1   Since (rainforests have many plants and animals) we must keep them safe.
2   Jason went to the marine park because (his father works there.)
3   Because (the oceans are getting warmer) some coral reefs are dying.
4   Emma is going to the tundra since (she wants to study the animal life there)

Write

- Direct the students to the Workbook for further practice.

Further Practice
Workbook pages 168–169
Online practice Unit 18 · Communicate
Oxford **iTools** Unit 18 · Communicate

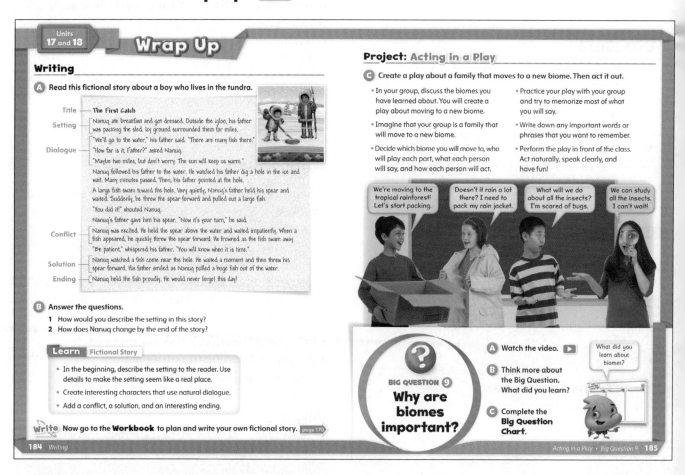

Summary

Objectives: To show what students have learned about the language and learning points of Units 17 and 18.

Reading: Comprehension of a fictional story

Project: Acting in a play

Writing: Write a fictional story

Speaking: Talking about acting in a play

Materials: Big Question DVD, Discover Poster 9, Talk About It! Poster, Big Question Chart

Writing

A Read this fictional story about a boy who lives in the tundra.

- Read the story together.
- Review the labels along the sidebar (Title, Setting, Dialogue, Conflict, Solution, Ending).

B Answer the questions.

- Have students find the answers in the text.
- Check the answers with the class.

ANSWERS

1 The icy tundra   2 He learns to be patient

Learn: Fictional Story

- Read the directions in the *Learn* box together.
- Explain that students should choose an interesting event for their stories.

- Remind students to follow these guidelines when they plan and write their stories.

DIFFERENTIATION

Below level:

- Focus on basic comprehension of the story:
  Character: *What does the author tell you about Nanuq? What does the author tell you about his father?*
  Plot: *What are the main events in the story?*

- Have students identify and underline the conflict and solution in the story (*Nanuq couldn't catch a fish and then he learned patience from his father and caught one.*)

At level:

- Discuss how the author meets the requirements of the *Learn* box:
  Describe the setting: The author uses descriptive language (Icy ground surrounded them for miles.)
  Create interesting characters: Nanuq's character is dynamic (he changes).
  Use interesting dialogue: Have volunteers read aloud the text within the quotations. This language sounds natural, like someone is actually speaking.
  Use a variety of verbs, adjectives, and adverbs: Ask students to find interesting and descriptive words the author uses in the story, such as *surrounded* and *impatiently*.
  Add a conflict and solution: Ask *What is the conflict? What is the solution?*
  Write an interesting ending: The sentence *He would never forget this day!* is interesting and engaging.

Above level:

- Challenge students to go beyond the guidelines in the *Learn* box for C:
  Conflict and possible resolutions: Revisit the Reading Strategy lesson on "Conflicts and Resolutions" in Unit 14, page 137. Ask students to include a few possible resolutions to the main conflict in their story before presenting the final solution.
  Open-ended questions: Tell students to write their stories without explicitly telling the reader everything. Can they hint at certain character traits or events?
  Writing skills: Encourage students to revisit the Word Study lessons in Unit 18 and throughout the Student Book. Can they include some of these targets in their story, such as complex sentences with *until* or phrasal verbs?

Write

- Direct students to the Workbook to plan and write their own fictional story.

CRITICAL THINKING

- Explain that sometimes authors use their own experiences for inspiration in their writing, but they elaborate and change details to make the experiences more interesting and exciting.
- Tell students they may use people they know, places they've been, and experiences they've had for ideas, but they should feel free to elaborate or change the details to suit the needs of their stories.

Project

C Create a play about a family that moves to a new biome. Then act it out.

CREATIVITY

- Read the directions together. Assign roles for each group, such as secretary, director, monitor, scriptwriter, set designer, etc.
- Have groups work through the steps together.
- Read and practice the sample speech bubbles as examples of how students can perform their plays.
- After groups decide which biome they will move to, have them revisit the Speaking lesson on page 182 to discuss what they will need and what they will need to do. Have the group secretary write these down to include in the final script.
- Some groups may prefer working with a script, and other groups may prefer improvising. Either is fine, as long as they practice and incorporate target ideas and language.

Units 17 and 18 Big Question Review

A Watch the video. ▷

- Play the video and when it is finished ask students what they know about the way biomes work now.
- Have students share ideas with the class.

B Think more about the Big Question. What did you learn?

COMMUNICATION

- Display **Discover Poster 9**. Point to familiar vocabulary items and elicit them from the class. Ask *What is this?* Ask students *What do you see?* Ask *What does that mean?*
- Refer to all of the learning points written on the poster and have students explain how they relate to the different pictures.
- Ask *What does this learning point mean?* Elicit answers from individual students.
- Display the **Talk About It! Poster** to help students with sentence frames for discussion of the learning points and for expressing their opinions.

C Complete the Big Question Chart.

COLLABORATIVE LEARNING

- Ask students what they have learned about biomes while studying this unit.
- Put students into pairs or small groups to say two new things they have learned.
- Have students share their ideas with the class and add their ideas to the chart.
- Have students complete the chart in their Workbook.

> **Further Practice**
> Workbook pages 170–172
> Online practice • Wrap Up 9
> Oxford **iTools** • Wrap Up 9

Audio Script

Listening Transcripts

Here are the listening transcripts from all the listening, speaking, and word study sections of the Student Book. It can be useful to ask students to read along as they listen to the audio CD, as it provides support for listening skills.

Unit 1

Page 14 `Listening`

1.05 A.   1.06 B.

Wow, just look at all those stars in the sky!

I know. Here at Grandpa's farm, they're so easy to see.

Why are they so easy to see, Grandpa?

There's less light pollution, Andy. Light pollution is all of the lights that shine in a big city at night. It's hard to see the stars there.

Hey, look at that really big star in the western sky.

That's not a star, Jenny. That's Venus. It's a planet in our solar system.

Why is it so bright, Grandpa?

Well, Venus is close to the Earth right now. And it's covered in clouds, so sunlight bounces off of it and shines back to us.

Grandpa, do you see that fuzzy white belt across the sky? What is that?

That's the Milky Way, Andy. It's the galaxy where we live.

But if we're in the Milky Way, how can we see it?

The Milky Way is shaped like a disk. We're in the disk, looking through it. What you are seeing are billions of stars in that disk. There are so many, it looks like milk!

Oh, that's why they call it the Milky Way.

That's right, Jenny.

Page 14 `Speaking`

1.07 C.

In the first picture, I see the Milky Way.

In the second picture, I see a comet.

The first picture has a quarter moon.

The second picture doesn't have a quarter moon, but it has a full moon.

I see Venus in the first picture, but I don't see it in the second picture.

The second picture has an owl but not the planet Venus.

Page 15 `Word Study`

1.08 D.

1. The woman wore a veil at the wedding.

2. There were over eighty people in the theater.

3. Hold on to the reins when you ride a horse.

4. Elephants weigh more than any other land animal.

5. Dad and I rode a sleigh in the snow.

6. Large ships carry freight across the ocean.

Unit 2

Page 22 `Listening`

1.12 A.   1.13 B.

And now a report from our science editor, Sharni Kapoor.

Just how fast is the speed of light? Well, the light from the Sun takes only 8 minutes to reach the Earth. It can do this because it is moving at a speed of almost 300,000 kilometers per second!

If light travels this far in one second, imagine how far it travels in one year! The distance is very difficult for us to understand, so scientists just call it one light-year. As you can imagine, it is a very long distance.

If you moved as fast as light, how long would it take you to travel around our solar system? Well, here are some examples. You could travel from Earth to Mars in just 4 minutes! You could travel to Jupiter in 35 minutes, and to Neptune in about 4 hours.

Some scientists believe that we will travel at the speed of light someday. However, if we reach this goal, it will still take 4 years to reach the nearest star to our Sun. If you wanted to travel across our own Milky Way galaxy, it would take thousands of years.

Page 22 `Speaking`

1.14 C.

How many stars does our solar system have?

It has one star, the sun.

How much water is in our solar system?

I'm not sure, but there is a lot of water on Earth!

Page 23 `Word Study`

1.15 D.

1. This flower has a nice fragrance.

2. We should try to have knowledge, not ignorance.

3. Arrogance is not a good thing to have.

4. The ignorant man never went to school.

5. No one liked the arrogant boy.

6. She always buys very fragrant soap.

Unit 3

Page 34 `Listening`

1.19 B.   1.20 C.

Good morning, class. Tanya, Lucas, and Dina will now tell us about an ancient town in Bulgaria. They got this information through many news reports on the Internet. As you listen, you will notice some similarities and differences between that time and the way we live today. Tanya will begin.

Thank you, Miss Elliot. Archaeologists recently uncovered an ancient town in Bulgaria that is over 6,000 years old. It is near the modern town of Provadia, near the Black Sea. It had a large stone wall around it to protect it from robbers. As you know, modern towns don't need stone walls to protect people.

That's true, Tanya. Thank you. Lucas, what can you tell us?

Well, this town made bricks out of salt. Salt was valuable then, because it kept meat and other foods fresh. Today people choose to keep food fresh with refrigerators. We still use salt in our food today, but it is cheap and easy to buy.

Thank you, Lucas. Dina, can you tell us more?

Yes, Miss Elliot. Archeologists discovered that this town had two-story houses. That means they had a downstairs floor and an upstairs floor. We have many two-story houses in our towns today as well.

That's true. Thank you, everyone. We learned a lot today.

Page 34 `Speaking`

1.21 D.

I'd like to go back to ancient Greece.

Why would you choose that place?

I'd like to see all the beautiful buildings in Athens. What about you?

I'd like to go back to an ancient Maya city. I want to see how Maya people made pyramids.

Page 35 `Word Study`

1.22 D.

1. The cartoonist is very good at drawing.

2. Erica wants to be a pianist, and she has lessons every day.

3. The florist wrapped the flowers in pretty paper.

4. If you want to be a cyclist, you need to ride a bike often.

5. In the office, the dentist cleaned my teeth.

6. The tourist has a map and a camera.

Unit 4

Page 42 Listening

1.26 A.   1.27 B.

A myth is a made-up story that explains something in the world. Myths are not true, but they can help us understand what people thought a long time ago. Here is a myth from the African country of Nigeria. It is called "Why the Sun and the Moon Live in the Sky."

Many years ago, the Sun was married to the Moon, and they lived in a house together on Earth. The Sun was very good friends with the Ocean, and he went to visit the Ocean often. However, the Ocean never came to visit the Sun. "I am too big for your house, Mr. Sun," he said. So the Sun decided to build a much bigger house, and then asked the Ocean to visit.

The next day the Ocean came to the house. "May I come in?" he asked. "Please do," said the Sun and the Moon. Soon the house was half full of water. The Sun and the Moon moved to the top of the room. "May I still come in?" the Ocean asked. "Please do," said the Sun and the Moon. The Ocean continued coming inside. Soon the house was filled with water. The Sun and the Moon climbed on to the roof and went up into the sky. They never came back to Earth again.

Page 42 Speaking

1.28 C.

What does a dinosaur bone feel like?

It probably feels rough. What do you think seaweed tastes like?

I think it tastes salty.

I agree.

Page 43 Word Study

1.29 D.

1. I felt relief after I finished the test.

2. Luke bought a birthday present for his niece.

3. The archaeologist found a piece of bone in the dirt.

4. This ride was fun, but it was too brief.

5. The woman was full of grief after her grandmother died.

6. A thief stole my bicycle!

Unit 5

Page 54 Listening

1.33 A.   1.34 B.

Hello! I'm Jan, and I only eat food that comes from plants. There are five kinds of food I eat.

The first kind is whole grains. People use whole grains to make many types of food, such as bread, spaghetti, and rice. About 35% of my daily food comes from this group.

I also eat many vegetables. Most of the vegetables that I eat are green, such as spinach and broccoli. However, I also like different-colored vegetables such as carrots. About 30% of my daily food comes from vegetables.

Next, we can't forget fruits! They often have a lot of sugar, so only about 15% of my daily food comes from this group. My favorite fruits are apples, blueberries, and oranges.

The fourth group is beans. People use soybeans to make many products, such as tofu. I eat that a lot. Also, I love chickpeas and black beans. About 10% of my daily food comes from this group.

Last are nuts and seeds. I love almonds, flaxseeds, and pecans. 10% of my daily food comes from this group.

Of course, some people like to eat meat, but I choose to get my food from plants. Remember, food from plants is very delicious, and it's good for your health!

Page 54 Speaking

1.35 C.

Do you want some fruit?

Sure. I love fruit. Thank you.

I have apples or mangoes. Which one do you like?

I like both, but I prefer mangoes because they are very sweet. What about you?

Unit 6

Page 62 Listening

1.40 A.   1.41 B.

I'm speaking today from a beautiful terraced rice farm in Vietnam. People make terraced farms by cutting flat strips of land, called terraces, out of the side of a hill or mountain. Then they grow plants there such as rice. You can see terraced farms in south Asia, in Europe, and even on islands. These farms are good because the soil doesn't wash away when it rains. It's also good for plants that need lots of water, such as rice.

Welcome to Belgium! I'm visiting a hydroponic lettuce farm. A hydroponic farm doesn't need soil for its plants to grow. The plants grow very well in water that has food, or nutrients, put in it. Hydroponic farms are good for two reasons. First, they don't need soil. Also, the water stays in containers, so plants need less water to grow than they do in soil.

Welcome to Hong Kong, where I am on the roof of a large building. In front of me is a rooftop vegetable farm! Rooftop farms are becoming very popular in cities around the world. Rooftop farms are good for cities. They collect a lot of rainwater, and they keep buildings cool by protecting the roof from the hot sun. Also, fewer trucks need to bring food into the city because food can now be grown here!

Page 62 Speaking

1.42 C.

People often grow apples where I live.

What do people make with them?

Many people make apple pie or applesauce.

Do you like apple pie or applesauce more?

I like apple sauce. What about you?

I like both, but I really like apple pie when it's warm.

Unit 7

Page 74 Listening

2.05 A.   2.06 B.

Hi! My name is Stella, and I live in Northern Sweden. I like to make jewelry, especially bracelets. I weave wire and leather together. This is called Sami jewelry. My grandma is an expert and teaches me. We can relax together while we make the jewelry. We are also continuing our family tradition.

Hi! I'm Juan, and I'm from Paraguay. I like to make junk art from recycled materials. I do this because I want to make a difference in the world. Trash is my treasure. I can make art out of anything! When I find something interesting, I ask myself, "What should I make?" I like being creative.

Hi! My name is Neema, and I'm from Tanzania. I like photography because I can capture the magic of things. I took some great photos of animals from the Maasai Mara. From our special bus, I took a photo of a mother lion with her paw around her cub. It was so cute! Photography is like a treasure hunt. I never know what special moments I'll catch on my camera.

Hi! I'm Marko, and I come from Croatia. I love creating art on my computer because almost anything is possible.

When I open a blank page, I can let my imagination soar. I like making abstract patterns. You might think they look mathematical. By creating art on my computer, I can challenge myself to make all sorts of patterns.

Page 74 Speaking
2.07 C.

What are the children doing?
They're painting.
Are they painting inside or outside?
They're painting outside.
Does it look warm or cool outside?
It looks warm.

Unit 8

Page 82 Listening
2.12 A.   2.13 B.

Hello, everyone. Welcome to the Marmottan Monet Museum here in Paris. Our museum has 300 works of art by Claude Monet, the famous Impressionist painter.

Here in front of us is Monet's famous painting, "Impression: Sunrise." He painted it in 1872. This work is very important. It shows the artist's special way of painting, which is called Impressionism. There are three reasons why Impressionism is special.

First, Monet painted outside almost all of the time. He wanted to show the light and color of nature in his paintings. He painted outside so that he could see this light and color clearly. Traditional artists often painted inside, even when they painted landscapes.

Next, Monet painted this scene by moving his paintbrush in a short, quick way. We call these "brushstrokes." Do you see the short colorful brushstrokes in this painting? There are no clear lines, and there is not much detail when you look closely. Traditional painters in Monet's time painted with a lot of detail.

Finally, most painters mixed their colors, but Monet did not mix colors very often. Each of his colors is side by side with other colors. It looks strange when you look at the painting closely. However, when you step back, all of these colors mix together. Suddenly, the painting looks very alive and real.

Because he chose to paint in a different way, Claude Monet is now one of the most famous painters of all time.

Page 82 Speaking
2.14 C.

I wish I could go to Berlin.
Why do you want to go there?

I want to visit the museums there.
That sounds fun. I wish I could go with you!

Unit 9

Page 94 Listening
2.19 A.   2.20 B.

Do you notice how many important cities are built near rivers, lakes, or oceans? There are very good reasons for this. Here are three examples:

The French capital city of Paris surrounds The River Seine. The first people settled there thousands of years ago on the present island called Ile de la Cite. They were called the Parisii, which means "boat people." The river gave them fish for food and water to drink. Today, the city of Paris has over 12 million people.

Mexico City began almost 700 years ago as an Aztec city on an island in Lake Texcoco. This lake helped protect the Aztecs from invaders. Today, Mexico City rests on the dry land that used to be Lake Texcoco. It has over 20 million people.

Istanbul, Turkey was the capital city of four empires in the past 2,000 years. Its location is very important. Istanbul became a city on both sides of a narrow body of water called the Bosphorus. The Bosphorus connects the Black Sea to the Sea of Marmara, and separates Europe and Asia. Transportation along this water route was very important, and still is today. Istanbul now has over 13 million people.

Page 94 Speaking
2.21 C.

My city grew because it is next to a river. The river was important because people used the water in many ways.

That's really interesting. My city grew because there is an ocean nearby.

How did that help your city grow?

It helped my city grow because people could catch fish in the ocean.

Unit 10

Page 102 Listening
2.26 A.   2.27 B.

What do cities have that small towns don't? Here are four answers. Toshi lives in Tokyo, Japan.

One great thing about cities is their zoos. Here in Tokyo, we have the Ueno Zoo. I like the pandas there. Pandas are the most beautiful bears in the world. The Ueno Zoo also has black bears and polar bears.

Gaby lives in Sao Paulo, Brazil.

I like living in a big city because of the restaurants. There are so many great places to eat. Here in Sao Paulo you can eat Brazilian food, Italian food, African food, and even Japanese sushi. Nothing is better than sushi for dinner!

Alina lives in Moscow, Russia.

Well, I like cities because of their parks! Here in Moscow, we have almost 100 parks! Per person, we have more park space than Paris, London, or New York. A park is the best place to read a good book.

Omari lives in Cairo, Egypt.

I love professional sports, and cities are great places for that. Here in Cairo, soccer is very popular. Our two top soccer teams play their home games here at the Cairo International Stadium. We also have excellent squash players. Squash is the most exciting sport in the world.

Page 102 Speaking
2,28 C.

What does a mayor have to do?
A mayor has to work with City Council to fix problems in a city.
Does a City Council member have to work with other people?
Yes, I think a City Council member has to work with lots of people.

Unit 11

Page 114 Listening
2.33 A.   2.34 B.

This is a public service announcement from the Department of Health.

Hello, everyone! The flu season is here, which means that some bad viruses may be in the air and on objects around you. Fortunately, you can keep yourself protected from these tiny, dangerous viruses with a few simple daily habits.

First, wash your hands often each day. Be sure to wash the front, the back, and between your fingers for at least 15 seconds.

Next, don't touch your eyes, nose, or mouth with your fingers. These are places where viruses can go into your body and infect you.

Also, if you have to cough or sneeze, cover your mouth and nose with a tissue. This will keep the virus from going into the air.

Finally, stay healthy by taking care of your body. Get enough sleep, try to exercise each day, and eat healthy foods.

Follow these four steps throughout the flu season. With a strong body and good health habits, you can protect yourself and others against influenza. Thank you.

Page 114 `Speaking`
2.35 C.

What do you do when you catch a cold?

I drink a lot of water and sleep as much as I can. What do you do?

I usually eat soup and drink tea.

How do you stay healthy?

I try to exercise each day. What about you?

I usually eat a lot of vegetables and wash my hands often.

Unit 12

Page 122 `Listening`
2.40 A.   2.41 B.

And now for a student report on bones.

Eduardo: Did you know that when you were a baby, you had about 300 bones? Later, some of those bones became one bone, so as an adult you have 206 bones. The largest bone in your body is the femur, which is in the top half of your leg. The smallest bone is in your ear!

Wendy: When you touch the middle of your back, do you feel bumps? That's your spine! The spine is one of the most important parts of your body, because it lets you stand up! It is made up of 26 bones, called vertebrae. They are shaped like rings.

Kaya: Feel the top of your head. Does it feel hard? That's your skull! The skull is actually made up of different bones. The only bone that can move in your skull is your jawbone, which lets you open and close your mouth. The skull protects your brain and gives shape to your face.

Subin: Your hands and feet have the most bones in your body. Each hand has 27 bones! Each foot has 26 bones! Your thumbs and your big toes have two bones each. The other fingers and toes have 3 bones each. There are many other bones that help your hands and feet move easily.

Page 122 `Speaking`
2.42 C.

What is the heart?

It's the part of the body that pumps blood.

What is a hospital?

It's a place where doctors and nurses help sick people.

Unit 13

Page 134 `Listening`
3.05 A.   3.06 B.

Hi! My name is Tina. I'm nine years old, and I have my own blog! You can have your own blog, too. Just follow these directions.

First, set up your blog. There are many simple blog websites where you can make a blog. You can also use blog sites that are just for children. My blog is on a children's site.

Next, decide what to write about. A good blog will teach people and entertain them. I like to write about nature in my city.

After that, set up a writing schedule. This will help people know when you will be writing new information. I write on my blog every Saturday afternoon.

Next, be professional. Keep your writing clear and easy to understand. Make sure you check for grammar and spelling mistakes.

Finally, be safe. Don't put photos of yourself on your blog. Don't use your last name, and don't give your address or phone number. The only contact I give is my parents' email address.

Blogging is a great way to build your writing skills. So get started, and have fun!

Page 134 `Speaking`
3.07 C.

My dad gets news from the newspaper.

My dad usually uses the Internet to check the news.

That's interesting. My mom prefers to get news from magazines.

My mom uses the radio to get her news because she can listen to it in the car.

Page 135 `Word Study`
3.08 D.

1. Some people kneel if a king walks by.

2. In the book, the brave knight protected the town.

3. The ball hit my hand and hurt my knuckle.

4. Stacy learned how to tie a rope into a knot.

5. My mom knit me a warm hat to wear in the winter.

6. Schools and books give people knowledge.

Unit 14

Page 142 `Listening`
3.12 A.   3.13 B.

Welcome to Westview Elementary Grade 4 news! I'm Fran. Today is Monday, October 9th. For school lunch today, the cooks will serve spaghetti with tomato sauce. Spaghetti is the most delicious meal we have at school, so we hope you enjoy it.

Hi everyone, I'm Jae-sung, and this is the Grade 4 sports news! On Saturday, our 4th grade soccer team lost to Eastview Elementary 4–3 in overtime! Our team did their very best, but they just couldn't beat Eastview. Better luck next time!

Hello, I'm Kareena, and here is the Grade 4 weather news! Today is a sunny day, with temperatures around 25 degrees Celsius. Tomorrow, however, will be rainy. Bring your umbrellas and your happiest smiles tomorrow, because no one likes a rainy day.

Hi, I'm Omar, bringing you the Grade 4 events calendar. This coming Saturday, on October 14th, we will have our school sports festival from 10:00 a.m. to 4:00 p.m. It's the most exciting school event of the year, so please join us and have fun!

Page 142 `Speaking`
3.14 C.

I think reporters have a difficult job.

Why do you think that?

I think that because reporters have to interview people, get facts, and write stories about what they learn.

Yes, that's true. I think that editors have a difficult job because they have to make sure a reporter's stories are correct.

Unit 15

Page 154 `Listening`
3.19 A.   3.20 B.

My name is Dr. Demir, and I'm an earthquake safety expert from Istanbul, Turkey. Earthquakes often happen without any warning, so it is important to be prepared for one.

The first way to prepare is to make sure your home is ready for an earthquake.

For example, during an earthquake, large objects in your house or apartment can fall down, so it's a good idea to attach objects like bookcases or mirrors to the wall.

It is also important to decide on a safe place in the house that you will go to if there is an earthquake. This could be under a large table, for example.

Electricity and running water can also stop during an earthquake. Prepare for this by keeping enough food and water in your house for three days.

The second way to prepare is to know what to do when an earthquake happens:

If you are indoors, stay indoors. Get to the safe place you chose beforehand.

If you are outside, get away from buildings and trees. Stay low to the ground.

After the earthquake, use a radio or smartphone to get important emergency information.

Earthquakes can be scary. However, by preparing before an earthquake happens, you can stay calm and know exactly what to do.

Page 154 Speaking

3.21 C.

What will the concert be like?

It might be loud.

What will the shopping mall be like?

I think it could be very crowded today.

Unit 16

Page 162 Listening

3.26 A.   3.27 B.

This is an announcement from the Ohio weather service. At 4:23 p.m, a tornado was seen 5 kilometers west of the town of Greenhills. If you are in the Greenhills area, please seek shelter immediately. Go to the basement or to a room near the center of your home. This tornado warning will continue for the next 60 minutes. Thank you.

The Canadian Weather Service has issued a blizzard warning for Toronto and Southern Ontario. This blizzard will bring strong winds and cold temperatures, and up to 75 centimeters of snow may fall. We ask residents to stay home during this time. If you must drive, keep blankets, food and water in your car.

The German weather service has issued a severe storm warning for the southwest part of the country. Rain, hail, and powerful winds are possible. Some trees may fall down. Stay indoors and away from windows. Do not drive unless you have to.

The Egyptian government has issued a sandstorm warning for the Alexandria area for the next three hours. If you are on the road, please drive slowly since it may be difficult to see. Everyone in the area should stay indoors if possible during this time, closing all windows and doors and shutting off any air conditioners. If you must be outside, carry goggles and a dust mask.

Page 162 Speaking

3.28 C.

We need to get water bottles.

We also need canned food.

I think we already have enough canned food.

OK, what else do we need?

We still need extra batteries for the flashlight.

I'll get the batteries.

Unit 17

Page 174 Listening

3.33 A.   3.34 B.

Hi, I'm Jake. Mandy and I are here to tell you about a food chain from the desert biome. Plants are usually the lowest part of any food chain. Plants get their energy from the sun. One desert plant is the shrub, which makes seeds.

Hi, I'm Mandy. Next on the food chain are animals that eat seeds. Desert quails are birds that eat shrub seeds. So you can see how energy moves from the sun to plants to birds. And what do you think eats quails in the desert? Coyotes, which look a little like dogs. The coyote is the final animal on this food chain.

Hello, I'm Carlos. Fatima and I would like to tell you about another desert food chain. It begins with desert grass, which also makes seeds! Insects eat these seeds. And what eats the insects? Lizards, of course.

Hello, everyone! I'm Fatima. Did you know that snakes eat lizards? They are next on that food chain. And believe it or not, something in the desert likes to eat snakes! It's a large bird called a hawk. The hawk is the final animal on this food chain.

Page 174 Speaking

3.35 C.

In the spring, the trees are full of small leaves.

Next, during the summer, the leaves are bigger.

Then, in the fall, the leaves change colors and some fall to the ground.

Finally, during the winter, all the leaves have fallen off of the trees.

Unit 18

Page 182 Listening

3.40 A.   3.41 B.

Ricardo, what biome would you like to live in?

Hmmm. I'd like to live in the ocean biome. I would live on a sailboat and sail around the world. I'd also like to catch fresh fish to eat. How about you, Sophie?

That's easy. I'd live in the tropical rainforest. The rainforest is full of animals. Colorful birds are always singing, and the air is so fresh. The native people who live there take care of the forest. I want to live with them. Toru, what biome would you live in?

Well, my parents come from Hokkaido, Japan. There is a lot of snow there, and I love it, so I'd like to live in the tundra. I would take pictures of the beautiful mountains and make friends with the polar bears and seals there.

Make friends with a polar bear? I don't think so, Toru! How about you, Brigitte?

I'd like to live in a forest like you, Sophie, but I would prefer the temperate forest. I'd see the changing colors of the leaves and the four seasons. I like cute forest animals like squirrels and rabbits. I would live in a little house and plant a garden.

Page 182 Speaking

3.42 C.

We're going to the tundra. What will we need?

We'll need warm clothes and a lot of food!

What will we need to do?

We'll need to plan our trip.

Workbook Answer Key

Unit One

Page 2
A.
1 stars   2 moon   3 comet
4 asteroids

B.
1 telescope   2 spacecraft
3 observatory   4 universe
5 meteorite

Page 3
C.
1 T   2 F   3 F   4 T   5 T   6 T
7 F   8 F   9 T   10 T   11 F

D.
1 universe   2 spacecraft
3 meteorite   4 observatory
5 telescope

Page 4
A.
He travels through the universe with them in his super spacecraft.

Page 5
A.
Example sentences:
Yes, I think that in the future scientists will be able to invent a spacecraft for each person.

B.
Example sentences:
First: Earth was a beautiful blue ball behind Stanley's spacecraft.
Next: I saw the Milky Way galaxy shaped like a disk. It was filled with billions of stars.
Finally: I saw billions of tiny galaxies that made up the universe.

C.
1 Yes, they do. In 2099, every child on Earth has a spacecraft.
2 She went shopping on Mars, flew around some asteroids, and chased a comet.
3 She will remember it forever, because she saw the whole universe.

D.
1 specks   2 vast   3 disk   4 dwell

Page 6
B.
1 My little brother says he <u>will</u> (be) the first person to walk on Mars. (c)
2 Astronauts <u>will</u> (find) water on a planet someday. (d)

3 Another bright comet <u>will</u> (appear) in the sky sometime soon. (f)
4 Each child <u>will</u> (have) his or her own spacecraft in the future. (b)
5 Students <u>will</u> (take) field trips to the moon someday. (e)
6 Scientists <u>will</u> (build) even bigger telescopes in the future. (a)

Page 7
C.
1 Astronauts will travel to other planets someday.
2 Scientists will invent a spacecraft that can travel outside of our solar system.
3 Bigger telescopes will let us look deeper into space.
4 Spacecraft will fly through space at very high speeds.
5 People will take trips to the moon as tourists someday.
6 Astronauts will wear lighter spacesuits so they can move easily.

D.
1 P   2 F   3 P   4 P   5 F

E.
1 People will fly spacecraft through the solar system.
2 Astronauts will travel through the universe.
3 Small meteorites will hit the ground tonight.
4 Spacecraft will fly very fast someday.

Page 8
A.
1 Leah received a beautiful red (sleigh) for her birthday. (e)
2 The new telescope at school is over (eighty) kilograms, so you can't lift it. (a)
3 In the future, spacecraft may deliver (freight) to other planets. (f)
4 The young woman wore a beautiful white (veil) on her head. (b)
5 Esteban grabbed the (reins) and rode his horse through the rain. (d)
6 Space observatories don't (weigh) anything once they are in space. (c)

B.
1 sleigh   2 eighty   3 reins
4 weigh   5 freight

Page 9
A.
1 Can see it easily in the night sky.
   You can see it easily in the night sky.
2 Difficult to imagine.
   It is difficult to imagine.
3 A large icy object.
   It's a large icy object.
4 Told me last night.
   He told me last night.

Unit Two

Page 10
A.
1 core   2 gravity   3 unique
4 surface   5 diameter
6 space probe   7 astronomer
8 distance   9 matter
10 craters   11 orbit

B.
2 8 1 5
3 6 4 7

Page 11
C.
1 matter   2 unique   3 gravity

D.
1 craters   2 astronomer   3 gravity
4 orbit   5 diameters   6 distance
7 space probes   8 surface
9 matter   10 core   11 unique

Page 12
A.
It is the largest moon in the solar system.

Page 13
B.
Different
Ganymede:
1 It's the largest moon in the solar system.
2 It is far from Jupiter.
3 One orbit takes 7 days.
4 It might have an ocean.
Our Moon:
1 It's the fifth largest moon in the solar system.
2 It is close to Earth.
3 One orbit takes 27 days.
4 It has no ocean.
Same
1 Ganymede and the moon have craters.
2 The cores of Ganymede and the moon are hot and made of metal.

3 The gravity on Ganymede and the moon are similar.

C.
1 T   2 F   3 T   4 F

D.
1 bodies   2 outer   3 inner
4 explored

Page 14

B.
1 If scientists continue to study Ganymede, they will learn much more about it.
2 If scientists don't find water on Ganymede, they will be disappointed.
3 People will travel through the solar system if we create fast spacecraft.
4 Kenan will build a model solar system if he finds the right materials.
5 If Jackie doesn't finish her homework, she won't use her telescope tonight.
6 If the space probe continues at this speed, it will fly by Ganymede next month.
7 The large meteorite will make a big crater if it hits the moon.
8 If the sky is clear tonight, we will see Venus, Mars, and Jupiter.

Page 15

C.
1 b   2 c   3 d   4 a

D.
1 If you don't study science, you won't become an astronaut.
2 If you look at the sky tonight, you'll see Venus and Mars.
3 If you read about Ganymede, you'll learn many interesting facts.
4 If you don't look through the telescope, you'll miss seeing Jupiter's moons.

E.
Examples:
1 If the sky is clear tonight, I will look for Venus in the western sky.
2 I'll stay home and read a book if it rains this weekend.
3 If I have a test next week, I'll study very hard the day before.
4 My parents will congratulate me if I get good grades this month.

Page 16

A.
1 After she won the race, her arrogance was really bad. (d)
2 Some flowers are very fragrant, while others are not. (a)

3 Tom studies a lot because he doesn't want to be ignorant. (f)
4 An orange tree in the spring can have a lovely fragrance. (b)
5 He acted arrogant, and his friends didn't like it. (c)
6 Ignorance can cause low test scores. (e)

B.
1 fragrance   2 ignorant
3 fragrant   4 arrogant
5 ignorance   6 arrogance

Page 17

A.
1 Is a galaxy a star or a group of stars?
   A galaxy is a group of stars.
2 Is Ganymede's orbit around Mars or Jupiter?
   Ganymede's orbit is around Jupiter.
3 Does a moon go around a planet, or does a planet go around a moon?
   A moon goes around a planet.
4 Does our solar system have seven planets or eight planets?
   Our solar system has eight planets.

Page 18

A.
title, introduction paragraph, second paragraph, third paragraph, fourth paragraph, conclusion paragraph

Page 19

A.
Across
4 disk   5 sleigh   6 asteroids
8 moon   10 fragrance   11 eighty
Down
1 body   2 astronomer
3 telescope   6 arrogant
7 core   9 unique

Page 20

B.
1 Space probes   2 If   3 will
4 solar system   5 inner   6 outer
7 diameter   8 observatory
9 matter

C.
1 Thousands of craters!
   It has thousands of craters!
2 Or to Ganymede.
   Someday I want to travel to Mars or to Ganymede.

D.
Examples:
1 I will remember that our solar system has eight planets.
2 I would prefer to be an astronaut because I like to travel.

Unit Three

Page 21

A.

3	11
1	4
8	6
9	10
2	5
7	

Page 22

B.
1 army   2 tomb   3 archaeologists
4 clay   5 uniforms   6 armor

C.
1 emperor   2 treasure   3 jade
4 soldiers   5 peasants

Page 23

A.
They found a 2,000-year-old Roman fort.

Page 24

B.
To inform: 1, 3
To entertain: 2, 4

C.
1 F   2 T   3 F

D.
1 general (d)   2 coffin (a)
3 battle (c)   4 ancient (b)

Page 25

B.
1 Raji chose to write about the first Roman emperor for his history report.
2 The Treveri people didn't expect to see such a large Roman army.
3 Do the archaeologists plan to dig in this area much longer?
4 What time and place in history did you decide to research?
5 Gabrielle seems to be unhappy with her history test score.
6 The general didn't appear to be nervous before the battle.
7 Did Diego agree to take you to the museum?
8 What did the students learn to do at the archaeological site?

Page 26

C.
1 The archaeologist didn't forget to label each of the items.
2 Julius Caesar chose to attack the Treveri army.
3 Do the archaeologists hope to find more Roman treasure?

4 What did the Roman shoemakers learn to make so well?

5 The fort near Hermeskeil seems to be a real Roman fort.

D.

1 He promised to study harder.

2 She didn't expect to find the treasure.

3 Did you plan to visit the museum?

4 Where did they agree to meet?

E.

Examples:

1 I hope to visit the lost city of Machu Picchu.

2 I first learned to speak English in kindergarten.

Page 27

A.

1 cyclist 2 tourist 3 cartoonist
4 pianist 5 dentist 6 florist

B.

1 dentist 2 tourist 3 cyclist
4 cartoonist 5 pianist 6 florist

Page 28

A.

1 began
  was decided stop

2 takes
  look discovered find

3 look
  find used make

Unit Four

Page 29

A.

1 skull 2 examine 3 discover
4 ravine 5 dinosaur 6 layer
7 pastime 8 ash 9 excavate
10 paleontologist
11 sedimentary rock

B.

| a 3 | b 2 | c 6 |
| d 5 | e 4 | f 1 |

Page 30

C.

1 paleontologist, skull
2 layers, sedimentary rock
3 pastime, dinosaurs
4 ravine, ash
5 examine, dinosaur
6 discovered, excavated

D.

1 paleontologists 2 excavate
3 dinosaur 4 discover 5 examine

E.

1 T 2 T 3 F 4 T 5 T 6 F
7 F 8 T

Page 31

A.

It has many plant and animal fossils.

Page 32

A.

Students' own answers

B.

Prediction examples:

1 Paleontologists will excavate the ravine to find more bones.

2 Karen will hike with them and show them where she found the skull.

3 She will become a paleontologist like her father.

C.

1 They want to see fossil samples within the layers of sedimentary rock and ash.

2 The skull was from a new dinosaur they didn't know about, and Karen discovered it.

D.

1 determine 2 tripped 3 favorite
4 dream

Page 33

B.

1 Jacob didn't start building his dinosaur model yet.

2 Karen likes looking at all the bones in her father's office.

3 Did Miguel finish examining the skull this morning?

4 Karen's father enjoys taking her on hikes in the Karoo.

5 Where did you practice digging before you went to the site?

C.

1 I enjoy watching films about ancient history.

2 The people in the Karoo like showing visitors their area.

3 Lars stopped doing research for his dinosaur report.

4 I recommend taking a break before we label these items.

5 Marin considered studying paleontology at her university.

6 Natasha disliked getting her hands dirty when she looked for bones.

Page 34

D.

1 reading 2 finding 3 digging
4 talking 5 studying

E.

1 Sarah likes visiting the science museum.

2 Karen enjoyed hiking with her father.

3 The paleontologists finished taking pictures of the skull.

F.

Examples:

1 I prefer eating cereal and toast.

2 I enjoy playing sports with my friends in the park.

3 I finished writing a history report recently.

Page 35

A.

1 niece (e) 2 grief (a)
3 brief (c) 4 thief (f)
5 relief (b) 6 piece (d)

B.

1 niece 2 grief 3 thief 4 brief
5 piece 6 relief

Page 36

A.

1 is (C) 2 excavate (C) 3 is (NC)
4 has (C) 5 washes (NC)
6 visit (C) 7 helps (NC) 8 goes (C)

Page 37

A.

title, introduction paragraph, body, conclusion paragraph

Page 38

A.

4	1
7	9
3	6
8	2
10	5

B.

1 excavate, skull
2 dentist, examined
3 jade, treasures
4 layer, ash
5 tripped, piece

C.

1 to excavate 2 to discover
3 examining 4 to label 5 letting
6 to like

D.

1 seems 2 are 3 look 4 are
5 remains 6 stays 7 changes
8 are 9 are

Unit Five

Page 40

A.

4	10
6	7
1	9
5	8
2	11
3	

Page 41

B.
1 Cinnamon 2 steamship
3 vanilla 4 Leopards 5 spoil
6 ingredients 7 butter
8 Sugar cane 9 wheat
10 plantations 11 bark

C.
1 steamship 2 cinnamon
3 plantation 4 butter
5 ingredients

Page 42

A.
He needs cinnamon, butter, wheat, sugar cane, vanilla, and apple sauce.

Page 43

A.
Students' own answers

B.
1 Pierre doesn't earn much money as a baker.
2 The best ingredients make the best cookies.
3 Many people buy the things that Pierre and Audrey bake.

C.
1 F 2 T 3 T 4 F

D.
1 peel 2 coax 3 gathered
4 introduced

Page 44

B.
1 Grace is baking a chocolate cake tomorrow for her mother's birthday.
2 The steamship is bringing sugar cane to Shanghai tomorrow afternoon.
3 Are you putting fresh cinnamon on the cookies soon?
4 I'm not making spaghetti tonight because I don't have any pasta.
5 Where is Sophie buying the fruit for the party on Friday?
6 They aren't baking cookies after dinner because they're too busy.
7 Is he driving to the supermarket at 3:00 p.m. to get the ingredients?
8 Why are you making peach pie without fresh peaches this weekend?
9 Jack isn't going to cooking school next fall because it's too expensive.
10 Who is eating vanilla ice cream with apple pie after dinner?

Page 45

C.
1 are shopping 2 isn't planting

3 are baking 4 are visiting

D.
1 am taking 2 is planting
3 are picking 4 is giving

E.
1 Chris is working on a sugar cane plantation next fall.
2 Is Natalie taking three cooking classes next spring?
3 Mrs. Miller isn't planting potatoes in her garden next April.
4 Anna is buying eggs next spring from her aunt, who has chickens.

Page 46

A.
1 out 2 by 3 off 4 back

2   4
1   3

B.
1 dropped by 2 dropping out
3 dropped back 4 drop off

Page 47

A.
1 vast 2 towering 3 exhausted
4 delicious 5 steaming 6 juicy
7 icy

Unit Six

Page 48

A.
1 convenient 2 export
3 corporate farm 4 local
5 process 6 package
7 agriculture 8 decrease
9 century 10 farmer's market
11 chemical
Secret message: I like healthy food.

Page 49

B.
1 corporate farm 2 century
3 chemical 4 farmer's market

C.
1 e 2 g 3 a 4 c 5 d 6 b
7 f

D.
1 farmer's market – local
2 agriculture – corporate farms
3 century – chemicals
4 package – decrease

Page 50

A.
Olive oil is delicious and healthy. People can buy it around the world.

Page 51

A.
Students' own answers

B.
Who produces olive oil?
Countries around the Mediterranean Sea produce most of the world's olive oil. These countries include Spain, Italy, and Greece.
How is it processed?
People or machines grind the olives into a mixture. They stir the mixture, and then press it to remove the oil.

C.
1 They use it for cooking, and they eat it with food such as breads and salads.
2 People now use machines more often to process the olive oil.
3 Machines can process olive oil faster and cheaper than people can.

D.
1 organic food 2 grocery store
3 food labels 4 whole food

Page 52

B.
1 Would you like to see where they grow olives in Italy?
2 Would you like a little olive oil on your salad?
3 Would you like to make fresh lemonade with these lemons?
4 Would you like a cup of tea with your cake?
5 Would you like two cookies with your milk?
6 Would you like to buy some organic peaches at the farmer's market?
7 Would you like to plant tomatoes with me this afternoon?
8 Would you like some strawberries from Spain?
9 Would you like to read this book about organic food?
10 Would you like some delicious chocolate from Belgium?
11 Would you like to package these green beans with me?
12 Would you like to go to the grocery store with me?

Page 53

C.
1 to 2 a 3 a 4 to 5 a 6 to

D.
1 Would you like to pick some kiwifruit today?
2 Would you like to buy a kilogram of beef?
3 Would you like some pepper on your salad?

E.

1 Would you like an orange?

2 Would you like to try some kimchi from Korea?

3 Would you like some cheese from Holland?

4 Would you like to work on a farm with me?

Page 54

A.

1 geography (d) 2 introduction (f)

3 dictionary (a) 4 photographer (c)

5 conversation (e)

6 environment (b)

B.

1 photographer 2 conversation

3 geography 4 introduction

5 environment 6 dictionary

Page 55

A.

1 between 2 next to 3 under

4 behind 5 on 6 near

B.

Students' own answers

Page 57

A.

1 butter 2 cinnamon 3 vanilla

4 wheat 5 chemicals

6 conversation 7 steamship

8 leopard 9 photographer

10 farmer's market

11 grocery store 12 food label

Page 58

B.

1 introduced 2 agriculture

3 convenient 4 export

C.

1 dropping off – package (this afternoon)

2 gathering – ingredients (tomorrow morning)

3 environment – organic food (next summer)

4 geography – drop by (tonight)

D.

It is a pretty (beautiful) morning. I reach (behind my bed) and get my old (tattered) work clothes. It's time for me to do some gardening. I eat a nice (delicious) breakfast and walk outside. The sunlight is warm (brilliant). I see that there are some bad (horrible) weeds (near the carrots). My shovel is (next to the garden) so I pick it up and dig out the weeds. The flowers look dry (parched), so I water them. Then, I rest (under a tree) because I'm tired (exhausted). I don't mind working. Gardening is fun (enjoyable)!

Unit 7

Page 59

A.

1 carpenter 2 street painter

3 prodigy 4 sculptor

B.

1 canvas 2 pastels 3 string

4 paintbrushes

5 three-dimensional 6 shapes

7 sketch

Page 60

C.

1 d 2 e 3 a 4 b 5 c

3   1   4   2   5

D.

1 street painter, paintbrushes

2 prodigy, sculptor

3 carpenter, canvas

Page 61

A.

They want to express the beauty they see in the world.

Page 62

A.

Students' own answers

B.

1 d f 2 a i 3 e g 4 c j 5 b h

C.

1 She shows that many things are still useful.

2 He shows the beautiful scenes of Africa.

D.

1 fascination 2 combines

3 complex 4 washable

Page 63

B.

1 Someone 2 Everyone

3 anyone 4 everything

C.

1 b (anyone) 2 c (anything)

3 a (someone) 4 d (something)

Page 64

D.

1 everyone 2 Anyone

3 everything 4 something

E.

1 Does everyone have a paintbrush?

2 Sculptors can make anything from wood.

3 I bought something from the art museum.

4 Is anyone painting in the park?

F.

1 There is something I would like you to do.

2 Everything used for this work of art comes from trash.

3 I met someone yesterday who is a street painter.

4 Anyone can go to the city art museum. It's free of charge.

Page 65

A.

1 d (disproved) 2 a (disorganized)

3 f (distrusted) 4 b (dissatisfied)

5 c (disability) 6 e (dishonest)

B.

1 dissatisfied 2 ability

3 disorganized 4 honest 5 trust

6 prove

Page 66

A.

1 As the sun rose, the artist went outside with his easel and began to paint.

2 Ashley drew a sketch of her house and gave it to her father for his birthday.

3 The street painter finished his painting and then stepped onto it.

4 My father builds houses on weekdays and makes sculptures on weekends.

5 The young prodigy won a painting competition and received a cash prize.

B.

Students' own answers

Unit 8

Page 67

A.

c	o	t	l	b	s	h	a	d	i	n	g
p	f	e	g	r	w	m	s	u	c	y	h
e	e	x	h	i	b	i	t	i	o	n	g
r	d	t	x	l	e	n	p	v	n	b	e
s	a	u	f	l	e	l	a	p	t	v	b
p	s	r	t	i	m	w	e	h	r	s	x
e	c	e	l	a	n	d	s	c	a	p	e
c	r	o	d	n	h	n	t	g	s	b	o
t	o	t	i	t	x	m	d	f	t	i	j
i	l	q	n	k	q	z	e	m	a	r	f
v	r	k	s	t	a	i	n	e	d	i	t
e	g	o	h	l	e	c	a	p	s	w	m

B.

1 h 2 c 3 i 4 a 5 g 6 e

7 f 8 d 9 b

Page 68

C.

1 brilliant   2 landscapes
3 perspective   4 exhibition
5 shading   6 stained

D.

1 texture   2 pale   3 frames
4 space   5 contrast   6 perspective
7 exhibition   8 landscape

E

1 T   2 F   3 F   4 T   5 T   6 F

Page 69

A.

Tam thinks her grandmother is beautiful on the inside and on the outside.

Page 70

A.

Students' own answers

B.

Tam
She enjoys what she does.
She sees beauty in others.
(Example) She isn't shy about painting.
Tam's Grandmother
She loves to sit and enjoy nature.
She is shy about who she is.
(Example) She loves her granddaughter.

C.

1 Tam loves to paint, so she finds many people and things to paint.
2 Tam's grandmother feels that she is too simple and old to be painted.
3 Tam's painting shows how her grandmother is wise and gentle.

D.

1 speechless   2 ignore   3 famous
4 worry

Page 71

B.

1 I'll take   2 Shall I paint   3 I'll ask
4 Shall I bring   5 I'll carry
6 I'll buy   7 Shall I draw
8 I'll wash

Page 72

C.

1 c will (I'll)   2 a Shall
3 d will (I'll)   4 b Shall

D.

1 I'll go to the exhibition with you.
2 Shall I paint a picture of you today?
3 I'll find a frame for you.
4 Shall I ask the teacher for another canvas?

E.

1 I'll meet you at the art studio at 9:00 a.m.
2 Shall I paint the mountains smaller to add perspective?
3 I'll add shading to your sketch.
4 Shall I bring your canvas and pastels to the art room?

Page 73

A.

1 b gifted, talented
2 c beautiful, pretty
3 a dreary, drab

2   1   3

B.

1 beautiful   2 pretty   3 talented
4 gifted   5 dreary   6 drab

Page 74

A.

1 an   2 The   3 a   4 the   5 a
6 a   7 The   8 a   9 the   10 a

B.

Students' own answers

Page 75

Students' own answers

Page 76

A.

Across
4 exhibition   5 sculptor   7 canvas
9 frame   10 space   11 prodigy
Down
1 beautiful   2 dishonest
3 dissatisfied   6 landscape
8 sketch

Page 77

B.

1 Shall   2 a   3 street painter   4 a
5 three-dimensional   6 anything
7 I'll   8 surrounded   9 Everyone
10 pastels   11 perspective   12 the
13 talented

C.

1 shapes – string
2 shading – contrast
3 ignored – tiny
4 complex – speechless

D.

1 Sumin cut out interesting shapes and attached them with string.
2 Karl took a pencil and added shading and contrast to the sketch.
3 Paula ignored the tiny mistakes she made and gave the sketch to Sam.
4 Ben finished his complex painting and gave it to Tara, who was speechless!

Unit 9

Page 78

A.

8	4
2	7
3	1
10	6
9	5
11	

Page 79

B.

1 architecture   2 antiques
3 street vendor   4 canal
5 shrimp   6 exotic fruits

C.

1 rickshaw   2 canals
3 souvenirs   4 architecture
5 shrimp   6 exotic fruits

Page 80

A.

It's an historic city with famous architecture, good transportation, and good food.

Page 81

A.

Students' own answers

B.

(Sample answers)
1 You can travel around Lisbon by bus, train, taxi, tram, or even bicycle.
2 The St. George Castle and the Vasco da Gama Bridge are interesting to visit.
3 You can bike along the Tagus River from Baixa to Belem on the "Poetry Bike Lane."

C.

(Sample answers)
1 It is one of the oldest cities in the world.
2 It has the longest bridge in Europe.
3 People in Lisbon eat more fish than anyone else in Europe.

D.

1 congested   2 haggle
3 countless   4 banned

Page 82

B.

1 Nobody   2 no one   3 nothing

C.

1 nothing   2 No one   3 Nobody
4 nothing

Page 83

D.
1 nothing   2 no one   3 anything
4 something   5 Nobody

E.
1 There's nothing interesting to see at the cinema.
2 There was nobody in the restaurant after 1:00 p.m.
3 I've got nothing to do, so let's go to the science museum.
4 No one found the keys that I lost at the department store.

F.
1 I bought nothing at the antique market this morning.
2 There is nobody riding a bicycle along the river today.
3 My little brother eats nothing that has shrimp in it.

Page 84

A.
1 (cinemas) f   2 (Cement) c
3 castles a   4 commerce b
5 corner d   6 (ceiling) e

B.
1 commerce   2 cement   3 cinema
4 corner   5 castle   6 ceiling

Page 85

A.
1 Lake Superior is the most western of the Great Lakes, reaching the city of Duluth.
2 The Arctic Ocean is the smallest of the world's five oceans.
3 The island of Dominica in the Caribbean Sea has a lake called Boiling Lake.
4 The Congo River flows past the city of Kinshasa as it heads to the Atlantic Ocean.
5 The Panama Canal reaches the Pacific Ocean at Panama City.

B.
Students' own answers

Unit 10

Page 86

A.
1 garbage collectors   2 mayor
3 equipment   4 assistant
5 citizens   6 city council
7 city hall   8 playground
9 president   10 volunteers
11 news conference

B.
1 news conference   2 city hall
3 playground   4 equipment
5 garbage collector   6 city council

Page 87

C.

People	Places	Things
city council	playground	news
garbage	city hall	conference
collectors		equipment
volunteers		
mayor		
assistant		
president		
citizens		

D.
1 mayor, news conference
2 president, assistant
3 citizens, volunteers
4 city hall, city council
5 playground, equipment, garbage collectors

Page 88

A.
Many of a city's schools, groups and organizations are in a parade.

Page 89

A.
Students' own answers

B.
1 Marcy, strength
2 citizens, weakness
3 artists, strength
4 chefs, strength
5 Mayor Wilson, strength

C.
1 They don't go out and do interesting things.
2 They can lose money, and sometimes they have to close down.
3 It reminded people that their city is an exciting and interesting place.

D.
1 speech   2 contest   3 members
4 ribbon

Page 90

B.
1 A city usually has lots of hotels for visitors, doesn't (it)?
2 Sushi restaurants are popular in Tokyo, aren't (they)?
3 The mayor will be in the parade tomorrow, won't (she)?
4 The soccer team didn't win the game last night, did (it)?
5 Thomas can visit the art museum this afternoon, can't (he)?
6 The garbage collectors don't work tomorrow, do (they)?

C.
1 doesn't it?   2 did it?

3 won't they?   4 does he?
5 isn't it?   6 can't they?

Page 91

D.
1 You enjoy looking at interesting architecture, don't you?
2 Sandra didn't take a boat ride on the canal, did she?
3 The mayor will have a news conference tomorrow, won't she (or won't he?)
4 Volunteers can paint the equipment, can't they?

E.
1 isn't it   2 does it   3 won't they
4 did it

F.
1 Istanbul is the largest city in Europe, isn't it?
2 The city council wants to build a new playground, doesn't it?
3 The Chicago City Hall burned down in 1871, didn't it?
4 Our city's baseball team will win the game, won't it?

Page 92

A.
1 took apart   2 took down
3 take up   4 take in   5 takes over
6 takes after

| 3 | 5 | 2 |
| 6 | 1 | 4 |

B.
1 took down   2 took apart
3 takes after   4 take up
5 take over   6 take in

Page 93

A.
1 or   2 but   3 and   4 but   5 or
6 and   7 or   8 but

B.
Students' own answers

Page 94
Students' own answers

Page 95

A.
1 F   2 T   3 T   4 F   5 T   6 T

B.
1 shrimp – tuna
2 took over – congested
3 volunteers – take down
4 mayor – members
5 president – news conference

Page 96

C.
1 The Mississippi River flows into the Gulf of Mexico, doesn't it?

2 Lake Baikal is the oldest and deepest freshwater lake, isn't it?

3 The Nile River flows north into the Mediterranean Sea, doesn't it?

4 Peru and Bolivia share Lake Titicaca's resources, don't they?

D.

1 nothing, but   2 and, nothing

3 No one, but   4 and, nobody

E.

1 nobody   2 it   3 or   4 won't

5 nothing

Unit 11

Page 97

A.

1 infect   2 microscope   3 bacteria
4 cells   5 common cold   6 paralyze
7 disease   8 virus   9 influenza

Secret message: Stay strong and healthy!

Page 98

B.

1 microscope   2 influenza
3 infect   4 common cold
5 diseases   6 bacteria

C

1 influenza   2 virus   3 infect
4 immune   5 microscope

D.

1 T   2 T   3 F   4 F   5 T   6 T

Page 99

A

It's trying to infect Sam.

Page 100

A.

Students' own answers

B.

1 b   2 c

C

1 You should wash your hands.

2 They stop viruses from infecting other people.

3 These things can keep your body strong.

D.

1 fluids   2 swallowed   3 scrapes
4 suit

Page 101

B.

1 a. opinion   b. color   c. kind
2 a. opinion   b. size   c. color
3 a. opinion   b. age   c. kind
4 a. age   b. color   c. kind

C

1 cotton   2 green   3 young
4 tiny

Page 102

D.

1 The medicine attacked the dangerous, new, blue pathogen.

2 This tiny, rectangular, green plant cell has very thick walls.

3 The curious, tall, young student made an important discovery.

4 Liz sprayed the beautiful, cup-shaped, yellow flowers to protect them from animals.

E.

1 Dr. Garcia gave Ben some good-tasting red medicine.

2 This powerful electron microscope can see viruses.

3 This simple cotton mask can stop viruses.

3, 1, 2

F.

(Sample answers)

1 I own a sporty, new, red bicycle.

2 I saw pretty, pink, cherry blossoms.

3 I'm wearing shiny, black, leather shoes.

Page 103

A.

1 inhale   2 live   3 shrink
4 expand   5 exhale   6 dead

B.

1 expanded, shrink   2 dead, live
3 inhale, exhale

Page 104

A.

(Sample answers)

1 Don't sneeze into the air. Sneeze into a tissue.

2 Don't stay here. Go to the nurse's office.

3 Don't eat with dirty hands. Wash them in the sink.

4 Don't go to bed so late. Try to go to bed earlier.

5 Stop playing so many computer games. Exercise with me!

B.

Students' own answers

Unit 12

Page 105

A.

1 lungs   2 trachea   3 diaphragm
4 arteries   5 veins   6 heart

B.

1 system   2 pulse
3 carbon dioxide   4 blood
5 Capillaries

Page 106

C.

1 lung   2 capillaries   3 trachea
4 carbon dioxide

D.

1 pulse   2 blood   3 capillaries
4 trachea   5 heart
6 carbon dioxide   7 veins   8 lungs
9 diaphragm   10 system
11 arteries

Page 107

A.

(Sample answer)

Exercise makes your body stronger and more flexible. You also feel better.

Page 108

A.

Students' own answers

B.

Step One	Step Two	Step Three	Step Four
3	5	7	12
2	4	9	10
1	6	8	11

C.

(Sample answers)

1 It produces carbon dioxide.

2 It keeps your body from becoming too hot.

3 It starts to pump (beat) more slowly.

D.

1 pumps   2 squeezes   3 major
4 tubes

Page 109

B.

1 d (used to eat)

2 f (used to swim)

3 a (used to go)

4 c (used to jog)

5 b (used to put)

6 e (used to think)

C.

1 ran   2 used to swim   3 had
4 drank   5 used to watch
6 thought

Page 110

D.

1 made, used to make

2 used to eat, ate

3 used to wear, wore

4 got up, used to get up

E.

1 Sonia used to eat two apples every day.

2 George used to weigh over ninety kilograms.

3 My grandfather used to walk to school every day.

4 Burak used to go hiking every Saturday afternoon.

F.

(Sample answer)

I used to eat sweets after school, but I don't do that anymore.

Page 111

A.

1 navigate **2** duplication

3 estimation **4** concentrate

5 exaggeration **6** graduate

| 2 | 3 | 6 |
| 4 | 5 | 1 |

B.

1 graduation **2** navigate

3 estimate **4** concentrate

5 exaggeration **6** duplicate

Page 112

A.

1 pumps **2** knows **3** works

4 want **5** has **6** goes **7** jumps

8 play

B.

Students' own answers

Page 113

Students' own answers

Page 114

A.

1 common cold **2** virus **3** mucus

4 inhale **5** exhale **6** swallow

7 trachea **8** lungs **9** pulse

10 heart **11** pumping

12 concentrating

B.

Does anybody (know) what this small, triangular, green object is under this microscope?

I think it's a plant cell, but nobody in my group (is) sure. I hope it's not a dangerous, new virus. Hopefully our talented, young science teacher can tell me what it is.

C.

1 used to dream, dreamed (dreamt)

2 did, used to do

3 used to bake, baked

4 exercised, used to exercise

D.

(Sample answers)

1 Don't eat so many sweets. Eat healthy food such as fruits and nuts.

2 Go to bed early and get up early. Don't stay up late every night.

3 When you are sick, drink lots of fluids. Stay in bed.

Unit 13

Page 116

A.

1 smartphone **2** newspaper

3 magazine **4** printing press

5 advertising **6** publisher

7 broadcast **8** blog

Page 117

B.

1 Web **2** mass media

3 broadcast **4** blogs

5 social networks

C.

1 smartphone **2** blog

3 magazine **4** mass media

5 publisher **6** broadcast

D.

1 Web – mass media

2 advertising – magazines

3 newspaper – smartphone

4 publishers – printing presses

5 blogs – social networks

Page 118

A.

(Sample answer)

It happened at a popular candy company, where many local people worked.

Page 119

A.

Students' own answers

B.

People in Canonsburg heard the news.	People in Pennsylvania heard the news.	People around the United States heard the news.
3, 5	1, 6	2, 4

C.

(Sample answers)

1 They smelled smoke, and then they heard a fire alarm.

2 Neighbors and friends of the workers spread the news.

3 The news about the fire was in the evening newspapers, on television, and on the Internet.

D.

1 radio station **2** latest

3 newsreels **4** journalist

Page 120

B.

1 has to **2** don't have to

3 didn't have to **4** mustn't

5 had to **6** have to

7 doesn't have to

C.

1 don't have to **2** mustn't

3 don't have to **4** doesn't have to

Page 121

D.

1 Students mustn't bring their smartphones into the classroom with them.

2 The students have to read newspaper articles in English class.

3 People who use social networks don't have to share news on the phone.

4 Pam's television isn't working, so she has to use the radio to get the news.

E.

1 The publisher has to buy a new printing press.

2 A blog doesn't have to have advertising.

3 People don't have to join a social network.

4 The mass media must broadcast important news.

5 You don't have to use the Web to play games.

Page 122

A.

1 (kneel) **2** (knot) **3** (knuckle)

4 (knight) **5** (knowledge) **6** (knit)

B.

1 knight **2** knuckle **3** knowledge

4 kneel **5** knot **6** knit

Page 123

A.

1 he **2** it **3** it **4** they **5** it

6 they **7** them **8** they

B.

Students' own answers

Unit 14

Page 124

A.

h	s	s	u	c	s	i	d	h	s	i	s
r	n	e	o	s	c	o	i	u	s	n	w
m	h	r	m	e	f	w	n	e	t	v	h
d	e	c	i	d	e	p	s	a	i	e	r
h	a	l	s	w	h	c	r	a	e	s	e
n	d	e	t	i	s	b	e	w	v	t	p
o	l	e	a	b	t	s	a	v	n	i	o
e	i	p	k	z	o	c	r	n	e	g	r
i	n	t	e	r	v	i	e	w	h	a	t
f	e	v	a	t	a	s	e	h	d	t	e
r	n	c	e	e	r	o	t	i	d	e	r
i	a	h	e	r	o	h	c	a	r	e	s

B.

| 3 | 6 | 1 |
| 5 | 2 | 4 |

Page 125

C.

People	Actions	Things
editor	investigate	interview
reporter	decide	website
hero	search	mistake
	discuss	headline

D.

1 website   2 discuss   3 reporter
4 search   5 editor   6 decide
7 interview   8 hero   9 investigate
10 headline   11 mistake

Page 126

A.

The hand cream and the cotton gloves were clues.

Page 127

A.

Students' own answers

B.

(Sample answers)

Conflict	Possible Resolutions	Actual Resolution
Madeline Mulrooney's diamond ring is missing.	The swimming coach took it.	Jack solved the case by finding the ring in a cotton glove in the garbage can.
	Mrs. Mulrooney sold it to get more money.	
	Mrs. Mulrooney lost it before she went swimming.	

C.

(Sample answers)
1 Jack's brother is a reporter.
2 The water isn't good for her ring when she swims.
3 She throws them away each morning.
4 The cream was slippery, so her ring came off with the glove.

D.

1 terrible   2 fair   3 mansion
4 donated

Page 128

B.

1 has found   2 has finished
3 haven't decided   4 have interviewed
5 hasn't discussed

C.

1 c   2 a   3 d   4 b

Page 129

D.

1 The reporter has searched for information.
2 The editor has changed the headline.
3 Amber has worked for a publisher.
4 The news program has won many awards.
5 The photographer has taken pictures for magazines.

E.

1 The reporter hasn't written the story.
2 Eduardo hasn't listened to news on the radio.
3 As an interviewer, Angela has spoken to some important people.
4 Fiona hasn't watched a newsreel, but her grandmother has.
5 Pedro has traveled for his blog.

F.

(Sample answer)
I've studied for tomorrow's English test.

Page 130

A.

1 b entire, whole
2 c special, unusual
3 a huge, immense

| 3 | 1 | 2 |

B.

1 entire   2 special   3 immense
4 unusual   5 huge   6 whole

Page 131

A.

1 made (I)   2 answered (R)
3 flown (I)   4 searched (R)
5 started (R)   6 brought (I)
7 bought (I)   8 turned (R)

B.

Students' own answers

Page 132

Students' own answers

Page 133

A.

Across
1 publisher   5 headline
8 unusual   9 huge   10 hero
Down
2 reporter   3 mansion
4 advertising   6 discuss
7 knowledge

Page 134

B.

1 Teresa doesn't have to update her blog tonight. She worked on it this afternoon.
2 The reporter made several mistakes in his article. He had to

correct them before the article went on the web.
3 Michael must finish the interview by 4:00 p.m. If he doesn't finish it by then, we can't broadcast it on the evening news.

C.

1 hasn't chatted   2 hasn't been
3 have investigated
4 have decided   5 hasn't printed

D.

I have <u>enjoyed</u> being a sports reporter for my school newspaper. I have <u>met</u> lots of people, and sometimes I have <u>interviewed</u> <u>them</u>. I also have to take pictures at sports events. Last night, I went to a basketball game. I <u>haven't</u> played basketball, and it looked difficult! I took pictures and put <u>them</u> on the school website. Today I <u>must</u> write an article about the game. I'm in a hurry, because we <u>have to</u> print the newspaper by Friday.

Unit 15

Page 135

A.

1 tsunami   2 blizzard   3 tornado
4 earthquake   5 hurricane

B.

1 thunderstorm   2 flood
3 power lines   4 victim
5 rescue worker   6 collapse

Page 136

C.

1 d, f   2 a, g   3 b, h   4 c, e

D.

1 rescue workers – victims
2 power lines – collapsed
3 tornado – blizzard

Page 137

A.

When people have time, they can protect themselves before an emergency.

Page 138

A.

Students' own answers

B.

1 c, e   2 a, f   3 b, d

C.

1 They measure waves and water pressure.
2 They leave the area.

D.

1 vertically   2 forces
3 horizontally   4 funnel

B.
1 Has / Yes, he has.
2 heard / No, I haven't.
3 ever / No, they haven't.
4 thanked / Yes, she has.
5 Have / No, they haven't.
6 hurricanes / Yes, they have.
7 ever / Yes, it has.
8 this river / No, it hasn't.
9 sunk / No, they haven't.
10 Have / Yes, I have.
11 Have / No, they haven't.

C.
1 Has anyone ever survived outside in a blizzard?
2 Have earthquakes ever happened in Greenland?
3 Have those power lines ever collapsed during a hurricane?
4 Have rescue workers in this city ever helped you?
D.
1 Have you ever been in a flood?
2 Has lightning ever struck this tower?
3 Have early warning systems ever failed?
3, 1, 2
E.
1 No, Tom has never been in a flood.
2 Yes, hurricanes have occurred in tropical areas.
3 No, Kelly has never felt an earthquake.
4 No, they have never experienced a blizzard.

A.
1 raindrops e 2 bodyguards a
3 haircut d 4 landslide b
5 snowfall f 6 teamwork c
B.
1 snowfall 2 landslide
3 teamwork 4 bodyguard
5 haircut 6 raindrop

A.
1 They've experienced many earthquakes in their country.
2 I've never been in a hurricane because I live far from the ocean.
3 She's met many rescue workers in her job.
4 The tsunami was powerful. It's damaged many coastal towns.
5 We've cleaned up the area where the power lines collapsed.

B.
Students' own answers

Unit 16

A.
1 emergency 2 storm shutters
3 supplies 4 bottled water
5 canned food 6 first-aid kit
7 batteries 8 flashlight
9 storm shelter 10 cash
11 sleeping bag

B.
1 d 2 f 3 a 4 b 5 c 6 e
C.
1 T 2 F 3 T 4 T 5 F
D.
1 cash, emergency
2 storm shutters, storm shelter
3 flashlight, batteries
4 canned food, bottled water
5 sleeping bag, first-aid kit, supplies

A.
You don't have time to decide what to do during an emergency. You should know what to do before it happens.

A.
Students' own answers
B.
1 d 2 c 3 a 4 e 5 b
C.
1 F 2 T 3 T 4 F
D.
1 landfall 2 inland 3 destroyed
4 trunk

B.
1 I've just put the batteries in the flashlight.
2 He's already returned from the storm shelter.
3 We haven't bought a new first-aid kit yet.
4 Have they already washed the sleeping bags?
5 Has the canned food become too old yet?
6 Have you just run out of supplies?

C.
1 already 2 just 3 yet 4 just
D.
1 Has the tsunami made landfall yet?
2 She's already bought canned food.
3 They've just built the storm shelter.

2   1   3

E.
(Sample answers)
1 I've already bought supplies.
2 I've just taken cash from the bank.
3 I haven't put batteries in the flashlight yet.
4 I've already talked to my family about what to do.

A.
1 turn in 2 turn back
3 turn down 4 turn over
5 turn up 6 turn on
B.
1 turn back 2 turn on
3 turned in 4 turn up
5 turned over 6 turn down

A.
1 loudly 2 violently 3 carefully
4 quietly 5 bravely 6 accurately
B.
Students' own answers

Students' own answers

A.
1 flashlight 2 bottled water
3 sleeping bag 4 batteries
5 rescue worker 6 canned food
7 supplies
B.
1 earthquake, tsunami
2 tornado, funnel
3 turned back, landslide
4 snowfall, collapsed

C.
1 She's just brought the first-aid kits to the storm shelter.
2 We haven't had a big thunderstorm this summer yet.
3 The hurricane is fast. It's already made landfall.
4 They haven't shown good teamwork yet.
5 He's just turned up the radio to hear the news.

D.

1 Have you ever seen a tornado spinning vertically across the ground?
2 Has the bodyguard ever protected the singer quickly during an earthquake?
3 Has he ever seen this river rising slowly until it became a flood?
4 Have raindrops ever fallen loudly on this metal roof?
5 Have these power lines ever shaken violently during a hurricane?

Unit 17

Page 154

A.

1 desert   2 freshwater   3 sloth
4 tropical rainforest   5 cactus
6 grassland   7 tundra
8 temperate forest

Page 155

B.

1 tundra   2 cactus   3 taiga
4 desert   5 tropical rainforest
6 grassland

C

1 tropical rainforest – sloth
2 freshwater – biomes
3 desert – cactuses
4 tundra – equator
5 taiga – temperate forest

Page 156

A.

(Sample answer)
Biomes give people many things, such as oxygen, clean water, and new medicines.

Page 157

A.

Students' own answers

B.

Tropical Rainforest	Grassland	Freshwater
1, 4	3, 5	2, 6

C.

(Sample answers)
1 They take away carbon dioxide.
2 Some of it blows away, and some of it is washed into rivers.
3 Animals and plants there start to disappear.

D.

1 hatches   2 glides   3 scenes
4 Arctic

Page 158

B.

1 has hiked, since
2 have drunk, for
3 have eaten, for
4 hasn't had, since
5 has traveled, since
6 have been, for
7 has gone, for
8 haven't taken, since
9 have found, for
10 hasn't visited, since

Page 159

C.

1 for two weeks
2 since this morning
3 since 1987
4 for hundreds of years

D.

1 Sonya has lived in the taiga for two years.
2 We haven't sailed on the ocean since 2008.
3 This sloth has slept for twelve hours.
4 The scientist hasn't visited the tundra since last summer.

E.

1 How long have elephants lived in this grassland?
2 How long have they studied biomes?
3 How long have seals swum along this coast?

Page 160

A.

1 batch   2 catch   3 stitched
4 scratched   5 itched   6 patch

5   2   4   1   6   3

B.

1 catch   2 itch   3 scratch
4 stitch   5 batch   6 patch

Page 161

A.

1 The biologists hiked through the tropical rainforest until they found a sloth.
2 The lion ran through the grassland until it caught the zebra.
3 The freshwater flowed through the river until it reached the ocean.
4 The leaves fell from the trees until the temperate forest ground was covered with them.
5 The whale swam through the Pacific Ocean until it reached Hawaii.

B.

Students' own answers

Unit 18

Page 162

A.

1 snorkel   2 border   3 speedboat
4 parrotfish   5 sea turtle
6 seahorse

B.

1 marine park   2 petition
3 astonished   4 law

Page 163

C.

1 seahorse   2 parrotfish
3 snorkel   4 borders
5 petition   6 speedboat

3   5   2   6   1   4

D.

1 sea turtle – seahorse
2 snorkeled – astonished
3 manta ray – speedboat
4 marine park – parrotfish
5 law – border

Page 164

(Sample answer)

A.

The cut down the trees and sell them, and they turn the forest into farms.

Page 165

A.

Students' own answers

B.

1 a, c   2 b, d

C.

(Sample answers)
1 Brazil and Argentina share the Iguacu Falls.
2 He started a petition. This made the government pass a new law.
3 He wants to protect all of the Atlantic Forest someday.

D.

1 invited   2 difference   3 signed
4 managed

Page 166

B.

1 Did you study; did; studied
2 have never seen; haven't
3 has already snorkeled; did it
4 hasn't signed; signed
5 Have; ever found; found
6 has worked; has never worked

Page 167

C.

1 b   2 a   3 c   4 d   5 f   6 e

D.

1 Has, seen   2 have, swum
3 Did, ride   4 Have, changed

E.

1 The seahorses didn't come to this area last year.
2 The speedboat left the area five minutes ago.
3 The members of the city council didn't receive the petition this morning.
4 Did they snorkel around the marine park yesterday?

Page 168

A.

1 intelligent, intelligence
2 independence, independent
3 absent, absence

2   3   1

B.

1 absence, absent
2 intelligence, intelligent
3 independent, independence

Page 169

A.

1 The Atlantic Forest is disappearing because people are cutting down the trees.
2 Biomes are important because they keep our planet healthy.
3 Speedboats are bad for coral reefs because they scare fish away.
4 This fish is called a seahorse because it looks like a tiny horse.
5 We need laws to protect biomes because some people hurt them.

B.

Students' own answers

Page 170

Students' own answers

Page 171

A.

1 parrot fish   2 sea turtles
3 freshwater   4 tundra   5 Arctic
6 desert   7 grassland
8 tropical rainforest
9 temperate forest   10 laws
11 marine parks   12 difference

Page 172

B.

1 (for) / People in the tundra ate seal meat in the 20th century.
2 (since) / People didn't hunt elephants in this grassland in 1974.
3 (for) / Sea turtles laid eggs on this beach last year.
4 (since) / The sloth didn't move in the tree this morning.

C.

1 The students continued to sign petitions until the government passed the law.
2 Ken took pictures of the parrot fish until it swam away.
3 The speedboat moved quickly until it reached the border of the marine park.

D.

1 The government managed the taiga because (or since) people were cutting down too many trees.
2 The mother sloth scratched the baby's back since (or because) its back itched.
3 People need biomes because (or since) they keep our planet healthy.

Word List

Unit 1
disk
dwelled
speck
vast
asteroid
comet
galaxy
meteorite
moon
observatory
solar system
spacecraft
stars
telescope
universe
eighty
freight
reins
sleigh
veil
weigh
alone
chart
climb
grand
notice
often
pie
realize
secret
view
wondrous
wooden

Unit 2
bodies
inner
outer
share
astronomer
core
craters
diameter
distance
gravity
matter
orbit
space probe
surface

unique
arrogance
arrogant
fragrance
fragrant
ignorance
ignorant
giant
neighboring
path
recently
sink
strange
technology
thick

Unit 3
battle
coffin
generals
varnish
archeologist
armor
army
clay
emperor
jade
peasant
soldiers
tomb
treasure
uniform
cartoonist
cyclist
dentist
florist
pianist
tourist
archer
attack
bronze
cap
charge
craftsmen
elegant
moment
rank
shiny
thin
trace

Unit 4
determine
dream
favorite
tripped
ash
dinosaur
discover
examine
excavate
layers
paleontologist
pastime
ravine
sedimentary rock
skull
achievement
brief
niece
piece
relief
thief
age
contact
crash
energetic
enjoy
lift
province
rub
shout
volcanic

Unit 5
coax
gather
introduce
peel (v)
bark
butter
cinnamon
ingredients
leopard
plantation
steamship
sugar cane
suitcase
vanilla
wheat
drop away

drop back
drop by
drop off
drop out
drop through
amber
bushy
coop
enormous
grain
magnificent
mustache
pail
relieved
slyly
tractor
wonderful

Unit 6
food labels
grocery stores
organic food
whole food
agriculture
century
chemicals
convenient
corporate farm
export
farmers' market
local
package
process
reduce
conversation
dictionary
environment
geography
introduction
photographer
cause
company
cool
globally
information
last
plate
surprised

Unit 7
combines
complex
fascination
washable
canvas
carpenter
paintbrushes
pastels
prodigy
sculptor
shapes
sketch
street painter
string
three-dimensional
disability
dishonest
disorganized
disprove
dissatisfied
distrust
admire
bend
capture
crevice
disorderly
expert
flexible
inspiring
public
temporary
variety
weave

Unit 8
famous
ignore
speechless
worries
brilliant
contrast
exhibition
frame
landscape
pale
perspective
shading
space
stained

texture
beautiful
gifted
miniature
pretty
talented
tiny
astounded
comment
feature
nod
offer
rush
shocked
tattered

Unit 9
banned
congested
countless
haggle
antiques
architecture
batik
canal
exotic fruits
port
rickshaw
shrimp
souvenirs
street vendor
tuna
castle
ceiling
cement
cinema
commerce
corner
capital
carriage
district
dock
futuristic
inspect
motorized
original
packed
replace
wander
wonder

Unit 10

contest
members
ribbon
speech
assistant
citizens
City Council
City Hall
equipment
garbage collector
mayor
news conference
playground
president
volunteer
take after
take apart
take down
take in
take over
take up
confused
head
impress
promise
smoothly
snap
tap
terrific

Unit 11

fluid
scrape
suit
swallowed
bacteria
cells
common cold
disease
infect
influenza
microscope
mucus
paralyze
virus
dead
exhale
expand
inhale
live
shrink
acid
aid

defense
illness
powerful
rod
super
trap
underneath

Unit 12

major
pumps
squeezes
tubes
arteries
blood
capillary
carbon dioxide
diaphragm
heart
lungs
pulse
system
trachea
veins
concentrate
duplicate
estimate
exaggerate
graduate
navigate
carry
fist
heartbeat
in addition
remove
unit
waste product
wrist

Unit 13

journalist
latest
newsreels
radio station
advertising
blog
broadcast
Internet
magazine
mass media
newspaper
printing press
publisher

smartphones
social network
kneel
knight
knit
knot
knowledge
knuckle
absolutely
appear
cost
early
fashion
focus
sports
spread

Unit 14

donated
fair
mansion
terrible
decide
discuss
editor
headline
hero
interview
investigate
mistake
reporter
search
website
entire
huge
immense
special
unusual
whole
awesome
channel
gatehouse
maid
mysterious
own
save
tear down

Unit 15

forces
funnel
horizontally
vertically

blizzard
collapse
earthquake
flood
hurricane
power lines
rescue worker
thunderstorm
tornado
tsunami
victim
bodyguard
haircut
landslide
raindrop
snowfall
teamwork
atmosphere
average
climate
condition
disaster
property
receive
rich
rise
roof
spin
violent

Unit 16

destroyed
inland
landfall
trunk
batteries
bottled water
canned food
cash
emergency
first-aid kit
flashlight
sleeping bag
storm shelter
storm shutters
supplies
turn back
turn down
turn in
turn on
turn over
turn up
board
contain

declare
hang up
peninsula
remain
smash
storage room

Unit 17

arctic
glides
hatches
scenes
biome
cactus
desert
equator
freshwater
grassland
sloth
taiga
temperate forest
tropical rainforest
tundra
batch
catch
itch
patch
scratch
stitch
autumn
evergreen
frozen
occupy
reside
roam
temperature
wetlands

Unit 18

difference
invited
managed
signed
astonish
border
law
manta ray
marine park
parrotfish
petition
sea turtle
seahorse
snorkel

speedboat
absence
absent
independence
independent
intelligence
intelligent
dart
department
explain
fishery
glide
shore
turquoise
upset

OXFORD
UNIVERSITY PRESS

Great Clarendon Street, Oxford, OX2 6DP, United Kingdom

Oxford University Press is a department of the University of Oxford.
It furthers the University's objective of excellence in research, scholarship,
and education by publishing worldwide. Oxford is a registered trade
mark of Oxford University Press in the UK and in certain other countries

ISBN: 978 0 19 427820 1   Integrated Teacher's Toolkit
ISBN: 978 0 19 427841 6   Teacher's Book with online practice
ISBN: 978 0 19 427842 3   Teacher's access card
ISBN: 978 0 19 427926 0   Assessment CD-ROM
ISBN: 978 0 19 427932 1   Big Question DVD

Printed in China

This book is printed on paper from certified and well-managed sources

ACKNOWLEDGEMENTS

Illustrations by: Constanza Basaluzzo; Mike Dammer; George Hamblin; Jannie
Ho; Anthony Lewis; Margeaux Lucas; Q2A Media Services; Mick Reid; Jomike
Tejido.

*The Publishers would like to thank the following for their kind permission to
reproduce photographs and other copyright material*: POSTER 1: bravobravo/
Getty Images; Patrick Batchelder/Alamy; samyaoo/Getty Images; Cardens
Design/Shutterstock; Adastra/Getty Images. POSTER 2: Homebrew Films
Company/Getty Images; Berthold Steinhilber/laif/Redux; Arne Hodalic/
Corbis; Unknown/Corbis; Everett Collection/Newscom. POSTER 3: Andrew
Holbrooke/Corbis; Joe Mamer/age fotostock/SuperStock; Blend Images/
Masterfile; RBP Trust/Getty Images; Angels Tomás/age footstock. POSTER
4: KidStock/Blend Images/Corbis; Hill Street Studios/Eric Raptosh/Blend
Images/Corbis; Robin James/Cultura Limited/SuperStock; Fuse/Getty Images;
Danita Delimont/Getty Images. POSTER 5: Peter Dressel/Getty Images;
JUSTIN GUARIGLIA/National Geographic Creative; Keith Levit Photography/
Getty Images; Atlantide Phototravel/Corbis; Klaus Leidorf/Klaus Leidorf/
Corbis. POSTER 6: Rod Walker/Getty Images; Jose AS Reyes/Shutterstock;
Ianni Dimitrov/Alamy; Stocktrek Images, Inc./Alamy; SCIEPRO/Getty Images.
POSTER 7: © LOOK Die Bildagentur der Fotografen GmbH/Alamy; The Art
Archive/Galleria d'Arte Moderna Rome/Gianni Dagli Orti; Antoine Arraou/age
footstock; sellingpix/Shutterstock; CAMERA PRESS/Ken Rake/Redux. POSTER
8: age fotostock/SuperStock; Mark Downey/Masterfile; Dennis K. Johnson/
Getty Images; Jim Edds/Corbis; Layne Kennedy/Corbis. POSTER 9: Minden
Pictures/Masterfile; R Gemperle/age footstock; Matt Chalwell/iStockphoto;
MARK COSSLETT/National Geographic Creative; Minden Pictures/Masterfile.